LOVE MY RIFLE MORE THAN YOU

LOVE MY RIFLE MORE THAN YOU

Young and Female in the U.S. Army

Kayla Williams

with Michael E. Staub

W. W. NORTON & COMPANY

NEW YORK • LONDON

This is a work of nonfiction, and the events it recounts are true. However, the names and certain identifying characteristics of some of the people who appear in its pages have been changed. The views expressed in this book are the author's and do not necessarily represent the views of the Department of Defense or its components.

Thanks to Captain Brian Johns for permission to reprint his contributions to the chapter "How to Prepare for Deployment to Iraq."

For information about permission to reproduce selections from this book, write to Permissions, W. W. Norton & Company, Inc., 500 Fifth Avenue, New York, NY 10110

Manufacturing by Courier Westford
Book design by Dana Sloan
Production manager: Julia Druskin

Library of Congress Cataloging-in-Publication Data
Williams, Kayla.
    Love my rifle more than you : young and female in the
U.S. Army / Kayla Williams with Michael E. Staub.
        p. cm.
    ISBN 0-393-06098-5 (hardcover)
    1. Williams, Kayla. 2. Women soldiers—United States—
Biography 3. United States Army—Women—Biography. 4. Iraq
War, 2003—Participation, Female. I. Staub, Michael E. II. Title.
    U53 . W61752A3 2005
    355′ .0082′ 0973—dc22   2005012911

W. W. Norton & Company, Inc.
500 Fifth Avenue, New York, NY 10110
www.wwnorton.com

W. W. Norton & Company Ltd.
Castle House, 75/76 Wells Street, London W1T 3QT

1 2 3 4 5 6 7 8 9 0

For Brian—
Who gives me hope.

Cindy, Cindy, Cindy Lou
Love my rifle more than you
You used to be my beauty queen
Now I love my M-16.

—ARMY MARCHING CADENCE

CONTENTS

PROLOGUE

SOMETIMES, EVEN NOW, I wake up before dawn and forget I am not a slut. The air is not quite dark, not quite light, and I lie absolutely still, trying to will myself to remember that that is *not* what I am. Sometimes, on better mornings, it comes to me right away. And then there are all those other times.

Slut.

The only other choice is bitch. If you're a woman and a soldier, those are the choices you get.

I'm twenty eight years old. Military Intelligence, five years, here and in Iraq. One of the 15 percent of the U.S. military that's female. And that whole 15 percent trying to get past an old joke. "What's the difference between a bitch and slut? A slut will fuck anyone, a bitch will fuck anyone but you." So if she's nice or friendly, outgoing or chatty—she's a slut. If she's distant or reserved or professional—she's a bitch.

A woman soldier has to toughen herself up. Not just for the enemy, for battle, or for death. I mean toughen herself to spend months awash in a sea of nervy, hyped-up guys who, when they're not thinking about getting killed, are thinking about getting laid. Their eyes on you all the time, your breasts, your ass—like there is nothing else to watch, no sun, no river, no desert, no mortars at night.

Still, it's more complicated than that. Because at the same time you soften yourself up. Their eyes, their hunger: yes, it's shaming—but they also make you special. I don't like to say it—it cuts you inside—but the attention, the admiration, the *need*: they make you powerful. If you're a woman in the Army, it doesn't matter so much about your looks. What counts is that you are female.

Wartime makes it worse. There's the killing on the streets, the bombs at the checkpoints—and the combat in the tents. Some women sleep around: lots of sex with lots of guys, in sleeping bags, in trucks, in sand, in America, in Iraq. Some women hold themselves back; they avoid sex like it's some weapon of mass destruction. I know about both.

And I know about something else. How these same guys you want to piss on become *your* guys. Another girl enters your tent, and they look at her the way they looked at you, and what drove you crazy with anger suddenly drives you crazy with jealousy. They're *yours*. Fuck, you left your husband to be with them, you walked out on him for them. These guys, they're your husband, they're your father, your brother, your lover—your life.

I never thought I would feel this way—not about these guys, not about this war, not even about my country. I was a punk-kid rebel, and now I'm part of the most authoritarian institution imaginable. I thought this war was probably wrong, didn't want to go. The lies that got us there, that killed some of us, that wounded and maimed more of us: Only the most messed-up-patriotic-head-up-his-ass-blind-faith-my-country-right-or-wrong soldier believed them.

But now I watch a cheesy commercial for Anheuser-Busch of

civilians applauding troops returning from Iraq and I get all emotional. I also watch videos on the Internet, with combat footage—"Let the Bodies Hit the Floor" and "Red, White, and Blue (The Angry American)"—and it chokes me up. It's scary to think about how much being in the Army has changed me. That experience couldn't leave even the strongest person the same. Everything I thought I knew about what it would be like turned out to be wrong. Not reality.

So I wanted to write a book to let people know what it *feels* like to be a woman soldier in peace and in war. I wanted to capture the terror, the mind-numbing tedium; and the joy and the honor. Not overlooking the suicidal periods, the anorexic impulses, the promiscuity; and the comradeship and the bravery. The times we were scared out of our minds. The times we were bored out of our minds, too. No one has ever written that book— about what life is like for the 15 percent. Don't count Jessica Lynch. Her story meant nothing to us. The same goes for Lynndie England. I'm not either of them, and neither are any of the real women I know in the service.

In a dress, away from the base, you'd never guess I was a soldier. Always been a girl that catches a guy's eyes. And yet I do fifty-five push-ups in under a minute. Tough, and proud to be tough. I love my M-4, the smell of it, of cleaning fluid, of gunpowder: the smell of strength. Gun in your hands, and you're in a special place. I've come to look forward to that.

It can turn you, though. Women are no different from men in their corruptibility. Women are just as competent—and just as incompetent.

As I write this in the early months of 2005, 91 percent of all Army career fields are now open to women, and 67 percent of

Army positions can be filled by women. Women are currently authorized to sign up for 87 percent of all enlisted military occupational specialties (MOS). But isn't Congress keeping women out of combat? There are no women in artillery, no women in the infantry. We are not permitted to drive tanks. We can't be Rangers or Special Forces. There are also some teams we rarely go out with because the gear is considered too heavy for the average female to hump on her back.

So people conclude that girls don't do combat zones. That we're somewhere else from where the action is. But that's bullshit. We are Marines. We are Military Police. We are there as support to the infantry in almost every way you might imagine. We even act in support roles for the Special Forces. We carry weapons—and we use them. We may kick down doors when an Iraqi village gets cleared. We do crowd control. We are also often the soldiers who negotiate with the locals—nearly one third of Military Intelligence (MI), where I work, is female.

Insurgents' mortar attacks reach us, too. In fact, because insurgents strike supply routes so often, it's frequently the non-infantry soldiers like us—with fewer up-armored vehicles—who end up getting hit and engaging in combat.

In Iraq, I cleaned blood from soldiers' gear after a roadside bomb hit a convoy. I saw the bloodied bodies of locals—civilians caught in the wrong place at the wrong time. I saw death. I speak Arabic, so I participated in interrogations. I had to deal with the tension between wanting to help the locals and having to do battle with them. I pointed my weapon at a child. I've understood things and seen things I need to forget: Humiliation. Torture. It was not just Abu Ghraib—it happened elsewhere, too.

Sometimes I wake up and I feel frightened all over again. The darkness is like the blackest night on the mountains west of Mosul, no moon, no stars, no light anywhere in the whole freaking world. I want so very much to vanish from the planet. Just evaporate like vapor trails after the jets have gone.

The smell of dead animals being burned. Dogs barking as I pull guard in the night. The different soils. The day we found dead white chickens everywhere and thought it was due to a chemical attack. How the faces of local women, and especially little girls, just *lit up* with pleasure at the sight of a female soldier: shy smiles. Saddam's palaces—marble, multiple colors, cut into designs and layered, incredibly beautiful and obscenely expensive.

I don't forget. I can't forget any of it. From basic training all the way to Iraq and back home again.

QUEEN FOR A YEAR

Queen for a Year: **1 a:** any American female stationed overseas in a predominantly male military environment. **b:** a female soldier who becomes stuck-up during her deployment due to an exponential increase in male attention—used disparagingly.

RIGHT INTO IT: Sex is key to any woman soldier's experiences in the American military. No one likes to acknowledge it, but there's a strange sexual allure to being a woman and a soldier.

I mean sex while in Iraq. At war. While deployed.

Take this one girl. I heard from reliable sources in Iraq she gave head to every guy in her unit. I mean, I heard it from guys who were there. Participants. No rumor. Truth. Guys who'd meet me and say: *Hey, Kayla, I'm told* all *MI females really like to* . . .

Don't get me wrong. I've never much minded the taste of it myself. I just had to wonder: Where was the pleasure in this for *her?* Was she nuts? And meanwhile, she's making my life tons more difficult. Making it tougher for the rest of us females to get our work done without having guys insinuate that *blow jobs* was part of our Advanced Individual Training. It totally sucked, pun intended. It made it easy for guys over there to treat females as if we were less reliable. Which is enraging, since our skills as *soldiers* are what landed us in this war in the first place. Anyway, this particular girl got caught in the act, I guess you could say. More than once. Reprimanded for dereliction of duty. Almost comical when you really stop to think about it.

Or the twenty girls from this one unit who got sent home from Iraq pregnant. Knocked up. I heard a number of married guys were involved in this situation. Now that's a violation of the Uniform Code of Military Justice. Single girls and single guys can do as they please. Technically.

A woman at war: you're automatically a desirable commodity, and a scarce one at that. We call it "Queen for a Year." Even the unattractive girls start to act stuck-up. It's impossible not to notice.

"Queen for a Year." You won't find the phrase in the dictionary or any compilation of military terms. But say it among soldiers, and they'll know immediately what you mean. That's what we've called American women at war since nurses traveled to Vietnam in the sixties.

There's also this "deployment scale" for hotness. Let me explain. On a scale of ten, say she's a five. You know—average looks, maybe a little mousy, nothing special. But okay. Not a girl who gets second glances in civilian life. But in the Army, while we're deployed? Easily an eight. One hot babe. On average *every* girl probably gets three extra points on a ten-point scale. Useful. After you're in-country for a few months, all the girls begin to look good—or at least *better.* It changes—how should I say this?—the *dynamics* of being deployed.

You could get things easier, and you could get out of things easier. For a girl there were lots of little things you could do to make your load while deployed a whole lot lighter. You could use your femaleness to great advantage. You could do less work, get more assistance, and receive more special favors. Getting supplies? Working on the trucks? It could be a cinch—if you wanted it to be. It didn't take much. A little went a long way. Some of us worked it to the bone. Who says the life of the Army girl has to be cruel?

Lots of girls succumbed to temptation. The younger girls were the most susceptible. Many thrived and fed on the male attention they were getting for the first time in their lives.

I did my personal best to resist. So did my friends and the girls I respected. (That's why I respected them.) But many girls became full-fledged Queens for a Year. We saw it. And the guys talked.

The guys loved to talk. It didn't even especially matter what girls did or did not do. By the time it circled back to us (and in Iraq, everything that went around came around extra-fast), it might as well have been true.

"I watched her doing PT today. She was doing dips. She wants it!"

"I saw her in line for chow—she was wearing a tight brown T-shirt. She's looking for some action!"

Creepy.

And the locals? Even worse than Joes. At least some American guys have learned some subtlety about staring at our tits. They'd look out of the corner of their eyes. Or when we were looking away. Either Iraqi guys didn't care or didn't have the practice. They just blatantly and openly stared at our tits. *All the time.*

Apparently Iraqis asked our guys if we were prostitutes. Employed by the U.S. military to service the troops in the same way the Russian army managed sex for its soldiers in Kosovo. I didn't want *anyone* to think we were the U.S. equivalent of that!

None of this means that life in the Army while deployed to a combat zone has to be celibate. "What goes TDY stays TDY." It's a longstanding military tradition. License to do as we please while on "temporary duty"—that is, while away from our permanent post. And it stays TDY when we return home.

Sex is not specifically prohibited for deployed soldiers. It's just *implied* that it is not allowed. Yet the PX in Iraq sells condoms. The general attitude is: "Don't get caught." The one rule is: "Be discreet." Probably most of the single girls do it. Most of the single guys, too, if they ever get the chance. It becomes a simple matter of supply and demand.

And even though it's not okay, it's true—if a girl was indiscreet, if she got caught, or people knew, everyone lost respect for her. Like she was some slut. It was different, of course, for the guys. Somehow everyone got it that getting laid was okay for the guys.

So get real. The Army is not a monastery. More like a fraternity. Or a massive frat party. With weapons. With girls there for the taking—at least some of the time.

The guys are there for the taking too. And we took. I took.

But mostly I chose to be a bitch. I was nowhere as young as most of the other girls over there. Nowhere as innocent—at all. I'd hung around guys almost all my life; my punk rock scene in high school was overwhelmingly male. I'd dealt with sex from a young age. I'd been married.

In Iraq I felt I could deal with being Queen for a Year. But it still got to me. It still got me angry. Sometimes. I remember walking through the chow hall (once it was built) at the airfield was like running a gauntlet of eyes. Guys stared and stared and stared. Sometimes it felt like I was some fucking zoo animal. Guys hitting on us or saying inappropriate things—just *constant.*

Then sometimes I got in the mood. I'd enter the chow hall with a swing to my step. Check me out. Look. Don't touch. So occasionally it went to my head.

The girls joked, too. Some guys we met in Iraq were no prime specimens themselves. Funny nose, bad posture, bad teeth, whatever. But they also looked better. Always. So it worked both ways. Location, location, location. It played with all our minds.

It was like a separate bloodless war within the larger deadly one.

Let me tell you a story.

"Hey, Kayla! Show us your boobs!"

I was on a mountain near the Syrian border. At this time, I may well have been the most forward-deployed female soldier in Iraq. You could lose yourself in the view from up there, especially at dusk or dawn, when the sheer impact of the vista made your head spin.

I was alone. Alone with the guys, that is. For weeks.

They're frustrated. Horny. Talking openly about jerking off.

We sat in the blazing sun—*hot*—not doing much.

"Show us your tits, bitch!" Trash talk.

"No."

"C'mon, Kayla. Lift your T-shirt. For a second. Please! Let us see what you've got!"

"No."

I had no *principled* objection. I'd modeled nude for art classes in college. I had no qualms about showing my body.

Then the guys made what I considered their first real mistake. They started to ante up. Ten bucks. Twenty. Forty. Sixty-five. Eighty bucks. It went to eighty-seven dollars, and then a smart-ass threw in some M&M's he'd stashed.

They came to me with their proposition.

"C'mon, Kayla. This is hard-earned American money. Uncle Sam's almighty dollar. Plus M&M's. We know how much you like M&M's. Now show us your damn tits!"

"Fuck off, assholes!"

It was over. Because I might *remotely* have done it for free. I would *never* do it for money. What did these guys think I was? A whore?

WHO I WAS

HOT.

As a small child, I reached up to touch the stove. To play with fire. Then pulled back in a flash. And spoke my first word.

"Hot."

I always liked this detail about myself. That I neither cried in pain nor called for *mama* or *dada*. I always thought it said something about me, though I've been torn about what it said. That I was willing to venture out and take the risk, and report clearly on what I had learned? That's the perspective I prefer and like to think is true. But on darker days (and there have been plenty of those), I think this early encounter with fire left me deeply hesitant to take risks for fear of pain. As a consequence I've always believed that I have something to prove.

Especially to myself.

It's a terrible thing to think that fear of pain or of failure shadows your entire existence. It's a worse thing to believe that you must struggle against those fears *every day of your life*. To prove to yourself and the world that you can do it. You can take risks. You are not afraid and will never be afraid.

I can admit it. I've been afraid. I've always been afraid. But

I'm most afraid I'll pass up a chance to overcome my fears.

Hence the Army? Not so fast. Nothing is as simple as that. We'll get there when we get there.

Growing up, my favorite drug was LSD. If you think about it, this makes sense. Marijuana made me groggy and slow-witted. I could never concentrate when I was high. Everything moved in absurd slow motion. People giggled like idiots and acted all profound while making no sense at all. I hated the experience. Who wanted to sound stupid? Not me. So I dropped acid, and it delivered a crystallized sense of lucidity in which my brain spun so quickly and lurched here and there in ways I could barely keep up with. But I did keep up. I always kept up. I don't recall having the notorious bad trip, only the lukewarm trip—the one that left me unenlightened (but hardly undeterred). But acid always made me think. And I loved (and love) to think.

Life in a combat zone made me think, too. Deployment in Iraq was like this yearlong invitation to think, though a year was probably way too much time. There was the war, but the war (as reported at the time) ended in May 2003. We'd only been in-country for a couple of months. Then came supposed peace. And during the peace, at least until the war began again, there was more time to sit around between missions. You started to go crazy with the thinking and the waiting and the sitting around. And the bullshit. You wondered what life might be like without so much time to think. You thought about how much you were thinking. You thought about thinking about thinking. Like an acid trip without the acid or the trip. Just thoughts. What fun was that?

I can't explain my attitude toward risk taking. Is it contradictory? There are things I've done, and there are things I'd never do. For instance I've gone to bars and drunk since I was thirteen. But I refused to get my first tattoo until I was eighteen, when it was legal to do so. (I now have six.) I would not get in a car with a drunk driver. I would never take that risk. But I've had lots of unprotected sex over the years. And I've let homeless guys I've never met before stay over in my house. Those risks I would take.

But before I get too far, let me say a few words about Mom and Dad.

My mom was a Republican with an antiauthoritarian streak, and my dad was a former pot smoker with anger-management problems. Mom had been married twice before; her first ex-husband had custody of her kids, and she didn't see them much. Dad had been divorced once; his ex-wife was a hippie who had lived on a commune in Washington State. Many years later, long after my folks split up, we all went out to Washington to attend the wedding of his daughter from his first marriage. We stayed with his ex-wife. Everyone got along fine. My mother, my step-mother, and my dad's first ex-wife liked to joke "There are three Mrs. Williams in the room."

Dad's daughter, my half-sister, Yarrow, was the sane one in my family. Kind and loving and generous, she was twelve years older than me. Mom said that when she'd first met Yarrow, she'd immediately thought about my dad: "This guy's got good genes." And decided she wanted his child. Years later Dad told me he'd felt used by Mom—tricked by her—and that he had not wanted another child then. I didn't really want to hear it. But at that point he wanted to come clean and build a better relationship with me.

My parents married, and I was born a couple of years later.

And a year or so after that, Mom bundled me into her car and left my dad. Said she wanted to raise this child alone, maybe as recompense for losing her other children to her first husband. Who knows?

Anyway, so ended the story of Mom and Dad. I certainly continued to see Dad throughout my childhood, and he certainly continued to have his tantrums. When I was still small, he grabbed me by my ponytail and threw me onto my bed so hard I smacked my head. Or the time I got muddy once while we were camping, and he ordered me to strip. So I lay huddled, freezing and naked, in the backseat of our car while he washed my clothes at a Laundromat—all the time berating me for ruining our vacation. I must have been five or six. Though he could be kind sometimes, too. I remember he made me this excellent robot costume for Halloween once, and he made cool snow dragons (instead of snowmen) and sprayed them with green food dye and gave them red tongues. He was always *trying* to be a good dad, even though it was obvious it didn't come naturally to him.

Mom was an artist from a well-to-do family, but she seemed intent on having us slide down the social ladder as much as possible. Her life played like Horatio Alger in reverse: riches to rags. Maybe it wasn't her fault, I don't know. At first things were good, though the neighborhood in Columbus, Ohio, she found for us after she left Dad was so sketchy some of my friends from school were never permitted to visit. But Mom got me into an outstanding private school with all these wealthy kids. So I moved between these two worlds—privileged and poor.

The school was multicultural and had a terrific curriculum. I started French lessons when I was really young, and Mom was so pleased that she somehow managed to take me to France twice so I could improve my language skills. Awesome experiences. So she clearly cared that I become intellectual, and put energy into that. I enjoyed being around all these bright kids during the day, and I did well in school. Meanwhile our finances remained okay for a while. She had solid connections in the gallery and crafts-show scene, and her sculptures and carvings sold.

Everything changed when I was nine or so. A serious financial setback coincided with health problems for my mother, and things got very rough. I remember peering around the doorframe, watching her going through the bills, trying to make her money stretch. Crying that we were three months behind on rent.

Things never got good again after that. We never regained our footing. There was not much money for toys, movies, vacations, treats; no money for new clothes for me at the start of a new school year. Little money for food, even, and eventually we had to collect food stamps so we could eat. Mom—a Republican, remember?—hated that we were living on public assistance. She hated people on public assistance, and now here she was, one of those people. She thought people on public assistance should wear orange jumpsuits and live in workhouses. Still does.

My mom—coming from Oklahoma country—felt it was an obligation for any child of hers to learn how to shoot a gun. Essential life skill, that's all. So when I was ten years old, the time came for me to learn. She drove me down to some weirdo's private land, and the people there handed me a .22. The thing felt *heavy*. Then they gave me a .38, and finally a rifle—but that was too much for me to lift. I never forgot how to handle a weapon. More than a dozen years later, at boot camp, these memories came right back again like déjà vu.

———

Age twelve: I switched to public school for high school to save money. Suddenly I was this brainy geek, feeling rejected because I was smart. So I rejected everyone instead. And became a punk. A lot of punks I met were the same way.

I got into the punk and alternative scene when I was thirteen. I loved the music. (Still do.) Jane's Addiction. Violent Femmes. Fugazi. The Dead Kennedys. I began to hang around seventeen- and eighteen-year-old high-school dropouts. Everyone so fucking *angry* all the time. Ronald Reagan had fueled our collective rage at societal injustice. We got pissed off about racism and classism, but mostly it was about the music. We saw all the shows. I attended the first Lollapalooza back in 1991. And since the punk movement in Columbus was so small, it overlapped with every other marginal scene—Goth, Skater, even neo-Nazi—and we all ended up together at the same shows. So things blurred.

I wore the combat boots. I looked tough. Intimidating. People locked their car doors when I walked by. That was cool. But it also infuriated me. I believed this was prejudice. I developed a sense of kinship with black people. People judged me on my appearance—just like white racism. I didn't think: Lose the look and I'd be just a good lily-white girl again. I thought: Fuck America! I was thirteen. There were a lot of things I didn't fully understand.

I did understand that the punk scene got me out of the house. Gave me a community. Like a family. And got me into a few tight situations. Like when I ran away from home for a few weeks the summer I was thirteen.

That was a risk that made sense to me.

As a runaway, I hung with Allison. Allison was fifteen with a

Mohawk and braces. Allison was convinced that Missing Persons had photographs of her, and so Allison decided to alter her appearance. I remember the night I watched her untwist her braces—she pried them off with scissors. She was so proud of herself when she got them off. And I looked at her and I laughed. Here's this fifteen-year-old girl with a fucking Mohawk who somehow thought that undoing her braces was going to help her escape notice.

We got ourselves into a bad situation toward the end. We stayed at a house we called the Dog Shit House because there were pit bulls everywhere and no one picked up the shit. The place was disgusting. We crashed there until I found a box of literature and began to look through it. It was neo-Nazi propaganda, and I was still a little too naive to be sure what I was reading. I remember here I was with Allison—a Jewish girl—in this neo-Nazi filth palace. Then one of the neo-Nazis found a picture in my bag of an African American friend from my school. "Who the fuck is this?" Then all the guys began to flip out on Allison and me. "Who the fuck is this nigger?" One of them grabbed my bag and set it on fire, while another one got a gun. But no bullets. Ended up throwing the gun at me while they chased me down the street. (Allison stayed at the Dog Shit House, but she had to fuck a guy to do it.) I ran to a house and begged the people to let me in. "I'm being chased by neo-Nazis!" I slept on their couch and returned home the next day. But my mother had changed the locks on me.

A couple of years after that, my mom ended up throwing me out of the house. She'd found evidence I was using drugs and wanted me out immediately.

That's when I moved to Kentucky to live with my father. But

I was already thinking: If this didn't work out, if my father threw me out of *his* house, I'd be homeless. And *that* was not a risk I was willing to take. I knew I couldn't handle a JDC (juvenile detention center). The very thought freaked me out. Scared me straight, I guess you could say. So I graduated from high school at sixteen and went directly to college.

But I couldn't see any point to it. I felt overwhelmed, so I dropped out of college after freshman year. Moved back to Columbus, and heroin had hit the streets. Everyone had just seen the film *Trainspotting* and deemed it exceptionally cool. Shooting heroin was suddenly very cool. A lot of my punk rock friends and acquaintances were using, and here I was trying to hold down a job as a secretary. I was hanging around homeless punks at night and on weekends, many of whom were doing hard drugs, and I was going to an office during the week.

I had vowed I would always support myself. And here were my friends calling me a poser because I worked in an office and dressed in nice clothes. I didn't know what to say besides, "Fuck off! You're eating my food. At least someone here has a job." Around this time, too, I noticed the sexism of the punk rock scene. I'd taken a couple of women's studies courses that made me think more about issues like feminism and misogyny. And here were these punk rockers treating me like a girl, and I hated it.

"How you gonna dis your bros for just some girl?" they'd say to one another. So that's all I was to them. *Just some girl.* That's all I'd ever been to them. It really pissed me off. That and the fact I was hanging around a guy, Douglas, who was knocking me around, persuaded me to finish college after all. Get out of Columbus. Get a degree. Not end up a loser like these losers.

I graduated from Bowling Green State University when I was

twenty. I graduated cum laude with my entering class even though I had missed a year. By the time I was twenty-two, I was employed in Tampa, Florida, by Infinite OutSource, a fund-raising collective funded by the Corporation for Public Broadcasting. I was raising more than five million dollars a year through direct mail and telemarketing for fifteen television and radio stations nationwide. I owned my first house, and I earned a salary of thirty thousand dollars a year. I was getting job offers in the nonprofit world for twice as much money. But I was also wanting to make a change.

I was feeling as if I had never really challenged myself. I felt I'd never learned how to fail. I'd never lost my fear of failure. I was at a point in my life when I felt that if I didn't do something drastic, I was going to wake up in a house with a white picket fence and a minivan and kids who hated me.

My love life? Complicated as always.

Before I got my house, I had rented a room in my apartment to a girl who worked as a stripper. She started to date a Saudi. Tariq was a friend of the Saudi guy. That's how he and I first met.

It's funny. Meeting a Muslim through a stripper strikes me as funny.

Tariq—everyone called him Rick—came over and we'd talk. We went on a first date. (He forgot his wallet and insisted I wait at the restaurant while he drove home to get it so he could pay for dinner.)

Rick observed Ramadan—kind of. He wouldn't drink alcohol or smoke cigarettes during the day. But he worked in a liquor store. He would not have sex if the Koran was in the room with us. So we moved it out.

Rick was Muslim in the way that most Christians are

Christian. Christians believe all kinds of things. "I believe premarital sex is wrong." But they don't follow their beliefs. "Yeah, I *believe* it's wrong—but I'm still going to do it."

We never lived together. But eventually he began to stay at my house every single night. We also shared a car for a while, when his car broke down. But he always kept his own apartment. I'd suggest: "We could pool our resources." But it was important to him to maintain his own space.

Rick's rich Kuwaiti and Saudi friends had everything. Ahmed's father bought him a Porsche. The other Ahmed's father bought him a house to live in for a year even before he started college so he could practice his English. Their families bought them everything. But aside from coming to America to get a fantastic education, these guys were also in the States to sleep with American women. To get it out of their system, so they could go home and marry good Muslim girls. They even admitted it. "Yes. That's exactly what happens." They couldn't fuck around with good Muslim girls back home. So they came to the States. They went to college. They slept with American girls. Then they went home and settled down.

They didn't think twice about it. Same with most Arabic women. They boarded a plane for the States and changed out of their *hijabs* in the cramped lavatories—and put on make-up, Chanel dresses, and high heels.

Rick was nothing like his friends. Rick worked two jobs so he could afford community college. I respected him for trying to make his own way in the world.

Rick was gifted at languages. He spoke Arabic, Greek, English, French, and Russian. Born in Jordan, he spent the first five years of his life in Lebanon. His mother told me stories of

Beirut during the civil war. She described how her five- and seven-year-old children buried their faces in her lap and wept while bombs fell around them. She said she prayed simply for her family to survive each day. I could not imagine what this would be like for a mother.

She made me think about how we—as Americans—are so willing to bomb other people's countries.

Rick and I were together for two years. He taught me words in his dialect in Arabic. I shopped for vegetarian products in the neighborhood Middle Eastern stores. I learned to love the cadences of the language. All the people in the shops were so encouraging and helpful. Was I married to a Muslim? Or was I Lebanese myself? Apparently my eyes and skin tone allowed me to pass for Lebanese, which surprised me. "No. I'm not Lebanese." But they remained just as friendly and kind. Just as eager to help me improve my few Arabic words.

I saw an intimacy to the Arab community in Tampa that I envied. Everyone was so close in a way I never experienced in white America—certainly not at college or growing up in Columbus. You need a new carburetor for your car? Take it to a friend's garage and get it replaced extra cheap. You need money? Friends lend it to you. The community was like a family, and people respected and trusted one another more than I'd ever experienced. Maybe in small towns it's like this, or certainly in some other ethnic communities you still see it. And when my older sister, Yarrow, was dying of cancer, I saw how members of her church brought food to her husband and made sure he was doing okay. But in big cities or many other places in America? Forget it.

It wasn't until I joined the military that I experienced anything like this again. In the military you'd be moving into your barracks, and you'd be having trouble hauling your shit, and someone would immediately drop everything to help you. They don't know who you are. They don't give a fuck who you are, but you're wearing the same uniform and they immediately help you. That's the way it works in the military.

I came to love Rick's willingness to share his community with me. I was honored to be a part of it for the two years we were together. It was tough, really tough, to let go.

As our relationship became more serious, we began to look at each other a little differently. I started to ask myself: Could I marry this person? If we're going to have a committed future together, how do things need to be between us?

I criticized Rick, but if anyone else criticized him or how he treated me, I got defensive. We'd been dating for six months when he picked me up from work. My coworkers knew I was dating a Muslim. And I thought they knew me. The very next day a woman from work said to me: "Oh, he doesn't look like anything I expected." At the time Rick had a ponytail and an earring. I snapped at her: "What did you expect? A turban and a camel?" Whether she could admit it or not, that was absolutely what she expected. She thought: Muslim. One word. And instantly she had a picture in her head.

My mom told me: "You shouldn't marry Rick because your aunt's husband is Muslim—and that's been so hard for her." I said: "They're still married after thirty years! They're happy and love each other. You've been divorced three times. Do you think I am really going to listen to marriage advice from you?!"

At the same time Rick said that if he had kids he didn't know if he'd want to raise them in America. I understood what he meant. If I had a daughter, I don't know if I would want to raise her in the circumstances I'd known as a girl. Once Rick and I were in Sears waiting for my alternator to get fixed. A man and a woman and their kid came into the garage office. The girl was about ten years old. Way prepubescent. She wore low-slung tight hip-hugger jeans, a pink skin-tight tank top with little straps, and little strappy sandals. She swayed her hips when she walked. Rick shook his head. Disgusted by the extent to which we sexualize children in our society—and the extent to which we allow children to sexualize themselves.

On other occasions Rick said to me: "You know, you shouldn't wear that tank top. If you wear that tank top, people will judge you in a certain way. They are not going to listen to what you have to say. And you're smart. I want people to judge you for what you have to say—not just for how you look."

Rick acted more like a traditional—or stereotypical—Muslim the longer we were together.

When I was just an American chick he slept with—or whatever—it was no big deal for him. What did he care what I acted like? But as things got more serious and I started to look more like wife material than fucking material, he wanted to control me more.

He'd say: *You can't behave like this. . . . You can't do this. . . . You can't wear that.*

Don't get me wrong: I've dated Catholic guys who were far worse.

When a personality conflict with a new female superior got me fired from my job in October 1999, I fell into a bad depression. Rick took care of me. He brought me flowers and orange juice. He mowed my lawn and made sure I was okay. I appreciated how *genuine* he was—how it was never just words with him. He never gave me a line about how he felt. He told me exactly how he felt, and I could always trust he meant it.

"I'm married."

When Rick finally told me, it felt like a violation of trust. What if I had gotten pregnant? What if I didn't want to have a child out of wedlock? I understood why he had hesitated to tell me. How do you explain when you haven't been dating somebody for very long? *I'm married. I don't even really know the woman I married; we never slept together. It was arranged so I could stay in the States; she's my old roommate's girlfriend. And by the way, I just gave you the power to get me deported.* But then, once you've been dating somebody for a while, and you trust her enough to tell her, how do you explain? *By the way, we've been dating for a long time, and we're pretty close, but just so you know, I'm married.*

It freaked me out.

On another occasion he said: "In my faith the children take the mother's religion. But you don't have a religion. So if we did have children, of course we would raise them Muslim."

I didn't appreciate that, either.

And there was another thing. I asked Rick sometimes about Islam. Once he told me about their end-of-time beliefs, which seemed to resemble the Christian notion of apocalypse. In the end of days, Rick said, all Muslims would rise up and kill all non-believers.

So I asked: "Would you kill me? Would you rise up and kill me?"

And he said: "I don't know."

"*You don't know?*"

That was a big deal to me.

"How can you *not know?*"

He was being honest.

When I enlisted in the Army as a linguist and told him I might be assigned to learn Arabic, he said I was planning to spy on his people. I believed him when he said that if I pursued a military career, there was no way he could be with me.

When I was in fact assigned Arabic, I announced: "Well, we're breaking up."

And he said, "No, I don't want to break up. I still want us to be together. I'm changing my mind."

During boot camp, whenever I was given permission to use the telephone, I called Rick. My decision to join the military was not just a decision to get away from him. In part it was. I admit that. But certainly not entirely. I hated that we were separated. When I completed basic training, he came to see me graduate. By then he'd grown this really long and wild goatee, and he looked like a cross between some crazy terrorist and a hip college kid. My parents didn't know what to make of him at all.

Everything got really complicated. In the end, once I moved to California, it was my decision to start dating other people that finally broke us up. After that Rick would never speak to me again.

It's hard to have someone with whom you've spent two years of your life, and cared about, hate you and want nothing to do with you.

But Rick was also a big part of my decision to enlist, because he gave me confidence that I could handle the Army. He had *so much* confidence in me. He certainly would have wanted me to do something else. Anything else. But the respect he showed me and the confidence he had in me helped me believe that I was capable of doing something I never thought I could do.

I owe him that. Despite how much he hated what I did, I don't think I could have done it without him.

ENLISTED

THERE WAS ONE more reason I enlisted in the Army.

I wanted to prove a former boyfriend wrong. I had dated Douglas when I was eighteen. A real arrogant son-of-a-bitch who wanted to be a Marine, he told me, and liked to yell at me—as if yelling at *me* was good practice for his Marine duty. He'd yell at me about how I could never make it in the military because I could never handle people yelling at me. Anyway, Douglas and I had this very unhealthy relationship that involved a fair amount of violence. I'm ashamed to admit it, but I was pretty into Douglas for a while, and that was hard, because I *hated* how Douglas made me feel—which was weak and vulnerable. I hated that he acted like he knew something about me that I couldn't contradict. Maybe he was right. Maybe I could never hack the military, how could I say for sure? As for the yelling, Douglas turned it into this twisted deal where I was supposed to *like* that he was cruel to me—as a way to prove to him I could handle it. I'm not proud I stuck with Douglas as long as I did, but lots of women stick in marriages far longer where worse stuff is happening. (And that sucks, too.)

Of course Douglas never became a Marine. For all I know he's drunk facedown in some gutter somewhere.

Eventually I got out of town. I returned to college in Bowling Green, and I got away from Douglas in the process. Leaving town has tended to be my way of ending relationships that I otherwise had no idea how to end.

So, five years later, I thought of Douglas when I enlisted. And even later still, during basic training, when I wanted so badly to quit, I thought of him yelling at me. Taunting me how I could never make it in the military. And I'd think: Fuck you, Douglas. And I kept at it—to prove him wrong.

After I lost my job, no one could console me. I just felt shitty all the time. As if someone had torched my house and the arsonist had gotten the insurance money.

In January 2000, in what was still Bill Clinton's America, I joined the Army Reserves to train as an interpreter. The thought that I might go to war was pretty distant.

The reservists I met were actually cool. I was impressed by how smart and well educated they were. Many had already done active duty, and they enjoyed what they did. They also talked up the benefits of enlistment—the cash bonus, the money for graduate school when I got out. It all sounded good to me.

Enlisting meant I would not be geographically stable, but I would be financially stable. This is certainly one big reason that there are so many low-income whites and minorities in the military. There are many reasons to join the Army. But without a doubt it's a great way—leaving aside the whole prospect of getting maimed or killed—to better your career prospects.

I learned that if I enlisted I'd be gone for two years of training. Two years away from my house. Two years away from my life. It felt like a huge risk.

It appealed to me. It was a risk I was ready to imagine.

I enlisted in the late spring of 2000. I was twenty-three. The minimum contract at that time was two years active duty; six years was the maximum. Due to the extensive training for my MOS (military occupational specialty) as a linguist, my minimum enlistment option was four years. But four years meant no signing bonus. If I committed to five years active duty, however, I'd get fifteen thousand dollars cash for signing plus fifty thousand dollars for grad school. If I signed for six years, I'd get an additional five-thousand-dollar cash bonus. But I understood earning potential. If anyone imagined I'd settle for five thousand dollars for one more year of my life, they could kiss my ass. I signed for five years.

The ride to boot camp at Fort Jackson, South Carolina, was a fair sign of what was in store. Pouring down rain the entire way, cramped in this awful van with holes in the seats and holes in the floor. The windows leaked and the engine rattled.

Basic training. It was like going to the movies when the picture is totally out of focus. Or the projectionist left the image off-kilter, and the actors' faces are all split in two. And you're sitting there in the middle of a row toward the front. You've got your popcorn, your soft drink. You're settled. And when the film rolls you think, No problem. Someone near the exit will get up and tell the kids at the concession stand to fix the goddamn picture. But no one moves. The audience sits there. Everyone just kind of adjusts to the situation. Like they squint or turn their heads a certain way. Deal with the fuzziness or that the actors' foreheads are below their chins. Maybe the movie is *supposed* to be that way?

I understood that basic training was indoctrination. I understood the aim was to break us down and rebuild us into what the Army wanted. But I was not too amenable to the concept.

It was generally frowned upon to challenge our drill sergeants, but I remember in an Army Values class I could not keep quiet. The drill sergeant was complaining about American antiwar activists: "Those damned antiwar protesters don't know anything. They don't understand how wrong they are and how wrong it is that they do that. They shouldn't be allowed to protest." And so on.

So I responded: "The right of American people to say whatever they want is one reason I joined the military. It's one reason I am willing to die for my country. Those protesters are exercising their ultimate responsibility as Americans by expressing their political opinion."

The drill sergeant did not yell at me. I got the impression it caused him to think—if only for a moment or two.

Mainly I found the drill sergeants to be okay. They respected me as a slightly older, more mature soldier-in-training. A lot of the other new recruits had never lived away from home, had never paid a bill on their own.

On the other hand some of the drills themselves were ridiculous. Take bayonet training.

Drill sergeant: "What is the spirit of the bayonet?"

Us: "To kill! To kill! To kill without mercy, Drill Sergeant!"

"What makes the green grass grow?"

"Blood! Blood! Bright red blood, Drill Sergeant!"

We all screamed "Kill!" in unison and stabbed at tires stuck to four-by-fours.

There were other memorable moments. Like learning to throw a live hand grenade. Or the drill sergeant who explained his personal theory about guns and girls.

"Females do better on the firing range," he bellowed at us one afternoon. "You know why? Because females know how to follow instructions. Having never touched a weapon before, they have to pay attention. Like good soldiers should. As for you men? You could learn a thing or two by watching the females learn."

I neglected to tell him I already knew how to shoot. At Fort Jackson I fired a weapon again for the first time in more than ten years. I was surprised; it felt good. Empowering. I liked having a weapon in my hands again.

I felt like a freak until I realized that so many of us were freaks in one sense or another. I found people at boot camp who appreciated the same alternative music I did, and felt the same cynicism I did about fitting the Army mold. The guys in particular were basically good guys, though they gave us females endless shit for the differential female standards on PT tests: *Girls get off easy. . . . Girls can't hack it.*

They had a point. Females got twenty minutes to run two miles compared to fifteen minutes for males. Push-ups: We needed a much lower minimum to qualify; the guys had to do more than twice as many. But guys couldn't bitch if we passed the male tests. That was my response. I was eventually able to surpass the male minimum standard for push-ups for my age group. I also worked hard to get my run to where I'd meet the male standards. Other girls didn't give a shit. They'd argue that our body types were different, that females tended to have strong abs, but we didn't usually have the same innate upper-body strength as most guys. And some guys understood that.

It's poetic justice that of the two people who didn't make it through Basic, one was male and one female. The girl collapsed quietly; the guy lunged for a drill sergeant's throat and had to be dragged away kicking and screaming by Military Police.

There was tremendous variety among the women in my company. I especially admired some of the older women. One African American was thirty-two and a nurse. She was tough, and the younger black women turned to her for guidance. Another woman was thirty-four, with six kids. Six kids—can you believe it? I have no idea why she enlisted. Allergic to the regulation black socks we wore, her feet got so horribly raw and bloody they had to send her to the hospital for a couple of days. But when she returned she finished the final ruck march. She made it through.

The younger girls were more of a pain. One cried and cried, claiming her recruiter said she'd never have to handle or fire a weapon in the Army because she was a female. Said she'd been horribly misled. Was anyone really this dumb? Had she honestly thought the Army would not make her learn to shoot?

Other girls fixated on appearances. They polished and polished their boots until they motherfucking shone. You could see your reflection in them. I never was that kind of soldier. When it came to appearances, I was going to meet—not exceed—the standard. If a sergeant told me to spit-shine my boots, I did it. But I never did it just to do it. Who gave a shit?

I did not see girls bond at boot camp. Sharing a shower head with another girl was no big deal. We got used to it. But require us to share three washers and dryers for nine weeks? "Who's the owner of this skanky thing?" Girls cut in front of one another all the time. Forced into close quarters, we just got catty. Very catty. I really hated living with females.

"I miss my mom." How many times did I hear this from some newly enlisted teenager? Not me. What *I* missed: Rick's arms around me. My strong and sexy man, so smart and tender. So mine. My dogs: Karma's waggy butt, Kinski's soft fur. Pizza and ice cream. Thai food and beer. Wine. Omelets. Popcorn. Television. Cigarettes. Making love. Being naked. Taking walks. Going to the park. Watching movies. Being alone. Going shopping. Taking a hot bath. Driving my car. Swimming. Cooking. Sleeping late. Calling friends. Air-conditioning. Normal clothes. Privacy.

But I discovered at Fort Jackson I could do things I never knew I could do. Endurance, stamina, willpower. You name it. I found I was strong beyond all my prior understanding. I learned what I could do, because I had to do it.

I also learned to follow the Army's rules, whether I liked them or not.

"What are those streaks in your hair, Private?" A female superior confronted me.

"My hair, Drill Sergeant?"

"Your hair, soldier. What are those highlights doing in there?"

"It's the sunshine, Drill Sergeant. It's put streaks in. I used to dye my hair cherry red, but this is my natural color."

She peered to get a closer look.

"Faddish highlights are not allowed in the Army, soldier. Get rid of them. Dye your hair a uniform shade."

"Yes, Drill Sergeant."

I dyed my hair dishwater blond that night.

I moved to the Defense Language Institute in September 2000. Only then did I learn that my score on the DLAB (Defense Language Aptitude Battery) qualified me for a Cat IV language, the more-difficult-language category. As Rick predicted, the Cat IV language selected for me was Arabic. I began my sixty-three-week course and, due to a few additional weeks of break built into the schedule, I ended up living in Monterey, California, until February 2002.

DLI was like a college campus for soldiers. A surprising number were Mormons. Apparently Mormons frequently did missionary work overseas, for which they were required to go through a language-immersion course. A clean-cut crowd that avoided cigarettes, coffee, and alcohol. Not like the rest of us.

Aside from the thirty hours of language class each week, and PT and other training, we had a lot of freedom. For instance, we could drink in our rooms after an initial period when it was forbidden. As a joint-service environment we were also a diverse bunch. There was even one arrogant jerk with a master's in philosophy from Dartmouth.

I'd always been good at school, and DLI was no different. I got good grades and made dean's list each semester. So when I needed to find a way to pay my bills, I was granted permission to get a job outside. I found part-time work at the Borders bookstore in town. I also volunteered for a Big Brothers/Big Sisters program and hung around with a ten-year-old named Ellen. Took her horseback riding. Brought her to the gym with me when I worked out.

———

I also made a close friend at DLI, although it took awhile. Zoe remembers the first time she saw me. She didn't like me very much. It was a Sunday night meeting arranged by the floor sergeant in charge of cleaning the barracks. The floor sergeant's job was to announce the cleaning duties for the week and ensure they were done on time and to standard; we didn't have a janitorial staff. We were our own janitors.

That weekend I'd been permitted to go off post for the first time. When you initially arrived at DLI, you were placed on restriction. This meant you wore your uniform all the time and you never left the installation. But as soon as I got my first day pass, I checked myself into a day spa for a massage and a facial. I had recently completed boot camp, and my body felt completely beat up.

Right before the floor meeting, where we were supposed to talk about cleaning the bathrooms and sweeping, mopping, and vacuuming the floors, I said: "Hey, I went to the spa today. It was so great. They totally pamper you."

Zoe was appalled. She told me later that she'd thought: Who does that bitch think she is? What a snob! Who does that? Who goes to a fucking day spa? And she could not believe I was wearing an ugly green cardigan. (Of course, years later Zoe is a completely different person. Now Zoe *loves* going to the spa.)

The first time I remember her, we were at a party in somebody's apartment. A girl with curly red hair. Tattoos. An expressive face, an expressive voice. I was sitting on top of a dryer in the kitchen. (In military housing in Monterey the washers and dryers were always in the kitchen.) We got to talking. I was getting wasted, so I have no memory of what we discussed. Probably music and men. That's a good guess.

It's unusual for me to pursue a friendship with another woman, but I really liked Zoe. We'd run into each other and talk. Then we started to go to the farmers' market together. We'd buy ourselves flowers and fresh fruit. There was an Indian place in Monterey that sold Indian burritos. (What's a burrito when it's not a burrito? A nan burrito.) We'd have nan burritos together— and talk. I soon came to feel, though not always in the details, that Zoe was like a younger version of myself.

Beautiful and amazing Zoe. Crazy and wild. Small tits. Great ass. Later guys would joke that the two of us put together would make the perfect girl. My rack, Zoe's ass.

She'd joined the Army when she was seventeen. She'd gotten out of high school and didn't want to go to college right away. She didn't see any way to support herself. She knew the military was there. She knew she could get paid to learn another language. So she picked the same job her mom had in the Air Force, only her mom had been a Russian linguist, while Zoe ended up an Arabic linguist.

In my experience people who have family members in the military are more likely to join the military. It just seems normal. In Zoe's case she saw the benefits of a military life. She'd lived in Japan, Germany, England, and Texas. Her mom retired as a master sergeant after twenty years in the Air Force and then went to law school. Her mom did very well for herself. In the military she was able to raise a kid on her own.

Zoe's folks divorced when she was still a baby. Her dad was not around when she was growing up. Like lots of girls with absent fathers, she's had a tough time forming decent relationships with men. Or trusting men. Or even knowing how to deal with men. Like me, she's been hurt. And like me, she's had difficulties maintaining female friendships. She tended to assume that every relationship would get yanked away from her. So if you wanted to stay friends with Zoe, you had to keep after her.

Zoe also wanted to party a little more than I did at DLI. She was still at that stage where she wanted to go out to bars, get drunk, and meet random men. When I was at DLI, that was not something I did too often.

I watched Zoe grow up in the military. When we met at DLI, for example, she wanted to have a baby. Right away.

"Why shouldn't I get pregnant and have a child? Why not have a baby to love and take care of?"

I was adamantly opposed. "No single motherhood when you're eighteen! Not a good idea."

"But my momma raised me by herself in the Air Force, and that worked out well."

She moved away from that position gradually.

So Zoe and I became great friends. And she was the only person who attended my wedding, besides my husband's parents. At the time she was really my only friend.

As the wedding approached, she was supportive.

"You sure you want to do this? Okay, if you want to do this, I'm there for you."

Maybe it was because of Rick that I couldn't quite imagine myself with an Army guy. Or maybe because the DLI guy I had been dating was so damned competitive with me. In any case, I ended up marrying the anti-Army.

It was at Borders that I'd met my husband. He was my manager. A sweet and sensitive civilian who began to urge me to end my Army life. (Especially after we were married and we saw *Black Hawk Down:* I had been assigned to an air assault division, and when he saw the helicopter crash in the movie my husband freaked over what might happen to me in a combat zone. *I* was freaked because the movie made him cry—in public. There were people I knew in the audience. It made him look like a big pussy.)

A few months later the marriage ended. Zoe remained just as supportive.

"You're way too good for Mark, anyway. He's short. He's bald. Trust me. You'll do better."

Would I? I was confused. Not so confident.

Zoe graduated from DLI a few months before I did and left for her advanced individual training at Goodfellow Air Force Base in San Angelo, Texas. She then left Texas the week after I got there. We both knew we were going to Fort Campbell, and we agreed that when I arrived at Campbell we'd find a place and move in together.

"ARE YOU GOING TO WAR?"

"Are you going to war?"

I was already awake and getting dressed at 5:30 A.M. I had just switched on the television when my cell phone rang. An old friend from my high school days. Her voice tight with anxiety. Worried out of her mind. For me.

September 11, 2001. And there they were. The Towers. A stunning Tuesday morning in New York City. How many dead we had no idea. Later that day I wrote in my journal: "Humpty Dumpty falls off the ledge and all the king's horses and all the king's men can't put him back together again. And he's just an egg, right?"

A funereal hush at chow. Formation tense. The post closed. All noncommissioned officers yanked for gate guard duty. We moved to a high-threat alert. In class the television monitors remained tuned to Al-Jazeera and to the Lebanese channel. (That's what total-immersion technique means. No *Good Morning, America* for us.) Totally surreal to be watching this news from Al-Jazeera's perspective.

Suddenly Arabic is the most important language to know in the world.

A guy in tears in the corner said his sister fucking *worked* at the World Trade Center. Couldn't get his cell phone to function, so I lent him mine. When our Egyptian American teacher arrived, he told us that his lovely American neighbor had spat on him as he got into his car to come to work.

My phone returned to me, I called Tariq in Tampa, but there was no answer. I didn't leave a message. What could I say? I was still so angry at Rick for cutting off contact, even though I also sympathized because I knew what troubles he was going to face if this tragedy had been instigated by Arabs. Why didn't he try to call me? Why did he never try to reach me in the weeks or months after 9/11?

Moving around DLI from building to building became a cruel parody of Checkpoint Charlie. Guards everywhere. *Show your ID. Don't leave your bag. What's in the backpack? What business do you have here? Let's see your ID.* As if the next attack might be here—in Monterey.

I would be lying if I said I was completely surprised or shocked that day. Already at boot camp, the people who trained us had been deployed. The First Gulf War. Somalia. Haiti. Kosovo. They'd gone overseas and done real-world missions. Already then I realized I was probably going to go. Somewhere. The longer I was in, the more inevitable deployment felt.

So 9/11 confirmed that reality for me. I already knew who Osama bin Laden was. At DLI we talked about the terrorist networks that existed in the world. We knew it might happen. We knew it could happen.

During class that day, as we followed the coverage on Al-Jazeera, a Marine yelled out: "Kill 'em all! I can't wait to get those bastards!"

We knew he'd get his chance. We knew we all would.

———

I completed my advanced individual training at Goodfellow Air Force Base. Stuck in a windowless facility where I learned the ins and outs of being a cryptologic linguist (98G). A kind of glorified way to say eavesdropper. Or spy—just as Rick had said. A job whose aim was, among other things, to provide early warnings of potential threats for our troops.

Goodfellow was all basic training all over again. No cigarettes, period. No alcohol in rooms, though we could still go out to drink. (Even drive to Austin to party now and then.) No opposite-gender visitations in our rooms. For the ones who came directly from basic training, Goodfellow was more of the same or maybe somewhat better. For the rest of us who came from DLI, it was a real pain in the ass.

During this time I filed divorce papers myself because my husband refused to do it.

I celebrated my divorce in Texas. Official: 06JUN02.

I got a new haircut. A new car. Two very cool new tattoos, one on each shoulder. (Mark had never wanted me to get any more.) And once I got to Fort Campbell, in July 2002, I also got a new house.

At the barracks at Fort Campbell, the woman who showed me my room said: "Make sure all the ceiling tiles are set right. Some soldiers hide drugs up there, so some ceiling tiles might be crooked." She also said: "Make sure all the tiles are fit really snug, so the rats don't get in." Rats? I really didn't want to live with rats. (I ended up living in Iraq with things much worse than rats. Like camel spiders: huge and hideous, they completely freaked me out.) Driving around with a realtor, I probably looked at five houses before I said: "I'll take that one."

As we planned, Zoe moved in.

It took a month for my stuff to arrive from Monterey. The Army paid for shipping my stuff, but they delivered it at their leisure. For a solid month I lived on an air mattress on the floor with my laptop propped on a box so I could watch DVDs. I had plastic plates, plastic bowls, and plastic tableware. I had a microwave—and that was it.

At Campbell I began to party. Even though my husband and I had been married for less than a year, it was still tough for me to deal with feelings of failure. Like I wasn't good enough because I'd been unable to make the marriage work no matter how hard I'd tried.

Easily half the people in my platoon hung out together on the weekend. Every weekend there was a party at my house or at Sergeant Biddle's house. We alternated. So every weekend there would be a party with lots of beer and people getting drunk. Puking in the driveway. One night we went to Waffle House and when we got back, there was a dog eating the puke in my driveway.

We knew we were deploying. We knew we might die. We didn't give a shit. We drank heavily all the time. There was a lot of random sex. We didn't care. We were going to war. I partied with these guys a lot.

I ended up partying more than I had in several years. I'd partied some in college, but really not that much. When I was with Rick, I certainly didn't party; I didn't go out and do anything crazy. But during this period at Campbell, I wanted nothing to do with emotionally committed relationships. I absolutely insisted that if I was going to have sex, there be no emotions or intimacy involved. At all.

Sometimes I slept with Connelly, who was one of Sergeant

Biddle's roommates. Connelly was twenty-one and a raging alcoholic, but I chose him because I knew he would not be able to form a connection with me. If I went on a date with anyone else, I made clear to the guy I was not going to provide a relationship. It was not going to be intimate. It was going to be casual. I made that very clear.

FTA

FROM SMALLEST TO largest unit, the infantry is organized like this: team, squad, platoon, company, battalion, brigade, division, corps, Army. I was assigned to the 2nd Prophet Team of 3rd Platoon, Delta Company, 311th Military Intelligence (MI) Battalion attached to 3rd Brigade in the 101st Airborne Division (Air Assault). Soldiers in the 101st are known as the Screaming Eagles. (They used to take an eagle as a mascot into battle with them.) Soldiers in 3rd Brigade (187) of the 101st Airborne Division (Air Assault) are known as Rakkasans. It's a name they earned from the Japanese during World War II; it means "falling umbrellas." That's presumably how the Japanese saw them as they parachuted from the sky.

I am proud to be a Rakkasan and proud to be part of the Screaming Eagles. The Screaming Eagles have a great tradition. I'll be proud of this for the rest of my life. If anyone ever asks: "What unit in the Army were you in?" I'll be able to say I was in the 101st and people will know right away what I'm talking about.

"That's Fort Campbell," they will say. "They served with pride in Vietnam and World War II."

But when it comes to day-to-day life, your team is what counts.

The team is the smallest and most fundamental unit in the military. During any deployment, it is almost always the most important. When you get deployed, your whole life—everything—is intimately bound up with the people on your team. These are the people with whom you live, sleep, work, eat, fight. You know them better than you know your lover or your spouse. You know what music they like. You know what they eat. You know their shitting habits. And you trust them with your life. You have to.

So if there's a problem within your team, it can be extremely difficult.

I was assigned to a team, but the team shifted several times over the course of the next few months. So I and the people I went to war with never really got a chance to know one another before we left for Iraq.

A Korean linguist, Specialist Geoff Quinn showed up from Korea but then left for a leadership development course for new noncommissioned officers. He returned in December as a brand-new E-5. A buck sergeant with no real leadership experience who tended to rub people the wrong way.

When we did the PMCS (preventive maintenance checks and services) on our truck, for instance, he filled every single thing to the top—including the radiator fluid.

I told him, "You don't do that."

"I'm a sergeant. You're a specialist. I don't see why I should listen to what you have to say."

"But you've never PMCSed a truck before. And I have."

Of course, when SGT (Sergeant) Quinn started the truck, radiator fluid burst out everywhere.

And then our team leader got in *my* face.

"Why did you let him do that?"

"Let him? I couldn't stop him! He wouldn't listen to me!"

(One positive thing I can say about Sergeant Quinn. He got better over time. He did learn. It just took awhile.)

So Quinn was no buffer for our team leader's weaknesses.

Our team leader, SSG (Staff Sergeant) Moss, had not been at Fort Campbell when I first arrived. She'd returned to DLI in California for an intermediate Arabic course. So I didn't meet her right away, but I met people who knew her. They'd laugh about her, but I had no idea why.

Then SSG Moss returned. A small woman who looked confused all the time. She immediately made clear how much she loved physical training. She'd burst out: "Hooah PT! Hooah PT! Hooah PT!" (Hooah in this context meaning "Awesome.")

That fall, we practiced our deployment. We loaded our equipment on our truck. Got it weighed. Got it ready for rail-loading. We banded our equipment with metal bands so it wouldn't shift around or fall out. We taped the lights. Simple things. But SSG Moss had a very hard time. She never quite grasped that the bands had to go *around* the equipment and *through* rings on the truck. She banded the equipment to itself or to other equipment.

SSG Moss also thought we could fit more equipment inside a space than was possible. She drew up a load plan and then taped the plan to the outside of our truck. This enabled us to see immediately what was inside. But she never seemed able to gauge proportions accurately; she was determined to fit larger items inside smaller ones.

We gently informed her: "That obviously won't work."

She always responded with the same puzzled answer.

"Why not?"

"Look at it!"

It also worried me when she discussed the fate of her previous truck.

"Cursed," SSG Moss said. "Every time we went on a field problem, that truck got stuck in the mud."

"Who else drove the truck besides you when it got stuck in the mud?"

"Um, no one."

"But the *truck* was cursed?"

"That's right."

"You don't think your driving might have had something to do with it?"

SSG Moss did not make me feel safe at all.

The fourth and final member of our team showed up only in January. Like Sergeant Quinn, Specialist Lauren Collins was a Korean linguist; she came to us directly from her advanced individual training in Texas. Less than five feet tall, she looked like the sweetest little thing.

I have the most vivid first impression of Lauren.

Lauren had been at Fort Campbell for less than two hours when Sergeant First Class (SFC) Fuller chucked a football right at her, missing her face by inches.

SFC Fuller liked to throw footballs at people. No fewer than three times, he hit me in the back of the head. He wanted soldiers to buck up. He wanted us to act tough. Be strong. A lot of people hated SFC Fuller.

"I will kick your fucking ass!" Lauren yelled at him.

Everyone froze. SFC Fuller was three ranks above her. He

grabbed her and started to drag her from the room. We were convinced he planned to kill her. Start beating on her right then and there.

Instead he told her: "I like to push people. Nobody has ever reacted to me the way you did. I really respect that. You've got one big pair of balls."

So that's my first impression of Lauren. One big pair of balls.

I'd had discomfort in my right foot since June, but the Army took its time with a medical diagnosis. Soldiers always attempted to sham injuries. Cry wolf. So the Army tended to stall diagnoses until things got serious.

My diagnosis was Morton's neuroma. In the ball of the foot there are nerve bundles that run and split down into the toes. A nerve bundle in my right foot was inflamed and, over time, the inflammation caused scarring in the nerve bundle.

I was given a choice. I could get immediate surgery and not deploy with my unit. I would probably miss the war and remain nondeployable until I was completely recovered. Or I could deploy and deal with the pain in Iraq with occasional cortisone shots.

I refused to deploy late. I would take the shots and put off the surgery.

Our unit deployed in February 2003. As world opinion spun on its axis away from support for the invasion of Iraq, we spun in the opposite direction—closer and closer to absolute certainty. We would go to war because that was the way it worked. We had signed a contract. We had given our word. It might not mean too much to give your word anymore, but that did not mean we would not keep ours.

For the longest time, though, we kept hearing the same refrain.

"There is no deployment order for the division."

We responded: "Uh-huh. But we are going to deploy?"

"No. There is no deployment order for the division."

"See those railroad cars with our trucks on them? Those cars are going to Jacksonville to get on a boat and take our trucks to Kuwait. That means we are going somewhere."

"No. There is no deployment order for the division."

"Just admit it! Tell us something like: 'Hey, look. We can't give you any dates. We can't give you any specifics. But we all know it's going to happen, so be ready for it.' Just say it!"

"There is no deployment order for the division. But you'd better go get your anthrax shot. Make sure your will is up-to-date. Get a power of attorney. Please update your life insurance policies. Be sure to set up automatic bill payments. Get a smallpox shot. And you females? If and when the order comes, be prepared to pee in a cup for your pregnancy test."

"Quit lying to us! A duffel bag with all our extra gear has already gone to the Middle East. We've been told to pack personal hygiene equipment for six months! We went to Wal-Mart and spent three hundred dollars on binoculars, batteries, cameras, books, and a solar shower! Extra fucking everything! And you're trying to tell us we're not going anywhere?"

"Roger that. There is no deployment order for the division."

Then the deployment order for the division was announced on CNN. It was lunchtime, and everybody's phones all started to ring at once. So we checked it. We went to CNN.com and printed out the web page where it said the deployment order for the

101st Airborne Division (Air Assault) at Fort Campbell had been published.

Our lieutenant came into the office. We confronted her with the news.

"So the deployment order is out."

She shook her head. "There is no deployment order for the division."

"It was on CNN. A major is quoted as saying that the division is getting deployed."

She got flustered. "Well, what does he know? Who's this major anyway?"

"He's the fucking public affairs officer! He's the person authorized to speak to the press for the division!"

"There . . . there's . . ." She stammered. "There is no official deployment order until we've had a formation and had a chance to announce it to you."

FTA. We said it all the time. Some soldiers even took a Sharpie and wrote it on their duffels or their helmets or boots— any damn place they could find. *Fuck the Army.*

A week later I left for Kuwait as part of the advance party for our unit. Zoe drove me to post that day. It was a Sunday. A light snow fell. I had a rucksack and one duffel bag. My second duffel had already gone with our trucks.

We hugged a tearless good-bye.

"Now don't go and start the invasion without us. Be safe."

Except for a brief time in Kuwait, I wouldn't see Zoe again for six months. Until after the war proper ended, and the president had stood on an aircraft carrier in front of a banner that announced: MISSION ACCOMPLISHED.

HOW TO PREPARE FOR DEPLOYMENT TO IRAQ

1. Every night until you deploy, sleep in your vehicle. Or sleep on a cot next to your vehicle.

2. Sandbag the floor of your vehicle as protection against improvised explosive devices.

3. Get your semiautomatic rifle and empty a round into the side of your house. And spread gravel throughout the house and yard. For atmosphere.

4. Find the most annoying alarm sound on your cellphone, and set it to go off at least once each night. At different hours.

5. Arrange for neighbors to wait until you are sound asleep then come outside and beam a flashlight into your face. Have them tell you that there's an emergency but then immediately change their mind and announce it was a false alarm.

6. Hire a garbage truck to run all day and all night in your driveway for correct ambient noise. Keep a pit of manure burning for proper fragrance.

7. Practice being physically separated from your spouse or

your girlfriend or boyfriend. Communicate with him/her only via cellphone, e-mail, and snail mail.

8. Ask two hundred people you don't know and don't necessarily like to live with you for a month. Make sure there are at least five times as many men as women.

9. When it rains, go dig a hole in your backyard. Fill a pail with dirt and stir it with rainwater. Slowly pour this mixture over your entire body.

10. Once you are good and filthy, use baby wipes to clean yourself. Don't take a proper shower for two weeks. Pretend you don't know what you look or smell like.

11. Handwash some clothes in dusty water only. Mix and match them with sweat-stained and torn clothes. Wear the combined outfits proudly when you meet with your boss or go to a dinner party.

12. Never clean your toilet and be sure always to urinate on the bathroom floor. Remove the toilet paper entirely. Better yet, walk to the bathroom at a gas station at least half a mile away. Always carry heavy equipment, a weapon, and a flashlight.

13. Whenever you feel you have to pass gas, go to the bathroom "just in case." Every time.

14. Take your once-every-two-weeks showers in public, preferably on your front lawn; pretend not to notice that people are staring when you strip.

15. Only eat food that has been prepared by strangers, making sure that you never have any idea what it is. Or what's in it.

16. If you drink coffee, be sure to let it sit for several hours before drinking.

17. Drink all beverages—including water, milk, and soda—either lukewarm or very warm.

18. Attach a flashlight to the bottom of your cot. Whenever you want to read or write at night, crawl under the cot.

19. Before you use the telephone, have a family member unplug the phone from the wall so there is no chance you can get through. Attempt to make phone calls anyway. Don't let this affect your morale.

20. Tell your neighbors that every dog on the block may be rabid. Gather up the dogs, shoot them, and burn them.

21. Travel in convoys with your neighbors. Drive very slowly, careful to avoid plastic or paper bags in the road (in case they are explosives). Carry your weapon with you at all times. Point it at anyone suspicious. Stop at every bridge and overpass and inspect them for bombs before driving over them.

22. Travel to the most dangerous neighborhood you can find in an up-armored Humvee. Dig survivability positions with overhead cover. Unroll concertina wire in the streets. Establish checkpoints on every block and tell anyone who wishes to pass through that they will have their vehicles searched upon demand. Tell residents that you are there to improve their situation.

23. Detonate unexploded ordnance in this neighborhood in the middle of the night. If residents are upset, tell them not to worry, things are going according to plan. If they complain that their living room windows have been shattered by the blasts, reassure them and inform them that plastic should work fine. Tell them glass windows were too dangerous, anyway.

24. When your child asks for a ball to play with, have him find the precise one he wants on the Internet, type up a Form 9, attach a printout of the web page, put everything in an envelope, mail it to a third party for processing, and tell your child the ball will arrive in just a few weeks.

25. Just when you think you're ready to resume a normal life, do everything on this list again in order to prepare yourself for the unexpected extension of your deployment.

FULL BATTLE RATTLE

OUR ADVANCE PARTY arrived at a commercial airport in Kuwait on February 18, 2003. It was an astonishingly long trip—more than twenty-four hours of travel, from Nashville to Chicago to London and Dubai and into Kuwait. I read an entire book on the way and realized that I might have seriously underpacked reading material.

We were in civilian clothes on civilian flights, so we could drink—which I knew was lucky; the rest of the unit would not have that privilege. They would fly over in full gear, packed on chartered planes, with no chance to soothe their nerves. I had a few beers along the way. The flights looked maybe half military. The British soldiers got drunk. We stood out, even in civvies. Especially the guys, with their buzz-cut hair. When we stopped briefly in Dubai for "security reasons," no one was allowed off the plane, even to smoke. One of the Brits—who had already been chastised for smoking in the bathroom—lost control at this indignity and ended up shaking the seat in front of him, reminding me of a caged monkey.

At the Kuwait airport no one was there to meet us, and we waited several hours before we finally made it through customs and someone showed up to take us to the local U.S. Army base, Camp Doha. While waiting, we wandered the airport a bit, got coffee, looked at shops.

When we were finally loaded into SUVs and on our way, SSG Moss, who had been relatively quiet and controlled on the trip, perked up.

"I'll be running you folks up to Camp Doha," the driver informed us.

"Run?" our team leader interjected. "Will there be an opportunity to run?" I looked across at her, silently pleading with her not to embarrass us.

"I'm sorry, Sergeant?" the driver asked politely.

"Running might get some of these knots out of our necks, you know?" she announced, apropos of nothing.

"We're passing Checkpoint Alpha," the driver said into his cell phone, no doubt alerting someone at the camp that we had arrived and were safely on our way.

Our sergeant was not listening, or not following what was going on, and I was beginning to feel the urge to throttle her. "I'd love a good run," she said to no one in particular. "Won't that be great? When we get there? The last time I was here I ran the perimeter every day. Can you still do that?"

The driver again called in our position. "We're passing Checkpoint Bravo," he said.

"Oh, really?" she answered.

A minute passed and she got it. "Oh. . . ." We all exchanged glances, sighed, and shook our heads.

Camp Doha. A world of sand and grit, thick enough some days to stick between the teeth and cloud the air to hazy white. The sun was incredibly hot. Inside the camp things weren't so bad. They had movies, a rec room, a library, a PX. A good chow hall where they periodically served lobster. My vegetarianism did not preclude my digging into a little crustacean, though I couldn't deal with the removal of its exoskeleton, and asked someone to do that for me.

We trained on new equipment for a few days before we pressed on to Camp Udairi. The amenities were fewer out there, but it was still pretty comfortable. There were tents with cots to sleep in, trailers and showers a ten-minute walk away. Larger tents served chow. In general, though, there were simply fewer distractions from the mission to come and the unpleasant thoughts that crowded in.

Waiting. That's all this was. Waiting. There was no doubt in our minds that this war was on. Time was the only variable, the only question mark. Not if, but when.

We heard reports of the worldwide protests against the invasion and the war. It was hard to know how to feel. I was positive that some of my civilian friends were among the protesters. And *of course* I didn't want to be here, either. The thought that I might possibly die in the desert . . . and for what? For whom? I was here because of my loyalty to my unit and my fellow soldiers. That was the beginning and the middle and the end of my sense of loyalty at the moment. That was what mattered. That was what kept me going: hoping I could make a difference; hoping I could provide good intelligence that saved even one life.

At the end of February we headed out to a site near the Iraqi border for three days of pulling live mission. We were living in more primitive conditions—not even Porta-Johns out there, just "field-expedient" shitters. These involved a toilet seat bolted to a chair frame and a plastic bag. It worked remarkably well. I was impressed by the ingenuity. The unit with which we'd been training also had generators, a luxury we appreciated for the heaters they powered; it was still cold at night.

My first sight of Iraq was a hill in the distance with a tower on it. Through binoculars we could see the Iraqi soldiers near the tower, no doubt looking back at us looking at them. We were teamed with a SECFOR (security force), infantry boys in their Bradleys, all ready to get out of this limbo and into combat. They were from Third Infantry Division (3 ID), out of Fort Stewart, and had already been at this site on rotation for a few months. On the drive there and back, I studied the landscape. The hesitant patches of green on the desert, from a distance like hints of stubble on a man's chin, but closer up looking like patches of mange.

Things were remarkably quiet. Under the circumstances, you could say it was spooky how ordinary life was. For the most part we were each left to our own thoughts while not on shift. Not that we had privacy. It was a given that someone could amble over and talk—about this, about that, about nothing. Mainly you took it for granted. Sometimes, though, it could get pretty strange.

"Hey, Specialist."

It was one of the 3 ID guys. I was bored, so I didn't mind the company.

"Hey," I answered him. He was a mechanic, a good guy so far as I knew, just someone everyone liked to joke around with.

"Y'all having a good time yet?"

"We're ready to end all this waiting. And just go. You ready?"

"Ready?" He cast me a big smile. "We're ready for anything. Bring it on, I say."

There was a little bit of an awkward silence then. But I was still feeling basically fine about the chatter.

"You know, my wife," he started, out of nowhere. "My wife and I, we like to do it hard, if you know what I mean?"

"Excuse me?"

"We like it rough, if you follow me? The rougher the better, so far as she's concerned, and who am I to complain? It works for her, it works for me."

Had I said or done anything to indicate I wanted to hear any of this?

"Yeah," I said, but I'm thinking *no*.

"Like if she were here right now," he said, then stopped. "Let me put it to you this way. She's not here. So I'd love to break the back axle of that Humvee there on you. If you get my drift."

"Uh, I'm sorry. I'm not really interested."

"I'm just saying," he said. "We see you girls in your T-shirts. We can see your boobs. You know we're watching."

I walked away.

Later on I seriously reflect on whether guys actually believe that talking to girls like this *works*. Or whether it's some kind of obnoxious ritual, some kind of compulsion to say anything—like dogs feel the need to piss on a tree and call it their own. Must guys say everything that comes into their pea brains when they're feeling horny—or whatever? That is, if what this guy was feeling was horny. I'm not so sure. Granted, we were on the edge of war and all that might mean. Sure, it must have made some folks do or say crazy things. But was that an excuse?

After the three-day mission, it was back to Camp Udairi. I developed heat rashes between my legs and on my waist. Itchy inflammations—bug bites?—sprouted on my ankle. Blisters appeared on the arches of my feet where the sand got inside socks and shoes when we ran. We had to carry our gas masks while we ran, which was worse. The rubbing and chafing of the weight could only be offset by gripping the mask when you moved. But that meant you couldn't swing your arms as you ran, and you lost rhythm as a result. I was realizing fast that being deployed was like being in the field: You had more time to focus on your body, its functions and complaints.

In the tents where we worked, shifts in the wind pushed the sides so it felt as if we were on a boat. Watching the shifting walls of the tent move somehow tricked my inner ear.

Insatiable thirst marked each day. All you could do was attempt (and fail) to quench it with water that also tasted like dust.

Sand stretching into vastness. A harsh, stark, desolate kind of beauty. The distance clouded always by dust, dust, dust. I wondered if there were names for the different types of sand, like we have for different types of snow or rain. There was the sand that was packed firmly, and that must be slogged through. And there was the sand that was delicate like confectioner's sugar or flour, so powdery you sank in and it billowed up in puffs when you stepped into it. There was fine blowing sand that misted your face lightly, and harder granulated blowing sand that stung when it hit your face.

Oddly, though, it was all almost relaxing. There were no bills to pay, no phone calls to answer, no friends or family to see, no daily chores to mind, no shopping to do. Daily life was nothing like *real* daily life, and while this was no vacation, it was also not so bad, either.

———

In early March the rest of my unit arrived in Kuwait, and we joined them at Camp New Jersey. It was very similar to Camp Udairi—sleeping in large, open cloth tents, with segregated male/female sleeping areas. There was a lot of down time. People played a lot of cards. The weather kept getting hotter, and it became so oppressive that all you wanted to do was lie still.

Our vehicles, shipped over on boats, finally arrived a couple of days after we got there, and we bused down to the port to drive them back. We were given a convoy brief prior to the drive back, detailing the route, speed, and rules of the drive. During this brief I noticed movement behind me and turned. A soldier had a nosebleed and was stanching it. No big deal. Glancing down, I saw his blood on the sand. The brilliant red stood out so much against the bland beige, I couldn't help but stare. *Please,* I begged silently. *Let this be the last time I see blood on sand.*

When we were trying to link up with the Kuwaiti police escort that would accompany our convoy back, I was called upon to translate. And found myself horrified at the deterioration of my Arabic skills since I graduated from DLI. It had been almost a year since I left Monterey, and there had been no language training at Fort Campbell. (For many of us this had been a big concern; language is such a perishable skill. There should be a mandate that military linguists and interpreters continue to receive language training at their permanent-duty stations.)

We stopped at a checkpoint, and I needed to ask the police manning it where the police escort for our convoy was. I was reduced to asking, "Where are the police for us?" since I couldn't remember the words for "escort" or "convoy." The cops must think I'm stupid, I thought, when I asked them, "Where are the police?" Just hearing and using the language, though, started to bring it back. We linked up. Nonetheless the experience still left me nervous about my language skills, and fearful that I would be useless.

Having our vehicles and equipment gave us more to do, getting everything prepped. Practicing, packing, seeing what would work now that we knew exactly what we had to take. The number of DOS (days of supplies—of food, water, batteries, and so on) we had to carry kept getting bumped up—five to seven to ten— necessitating several reorganizations of our gear. At least we were doing *something*.

The chow tents were a few hundred meters away, and long lines formed before they even opened. They were open for breakfast and dinner; lunch was an MRE (meal ready to eat). The food was typical for institutional dining. A small shopette run by AAFES (Army and Air Force Exchange Service) in a trailer was stocked periodically, and sold out almost immediately of the items people most wanted— cigarettes and pogey bait (civilian food).

There were occasional sandstorms. It became hard to see as painful grit pelted the eyes. One evening the blowing sand got so awful that some people put on their gas masks to shield their eyes and ease breathing while walking back from chow.

On March 12 we moved to full battle rattle. Everything on (or carried) all the time. In case of attack we needed to be prepared.

Kevlar: a flameproof lightweight fiber first developed to reinforce the tread of radial tires. Our soft Kevlar flak vests protect the upper body, the shoulders, and back, and are sewn together inside a nylon shell. There are supposed to be ceramic bullet-proof plates that slide into pockets in the front and back of the vest, protecting the heart and lungs, but the majority of people in my unit never had these. (There simply aren't enough to go around, so those considered more likely to be in high-risk situations get them.) A vest without plates can stop bullets from handguns and fragments from mortars and hand grenades. A vest with plates can stop bullets from high-powered rifles. In addition many of us had a load bearing vest (LBV), if we had old-style equipment. (As I did.) This held our ammo pouches, canteens, and so forth.

The Kevlar vest weighed nine pounds without plates. Add a four-pound Kevlar helmet, and we were already thirteen pounds of gear, plus mask, weapon, and a basic load of 210 rounds of ammunition. We also carried, in a bag, our joint-service lightweight integrated suit technology, or JSLIST (pronounced just *J-List*), that is, the suit that was going to protect us from biological and chemical attack. It was particularly frustrating in the chow tents, too much gear in too little room. A high-ranking officer was quoted as saying that carrying all our gear "improved morale." I thought this was crazy.

In my Kevlar helmet, I carried a medevac card so I knew how to respond in case someone in my unit required a medical evacuation. I carried a casualty feeder card in case I was seriously injured or killed in battle. (I was instructed to fill out the personal data on this card, but I couldn't bring myself to do it. I was superstitious about this detail.) I carried a copy of the ROE (rules of engagement). I carried a code of conduct (first developed when Eisenhower was president) in my Kevlar in case I was captured as a prisoner of war.

I memorized the code of conduct:

I am an American, fighting in the forces which guard my country and our way of life. I am prepared to give my life in their defense. I will never surrender of my own free will. If in command, I will never surrender the members of my command while they still have the means to resist. If I am captured, I will continue to resist by all means available. I will make every effort to escape and aid others to escape. I will accept neither parole nor special favors from the enemy. If I become a prisoner of war, I will keep faith with my fellow prisoners. I will give no information or take part in any action which might be harmful to my comrades. If I am senior, I will take command. If not, I will obey the lawful orders of those appointed over me, and will back them up in every way. When questioned, should I become a prisoner of war, I am required to give only name, rank, service number, and date of birth. I will evade answering further questions to the utmost of my ability. I will make no oral or written statements disloyal to my country and its allies or harmful to their cause. I will never forget that I am an American, fighting for freedom, responsible for my actions, and dedicated to the principles which made my country free. I will trust in my God and in the United States of America.

I believe it was John McCain who said that the code of conduct helped him get through his time as a POW.

On the band of my Kevlar, I also had my blood type written. Our blood type was on our dog tags, but a lot of soldiers also wrote it on their T-shirts and their boots. When you enter a combat zone, you think to put it everywhere. (All soldiers know their blood type.)

We also should have carried forms in case we confiscated

enemy equipment. And we should have had forms in case we took prisoners. But no one I knew had those forms at the beginning.

At full battle rattle we ran drills periodically in which everyone huddled into the back of a MILVAN, which resembled nothing so much as a metal truckbed. (Officers got into concrete bunkers, where, I imagine, they had a higher chance of survival.) The story was that a MILVAN would protect us, either from incoming rounds or from chemical attacks, but this appeared quite unlikely. If a MILVAN took a direct hit, having us all together meant that the enemy would kill us all at once. We also put on gas masks while standing inside these metal containers, so it became extra uncomfortable and difficult to breathe.

The whole thing would have been completely insane if it hadn't also been incredibly real.

Specialist James Reid was not on our team, but he was in our platoon. He joined us at Fort Campbell almost immediately before we deployed for Iraq, so no one knew him real well. He was always very laid back and calm. Quiet. Quirky. Funny once you got to know him. I always felt as if I got on his nerves because I could be so intense and excitable much of the time.

If I was happy about something you'd know about it.

"Oh my God, the sunset was so beautiful! You totally should have seen it! It was so cool looking!"

Or if I was mad, you'd know about it too.

"I can't stand that fucking bitch! I hate being around her! I'm so pissed off!"

But Reid always stayed cool.

"Yeah," he'd say, real slow and calm. "Yeah, she can be a real pain sometimes. I don't know about her."

That was about as demonstrative as he ever got. In the course of an entire year in Iraq, I never saw Reid lose control.

Later, once we got to the mountain site, some of the soldiers got to calling Reid "Lawyer" because he'd gone to law school and passed the bar in Kentucky. Having no interest in practicing law, Reid had joined the Army and ended up a Korean linguist who, like Sergeant Quinn, came to us direct from a year in Korea.

But calling Reid "Lawyer" was not a disrespectful thing. Everybody liked him.

So sometime after we go to full battle rattle, Staff Sergeant Moss, Reid, and I pull guard shift together from 2400 to 1200 hours. Our straightforward task is to watch the ammo dump. It's too easy.

"Be at the vehicle at 2345," SSG Moss tells me.

I'm there. She's a no-show. I'm tired and impatient and I'm thinking maybe she means *Zulu time.* Whatever. I head back to bed. At 0010 she comes to get me.

"You're late," she says in a supersnotty voice. "Get Reid and meet me at the vehicle."

I keep the peace and say nothing. I just get my gear together and go outside so I don't wake everyone up.

"Let's move, soldier," she says.

I stare at her.

"Can I put my gear on first?"

"I don't want to hear any attitude," she says, giving me truck-loads of *her* attitude.

We get Reid, and the three of us move to the perimeter and settle down for the night. Reid and I locate positions for the night, leaving SSG Moss in the Humvee, which she randomly moves about five times, reparking it. At some point I swear I hear her talking to herself in the truck. Weird. I light a cigarette. Finally she gets out of the truck and comes over.

"You'll have to move," she says, pointing to my cigarette. "Twenty meters away from the ammo. A precautionary measure." She turns and starts to go. Then turns back again. "And come tell me first."

"Come tell you what?"

"Williams," she says. "Watch your attitude. I've already asked you once. Don't make me tell you again."

I throw the cigarette down into the dust, too tired to deal.

"Sergeant," I say as calmly as I can. "I'll just sit here and stare at the ammo. Okay?"

"And change the way you're sitting," SSG Moss says. "I've been watching you. Leaning down on one hip like that. Shifting back and forth. Our platoon leader could come out here and think you're drifting off. Not paying attention."

I stare at her in disbelief. She's criticizing the way I *sit*? But I maintain control.

As the night drags on, SSG Moss never leaves the vehicle. Not once. Every hour we have to make reports to the battalion tactical operations center (BNTOC), and I expect the three of us to rotate this chore. Foolish me. SSG Moss says Reid and I will make the hourly fourteen-hundred-meter round-trip walk together. This we do—eleven times—with full battle rattle. Adds up to more than fifteen klicks (that is, fifteen kilometers) of walking.

My foot problem was horribly painful, more so when I had to

carry weight. As a good *soldier*, I sucked it up and did what I was told. As a good *leader*, Sergeant Moss should have remembered my problem and considered it. After all, we had a damned truck!

But SSG Moss never relieved us, never made the walk, never used the vehicle provided. Just bitched now and then about the shitty detail. Somewhere in there she tells us she's got a headache and could we go farther down to pick up some Motrin for her?

When it's time for breakfast, SSG Moss orders that we can't go for hot chow. We could leave the prescribed route for her needs but not our own. When our shift comes to an end, a captain from BNTOC arrives and tells us we're done for the day. Incredibly, she makes us walk one last time back to BNTOC to confirm that this is accurate information. Ridiculous! I am so angry and hungry I want to bury my head in my hands and cry in frustration. When the shift finally does end, that is exactly what I do, alone and secretly, on my cot.

IN-COUNTRY

MARCH 21, 2003—the day before the invasion. We were back at Camp Udairi, linked up with the rest of our GAC (ground assault convoy). Tomorrow, Iraq. No time to think about that, though, with alarms going off repeatedly, all day, all night. Three quick car horn honks signaled an al-Samoud missile overhead—gas. A little unnerving. Seven seconds to mask up, in case our Patriot missile missed the al-Samoud. The masks stayed on until we heard the all clear. Problem was SSG Moss never seemed to notice it. We took to demasking without her authorization. Then at some point she'd suddenly yell at us to demask, apparently oblivious that we already had. Was she going to be this slow the entire time we're deployed?

Saturday, March 22. I entered Iraq for the first time, in the second vehicle in the 4th GAC of the 101st Airborne Division (Air Assault). We were behind the Army's Third Infantry Division, which had left for Baghdad on Thursday night. We stretched endlessly across the desert, averaging between fifteen and twenty-five kilometers a hour, like the most intense traffic jam in the world.

It went slow. And it stayed slow, and hot, and mind-numbingly dull. Drive and drive and drive. I saw no resistance. We were advancing, and we would keep moving as long as it took to get to FARP Shell (our forward arming and refueling point)—at least two days of near-constant driving.

My weapon was loaded. My mandatory protective gear was on. But there was no resistance. Nothing at all. We saw burned-out vehicles on the side of the road, damaged buildings—but weren't even sure if these were from this war or the First Gulf War.

My team was lucky. We GACed with 101 Aviation, which meant pilots were in charge. Pilots were more laid back than other commanders. So a couple of times we were able to stop for a few hours; drivers were allowed to sleep. The pilots gave us extra batteries and T-Ration waffles, a welcome break from MREs. There was an embedded reporter in the lead vehicle, Colin Soloway from *Newsweek*. He was very bright, an engaging conversationalist, and highly knowledgeable about the region: talking to him was a real pleasure. We had an electric outlet in our vehicle that he used to charge his satellite phone. In exchange he let us call home, and gave us hot water made on the one-burner camp stove he'd had the forethought to bring. It was a little thing. But in this kind of situation, a little thing was incredibly important.

Then there was SSG Moss. She messed with a key piece of equipment and somehow busted it. "Oops," she said, the vital piece in her hand, "I broke the card in the computer." We had been repeatedly instructed never to touch the card, so I asked: "Why did you touch it?" "But you *can* touch it," she replied. "Yes, but they instructed us not to," SGT Quinn said. "But you *can*," she insisted.

This continued for a few minutes, obviously in vain. The air grew tense in our Humvee. We tried to raise anyone from our platoon on the radios, to get a message relayed back for a replacement. But we couldn't get through at all.

"The vehicle in front of us," I volunteered, "they've got a satellite phone. We could call in."

"I don't know," SSG Moss said lethargically. We continued to try the radios. She ate and chatted with people around us.

Luckily, during refueling, we found a tech able to do an emergency repair job and got our system back up.

That wasn't the end of Staff Sergeant Moss's unpredictability. She drove the Humvee erratically, pressing too close to or staying too far from the vehicles in front of and behind us. We could barely stand to watch. She wouldn't let Lauren drive since she didn't have a military driver's license, and we agreed that SGT Quinn shouldn't drive because his vision was so bad. He didn't have the plastic adapter to hold his special glasses inside his mask, so if we were chemically attacked and he had to mask, he'd be driving blind. So I drove almost the entire way across Iraq, while Quinn sat beside me working the radio, and SSG Moss in the rear seat running ops (operations).

Outside the scenery changed from dust and sand to green and greener. Not at all what I expected. The second day we were back to dust and sand.

Stops to go to the bathroom weren't pleasant. On the first day, we females opened the doors on one side of the vehicle and hung up a poncho to create a little privacy. But this didn't last. The poncho went first, and not long after, any hint of modesty. You just dropped your pants and squatted with your butt toward the truck on the side with the fewest people. Of course the guys pissed everywhere—or they went behind sad, straggly bushes to take a shit. It became impossible to care. How could you? Stops sometimes lasted fewer than five minutes, even though getting in and out of chemical gear took forever, especially with three chicks taking turns because you were also pulling security. Some guy getting a random peek at my butt quickly became meaningless.

Iraq was not just a giant cat box, as we called it. We also turned it into a garbage dump, leaving a vast trail of trash in our wake. We littered our way through southern Iraq and this brought out the locals, who were friendly and supportive—but also very hungry.

Those days we drove through small villages, and locals lined the streets, cheering for us. Curious and unafraid, the men and kids came right over to the slow-moving convoy and made their demands known. They wanted food. We'd been instructed never to pass an MRE out the window while we were driving, but it was tough to resist their pleas. These people clearly supported the invasion. And we were wasting so much food. Whenever we stopped, protocol demanded that we burn what we left behind. But Lauren and I sneaked a stack of MRE meal parts we wouldn't eat near a pile of trash. It was crazy to be here supposedly to help—and then not help those who needed it most.

Food. We all spent a lot of time in Iraq thinking about food. I certainly did. Of course it's tough to be a vegetarian if you're living on MREs. True, there are twenty-four different varieties, but most of them are entrees like Meat Loaf, Jambalaya, Country Captain Chicken, Thai Chicken, Hearty Stew with Beef, and Boneless Pork Ribs. Yes, there are vegetarian meals: Pasta with Vegetables and Tomato Sauce, Pasta with Alfredo Sauce, Cheese Tortellini, and Bean and Rice Burritos. But in Iraq you couldn't always get the meal you wanted. In fact, since the meals came in two different cases, twelve to a case, you could keep getting one kind of case over and over. That way you not only didn't eat what you preferred, you were also starved for variety. Sounds like a small thing, but over time, especially wartime, it takes on huge significance. Truth is, you'd be bumming after a while. Us, we kept getting Case A, Case A, Case A, Case A, Case A. So there would be these times we'd come across some other unit, and we'd get to talking. "We only ever get Case B!" they'd say. Time to trade. Doing a drug deal, we called it.

All over Iraq, soldiers did drug deals. You name it, it got traded. Once we swapped batteries we found on the side of the road with another unit for some maps. They didn't have batteries. We didn't have maps. And we constantly traded MREs. Big prize: a Lorna Doone shortbread cookie, or M&M's. When I'd get one of these treats, it would be awesome.

It totally pissed our team off when Staff Sergeant Moss *ratfucked* our cases of MREs. That's what we called it. She'd rustle through MRE after MRE, looking for the one that had the Lorna Doone. It drove us nuts.

Another unpleasant thing: MREs were essentially a fiber-free diet. Nothing accidental about that—the military wanted to stop you up, so you didn't have to go to the bathroom as often. Less interference with your ability to do your mission. And that was fine if you were in the field for a few days. But it became problematic if MREs were all you were eating for months—which is what we did. Possibly every MRE had fruit in it—diced pears in heavy syrup, or diced peaches in heavy syrup, or apple sauce. But an MRE *never* had green vegetables. Never. Fruits are full of sugar that give you an instant rush of energy. But green vegetables don't, plus they have almost no calories. So what's the point?

Over time we tried some MRE experiments. We learned to mix and match. I really liked to mix the minestrone stew with the mashed potatoes to put together a half-assed version of shepherd's pie. I'd go through our box of extras—the remains that others had not wanted to eat—and pull out the things I wanted. Keep in mind that maintaining my vegetarianism, which I was determined to do, meant there was very little I could eat. I was desperate. So I got creative. For instance, I couldn't eat the Mexican rice because it had beef stock in it, but I could eat the beans. I couldn't eat the Thai chicken, but I could eat the white rice it came with. So I'd mix the white rice with the beans. But no ingenious mixing and matching made up for the fact that there were only two vegetarian MREs in a case of twelve. That meant one out of six MREs was vegetarian, and I was one out of four people on a team. Even if I got every single vegetarian MRE, it would still not be enough for me. And in fact, I tried to be cool and polite, and took whatever was there. If it turned out not to be a veggie MRE, then I'd eat what I could from it—crackers and peanut butter or crackers and cheese. Then I'd put the remainder of my meal in the box for the others to dig into, and take what I could out of the box to supplement.

On Monday the 24th, we made it to FARP Shell. That was when we were hit by a tremendous sandstorm that lasted three days. The wind whipped the dust upward. The air grew thick. The sky turned a sickly orange and then suddenly almost black—so dense you could barely see. Within minutes dirt clogged up everything. Worse, it was in your eyes, your hair, your mouth. We couldn't sleep sitting upright in the cramped seats of our vehicle, so we finally fell into the back of the truck next to us, our exhausted bodies weirdly entangled, an arm here, a leg thrown there. It was dark and cold, and we listened to the crashing of the wind and sand, felt the truck shake. But we slept. When we woke, the dust had coated every orifice that was at all moist—eyes crusted shut, lips and nostrils caked in grit, and tongue and throat coated with a film of dirt. It was horrible.

Rain began to fall. We hoped it might weigh down the dust, or rinse off the filth. But when it started to beat on the windshield, we saw it wasn't water, it was mud. It was raining mud. By the time the storm ended, our green vehicle was brown. There wasn't even a thought of washing ourselves—water was rationed.

There were no showers. No rinses. No way to get this off you other than the ubiquitous baby wipes. I hated the smell of them. Staff Sergeant Moss used the scented variety; the rest of us used unscented. But either way the wipes didn't do a lot of good; you rubbed the spots that got dampest or dirtiest—groin, armpits, feet, hands—every chance you got. But it was a losing cause. You moved on. And you tried not to feel more than the absurdity of it.

But the awfulness of the filth paled next to our team leader's critical errors in judgment. Leaving her flak vest lying around when she left the area. Not donning her JSLIST top but bitching at me if I took mine off. Leaving her ammo rounds unsecured outside the vehicle at night. We didn't speak for days, except when absolutely required. And when we did speak, I would not stand at ease with her, even at her order. I told her: "Sergeant, I believe it is more appropriate for me to maintain military bearing with you at all times."

There was nothing she could do about it. I was demonstrating that I would respect her rank, but that was all—the ultimate show of *disrespect*. When she tried to open a conversation about my attitude, I shut it down. I knew that I could not be faulted for my bearing, since it was completely correct.

So there was little conversation. No one wanted to break the tension, so it festered. We all withdrew into our own personal shit, talking less and less, at least when she was around.

I considered all over again how someone like SSG Moss managed to become a noncommissioned officer. The military system puts everyone up for promotion after a specified period of time unless there is a paper trail flagging problems. In SSG Moss's instance her college degree, her motivation, and her enthusiasm for PT gave her points; in all other areas, she merely had to demonstrate passable skills and show proper military bearing. Which, apparently, she had.

Our shifts were six hours on, six hours off, staggered so that I had three hours with Sergeant Quinn and three with Lauren. This meant that there was always an Arabic linguist on shift—and that SSG Moss and I never had to work at the same time. But I was getting just three hours of sleep at night. During the day, with the temperatures above a hundred degrees and the sun blazing, it was almost impossible to sleep. Exhaustion was making me increasingly irritable.

After eight days, which felt more like five weeks, Lauren and I managed a solar shower with two precious bottles of water each. We rigged a poncho and got naked behind it—in itself a rather wonderful experience. I managed to wash my hair and body, and even though I scraped off only a top layer of crud, it still felt great.

———

From March 30th to April 5th, we colocated within FARP Shell with Alpha Company, 1st Battalion, 187th Infantry (1/187). They took good care of us, gave us supplies our unit had not been able to get. Lauren and I were big coffee drinkers, and they let us share their "cowboy coffee," made in big vats with the grounds stirred right in. Strong, gritty, but hot and good. Some of the guys almost fell over laughing as Lauren and I tried to dig a survivability position. We're both pretty small, so our survivability position was supposed to be approximately thirty-six inches deep (unlike a foxhole or fighting position, which would had to have been deep enough for us to stand in). But about a foot down we hit a thick, hard layer of salt. It had to be broken up and then removed, along with big rocks. Luckily the guys decided to show us how it should be done, and what strong men they were, and they did it for us. A rare moment when I took advantage of the benefits of being a girl.

By this time, I could already tell the difference between the smell of burning trash and the smell of burning shit, a skill I never really had the desire to acquire. The latter is more acrid, stinging the eyes and burning the nose. We burned our shit soaked in JP8 diesel fuel throughout our deployment. (And soon I learned that the smell of dead animals being burned is another smell entirely—the worst of all.)

One day I tried to use a military phone to call home. I spent an hour trying to get through, failing miserably. It was frustrating and upsetting, and I ended up wishing I had never tried at all. In this emotional state, I got lippy with SSG Moss, and then retreated into my shell of protocol.

"We can't do this," she says. "I need this to stop."

"What are you talking about?"

"You don't communicate with me. You lock up every time I approach you. I want this to stop."

"Yes, Sergeant." My eyes straight ahead. My posture stiff and proper.

"At ease, Specialist Williams."

But I am not moving.

"Williams, *please*—"

Is it happening? Is that what I think it is?

Staff Sergeant Moss is crying. It isn't anything huge. Just a tear or two. But I see it, though I might not have noticed if I weren't studying her.

The bitch.

She's crying in front of a subordinate, and I have even less respect for her now, if that's possible. You *never* cry in front of a subordinate. Especially if you're a woman in a position of authority. The guys already think we can't handle this. It just isn't done.

I don't say a word. Not a word. She stands there for a moment, a single tear running down her cheek.

Then she turns and goes. I should feel guilty, but I don't.

Later that day, our platoon leader, Lieutenant Malley, came over. She pulled me aside to talk.

"Specialist Williams, I know that you are not doing anything to Staff Sergeant Moss that anyone can fault you on," she told me. "But what you're doing is really hurting her feelings. And really, you should relax and try to be normal with her because it's getting hard for her to cope. It's getting out of hand. You can't go on like this. You really need to back down. Relax."

LT Malley was smart and efficient, if highly strung. She was someone I understood. A lot of people didn't. Later, she became our company's executive officer (XO), and she was great at it—very organized. But as a platoon leader, she'd micromanage like a motherfucker, and that was tough on a lot of soldiers. As a West Pointer, she also didn't trust noncommissioned officers. I've heard rumors that at West Point they actually teach officers not to trust NCOs.

Just because an officer attends college doesn't mean she knows shit about the Army or how things really work. So many West Point graduates have little real-world experience. They live in dorms for four years and then go straight into the Army, never having had a job outside, never having rented an apartment, never having had to be responsible or having to take care of themselves on their own.

So for instance here was LT Malley, West Point and two-and-a-half years of Army experience, and our platoon sergeant—with his seventeen years of experience—was technically serving under her. Guess who really knew what the fuck was going on?

One time, at Fort Campbell, when we were getting ready to go to Iraq, everyone was doing a million things at once. We were always frantic and rushed. We'd be at work from 4:30 A.M. until 8 P.M. Then the order came down to paint the bottom of our A bags and B bags tan, and then stencil them black with our last name, the last four numbers of our social, what unit we were in, and so forth. The bottoms of our B bags had to be done that day. I carried them outside to paint them, then went back in for a moment to get another bag. When I returned, LT Malley was sitting there, crouched in the parking lot. Painting bags.

"Ma'am, what are you doing?"

LT Malley was tense as hell.

"They said these had to be painted by eleven o'clock!"

Calmly I said: "I think I can handle it."

"But it has to be done!"

Again calmly I said: "Ma'am, I know I'm only a specialist. But I think I can manage painting some bags." Admittedly I was being a bit of an asshole here. "So why don't you go inside and do whatever it is that you do that makes you deserve so much more money than me."

I actually did say this. It was an inappropriate way for me to talk, but it jarred Lieutenant Malley. She looked at me. She took it in. We'd spoken off-line before, casually, a couple of times. So we'd already established that she understood I was competent.

"Okay. You're right."

I said I understood LT Malley because I'd had experiences not so different from hers. When I was twenty-two and working in Tampa, I had an assistant, but I was so young that I had no authority over her. If she showed up late, there was nothing I could do about it. It was an awkward position, and probably because this was my first job with real responsibilities and I was so young, I got extremely emotionally invested in what I did. If I made a mistake and something went wrong, I took it very much to heart.

So here was LT Malley in what was most likely her first job after college. She was twenty-three or twenty-four years old, and she had a platoon of over twenty soldiers she had to lead into combat. Combat. We might get chemically attacked. Some of us might die. Before we went to war, there were estimates of 30 percent casualty rates. (No official statistics: just rumors. If the Iraqi army had actually stood and fought, rather than run away, who knows what might have happened?) So LT Malley was looking at her soldiers and thinking: I'm in charge of them. I'm responsible for them. They might die right in front of me.

That had to be overwhelming. For someone who's a perfectionist, that had to be very tough. She wanted to do everything herself. (I'm not so different.) But as a leader, she had to learn to let other people do their jobs. She had to delegate responsibility. I knew it would have been hard for me.

So we understood each other. She pissed me off, but we could talk. We talked a bunch of times. And so on that day in Iraq, we talked about SSG Moss, my disgust with the situation. And Lieutenant Malley actually commiserated. Inappropriate for both of us, but she convinced me. Helped me see that my stubbornness was hurting the whole team. Also—to be honest here— I felt I'd won something. I'd proven my point, in a sense, and that freed me to bend. Some of the tensions eased, and SSG Moss and I started working somewhat better together.

We're pulled for a mission with Division, and get briefed. Then we're sent out into the field with other teams. Finding units in the field ought to be a no-brainer, but there's little coordination and poor planning. Our four-digit grid coordinates are vague at best, accurate only to within a square kilometer of our target location. Under these circumstances, it's amazing we find the first two locations. We drop a team at each site.

As we drive through random Iraqi villages, we see that it may not have been the best idea to send MI teams out without infantry support. We have only the most general sense of where we are going. A few hours later, we're lost. The town we are driving through is the same town we've driven through twice before. The same locals are sitting and watching us go back and forth. They're looking a little puzzled. What are those Americans doing now? It was a damn good question. We later heard rumors that this town had seen a few ambushes of American convoys. I am so glad I didn't know this at the time.

Locals come out to look at us. Waving white flags (as in "Don't shoot me" or "Go America," we can't be sure). Giving us the thumbs-up. Always the thumbs-up. The people we see seem so happy. Waving and smiling and pumping their fists in the air. But at the same time I recognize pro-Saddam graffiti on some of the buildings, though no one comments on the disconnect. Mainly we are relieved that the people appear to welcome us. Not hate us.

We go on. Suddenly they're waving dead white chickens.

None of us has ever encountered anyone waving a dead white chicken. None of us knows what it means. Are they offering us something to eat? Are they making an obscure reference to something about Americans, the United States, our invasion? Is it a gesture of resistance or of mockery? What the hell is going on?

I'm not talking one dead white chicken. Or ten. Or fifty. As we continue to drive, we are seeing locals waving dead white chickens *everywhere*. And now that you mention it, we are seeing dead white chickens in the road and on the roadsides by the hundreds. We drive and drive, and there are thousands of dead white chickens.

But that is not the strange part.

The strange part is that we have been trained how to recognize a chemical attack. And one of the first signs of a chemical attack is dead animals littering the roads. And so we consider the scenario and we ask ourselves: Should we suit up? Don our chemical protection gear? Are we under chemical attack?

But the locals are absolutely unfazed. They are smiling and laughing as they wave the dead chickens. That's the first problem. The second problem is the perfectly healthy-looking black and brown chickens scampering in our path. If this is a chemical attack, it has killed only the white chickens. The nonwhite chickens are all fine.

Has the evil dictator of Iraq devised a racist chemical weapon that only kills *white* chickens?

Soon someone on our team starts to laugh. And then we're all laughing. Laughing hysterically. Why? That's hard to explain. But there's something so blatantly bizarre about this situation. So manifestly hallucinatory. We don't feel threatened. We know we are not the target of a chemical attack. Just a cosmic joke. And given the scheme of things—our fatigue and frustration at having gotten so utterly lost—it's a huge relief.

A couple of weeks after the dead white chickens incident, the *Newsweek* reporter traveling with our unit does some independent research. He thinks he has an answer, and it's nothing like what we expect. Turns out that one of Saddam's sons, Uday or Qusay—no one can say for sure—had a chicken factory where he liked to breed white chickens. With the invasion, the factory had been abandoned by soldiers sympathetic to the regime, and the locals had overrun it. They'd decided to take out their anger at Saddam by releasing the chickens into the wild where—bred for captivity—they had no survival skills. And promptly died by the thousands. The locals, wishing to demonstrate their enthusiasm for the U.S. troops, waved the chickens to demonstrate their hostility to the toppled dictatorship.

Thousands of dead white chickens on the roads or not, we're still lost and frustrated. Soon the sun starts to set. We wander aimlessly back and forth on various roads through anonymous towns. We have no maps.

The sky is going dark, and this is nuts. A handful of MI soldiers with small weapons and no combat support in the middle of Iraq in the middle of an invasion. What *was* the plan, exactly?

We eventually locate an infantry unit that has dug in around an abandoned building by the road. A berm has been built for protection, and after being in the truck all day, it's nice to stand up and stretch, walk around a little.

They don't mind sharing their space with us, but they ask that we share guard duty. It sucks since we've already been on twenty-four-hour operations. But it's fair. We're posted around the perimeter and lie on the berm, peering out into the darkness.

We've got NVGs (night vision goggles), but no mounts on our Kevlar helmets, so we hold the goggles to our eyes with one hand while we grip our weapons with the other. When we squint through the goggles, everything goes luminescent green and black, a kind of shadowy glow is cast over everything. Occasionally, and over time, fatigue sets in and the mind plays tricks. Is that a bush? Or a man? Staring through NVGs all the time gets tiring, and there's some moonlight, so we switch back and forth. We're a little paranoid. Howling dogs roam everywhere all night long. Are we supposed to communicate with any suspicious person or persons, or are we supposed to shoot on sight? The rules of engagement aren't covered often, and we weren't briefed on any specifics that night.

———

In the morning, without much sleep, we press on. Continue the search for our location. Before too long we find the unit with which we are to colocate, pick a site, and resume a regular shift schedule for operations.

I see local women in the distance, and I watch them through my binoculars. A number of women collect sticks and carry them in bundles back to homes that lack windows and roofs. A few other women lead donkeys and carts piled with stuff. It's all so ordinary. An ordinary day for them, despite the war.

Before sunset, though, we learn that the other unit is not expecting us to spend the night. And might not let us stay.

"*What?*" We are incredulous.

Their commander gives no ground.

"I repeat: No one cleared this. We will need to check with higher about this."

"What do you expect us to do? Go drive around in the dark?"

"Just stand fast until we figure this out."

None of this inspires confidence in anything other than the certainty of military incompetence. Like death, like taxes, military incompetence is something you can bet on. (You know the World War II saying, right? *Snafu*—situation normal: all fucked up.)

After a while it gets straightened out. They let us stay.

Here's the good part: While we're with this unit, I discover halal/kosher meals.

I'm walking around and talking to infantry guys when I notice a case of them.

"What's that?"

"Those are kosher meals. No one wants the fucking things. We don't know what to do with them."

"Can I look?"

I open one or two, and I cannot believe it.

"Can I please have these?" I start to beg.

"Yeah, get 'em out of here. They're just in the way. We're tripping over them."

The vegetarian MREs I've been subsisting on provide carbs but no protein (except for peanut butter—and how much peanut butter can a person eat before feeling ill?). But these halal/kosher meals, all pork-free and approved by both Jewish and Muslim authorities, are amazing. In each case of twelve there are six vegetarian meals. I score two cases—a dozen veggie meals total. They actually taste good, and they are made with real food! (When I read the ingredient list, I know what everything is. "Chickpeas," "tomatoes," "flour," "water," and "beans," instead of whatever artificial ingredients are in the regular MREs.) All the accessory packs have real sunflower seeds and peanuts and raisins. It is all so much healthier. And the accessory packs also include black pepper, which is very exciting. I never used to like pepper, but it is a flavor I really grow to appreciate during my deployment.

Up to this point I've been getting fewer than twelve hundred calories a day, even though I need at least two thousand. After this, at least for a while, I am able to eat one halal/kosher meal almost every day. But it's still not enough to maintain my weight. I have been losing weight—a lot of weight. But now for the first time since I've been in-country, I don't feel like I'm starving.

"Halal meals? You are not authorized to have them." My platoon leader goes on: "The chaplain has said that there needs to be a religious reason."

LT Malley is following a precise rule, and not watching out for a soldier in her command. This infuriates me.

"I'm not getting enough protein." I hate trying to explain this to her.

"I can't make these sorts of special arrangements—"

"I'm not asking for special arrangements." I try to keep cool. "These meals are out there. And no one is eating them. They're getting thrown away, mostly."

"I'm sorry. I can't get these meals for you. And the chaplain agrees. You're not Muslim. You're not Jewish. I can't make these arrangements for you just because you have a personal preference—"

"I'm not—"

"What if every soldier decides she wants some special food?"

"Ma'am, I don't think—"

"Is that all?"

"Yes, Ma'am."

Later, I mention my problem to our supply sergeant. She says: "I can get you halal meals. No problem." It takes her twenty minutes to get me two cases.

So why the fuck could our supply sergeant do this, but our platoon leader couldn't? She has the rank. She could have gone to any supply sergeant and said: "I need these now. Put them on my truck."

Because in Iraq, doing the right thing isn't always the right thing.

Because Lieutenant Malley, like the good West Pointer she is, fucking followed the rules. You cannot always do that.

When I arrived in Kuwait, I weighed 140 pounds. Over the course of the next several months, I lost more than 25 pounds.

On April 8, a Tuesday, we got sent out with an artillery unit. We were finally realizing that we were going to get tossed around from unit to unit on a regular basis. It was frustrating never to get really comfortable with anyone, but it was simultaneously cool and interesting to see how a variety of units operated.

Pulling operations while artillery is being fired is not easy. My job is listening. Artillery is *loud*. Even though these were relatively small guns—105mm—whenever they fired, that was all I could hear. And if I was sleeping, it woke me without fail. I was amazed when I was on shift once and watched SGT Quinn sleep through a lengthy barrage. He snored. The closest gun was less than ten meters away!

While we waited for the convoy to get ready to leave, I met a local who wanted to talk to me—in Arabic—about the invasion. Tanks were rolling by his house, and there was an entire arty (artillery) unit parked in his backyard. He wasn't pleased. His children were scared. He wanted peace and freedom, but not this way. He wanted the U.S. Army to get out. What could I say? I'm sorry? I *was* sorry. *Maybe things will get better,* I told him. But I still felt pretty damn helpless. I left a bag of Skittles for his children— the only offering I had. I think this offended him even more.

Lauren may be the other girl on our team, but we didn't exactly strike up a warm friendship. Not at first, anyway.

She's careful around SSG Moss, and careful around me for disrespecting SSG Moss. So we're polite but have little to say to each other. Mainly, if we talk at all, it's to rag on Sergeant Quinn, since he's way too innocent. Like a lot of people, he wears his Birth Control Glasses in combat, but they look awful on him. We call them BCGs because these big thick plastic Army-issued glasses are so ugly; our thinking is that nobody will have sex with you if you're wearing them. I certainly avoid mine. (I figure if a chemical attack fuses my contact lenses to my corneas, it really won't matter if it happens moments before I die.) Lauren and I learn pretty fast that Quinn's probably never even slept with a girl, and once we get a good laugh when we tell him we've probably kissed more girls than he has. But he's too stiff to laugh, or smile, much. His promotion still sits uncomfortably on his shoulders.

Things change after our first direct encounter with small-arms fire. We're back with an artillery unit, just getting settled, and when we first hear it, I don't register immediately what it means. *Pop, pop, pop!* My first thought is: That sounds like the firing range. Then it clicks in my mind: They sound like gunshots because they *are* gunshots. The guys in the artillery unit take cover behind their vehicles.

We're slower to react, but SSG Moss, Lauren, Quinn, and I take cover in the dirt behind the vehicle on the side opposite the small-arms fire.

As I get my bearings, I realize the danger is pretty far off. We can't see who is firing, and are behind a lot of our own guys, so we wouldn't dream of shooting back. It's best to wait.

"Get up, Specialist Williams!" It's Staff Sergeant Moss.

"What?!"

She's facing me in the dirt, from behind the other tire.

What the fuck is she talking about now?

"Get in the truck and run ops." This sounds like a ridiculous order. She wants me to get in the truck, put on headphones, and start listening for enemy communications. I look at Lauren and she meets my eyes. In an instant I see that Lauren is getting it at last. *What is wrong with this woman?*

"Get up and go pull ops, Williams!"

I ignore this. It cannot be happening. NCOs are not supposed to make their soldiers do anything they won't do themselves, so I think she can get up and pull ops herself if it's that important. I watch the combat-arms guys, figuring I'll get up when they do. They're better trained at this than we are.

I am pretending I can't hear SSG Moss, and I look away. The enemy fire sounds weaker, ever more distant. The threat lessens with each passing second. But I am not moving. I am not going to stand up and walk around for no reason until we are completely safe.

"*Oh,*" Staff Sergeant Moss says with an odd emphasis, as if realizing belatedly why I stayed put. That the bad guys have been shooting at us, and our best strategy is to take cover. Follow the example of the artillery guys we can see.

I try to read her face, but there's a blankness there, a stunned incoherence that I don't understand at all. What is she experiencing at this moment? Is she afraid? Does she know that asking a soldier under her command to get up and move around to get into the vehicle while we are under attack is stupid? Or what the hell is going on? Is she trying to get me killed?

For what seems like the hundredth time since we've been in-country, I ask myself: How do people like SSG Moss survive in the world? Or let's put it another way: How am *I* going to survive working for this woman?

Two days later, traveling north with the same arty unit, we came to a site near Babylon, the ancient city on the Euphrates River.

We stopped near a statue of King Hammurabi, whose dynasty ruled this region almost six thousand years ago. We passed the area where the Tower of Babel supposedly stood. A lovely area, it was a tremendous relief after so much time in the desert.

We took a trip to one of Saddam's presidential palaces, a gigantic building with immense rooms, two elevators plus a service elevator. Each room had its own distinct design, with its own elaborately painted ceiling and its own chandelier. We'd never seen anything like it, and once we reached the balcony and looked out onto the huts below, we were blown away by how this splendor existed in the midst of outrageous poverty. The people were beyond impoverished. And every day they got to look up at *this*.

Near the palace I assisted a few American reporters as a translator so they could conduct interviews with locals. They let every soldier use their satellite phone for five minutes. I attempted to call my father and mother in the United States. This felt huge, and I got very excited. I'm at war in Iraq, and I'm calling home. When I got my mom's voice mail, my excitement turned to anger. Not at home? When I got my dad's voice message, I sank even further. Did I really expect them to be sitting around the telephone on the off chance I might call?

A few local boys joined us in the palace, and they latched onto Lauren and me. Asking us in Arabic if we had boyfriends, if they could be our boyfriends, or if the soldiers with us were our boyfriends. Clearly trying to puzzle out our relationship to this military situation. We laughed at them, and I joked with them, but even I had to admit that these boys reeked. It wasn't their fault; there was no running water in these villages. But still, I felt a little uncomfortable. Uncomfortable as well that I was having these feelings. Not wanting to fall into the attitude so many soldiers had about Arabs—that is, that they're smelly, awful people.

Once again Lauren and I filled a box with MRE remains— the stuff none of us wanted to eat—before we left, and I labeled it "nutritious food" in Arabic for the locals.

On the highway to Baghdad a disturbance brings our convoy to a halt.

Word comes down that the unit in front of us has come under small-arms fire. Usually you just push through, but the whole series of convoys has ground to a halt. We're at the tail end, and our instructions are to hold traffic. No one goes forward. No locals pass through. Everything stops.

Lauren and Quinn are Korean linguists with technical skills to do signal intelligence, but no Arabic-language skills. That leaves SSG Moss and me to deal with the language issues. I see the crowd gathering, and a handful of guys working to keep them in place, and I jump out to help.

Everywhere I've been I've made signs on MRE cardboard boxes saying, STOP. AMERICAN MILITARY CHECKPOINT. ENTRY FORBIDDEN. Made flashcards for guys manning roadblocks. Drilled people on basic phrases in Arabic. It's my duty to help whenever I can with my language skill—the Army paid for me to learn! So this is just another way for me to contribute.

"I'm not doing this," SSG Moss says. "You talk to them."

She's acting like it's a block party that's gotten unruly.

For the first hour or so the locals are understanding when I tell them that there is danger on the road and they can't move forward. They are interested in me, this blond girl speaking Arabic, this girl in the Army—I am an anomaly, a distraction. I keep putting them off: "Another half hour, God willing." It's a great phrase, one that they generally accept. It's out of my hands, all up to Allah.

After a while, though, coming from the north on the highway, other locals are telling those folks we have stopped that there is no problem, the road is safe and clear. The crowd grows. And it continues to grow.

Even though we have weapons, the people don't want to listen or respect us any longer. I tell them over and over to stay behind the rear vehicle, but they push forward, again and again.

"It's too dangerous to pass! *Dangerous!* Please listen! We'll let you go through as soon as it is safe to move!"

I'm almost alone out here with the crowd, there are maybe six guys with me, and I'm the only one who speaks Arabic.

Except SSG Moss. I run back to the Humvee.

"I seriously need help," I tell her. "Someone else who speaks Arabic to explain what's going on."

"I told you once," she says calmly. "I'm not talking to these people."

SGT Quinn tells me that the first sergeant also told SSG Moss how much we needed her help, but she refused to get out of the vehicle.

The crowd is getting more frustrated, with men pressing closer and starting to intimidate me. I'm not scared, exactly, but I'm stressed. And I'm wondering whether I can kill my team leader for leaving me to deal out here by myself.

I'm yelling now. Starting to get angry. And then I have an idea.

I go get Lauren.

Now Lauren is a tiny person. She's perky and cute, and

speaks with the gentle twang of someone from a small town in Texas, which is where she's from.

But she's tough when she needs to be. And she backs me up.

Did I also mention she's the one on our team with our most serious-looking weapon? It's an M-249 squad automatic weapon (SAW). This is a big gun capable of firing 750 rounds per minute. When this little woman with the stern look and the dark shades moves to my side and holds her SAW up for everyone to see, there's a real hush in the crowd.

This weapon says: *Respect me.*

Lauren sets it up facing them, and everyone makes a nice neat line behind the rear vehicle. I grin at her.

Soon enough the road opens again. And we move on.

AT THE MONASTERY

BAGHDAD. April 2003.

Our team settled into an abandoned compound, a sort of manufacturing plant, with 1st Battalion, 187th Infantry (1/187). There were military guards with guns sitting at the entrances to the compound; no one got in or out without passing a checkpoint. No locals were permitted on the base. Lots of big buildings with office supplies. Bathrooms were a hole in the floor and a spigot. But there was running water. Spigots lined the main road. When Lauren and I walked to the aid station, several dozen infantry guys were stripped naked in the street to wash at the spigots. We laughed and waved. They looked embarrassed. Then they laughed and waved back.

I am asked whether I would be willing to go out on missions with the infantry. They have no civilian translators. Translation is not my job, so I do it almost as a favor. In part it's better than just sitting in the compound. It's a chance to see the local area, meet the people, and experience the immediate results of my work. Though it is certainly *way* outside the realm of my official responsibilities.

Why else do I do this? Think about it.

Put yourself in the position of some eighteen-year-old infantry soldier with a loaded weapon in a country surrounded by people who don't speak his language. And these people come up to him and yell. They want to tell him something. And he doesn't know what it is. They might be saying to him, *I love you, and I am so glad you are here to liberate my country.* Or they might be saying to him, *I'm about to fucking kill you.* So this kid is eighteen and he's got his loaded rifle—and he doesn't know *what* they're saying.

In the Middle East, people have a different communication style than Americans do. Americans have this three-foot-space rule. We do not want anyone to invade a space within three feet of us when we talk. For most Americans this is standard. In the Middle East the space is much less—it's more like a foot or six inches. They get right up in your face. And they will yell. It looks to most Americans like aggression. But it isn't. It's friendly.

This is something I had to get used to while I was dating Rick. I watched him interact with his friends, and I often thought they were about to fight all the time. But they were having this casual friendly conversation.

No doubt my experiences with Rick gave me more sympathy, understanding, and respect for the people in Iraq. For starters I never looked at them as having some freakish or weird religion. I didn't look at them as being foreign. For me there were things that were comfortable and comforting about being around Arabs. I spent a long time with Rick and a lot of time with Rick's friends. So I acquired a familiarity with Arab men. Things that might offend other Americans about Iraqi men didn't bother me. Like how close someone got when they talked to you. It didn't upset me.

But there was something I did realize once I got to the Middle East. When I had been with Rick, his friends never looked at me sexually. They always treated me with total respect. So at the time I just thought Arab men were very respectful of women. But when I flew into Kuwait and walked around the airport in my civvies, these Kuwaiti men were staring at me. A couple of them followed me around. I was horrified.

"You're not allowed to do this!" I wanted to tell them. "It's against your religion. You're supposed to be respectful!"

That's when it hit me. Rick's friends' respectful and polite attitude toward me had *nothing* to do with their culture or religion. It had nothing to do with me. It had everything to do with Rick. They were being respectful of *him*—not me. They were showing him respect by showing respect for his possession. *Me.*

But my having known Rick did help me in Iraq. For one thing I never told locals that I learned Arabic because I was Military Intelligence. I never said I spoke their language so I could spy on them.

Locals asked: "How come you know Arabic?"

I said: "Because my ex-boyfriend is Palestinian."

Or I said: "Because my boyfriend is Palestinian." (This had the added benefit of making me "taken," and it prevented local guys from hitting on me.)

Either way I had some Arabic dialect from knowing Rick, so it was easier for people to believe me. It helped me feel safer saying I knew Arabic due to Rick—rather than saying I'm Intel. At times it could be difficult because there have been tensions between the Palestinians and the Iraqis. After all, here were a miserably poor people whose president was giving money to the people of another country. (Saddam Hussein gave "martyrdom bonuses" to families of Palestinian suicide bombers.) Still, my language skills and my ability to speak about Rick made things a whole lot easier for me. For the most part, locals treated me well.

One day in Baghdad, our platoon leader ripped Quinn a new asshole right in front of us. Our first sergeant was present. Our XO at the time was present. And Lieutenant Malley came up, and it was obvious something was wrong. You could tell.

"Sergeant Quinn, get out of the truck this instant! Get out of the truck and stand at parade rest!"

So she was screaming at an NCO in front of us, and I was lower enlisted. That's not appropriate. If she had a problem with a noncommissioned officer, she should have taken him aside. You do not hem him up in front of his soldiers. How was I supposed to respect him if I had to watch him getting hemmed up?

So we were all frozen, watching this. But that was how LT Malley was. For instance she'd come up to me when something got fucked up, and she'd start yelling at me about it.

And I'd be thinking: Don't yell at me about something being fucked up. I can't make these people do anything. You want to yell at me? You want me to be in charge of this shit? Promote me and put me in charge.

I'd say: "I'm not in charge. You can't talk to me about this. There's a noncommissioned officer right there. Sergeant Moss is right there. Sergeant Quinn is right there. You'll have to talk to one of them. Don't look at me. Don't talk to me."

We clear a school.

We've all heard the stories of Saddam and his army stashing

weapons in schools and mosques. Places we wouldn't attack without provocation, so we know that even these places must be searched. This is my first chance to see how the infantry works. I hang back a little. Stay out of the way. Wait until I'm called.

The school is a group of buildings inside a walled compound. I linger near the entrance with the radio guy, doing some loose crowd control—basically chatting with locals, doing my bit to be friendly and "win the hearts and minds." The children especially are fascinated by an Arabic-speaking, blond, female soldier. One little girl offers me a rose, and I hold her in my arms while her father takes our photo. I wear the flower in my flak vest all day.

Before too long a call comes over the radio to send in the linguist. I am directed inside to "three women" and asked to translate. One woman is hysterical and terrified. She carries a baby and holds a small girl by the hand.

"What is the problem?" I ask her as I am told to do. "Are there weapons in this school? What is your position here?"

She tells me she is a teacher, and that she knows nothing about weapons.

"I am afraid," she says between sobs, "of the men with guns."

She has no Intel value. She fears for her life and the lives of her kids. With the commander's permission, I lead her out of the compound.

"Don't be afraid," I tell her. "No one will hurt you. We're here to help you. Don't be afraid. Everything is fine."

Once we get outside, she runs crying into the arms of her mother. I try again to soothe her. Her family thanks me, and I return inside.

I move with the infantry guys as they clear rooms in the school.

We come across an older man, his wife, and their two children. He says he is the guard of the school, and that his family lives on the premises. He points to pallets of bedding on the floor.

The daughter is making bread when we find her. Her hands covered in dough, she wipes them on her clothes. She is desperately shy and will not look at me.

We gather the family together all into one room. I ask the same questions I asked the teacher.

"Are there any weapons here? Have you been asked to hide caches of weapons?"

The father begins to complain of chest pains.

It's all we need. Have this man die of a heart attack in front of his family.

"Medic!" I call out to the soldiers. "Get a medic for this guy!"

It takes awhile, but we calm him down. It's only an elevated pulse. Nothing serious. A couple of ibuprofen as a placebo, and he begins to breath normally again.

His grateful son voluntarily leads me to one old Soviet-era rifle his father has to guard the school.

I thank him, but he expresses concern that his father will get fired when he reports his gun missing. I write out a receipt in Arabic and in English that says the U.S. Army has confiscated this rifle. There are proper forms for this, but I don't have them. So I use scrap paper. It will have to do.

We clear a military compound.

It looks like a joint Iraqi/Palestinian training facility. There are paintings everywhere of the Iraqi flag and the Palestinian flag. There are posters glorifying the first Palestinian female *sha-*

heeda (suicide bomber). There is also a MOUT (military operations on urban terrain) site, for urban combat training, and an obstacle course. A couple of the rooms have UXO (unexploded ordnance), and a couple of rooms have been deliberately destroyed. I go through files looking for papers that may be worthy of DOC-X (document exploitation). There are files of Ba'ath party members and soldiers. I take a few training manuals, one on PT/hand-to-hand combat, one on weapons. We look over posters that explain how to fire a rocket-propelled grenade, and others on chemical warfare. Eventually, some civil affairs/psyop (psychological operations) guys show up, and they bring a civilian interpreter with them. I show him around, but I am extremely confused when he picks up the few unburned files on women and tears off the photographs, leaving the papers behind. He shows no interest in the men's files or photographs.

We clear a monastery.

I know on some level that Iraq has a small Christian minority, but finding this monastery astounds me. It certainly explains the many people in the neighborhood who ask if we are *mesihi.* Christian. It is a Catholic neighborhood—*catholiqi.*

We are in an area of Baghdad called Dura. It is quite lovely— trees, orchards, homes inside walled compounds. The doors, as in most of Iraq, are elaborately designed and often blue.

We go in the back of the compound. The grounds are lush, well tended and groomed. Around to the front of the building, which is beautiful and clean to a degree that is surprising. Amazingly the UN embargo and the ravages of two wars have somehow spared it.

We knock, and a man in robes ushers us inside.

In Arabic I repeat my by-now-standard questions.

"We must search this building. For weapons. Do you have any weapons here? Or caches of weapons and ammunition?"

The monk is polite. He smiles. He responds in English.

"We have nothing to hide," he says. "I am happy to show you our church. However, some of the rooms are locked. The man with the keys is leading prayers in a small room. There." He points to his right. "Perhaps you can search those rooms later? When prayers are done."

The lieutenant in charge of this mission is looking at me.

I look back at him.

We are all silent for a moment.

"Specialist Williams," the lieutenant says.

"Sir?" I respond, uncertain.

The monk stands there, a model of serenity and calm.

"What did this guy just say?"

I glance at the monk, but his expression does not change.

"He says they are in the middle of prayers, and the man with the key to the locked rooms is leading the prayers. When they finish prayers, he can show us the locked rooms."

"Oh," the LT says. "Okay."

But I can't take this.

"He's speaking *English,* Sir. You can ask him anything you want."

The lieutenant is uninterested in hearing my views.

Is it possible the lieutenant cannot understand the monk— simply because he *looks* foreign?

"Ask your commander," the monk says, still in English. "Ask him if he would like to join us. In an Easter prayer. Or whether his soldiers would like to join us in prayer."

"What's that?" the lieutenant asks. "What's he saying?"

"He is asking whether we would like to join them in prayer. For Easter."

"Yes," the monk says brightly. "Today is a holy day. Are any of these soldiers Catholics? Would any of the soldiers like to come and join us in prayer?"

"Huh?"

"He's asking about prayer. Whether any of us would like to join them in prayer."

A few soldiers shift restlessly, almost longingly.

"Can we, Sir?" one of them ventures.

"No!" the lieutenant says loudly. "No. We're at war. We have a mission to do."

I feel slightly sickened. These are Christians in a Muslim country. Haven't they been persecuted enough? Are we really spreading freedom and democracy to the Middle East by clearing this Catholic church?

"We can't wait," the lieutenant says. "Tell him we plan to begin searching the building. *Now.*"

"We could also offer you tea?" the monk suggests. "While we wait for services to end."

I don't even bother to translate this, expecting the usual response from the lieutenant.

"I'm sorry. We can't wait," I say to the monk. "We need to search the building now."

The monk nods, but I can see he is not pleased by this.

So we begin to move through the monastery to verify that everything is clear.

We start down a hall, and the lieutenant impatiently jiggles each locked doorknob. We reach an unlocked door that opens to reveal stairs.

"Ask him where these stairs lead."

"To the basement," replies the monk. "A storage space."

It appears to me, though I cannot be sure, that the monk has chosen to enunciate his English more slowly. As if he is speaking to a child.

The lieutenant rolls back and forth on the balls of his feet.

"What did the fellow say?"

I catch the eyes of a few of the soldiers standing around us. Some of them are also half smiling at the absurdity of the situation.

"To the basement," I repeat.

We go to the basement, where there are precious sacred icons. The only lights provided are the tactical ones attached to soldier's weapons.

There is a room filled with vats of sacramental wine. The smell, heavy and sweet and fruity, hangs in the air, cloying. None of us have had alcohol in a couple of months. We are stunned with desire for it. We move past this room quickly, unable even to articulate our desires to one another.

In the back there is a plywood sheet nailed against the wall. The edges look glued. This draws the lieutenant's instant suspicion.

"Ask him what's on the other side of this."

Wearily I repeat the question to the monk.

The monk nods.

"It goes to the outside."

"It leads to the outside."

"Hm." The infantry lieutenant thinks this over. "We are going to have to break it down. Tell him we don't believe him."

I repeat this to the monk, who is already shaking his head.

"Look," the monk says, pointing upward. "There's a window

to the outside. You can see that this door leads to the outside. There is nothing on the other side of this door."

I repeat this to the infantry lieutenant, who ponders things for a moment.

"No," he finally says. "Uh-uh. Tell your buddy here we are going to have to break it down."

"Please," the monk says. "Send some of your soldiers around to the outside and have them knock on the other side. We'll hear them. And then you can know that this door leads nowhere. It goes outside."

When I repeat what the monk has said, the lieutenant agrees. He sends two soldiers around to the outside.

But he remains suspicious.

"Ask him why this door is barricaded like this. Why did they block this door?"

The monk is becoming agitated. He doesn't wait for me to repeat what he already understands.

"We put it up in case of chemical attack. To keep gas out. This was our way to protect ourselves from a chemical attack."

This sounds too strange and sad even to me. But locals have lots of strange ideas about chemical attacks. I begin to repeat everything to the lieutenant.

"He believes that this plywood would protect them from—"

"Get in here," the lieutenant gestures to the soldiers who have joined us in the basement. "Bust this thing down! Now!"

It just feels wrong to desecrate this place.

By the time they've busted a few holes in it, soldiers begin banging on the door from the outside.

"Yeah," we hear them saying. "It's the outside! Like the priest said!"

We leave the basement and search the simple kitchen facility. We poke into a few of the rooms. Everything is disappointingly empty.

Returning to the foyer, the LT is pissed. The prayers continue. The head monk with the keys has not concluded the service.

"Ask him again if they have any weapons."

I speak Arabic this time.

Dejectedly the monk acknowledges—also in Arabic—that they do.

"We have one AK," he says quietly. "One Kalashnikov."

This is an ancient weapon at least thirty years old.

"And twenty rounds," he continues. "We have twenty bullets."

So that is how the monastery protects itself. What stands between the monks and the looters is one pathetic weapon with its twenty rounds.

I tell the LT about the rifle. He looks absurdly satisfied with the news.

"Find that damn rifle," the lieutenant says. "And confiscate it."

The monk retrieves a key and produces the weapon and its twenty rounds. As the rifle and the ammunition are removed from the monastery, the monk practically begins to beg.

"Please," he protests gently. "Please. We need this rifle. We need to be able to defend ourselves. We have the only computer in the entire neighborhood. And we have religious relics. Please. Everything will be taken."

The LT is slightly amused.

"What was he planning to do with the AK anyway? Shoot an armed mob?"

"Scare people away," the monk insists. "Not shoot people. *Never.*"

I know the LT's orders are to remove all weapons from mosques and schools and organizations. But orders can be interpreted. His orders at this point also stipulate that families can keep one weapon for self-protection. To protect themselves from looting. This lieutenant can make a personal judgment call on this. He can interpret his orders differently—if he wants to.

Again: The right thing isn't always the right thing. The right thing doesn't happen. Perhaps to justify this colossal waste of time or perhaps because this is an institution (and not a family home), the lieutenant is unmoved when I repeat the monk's plea. On the contrary, he takes his actions further.

"It's time to finish this," he tells me. "Tell him we are not going to wait any longer for those prayers to end. They're taking way too long. Tell him to get the keys for those rooms that are locked. We need to search everything. *Now.*"

So during Holy Week we cut mass short. We march into the room where the monks are praying. We order them to return to their rooms and open doors for us.

In this way we finish clearing the monastery.

We find nothing else.

As we pack to go, the monks gather at the front of the monastery. They see the lieutenant toss their AK in the back of the truck. He doesn't bother to glance back. Orders his men to climb in. The job here is done.

I linger as long as I can. I want to say something. Anything. But I can't think what to say. We are abandoning these poor monks to a fate I cannot imagine. I can only hope their building is considered too insignificant. But news travels. No doubt our search has been noted on the street. The word is out: The monks have been disarmed. I give them until dusk—maybe the night—before some gang or other comes busting through their door.

How does this qualify as liberating the people of Iraq?

I load up with the men. Looking back, I see the monk I've been translating for turn away from us, as if we are already gone.

It's over. We're out of here in a swirl of dust.

I never see those monks or that monastery again.

Maybe I told a captain I knew what had happened. How we had stripped these defenseless men of their one rifle. It would be a dramatic breach of military authority for anyone under these circumstances to *return* a rifle to the Iraqi people. Given the circumstances—that we are currently at war—what would it mean to provide a weapon to Iraqis? In plain cold terms, it would be a serious breach of military protocol. There would be *consequences*.

I don't say this happened, but it might have happened. The captain I told about this incident at the monastery headed out there later that day. He arrived at the monastery. Climbed over the back fence. Knocked on the door. Probably interrupted their evening prayers. The same monk came to the door, thinking: Now it begins. But also thinking: Looters do not knock. So he opened the door, expecting the worst, but was then confounded. It was an American captain. Silently and without ceremony the captain displayed an AK rifle. Not *the* rifle. But a good facsimile of it—some other crappy weapon confiscated in a sweep of some other poor soul's miserable dwelling. Hastily the captain handed the AK to the monk.

And he was gone again, even before the monk could thank the captain for this priceless gift.

THE EXPLOSION

Everything goes in alphabetical order in the Army. So Alpha, Bravo, and Charlie are dismounted units. They are the true grunts or foot soldiers who, as the cadence goes, "hump it on [their] backs." Meanwhile Delta Company has the mounted gun trucks. There's a good-natured rivalry between grunts and D Co guys. The foot soldiers say the gun-truck guys are "soft." D Co insists that grunts take too long to get anything done—which is true. Dismounted troops always have to get loaded onto LMTVs or civilian buses to get anywhere. Delta guys are often the QRF (quick reaction force). They go everywhere on short notice, and so when it came time to decide which unit should get my services, that's the argument they made. They were the ones who needed a translator most.

So D Co was the unit I frequently got to work with. Often they were accompanied by a combat-line unit, so I met a lot of Joes, but I was closest to the men in Delta, 1/187.

It turned out that I loved working with the infantry. During my year in Iraq those men in D Co were the single best group of soldiers I met. Their commander was a stand-up guy, honest, straightforward, and tough. A man who inspired loyalty. A leader who made you want to try harder and do better. He was clearly devoted to his soldiers and his mission. His solid leadership showed on all levels. I was treated like a professional. These D Co guys respected what I could do for them. A platoon leader asked me to teach his men a class on basic Arabic. I made up flash cards for them. I made up signs for them to use in crowd-control situations.

This unit was the *only* unit in which I never experienced any discomfort or harassment. No one made inappropriate comments or stepped out of line. Even months later, when I ran into those guys, they always said, "Hey! You were our linguist in Baghdad!" They never said, "Hey! You were that chick we had with us!"—as so many other Army guys did.

I was in Dura, the area on the outskirts of Baghdad where I'd been before. I was out again as a translator with Delta Company, 1/187.

We walked down the street. I talked to families one at a time and asked if anyone had weapons, knew of any caches, or was aware of any terrorists/criminals in the area. The people were friendly and open. They wanted to talk to me. The stories were remarkably consistent—no caches, no terrorists. There were only individual household weapons and several abandoned military pieces in the area, including artillery and an APC (armored personnel carrier).

As we went through the neighborhood, children swarmed around us. They experimented with their few words of English.

"What's your name? What's your name?"

"How are you? How are you?"

"One dollar. One dollar."

They clustered around, and after a time we grew more familiar. There was laughter and giggling. Everyone relaxed.

The last time I was here, I told a few of them my name, and now they chanted it: "Kayla! Kayla! Kayla!"

One boy, a little older, maybe a teenager, asked my name as well. When I told him, he said, "No! You are Britney Spears!" From then on he or his friends called out "Britney! Britney!" I laughed and shook my head. I don't even like Britney Spears, but I knew they meant it as a compliment.

Throughout my deployment I was constantly amazed at how far and fast American pop culture has spread. Even with sanctions in place, Iraqis all knew Britney Spears. And they all knew Michael Jackson and Shakira. (Shakira made sense to me because she's part Lebanese.) But there were also slews of VCDs imported through Asian countries. VCDs are these cheap knock-off DVDs. They have Chinese, Korean, and Arabic subtitles. Some of them are very badly done; taped with handheld video cameras from the screens in movie theaters—you can see the theater's exit signs in the corner. You can see people standing up and walking out. Once we settled in, soldiers bought stacks of these illegal VCDs. I bought *Finding Nemo* and *Dirty Dancing;* I managed to purchase *The Lord of the Rings—The Return of the King* on VCD even before it was available in theaters in the States. After a while, we were routinely picking up VCDs for very little money to play on laptops or portable DVD players. At some later point we also began to buy small Discmans that play VCDs when plugged into cheap televisions we also bought from the locals.

(Later families back home also began to send televisions to their sons and daughters in Iraq. The Army was never able to provide troops with enough air conditioners, so sometime in the summer, when temperatures reached 130 degrees, families began shipping air conditioners to Iraq. There was a story that one mom collected a lot of money and then shipped her son's unit something like a hundred air conditioners she'd bought at Wal-Mart.)

So we got to the end of the street and approached the APC. The families who lived in the nearest compounds came out and gave us dates and bread from woven plates. The food was delicious, a welcome break from MREs. I especially loved the bread—like pita but larger, maybe a foot in diameter, thin and still warm. Around the APC were scattered Iraqi army uniforms. As they deserted the soldiers apparently left even their clothes. I idly wondered if they had civilian clothes with them or if they ran off in their underwear.

We poked around the vehicle, retrieving unspent rounds. I looked through the record book. A few local men talked to the guards we posted. I was called over to translate. They explained how the men in the APC buried their extra ammunition by the side of the road in mounds of dirt. They showed us, and we started to dig. More men and boys joined us. It became a strange scene of soldiers and locals digging up box after box of 50-cal ammunition. Hundreds and hundreds of rounds.

The locals helped us load the ammo onto a bus to transport to the UXO pit where EOD (explosive ordnance disposal) teams would destroy everything. (These explosions, every day or so, were very jarring when unexpected.) The people did not want this stuff in their neighborhood. They worried—with good reason—that their children could get injured.

There were unexploded shells everywhere in this country.

Our shells, their shells—who knew? Bomblets from our cluster bombs were in fields, yards, gardens. When we found them we marked the locations and called EOD to come and destroy them in place. We warned locals to stay away. *Don't touch anything! Keep your children away at all costs!* But children in any country are hard to watch all the time, and forbidden fruit is always the sweetest.

So there was always a concern that some kid would get blown up. But what could we do? There weren't many EOD teams available, and there was a vast quantity of UXO waiting to be destroyed. We did our best but simply couldn't keep up. Several locals pointed out UXO to us, and we marked the areas with white engineer tape and *U-X-O* written on them. I told locals that "special soldiers" (I had no clue how to say EOD in Arabic) would come to take care of it.

They asked, "When?"

I could only say, "Soon, God willing."

There were five artillery pieces in the neighborhood, in addition to the APC and a BM-21 (a Soviet multiple-rocket launcher). We didn't want to leave anything there in usable condition for fear it could be turned against us. The locals didn't want it there anyway. Unfortunately we also didn't have the ability to take it all away with us, so what couldn't be towed had to be destroyed in place.

Dismantling the BM-21 was the coolest. I got to use my Leatherman to cut the wires at the back. This was particularly exciting because I had a pathetic Leatherman. It was very girly—my ex-husband gave it to me, and the gift may have contributed to our divorce. It certainly showed his lack of understanding of my position. I'm in the Army! But he gave me this wine-and-cheese Leatherman. The "Flair" variety. It actually had a shrimp fork, a butter knife, and (more usefully) a bottle opener and a corkscrew. But Army guys all kidded me about it. I called it my "chick Leatherman" or "fag Leatherman." So using it for this cool job of cutting the wires on a BM-21 was very satisfying.

A soldier set a thermite charge on the engine of the APC. It burned right through the engine block and smoldered for hours. They sent another charge down the barrel of one of the artillery pieces.

A few soldiers from the line company decided to shoot two AT-4 (antitank guided) missiles at the rocket launcher. As they set up to fire the missiles, everyone got a thrill. (We didn't do this sort of thing every day.) Eight guys got out cameras to take a picture of the one guy who shot the AT-4. The cameras all snapped at almost the same time. But the missiles did a surprisingly small amount of damage. Inadvertently a patch of underbrush caught fire.

Later that same day, we stopped at a field near the intersection of two highways. We saw kids playing soccer near an abandoned artillery piece. We drove right into the field and got out. We walked around for a few minutes. Then someone saw, or noticed, or realized.

"Oh, shit! This whole fucking field is full of UXO!"

And it was. UXO was everywhere, just littering the ground. And kids were running around. People were flocking to see these fascinating foreigners. The soldiers I was with were convinced that one misstep would blow us all to pieces.

Strangely I wasn't even afraid. It didn't seem like it could be real, exactly, and though I was extremely cautious, I wasn't terrified the way I might have guessed I would be. We all began to step in the footsteps of the person walking in front of us, and continued the mission. We checked the artillery piece, and I sought out the oldest among the locals—a couple of college kids—and explained to them the gravity of the situation.

In Arabic I said: "This place is very dangerous. You must not let children play here."

"Children are impossible to control," they responded. "You can tell them anything, but as soon as you look away, they do it anyway."

"But they could die!" I emphasized. "Explosion! Big danger! Bombs everywhere!"

"Clean it up," they suggested.

I tried to explain, again, about the scarcity of EOD.

A young lieutenant joined me as I attempted to persuade these college students. Again and again we emphasized the danger. We encouraged them to take the children and leave the area. No one moved. They continued to follow us. I could not understand. In America if you tell people they may die if they don't leave, they leave! Don't they? Do I fundamentally misunderstand American culture, or is Iraq just wildly different? After half an hour or more, they finally gathered the children and left.

Very carefully and slowly, we backed our trucks out over the tire tracks we had made on the drive in. On the road again, we breathed easier. We called in the grid coordinate, and waited for a while. Nothing happened. No one came.

I was not entirely sure what was going on but found myself sitting in the back of a Humvee with the very cute lieutenant with an angular nose. We weren't doing anything much, so I struck up a conversation.

I opened with: "So what route did you take to becoming an officer, Sir?"

I tended to ask this question whenever I met an officer, since there are basically three main ways to become one. These are: West Point, Reserve Officers Training Corps (ROTC), and Officer Candidate School (OCS). (For myself I never would have done West Point. It's basic training for four years. Really hardcore—stringent, extreme. It's not my personality. Nor was I the sort of person during college who would have participated in ROTC and then automatically been commissioned as an officer when I graduated. So my route would have been OCS.)

"ROTC," he said.

"So where did you go to college, Sir?"

"Austin. UT Austin."

"I majored in lit at Bowling Green State University in Ohio. What was your major, Sir?"

"History. And political science."

"Oh, really," I said, taking more of an interest. "A history major? Have you read *A People's History of the United States* by Howard Zinn? I really love that book."

The lieutenant smiled. I noticed that his blond hair was quite long for a soldier.

"Oh, you like Zinn, huh? You must read Noam Chomsky, right? And listen to the Dead Kennedys?"

He was teasing me, sure, but if you're a liberal and you do like Howard Zinn, then you probably read Chomsky, too. And you've probably listened to the Dead Kennedys if you're my age and his age. Still, I couldn't believe how he pegged me so quickly. I was intrigued. Even though I knew some bright people in Military Intelligence, I hadn't met an infantry soldier who could chat so casually about Chomsky and Zinn while sitting next to a field full of UXO.

That was how he signaled his own interests and political leanings. A little insider's reference that probably a lot of other people in the military would not necessarily get because most soldiers were not going to have a clue about Howard Zinn. It became this little bond between us.

We talked about his time in Afghanistan as part of Operation Anaconda. I'd heard a lot of scattered references to Anaconda that spring and summer from a number of soldiers, but it was one of those things that was bad enough that no one wanted to talk about it too much. Apparently they experienced a three-day firefight in the mountains. In the snow—with no resupply.

"You know," Lieutenant Samuels said, "I'm thinking that this field is the most UXO I've ever seen in one place. More than I ever saw in one place in Afghanistan, that's for sure."

I knew there were a lot of minefields in Afghanistan. So this impressed me. It also impressed me that he stayed so *calm*.

A few days later there was an urgent call for QRF (quick reaction force).

There's been an explosion.

Soldiers are down. Civilians are hurt. We need to move. *Now.*

We're getting there, and I'm thinking: Wait, wait. Fuck this. I know where we are—

It's the same road as a few days ago, the same streets, the same neighborhood. Only this time we're moving fast, very fast. Everything in overdrive, fast-forward motion. Honking around curves, kids in the streets leaping back and out of the way. People we pass way more subdued, but waving us around the blind curves, telling us it's clear. Like a retake of the same scene, only played for tragedy this time. I can feel myself tensing up.

Once there, I recognize it all. We were here. We marked the door to that compound with white engineer tape. *U-X-O.* The locals would not have any idea what these English letters meant, but the intention was to warn other soldiers who might be doing patrols. And to mark it for EOD. We don't bother to mark the UXOs in Arabic because it's usually the locals who call the unexploded mines to our attention.

We get out of the Humvees, and things are bad. The explosion was in a compound, but nothing else about the circumstances is immediately clear.

We find three locals on the ground, bleeding, already getting treated by other soldiers. Our wounded guys are being transported out in the backs of Humvees. Not so lucky are these locals, their bleeding stanched by field dressings, their legs already caked in dried blood. But everyone is doing their job— pulling guard or treating the injured. Focused.

My job: translate. But what and to whom? Everyone ignoring me. It's not a situation for which I have trained.

What can I do? How can I help?

A young local in a blue shirt, sweating, his hair slicked back as if for a prom. His English is clear enough.

"You need help."

It's a question, I know, but I take it wrong for a moment. He wants to help *me.*

"You speak English? Stay here and help. Yes," I say. "Thank you."

I ask the soldier in charge how I can help.

"Grab my Kevlar and weapon from over there," he points at

the ground a couple of meters away. He shouts at other soldiers in the vicinity. "Maintain your guard positions!"

I grab his stuff and hand it over. He puts on his Kevlar.

"What do you need?" I ask. "How can I help? I'm a translator."

"Tape. I can't find my tape." He's treating a local who is less seriously wounded. "In my CLS bag."

I look in his CLS (combat lifesaver) bag but I can't find tape. I notice the Delta Company first sergeant pulling away in a Humvee.

"First Sergeant, we need *tape*." I'm out of breath, no doubt looking a little wired. "Do you have your CLS bag?"

No. But he does have a big civilian first-aid kit, and that's probably better. He hands it to me. And he's gone. Not a word passes his lips.

I'm back at the scene again. Deliver the tape. Gloves on. Conscientious. Still feeling okay, despite all the blood. The mood remains tense. One guy on the ground—it's obvious—worse off than the others. The medic—that's who's been directing everyone—is starting an IV on the man he's treating. The man is relatively calm. I reassure him in Arabic as best I can and then move over to the other small group.

"Can someone please tell this guy to hold still?!"

A seriously wounded man is thrashing.

I step forward. Kneel. In Arabic I repeat the instructions. Over and over. "Stay still. Don't move. Please." The badly wounded man calls out to God. Moans. Writhes.

The two soldiers treating him have field dressings in place to stop the bleeding. They are attempting to start an IV to replace lost fluids.

I move in closer.

I beg him, "*Ya hajji, la t'hark.* Don't move." I try to explain.

In Arabic: "We're trying to help you. This will hurt a bit, but it's to help you."

Panicked, he looks through me, if he looks at me at all.

I ask the kid in the blue shirt to help me calm him. He tries. I get more supplies—a tube, another needle. But the soldiers can't find a vein. The dying man's veins are collapsing as he goes deeper and deeper into shock.

I'm in close now, so close I'm holding the badly hurt guy's legs, covered in drying blood. Holding the legs still until they can get an IV going.

It's not working. There are problems here. The man starts to scream again. I'm concentrating on helping this man, but we are not finding a vein. I'm holding his legs, holding them still. Hoping this is going to work.

The soldiers yell for the medic, but he calls back over that he can't or won't leave the guy he's treating.

"Just do what you can! Do what you are trained to do!"

I'm amazed at his focus.

My breathing is getting faster and faster, and one of the soldiers stares at me. I consciously slow my breathing.

They bring over the third wounded local, his leg broken in two places. I check on him.

I move between the three injured men. The first is doing pretty well. The young man in the blue shirt is holding an IV bag up for him. I kneel to reassure him that more help is coming. His pants are cut off, his dick and balls are there, and there's blood. Flies hovering everywhere, everywhere. No fucking respect for the crisis at hand, I think, even as I realize that this is illogical. Flies are flies. I brush them off the bleeding cut on his head.

When he realizes he is naked from the waist down, he feebly moves to pull his shirt to cover himself. I recognize the motion, and try to reassure him.

"My brother, that isn't important. Just hold on. An ambulance is coming. We're taking you to a hospital."

Periodically the medic yells: "Where the fuck is the FLA [ambulance]?"

More soldiers arrive. More medics. A medic orders the kid in the blue shirt to leave.

"Let him stay!" I'm yelling. "He's helping. He speaks good English. He's helping me!"

Among the new arrivals is a lieutenant colonel. He wants me to interrogate these wounded men.

"Ask him," the colonel is shouting at me. "Ask him why the fuck these ragheads took our guys to this compound *knowing* there was a UXO in it."

"Because of the UXO," I try to explain.

"Because of the UXO? They were trying to kill our guys?! Ask him!"

I look up, but I can't bring myself to speak. Why did the locals lead our guys to the UXO? I think. Like these guys *wanted* to hurt us? And now one of *them* is *dying*?

"You stupid asshole," I say, but my voice is only in my head. "They're scared for their kids." Out loud I mutter: "I am not interrogating the guy that's dying."

But the colonel's gone off. No one responds to what I say.

I hear an officer: "Fuck these motherfuckers. One of *them* set it off."

The colonel sees me again.

"Go tell those people not to go in there." He points at a

crowd gathered two hundred meters away by an intersection, kept back by the guards.

"We did that, Sir," I say as calmly as I can. "We did that. A couple of days ago. I'll mark the doors again—in Arabic this time. Maybe that will help."

He looks hard at me.

"Soldier," the colonel says. "Just do what I am telling you to do. Right *now*."

Lieutenant Samuels, the guy I met from a few nights ago who reads Zinn and Chomsky, is here too, and he sees I'm getting ready to fight. He sees that I am not noticing rank. That I just want to do what's right—even if it means yelling at some asshole colonel.

The lieutenant pulls me away.

"Leave it," he says in my ear. "Take a moment. Step *back*."

Hearing this, I do head down the street toward the crowd. And I explain again to the locals that no one should go in there. Avoid UXO. And so forth. Behind me I can *feel* the man dying, and I cannot fucking believe I'm here doing this—instead of helping him.

A local is right in my face.

"We told you about this bomb a couple of days ago." He is so close, I take a step back just to breathe. "Why didn't you fix it? Before it was too late? Now people are hurt."

Almost dead.

"Their family—" And he points. I don't want to look. But I do. A couple of men over there. Brothers, I am told. Women are crying.

I'm trying to explain. "It *was* marked. There is so much UXO. So few soldiers who can remove it. We're trying. We're *trying*."

We get permission for the brothers to come back with us. I gesture to them, and we walk back to the dying man. They see the dying man puke as a soldier gives him mouth-to-mouth. I'm shocked in a numb way that he isn't already dead.

I think: I've been pretty calm, I'm handling this well.

Someone hands me a bottle of water. I don't drink it—just use it to wash off some gore. The brothers talk. They want me to go back down the road. Some more family members have gathered. If the man is going to be moved to a military hospital, I explain, only immediate family can escort him. I go back down the road with them, and there are two wives. They want to come, and then they change their minds.

Moving back again, I see that finally it's time to move the injured men into an ambulance and take them back to the aid station, and take the brothers in a Humvee.

The man who was dying has now been covered with a poncho.

The medic tells me what to say to the other injured men. To keep them calm.

"Say he's only injured. He's very cold. He needs covering."

I repeat these lies.

In a Humvee we drive back to the "hospital," that is, the aid station in our compound. I sit in the backseat and I get to be still for a moment.

I just want to cry, but I don't. I can't. I have to be hard, strong, in front of these soldiers, these *guys*. I blink the tears back and breathe deeply.

I'm wondering: Why the fuck did soldiers go in there after we fucking *marked* it? That makes no sense. And the locals all saying it was a *soldier* who set it off.

Once we arrive, I get out of the Humvee. In what I think is

the smartest thing I've done all day, I reach out for support. I get help, sending someone to fetch another Arabic linguist I know, a friend of mine in Human Intelligence (HUMINT), to translate for one of the injured men while the doctors treat him. The main crisis feels over. Easing. Slowing.

I help as they treat the guy with the broken leg. His name is Mahmoud. He has three sons and a daughter. He gets morphine, finally, for the pain.

I go to talk to the relatives of the dead man. They tell me his name is Ali and that he has a son and a daughter.

His brothers ask, "What will the Army do for our family?"

Under Islamic law, there is a thing called *di'ah*. If you accidentally cause someone's death, you pay their family. It is your debt.

"We're the American Army, and we don't do that," I explain.

I feel terrible. I wish there is something I could do. I wish there was some way I could pay them myself.

Sergeant Quinn finds me and offers me Gatorade. He knows what has been going on, and he is more compassionate and gentle with me than I have ever seen him. I realize, drinking the Gatorade, that I haven't had anything to eat or drink in hours and hours. It has gotten dark. I feel, suddenly, shaken and drained.

Finally I am no longer needed. The injured men are being transported to a real hospital. I go back to our site. Staff Sergeant Moss tells me to take the night off, but she doesn't speak to me otherwise. I need to talk to someone—this is probably the only time I could have reached out to SSG Moss, but she acts disinterested. I tell Lauren the whole story, and I finally cry. She sympathizes and comforts me for a moment. I can't possibly sleep yet—still wired, full of nervous energy. Strangely I realize that all I want, the only thing I really want, is to be told that I did a good job out there today.

With a start I remember that I never asked if all of our guys are okay. I walk back to the aid station to ask a medic. He reassures me that they will all live.

At the aid station there is a chaplain. He sees me and walks over to talk. He tells me he was out there today. That he saw me. Watched me.

"You did a good job," he says. "You really comforted those men. It must have been hard on you—it was hard on me, and I was just watching. But you did a really great job."

I never have had much use for chaplains, but this man, Captain Bridges, somehow says exactly what I need to hear. I am reassured, calmed.

I go talk to my HUMINT friend who speaks Arabic. He tells me that they refused to allow the dead man to be transported back to his family in an FLA. This makes some sense, since an ambulance might be needed if more soldiers get injured tonight.

But then he tells me that they decided to transport the dead man in the back of a commandeered pickup truck.

I'm taken aback by this.

"Damn," I say, feeling tears again. "That feels real disrespectful. Don't you think?"

"Listen," he says. "It's way better than their first idea. They were debating whether or not just to strap the body to the hood of a Humvee."

NORTH

SUDDENLY AND UNEXPECTEDLY our team got pulled out of Baghdad, yanked back to D-Main to sit on our collective asses for several days. Given the supreme need 1/187 had for translators, and given a powerful lack of available Arabic linguists, this made no sense to me. Then we were moved south to join 1st Brigade (BDE), where we did nothing for a couple more days. Now at last we joined a convoy heading north toward Mosul. This was all frustrating beyond belief. The only constant in our lives was movement. Pulled here and there.

By this time, our shirts and DCUs (desert camouflage uniforms) were utterly filthy and salt stained. We just sat and sweated. When we entered Iraq we'd worn the JSLIST suits to protect us from biological and chemical attack. When we were finally allowed to take off these suits after three weeks or so, we switched to our second pair of DCUs and wore those until they stood up on their own. Then we put back on the DCUs we'd worn before we were in-country—uniforms we'd considered dirty before but that now appeared clean by comparison. Occasionally, a couple of times in Baghdad, we did do some hand-washing of clothes, but nothing ever felt clean.

The convoy commander was a prick.

"Today's drive will last between five and seven hours," he announced. "Three hundred kilometers straight from here to Qayyarah West Airfield. Q-West will be the main headquarters of 1st Brigade, and it is currently in poor shape. Dirt piles, cratered airstrips, broken concrete. You get the general idea." He paused. "Oh, one more thing. We're in a hurry today. There will be no stops. No breaks. Once we move, we keep moving. If you need to piss, piss in a bottle."

And with these words, off we went. I drove our truck, and I was thinking how this captain had given no consideration to the girls on his GAC. Had anyone informed him that peeing in a bottle for a girl was not the same as it was for a guy? Guys could pee out the damned door! (They didn't—but they could.) Nor had this guy considered how difficult it was for a girl to piss in a bottle while driving a Humvee. But "no stops, no breaks" meant "no stops, no breaks." So we started rolling and we kept rolling.

The scenery distracted us from yet another boring drive, at least for a while. There was a gentle transition from desert to rolling grassy hills as we moved north through Samarra and Tikrit. We saw scenic mountains in the distance, and men or boys herd fat fluffy sheep with a donkey or a dog in tow. We saw women in *hijabs,* and when they spotted us female soldiers, they smiled shy smiles. They waved, and we waved back. We saw brightly colored clothing flutter on clotheslines outside uniformly grayish brown houses. Children cheered us, though they were just as likely to beg for food or water by using the universal symbol: repeatedly raising their hands to their mouths. We passed open-air markets or city shops with stands piled high with vegetables and fruits. Despite the war, daily life continued. Roses in so many yards, flowers in so many gardens. Beauty carefully cultivated even amid such poverty and oppression.

North. The mood changed after a time. We slowly drove past 4th Infantry Division (4 ID) guys looking mean and ugly. They stood on top of their trucks, their weapons pointed directly at civilians. The civilians were moving tensely through ordinary activities. Acting as if there were no damned guns aimed at their heads—and these were women with children in tow! What could these locals possibly have done? Why was this intimidation necessary? No one explained anything, but it looked weird and felt wrong.

The drive was beyond dull after a while, and I was left to reflections. In Baghdad with D Co, the primary effort had been to build a bond with the locals, carefully nurturing relationships and building *trust*. We got to a point where locals in certain neighborhoods knew us, and knew they could trust us. Maybe because those guys had already been in "the Ghan," or maybe due to better leadership, they grasped the high stakes. They acted like the U.S. Army, not bulldozing in a minute what it takes months to build up.

In the last several days I'd heard all sorts of horror stories: soldiers busting down civilians' doors and dragging people into the streets; soldiers purchasing a damned sheep only to muzzle it and then beat it to death. Soldiers taking shots at people as they ran away, or shooting up entire cars of people as they approached a manned checkpoint (women, children, whatever) because they didn't stop in time.

We all knew that local women were afraid of soldiers and would not necessarily stop at checkpoints. They were not used to dealing with men, let alone American men. They would see

American men with guns and panic. If an American sees a checkpoint with armed soldiers, the American stops. Wouldn't she?
But in Iraq there was a lot of confusion. From what I heard,
things got out of hand pretty often.

Fucking mayhem was what it was. And meanwhile there
were *no signs* in Arabic to alert locals that they were approaching a checkpoint. No respect for the customs of the people, for
the rhythms of their lives, for the shit they've had to suffer.
There was way too little attempt to communicate with the people. Too many soldiers acting like it was *shoot-em-up* time. I
already missed 3rd Brigade. None of them ever said they
wanted to feel what it might be like to shoot someone. Or
thought killing a local might be cool. These 1st Brigade soldiers
made me uncomfortable.

Soon, however, reflections were overwhelmed by a serious
need to pee. It had to be psychological—the damned speech. If
the convoy commander hadn't said we couldn't, who knows? But
now after a few hours bouncing in the backseat, Lauren can't
take it any longer.

"I really have to pee," she said. "I can't hold it. I'm really
gonna have to piss. I cannot wait. I'm gonna have to do it right
here."

We all laughed as Lauren started to curse the convoy commander for forcing this indignity upon her. Cursing herself for
downing a big milkshake mixed with coffee right before we left.
Quickly Lauren sliced off the top of a water bottle with a knife,
dropped her pants, and pissed. A clean move. And then she
hurled the whole mess out the window.

Five minutes after the cup spattered in the dirt, a truck up
ahead broke and died. The convoy cruised to a halt for repairs.

And in the meantime dozens of grateful soldiers rushed to relieve themselves. Lauren could not believe her lousy luck. The guys in the truck behind us announced how impressed they were with her acrobatic feat.

I was spared a lesson in how to pee while driving. But I heard later some other girls do accomplish this maneuver. I didn't ask for details. It just did not qualify as something I really wanted to know.

We got to Q-West in the evening.

Soon afterward this random 1st BDE infantry guy sauntered over.

"Hey. You MI?"

"That's right."

"Welcome." He was like eighteen, nineteen. "Seen any combat yet?"

"A little." No one eager to talk. No one in the mood at the moment to humor this.

"Yeah," the guy said, puffing himself up and stretching his arms. A little yawn. Casual-like. "I got a kill just last week. Man, I gotta tell you. It was the *coolest*. To see what happens when this dude got it. I can't even begin to explain." He looked at us to see how we were doing.

Not one of us said a thing. Don't try, I'm thinking.

"I warned the dude," he continued. "I was yelling at him, 'Stop, motherfucker.' But he kept coming. He kept coming."

"Listen—" I began to say. I didn't want to get involved, but I didn't want to hear this.

"Man, it was so *cool*," the kid repeated. Cleared his throat. He sounded scratchy all of a sudden. Like the kid he really was.

Swapped tones on us, going from hard-core to altogether less macho.

"But it's my job and all, y'know?" he said, a little shaky. "I got a job to do. That's why I'm here. To get a job done. Y'know?"

After a moment he wandered off. Like that's what he came to say, and now it was done.

No one spoke. We moved into the night like it was a bad dream, which—in a way—it was.

I mean: What *do* you say?

Real packages arrived for the first time. Since we'd been kept moving, attached to one unit and then another and another, we'd been a hard team to find. Mail never seemed to get to us on time. And now boxes and boxes of stuff all at once for everyone. After so many weeks of nothing, this was amazing. *Real* packages with stuff in them. I got envelopes and treats. Potato chips. Cheese and crackers. Granola bars and Special K cereal bars. Sucky chewies. Pogey bait. Lauren got cigarettes, romance novels, and magazines. And she got some fine-smelling lotion, which was a very big deal for us.

Maybe because the war was pretty much over and all, or officially *announced* as almost over, the packages raised hopes that this signaled the beginning of the end of our time there. Everyone ready to go home. Rumors almost every day. Talk about a midsummer return or, if not, then certainly by Labor Day. Already folks were planning what they'd do when they got back. It all felt unreal to me, but there was no reason to doubt it *could* happen.

This day the packages arrived may not have made it Disney World, but it certainly felt like Christmas.

———

Lauren had a wisdom tooth out, which left her high on painkillers. Acting silly. Giggling all the time. So we chilled out near our position, reading our books and magazines, eating a little candy, and trying to stay in the shade, where it was a little cooler. The heat was brutal.

I vaguely registered some infantry guys walking over to drop trash in a burn pit about ten meters off. They lit it, and then they were gone.

A putrid smell of smoke, but that was not new. Still, after a few more moments it got our attention. We heard a strange crackling sound. Lauren looked up. "Fire!" she yelled. The dry grass around the burn pit had leaped into flames.

The fire was spreading with terrible speed and, with a breeze blowing, our truck with our stuff was going to get hit soon.

"What the hell? I thought those guys—"

"Incompetent bastards," Lauren said, still hazy.

The guys lit the fire not thinking it might jump out of the pit, and didn't bother to monitor it properly to make sure it didn't.

But it did. And here we were in the middle of it with no one around to help us put it out.

Fire moves fast over ground when it hasn't rained in weeks.

We ran. Right into the burning grass. We stomped and stomped, a crazy dance with our boots hitting the flames. We grabbed our e-tools (small folding shovels) and used them to beat the flames. The ground was too tight and dry to scoop handfuls of dirt to throw, so it was the rain dance we did. But we were losing the fight. The fire kept moving outward in every direction.

Quinn arrived to help us, but where was Staff Sergeant Moss? Who knew? She was always somewhere else when shit happened.

After a time some infantry guys—*not* the guys who set it—saw us out there dancing in the flames, and they joined us. It got scary, but the number of soldiers stamping made a difference. We halted the fire's progress and then got it under control.

So that was the scene. A bunch of soldiers putting out a grass fire. But before we stopped it, it burned a hundred square feet.

Man, were we *pissed.*

We got even angrier when one guy called out to everyone, "Great job, gentlemen!"

Hey, we're not all gentlemen! Lauren and I worked our asses off. We were first on the scene. But none of that seemed to matter at all.

Sergeant Quinn wanted to talk to someone from the unit that started the fire. So we kept our eyes on their bunker. Before too long a guy stepped out to smoke a cigarette.

"*Hey, you!*" Lauren yelled. "Yes, *you.* Get over here."

Now Lauren was this little person, as I've said, and she looked so sweet. But that was misleading. However, it was never a good idea to shout at a soldier when you didn't know him. Or know his rank. Like, for instance, as this soldier approached, we saw he was a first sergeant.

"What's the problem here?" he asked.

"Your damned men almost *torched* our position. They lit a burn pit and they didn't mind it and—"

He looked like we did have a problem, but it wasn't the problem we were talking about.

"Listen," he said angrily to Lauren. "Let me offer you some advice. Don't *ever* tell any of my men what to do. And don't bother me again."

He lumbered away.

———

The next day we got moved out beyond the perimeter to set up a listening post (LP) on a nearby mountain. All the buildings here were empty shells—walls with no doors, no windows, no ceilings. Lauren and I claimed a room, rigged a "roof" of ponchos for shade, and set up our cots. A degree of privacy for the first time since we'd been in-country. Resting in there when we were not on shift, we'd talk. Open up to each other more. I was finally beginning to feel like I had someone around I could trust.

It didn't last. After a couple of days, our team fell apart. Lauren's wisdom tooth wound had gotten infected, so she went back to Q-West to have a dentist look at it. Leaving behind her gear and personal stuff, she figured it was minor and she'd be back, maybe the same day.

But she didn't come back that day.

And then that same night SSG Moss got dysentery. It came with the country; everyone got sick at some point. Vomiting. Diarrhea. Everything running out of her at both ends, and it might have been funny if it hadn't been awful. A plastic bag attached to her ass, and another plastic bag for her mouth. She looked so pathetic and smelled so bad I began to feel sorry for her. Couldn't help it. I didn't want or need this. I didn't want her *useless*. This was bad for all of us, especially with Lauren gone.

So we were down from four to two. With running ops around the clock, and pulling security, this meant Quinn and I would be awake all night.

Now Sergeant Quinn was a guy I didn't much like at first. Stiff and official. Needed to prove he was right about everything. Made certain he always got the last word. He'd read a lot, knew a ton, but there was this need to let everyone know what he knew.

And basically leaving me feeling irritable around him much of the time. Testy and *tested*.

To cope with the inevitable, we fixed a huge amount of instant coffee mixed with cocoa powder and lukewarm water. A potent mix. Around 9 P.M. we began our dosage, and managed to finish our entire bottles by midnight.

The LP was a few kilometers off from Q-West on a hilly bedrock, elevated but remote. The air cooled down at night, and the softly swaying sound of the wind had a lulling effect. By this point, SSG Moss had passed out, her groans dissipated down to an open-mouth breathing we couldn't hear from where we were in the truck.

SGT Quinn started to twitch, but once he did, it wasn't long before I did, too. The cocoa and coffee having more of an effect than we bargained for.

"Listen," he said, but I couldn't tell if he meant *Listen, I hear something out there* or *Listen, I've got something to say.*

Playing it safe, I listened for both possibilities.

"Do you hear that?" I asked.

At 0215 hours there was a hissing sound somewhere, or I thought there was. Didn't I?

"Do I hear that?" Quinn asked, but I couldn't see his face. Was he mocking me?

"Listen," I said. "Do you see that?"

There was a shadow. Or maybe I just imagined I saw it. A slim crescent moon rose over the horizon, so darkness still prevailed.

"I don't mean to frighten you," Quinn said, frightening me.

"But?"

"But I was wondering—" He stopped for a full minute, and there was only silence. "I was reading about space aliens in this science journal. Something real, I mean. A real science journal. And studies show how likely it is. Likely that they exist, I mean. Space aliens."

"You're messing with me," I said, feeling messed with.

"No. I'm not," Quinn said. "Listen, it's probably bullshit. But I thought I saw—"

"That flashing light a few minutes ago?"

"You saw it, too?"

"What could it be?"

"Now you're messing with *me*."

Silence.

We talked about the movie *Signs* while listening to static on the radio. We got progressively more freaked out. It was absurd; we knew it was comic, laughed about it, but still were getting more nervous and jittery anyway.

"Any more coffee?" Quinn asked.

"I think we've had enough."

The night went like that. An early Halloween this year. Panic-inducing phantoms and crazy chatter about space aliens.

By the time the sun came up, we'd thoroughly freaked each other out.

But I really felt okay about Quinn after that. He's really all right, I decided.

We never told anyone about our paranoid night together tripping on coffee and cocoa, more spooked by aliens than a very real human enemy.

Lauren never came back. While she was at Q-West for her infection, she got word that her husband had gotten dangerously ill, something no one could say for sure what it was, and that she would be going home as well. It all happened so fast, she never had a chance to get back in touch with us. Left everything behind, and I was left to inventory her stuff.

After a few more days at our hillside LP, we also returned to Q-West. As barren and austere as it is, Q-West still felt like civilization after several days in the wilderness.

Pretty randomly I bumped into the first sergeant Lauren and I had yelled at. The one whose men had lit the fire that almost burned down our position.

"Where's the sparkplug?" he asked, holding a package.

"Who?"

"That tiny female who yelled at me. Don't say you don't know who she is."

"Yeah," I said. "I know her. But she's gone. Her husband is very sick, and she got sent home."

"Tough break," he said, sounding like he meant it. "Listen. This was for her, but maybe you could tell her I tried to get it to her. Or maybe you can all have it."

He handed me a package.

"Just some stuff we got together, the guys and me," he said. "A peace offering . . ."

I opened the box, and it was soap, toothpaste, chocolates, pretzels, Cheez Doodles, a *Maxim* magazine or two, and some cocoa mix.

"Hey, you don't have to—"

"Hey, take it. Our way to square this one away, okay?"

A good leader, I'm thinking. A good man. I'm already wanting to tell Lauren about it.

I missed her already.

MOUNTAIN TIME

"So what's this now again?" Quinn asks.

"It's the Femmes. The Violent Femmes."

"It's—cool. I like it, I think." He begins to remove the earphones.

"That's good, Geoff. But give it more time. Keep listening."

He's so tense looking. Stoic. It's odd to watch him. But also fascinating.

After a minute more, I wonder. He's sitting there motionless, like he's frozen solid. Has my MP3 player died? Is he faking me out?

He's looking so damned puzzled, it's almost sweet.

"Maybe we should try something else," he says.

"No, no," I demur. "Don't stop, Geoff. Give it a minute. Remember this is supposed to be a *lesson*."

"Maybe something else, though. What else you got?" Trying to act relaxed. Failing.

"Well," I consider, holding up the player for a look. "Let's think."

It's my music appreciation class for Geoff, and I'm giving it my best. He's a tough sell. Since the night at the LP when we shared that special moment freaked out together, I've relaxed around him. He still annoys me sometimes with his "I'm so smart" attitude, but I try to develop a little more compassion. Not judge so hard. And as I lighten up, he starts to share accounts of his very sheltered childhood in Ohio. We're both from Ohio; you'd think this means we have things in common. Not too likely. Here's a guy whose mother considered *The Simpsons* a bad influence. So she told Geoff not to watch *The Simpsons*. Okay. I know parents can be bizarre. That's not what gets me. The crazy thing is: Geoff has never seen *The Simpsons*. He grasps some rudimentary concepts about Homer and Bart. He knows it's a cartoon— but that's it. His mom says *no,* and Geoff says, *Okay, Mom.*

What twenty-one-year-old guy in his right mind avoids a cartoon show because his mother says he should?

We're into May, and Quinn and I have been stuck on the same team for months. Dealt with Staff Sergeant Moss and everything else. Got separated for a week or so in Baghdad when I was tasked out with D Co, but otherwise we've been together from day one. Honestly, I had zero tolerance for the guy at first.

So he's inexperienced and inept in all sorts of ways. Focused on narrow details he can get right, and understands thoroughly. But would not run from his cage even if someone left the door wide open. I almost pity him sometimes. Then sometimes he's just a jackass, and I feel he deserves what he gets. But after we stay up all night imagining spaceships and aliens, I work on seeing his potential. The inner Geoff. I gently try to encourage this guy to evolve in a more positive direction.

That means music appreciation class. Anyway, it's a start.

On the player I program tunes randomly. Let's give anything else a try. See what comes. I lean back in my seat to watch.

He actually likes some of it, he says. I then try to play my more "accessible" music, nothing too "out there." I'm glad he's giving it a shot.

We talk more now, too. I'm feeling pretty whiny and full of self-pity.

So I'm telling Quinn: "I am never going to find somebody to spend his life with me. People don't like me. Sooner or later everybody leaves me. Even my damn parents never cared for me. No man is ever going to marry me. I am terrible at relationships. My relationships always fail. So I have to face the truth that I am going to be single forever. I am really such a failure."

I'm feeling quite dramatic. Like a martyr doomed to a life without lasting love.

"And I hate it," I continue. "It frustrates me that those things that I consider my best qualities are the same exact things that everyone hates about me. Like the fact that I'm driven. Like the fact that I'm extremely organized. That I'm always pushing myself to learn better and do better and be better. And be more successful. And grow. I think that those are my very best qualities—the most admirable things about me. And almost all the men I've dated end up asking me 'So when are you just going to be happy with the ways things are? Why can't you just accept things? Why don't you just be happy with what you have? Why do you have to be like this?' So these guys always cut me down. Nitpick."

Quinn adjusts his glasses.

"You, you're a nice girl," he says. "You're a good person. You're really okay. You're smart. You're funny. You'll find the right person someday. Someday you'll find that special someone."

Quinn goes on.

"How do you think I feel? The things I believe are the most important things in life are to have a relationship and get married and have children. Or even just have a relationship. But this is something I have never done. Never. So how do you think I feel?"

That stops me. That makes me think.

I am thinking: This fucking guy who has not even *kissed* a girl! He's never found a girl who's even close to being "that special someone," while I've had how many failed relationships? And now he's telling me to hold on to hope?

Still, it's really sweet. Quinn telling me not to lose hope. It touches me. In an odd way his belief that I can find happiness does help me feel hopeful.

We get moved back temporarily to D-Main, where I'm called to appear before a promotion board, my first step toward becoming a noncommissioned officer. As my time in the military passed the three-year mark, it was time for me to become a sergeant. Meaning better pay, for one thing. Also greater responsibilities and authority. I got the maximum score on the board and was proud of myself—it was a tense experience for me, like it was for most people.

But then it looked like the Army screwed up my paperwork. It became anyone's guess how long this was going to take to straighten out.

We moved again to 3rd Brigade, where Staff Sergeant Gardner replaced SSG Moss. One Arabic linguist replacing another. Meanwhile Specialist Reid replaced Lauren. One Korean linguist replacing another.

So we've got Lawyer now, and that's cool. Reid never acted

like he was better than anyone because he went to college or law school. None of that. He never talked down to infantry or other MI.

Gardner replacing Moss at first seemed good, because he could talk about ideas and books. And he listened to a lot of the same music as me, and liked some of the same strange movies I liked.

Staff Sergeant Gardner was a very tall half-Korean in his mid-thirties, a military brat whose dad had also been Army. Gardner was a military man through and through. His wife was also a staff sergeant and an Arabic linguist. We quickly realized that Gardner's career was definitely fast track. And then we realized how pedantic he could be. If I talked to Gardner about practically anything, I was going to get lectured on how much he knew about the topic.

He would lecture me about literature. Which pissed me off—that was my major, after all. Eventually we had a conversation about politics, and it turned out he was this hard-core Republican. Very conservative. I'd cite statistics or facts about social conditions or political issues, and Staff Sergeant Gardner's response would always be the same.

"Can you prove that fact, Williams? I don't know how you can expect me to take that statistic seriously unless you're prepared to back it up with evidence."

And my answer was always the same, though I never said it exactly like this:

"I'm in fucking Iraq, Sergeant Gardner. I do not happen to have a goddamn encyclopedia in my fucking pocket. No, I can't prove it!"

Gardner inevitably said: "Well, I don't believe you."

Still, Staff Sergeant Gardner was a huge improvement over Staff Sergeant Moss. So the guy talked down to us. Big deal. He never almost got me killed.

We pulled mission in the Sinjar Mountains on the Syrian border, colocated with a Pathfinder unit in a small compound.

In other situations Pathfinders established drop zones and landing zones (DZ/LZ) for the parachuting of personnel and equipment. Here they were monitoring the border. Watching for suspicious persons coming across.

The Pathfinders kept to themselves while we were there. They worked with a few Peshmergas—guerrillas fighting for a free Kurdish state. The Peshmerga guys were friendly, but most of them spoke only Kurdish—and I sure didn't. Otherwise our compound was off-limits to locals, so it stayed secluded and *very* quiet.

The physical surroundings there were really quite beautiful. Fantastic vistas and incredible flowers. You could see the whole slope of the mountainside down to the patchwork plains below. You could see for miles. The plants inside the compound were amazingly varied. Pink flowers and purple flowers and pale green flowers that looked like little wontons, as well as bright red poppies that stood out from a considerable distance. There were also flowers I called the evil death bushes because they had really sharp thorns on them. Whenever I got up in the middle of the night to pee, I inevitably stumbled into one of these bushes and scratched my legs.

But there was nothing much to do off shift. Surrounded by hills and open space where we couldn't wander (for security reasons), it got a little tiresome.

The Peshmerga guys provided some minor distraction once in a while.

Once I got woken in the middle of the night because one of the Peshmergas was sick. He needed to speak to the medic who only spoke English. One of the other Peshmerga guys spoke some Arabic. So the sick guy would talk in Kurdish to the other guy who translated into Arabic for me, and I would translate into English to tell the medic. Then the medic would ask a question back, and we'd go to Arabic and then back to Kurdish. And back and forth. It took forever. After we finally gave the sick guy some medicine, suddenly all these Peshmerga guys appeared and lined up with ailments. They all wanted to tell us about their medical problems.

"I have a toothache."

"My stomach hurts."

Several of them pulled up pants legs or shirtfronts.

"Would you please ask the doctor to have a look at this scar for me? I got this in the Iran-Iraq war." (I don't know why, but Iraqis *loved* to show you their scars.)

And I was stunned. "What do you expect us to do?"

The Kurdish locals also played a game we called "rock," though this was certainly not its real name. It was a little like checkers. They would draw a grid on the ground and have sides with light rocks or dark rocks. Despite the immense language barrier, the Pathfinders learned to communicate. They learned how to play rock, for instance. Some of the Pathfinders got pretty good at it, too, and would win once in a while against the Peshmergas.

Occasionally the Peshmergas would cook for us. Though all I ever saw them prepare for themselves was a big vat of rice with chickpeas. No spices. Nothing. And that was truly all I *ever* saw them eat.

But mainly there was way too much time to think.

My own warped past came back to me as raw material for unpleasant thoughts and loopy dreams spinning through my brain: messy relationships with boys that in retrospect appeared utterly ridiculous. My lousy marriage. (What *was* I thinking?) My dad, too, who I heard from my stepmom was having a hard time with my deployment. Especially as we moved past the tenth anniversary of my sister's death, I worried about him. Might I be getting a Red Cross message soon—the way Lauren did? (Not to be morbid.)

Before things got too gloomy, we got pulled again. Within a week we went back down to the plains to Tal Afar, a desert airfield about thirty miles from the Syrian border and thirty miles west of Mosul, where we reunited with our platoon. The mountains weren't cool, exactly, but coming back to the desert you realized it was twenty degrees hotter down there. It could reach close to 130 Fahrenheit at the airfield. It was only May, and the heat was miserable. Day or night, you never stopped sweating. I'd walk to the shower tent and get clean and put on clean clothes. I'd walk back outside and within five minutes I sweated through everything again. As clothes dried they looked tie-dyed because the salt left a white residue. (You could see the outline of girls' bras this way.)

Eventually the airfield got swamp coolers for the thirty-man tents. You filled the swamp cooler with water, and it blew humid air into the tent. It might cool off the area in the immediate vicinity a dozen degrees or so, but from a temperature of 130 that's not a great help. That was as close to air-conditioning as they ever had in the tents.

I was not finding it easy to be around my own platoon. Guys in my platoon I drank and partied with back in the United States, but here it was not so easy to feel a connection. These guys were not even saying hello to me. They wouldn't even look at me. But they greeted the men on my team.

"Hey, Sergeant Gardner. Hey, Sergeant Quinn. Hey, Reid. Long time. How you been?"

I was getting shunned. The cold shoulder from guys I used to hang with all the time. I had no fucking idea why. No one was talking. No one was telling me anything.

Within a day we were sent back out on mission. I was just as happy to leave, and it wasn't just the heat.

Staff Sergeant Gardner stayed at base to discuss his reenlistment options. So it was only Sergeant Quinn and Specialist Reid and me out in the truck. Our mission was to colocate with a COLT team (combat observation and lasing team) that had an observation post on Sinjar Mountain.

The guys on a COLT team, I learned, were chosen from the best of their MOS, which is 13-Foxtrot, the fire support team or FISTers—an acronym they love. It's a competitive process to be selected for a COLT team. (So all COLT are FISTers, but not all FISTers are COLT.) The FISTers we were to meet were serving as forward observers to watch the Syrian border and call for artillery fire if necessary.

We took the road out of Tal Afar straight west. Everything was fine. We got to the end of the road—literally—and radioed the FISTers, who directed us more or less straight up a mountain.

Okay. Visualize this. It was *very* rocky terrain. Nothing but rocks. No road, no path, no trees or brush. Just rocks. The only differential was rock size. You've got really big rocks, the kind we might call boulders. And you've got smaller rocks, big enough to stop most civilian vehicles in their tracks. And I was driving.

Humvees are remarkable machines. They work almost everywhere and can do almost anything an off-road vehicle needs to do. But this mountain was rocky and it was steep. Very steep. We were going slow, maybe five to ten kilometers an hour, and I was creeping us up, holding tight to the wheel.

Then we slipped a little sideways.

"Hey," Quinn said, popping the passenger door. "Let me ground-guide you."

A sensible call. The goal here was to help avoid the larger rocks and steer us past them. But the wheels began to slip some more no matter where I turned, and there was a feeling in the front like the wheels were lifting slightly when I gunned the engine.

"Hey," Reid said, popping open the door in the back. "I'm getting out of this thing."

So now I was alone in the Humvee. This was unbelievable. The guys in my team out there walking up the mountain. Me in the Humvee feeling pretty confident the truck was about to flip over.

"You guys are fucking pussies!" I yelled.

No one contradicted me. No one volunteered to get back in the Humvee, either.

Whatever happened to moral support?

My legs started to tremble, and I clutched the steering wheel. Sweaty palms made a firm grip theoretical. Quinn was in front of the truck, waving right, waving left, doing something *useful*. I couldn't see Reid. Maybe when the truck flipped, it would flip right onto his lousy ass. Now, that would be poetic.

Things kept on in this vein for longer than I care to imagine—or remember. Up and up the damned mountain, my two team members safely out of harm's way. I'd downshifted into low-lock, and we made it up eventually. Quinn yanked big rocks from in front of the wheels sometimes. I swear the front tires lost touch with the ground once or twice when I pressed hard on the pedal.

Honestly, I thought this was the end of me.

Finally, though, when we arrived at the site, the FISTers were grinning. Said they'd been watching us through binos the whole way up. Said they were betting *for sure* we'd flip it. Surprised to find a girl behind the wheel.

"You going to help set up?" Sergeant Quinn asked.

"Are you fucking kidding?" I said. I was shaking so bad I could barely stand.

The other team cracked up laughing—but I could tell right away that they were laughing with me, not at me. I had won their respect by driving while the guys walked.

"Can I have a cigarette?" I asked them. I had been trying to quit smoking for a few weeks, but this drive tore my resolve.

"Boobs," a FISTer said, like it was some genuine insight. "Look, this one's got *boobs*."

The locals came to visit us on the mountain almost every day. Their visits livened things up. Only the men and boys; we never saw a single woman or girl. Full of curiosity about our stuff, they wandered onto our site while herding sheep and goats. Some stuck around for hours, asking if they could have a look through our binos at their houses in the valley far below. They made plain their gratitude for our presence. How delighted they were that

Americans had liberated Iraq! How grateful they were that Saddam Hussein had been pushed from power! Everyone had a story about how Saddam made their lives worse. How hopeful they were that our presence in their mountains meant there would soon be schools for their children, schools for kids who had never gone to school. So basically, they wanted us to stay—forever, if we liked.

These locals were Yezidis. They observed a religion that was not Islam. So far as I could gather, it was a nature-based religion that may predate not only Christianity but Judaism as well, and it also seemed to involve angels. They expressed an affinity with Israel I found surprising. They were not Kurdish, they told us, although Kurdish was their language.

We communicated with signs and gestures, but a few also spoke a little Arabic. So we communicated a little in broken Arabic as well. They visited so often that we soon counted on their visits and prepared presents for them in exchange for the presents they brought us.

They were an amazingly generous people despite their brutal poverty. They brought us tea, flat bread, and goat yogurt. When I asked for vegetables, they brought garlic, onions, tomatoes, cucumbers. They also brought butter and eggs—and once turkey eggs, which were amazing. The Yezidis fed me far better than my own unit did. For this I was immensely thankful. (Around this time I found a scale and discovered how dramatic my weight loss had been.) So the Yezidis brought me food, and we gave them old magazines, fruit, water, some MREs. For their wives and daughters I sometimes gave them a toothbrush and toothpaste—or hand lotion, shampoo, conditioner, deodorant, and dental floss. The concept behind some of these last items proved tough

At my graduation from
Basic Combat Training at
Fort Jackson, South
Carolina, September 2000.

Chris Williams

Stephanie McCoy

Studying Arabic at DLI, 2001.

Stephanie McCoy

Outside of the barracks at DLI.

Kayla Williams

Above: Heavy sandstorms during the GAC (Ground Assault Convoy) and at FARP Shell made the visibility difficult.

Left: Getting to know some locals in Dohuk.

Craig Sanchez

Sean Baker

Relaxing in the hammock in the back of our ISG's Humvee, spring 2003.

During a break on the GAC.

Our smallest team member carrying our team's biggest weapon.

Relaxing during a brief visit to a friend's site.

The Shrine at the second mountain site. A local and his dog, as seen from behind our c-wire (concertina wire), summer 2003.

Kayla Williams

Above: Guys on the COLT team reverify their zeros (check the accuracy of the sights on their weapons).

Right: Winds at the shrine atop Mt. Sinjar got strong enough to knock our antenna down—and make my hair crazy!

Justin Edgecombe

Justin Edgecombe

Rock climbing on Mt. Sinjar, summer 2003.

Kayla Williams

Left: Feeding Rak Hammer, the do we doted on for months, during summer 2003.

I played with a puppy on the floor of our building at Range 54, the first time I lived indoors since leaving Kuwait, fall 2003.

Justin Edgecombe

Down time in
Baghdad, 2003.

Sean Baker

I get pinned—my Sergeant
rank is pinned on when I get
promoted—December 2003.

Craig Sanchez

Craig Sanchez

Christmas in Tal Afar—our company poses with "Santa."

Stephanie McCoy

Happy to have made it home safely—right after the plane landed, February 8, 2004.

Brian McGough

Dressed up for a big night out back in Tennessee.

to explain in Arabic. One day, for instance, I watched this Yezidi guy apply deodorant directly to his shirt.

Jasu, a man about my age, came more frequently than the rest. He liked to ask me about the United States, a place he hoped to move to someday. America held endless fascination for him. Especially, I soon realized, the very different ways that men and women behave in the West.

Leafing through an old *Newsweek* one day, Jasu pointed to a cigarette advertisement. It was a photograph of a girl and a guy in swimsuits strolling on a beach holding hands.

"In America you see this?" he asked.

By this point I knew he didn't mean the *beach*. He meant the bikini the girl wore.

"Sure you see it. In the summer, when it's hot. Like now. You see it all the time."

Jasu reflected.

"And holding hands. You can do this?"

"Yes. You can hold hands."

Then he branched out.

"And women—they go to the cinema in America? Even when they are married?"

"Yes. Married women go to the movies."

"I want to go to America," Jasu announced. "Find another wife. A better wife."

A FISTer wandered over and dropped another magazine into Jasu's lap.

"Maybe she's in here, Jasu. Your better wife."

Jasu was so delighted he dropped *Newsweek* in the dirt. Who needed girls in swimsuits? He happily let me photograph him with this new discovery: a back issue of *Hustler* magazine.

Welcome to America.

Some other day, he and I talked about life in the mountains.

I rambled: "It's so beautiful here. So peaceful. So far from the world. You live in a special and amazing place. Your life is so simple. You're so lucky. You don't have to worry about so many things."

I went on like this.

Jasu looked at me. Softly: "We have no electricity."

He was way too polite. What he meant to say was: "Don't go and romanticize my poverty, my isolation, my 'exotic' existence. What I want is what you Americans already have: opportunities, a car, a television, an education for my little brother. Money."

A week after we colocate at the mountain site with the FISTers, Geoff pulls rank on me.

"Don't take this the wrong way," SGT Quinn begins, but it's no great way to start. "I've been reviewing your logs. Doing some counts. Checking to see who's doing what. And it's clear . . . um . . . that you're not . . . *productive* enough."

Not take this the wrong way? What way am I *supposed* to take this?

"What are you talking about, Sergeant?"

He's nervous, but he doesn't back down.

"The tally. Your shifts don't tally. You're not making the count. Not making the cut. I don't want you to take this the wrong way—"

"Sergeant," I start to say, astonished.

"I'm going to sit sidesaddle your next shift."

"Wha—"

"Today. Fourteen hundred."

This is so bullshit and so unexpected I'm blinking back tears, and I turn away. I am not going to let this bastard see me like this. Not now. Not ever.

Quinn's got me, and he knows it. And he's not done. He turns back.

"And Williams," he says. "One more thing. This—*fraternizing*. With the other team. Those guys over there." He juts his chin in the general direction of the FISTers. "I think . . . well . . . it's my opinion that it's not so great for our team's integrity."

So that's it. I get it now, suddenly. Quinn is *jealous*.

Tears switch clear to anger.

"Listen, Sergeant," I say, as calmly as I can manage. "You do your job, I'll do my job. We're all stuck out here together, right? Let's make it work, okay? I've got no problem with how you're doing things. Let me do things my own way." I let him take this in. "And—what I do and who I do it with when I'm off shift is my own fucking business, okay?"

"Grow up," is what I want to say. But I leave it.

"Fine," he responds after a moment. "I'm still going to be there on your next shift."

"Whatever," I say, but I'm definitely unnerved at how deeply his petty disrespect of my professionalism ticks me off.

I'm feeling shaken and ill. Why? Why is it I can watch a man die and not freak out? Then I have a powerful physical reaction to a small—and *completely* unjustified—hassle from a superior? I go to see Staff Sergeant Gardner, and he responds blandly that he'll take care of Quinn. Which, of course, he does not do beforehand. Which leaves me to deal with Quinn there on shift to determine why my numbers are allegedly low. Which they are not. I go through the logs and prove that I'm right. Halfway through, Staff Sergeant Gardner pulls Sergeant Quinn aside, and nothing like this happens again. But I still fume from the insult.

It all totally sucks.

Why do I feel so damned helpless and *vulnerable* at moments like this?

If I were a FISTer, I think I'd punch Quinn in the face.

Which is weird because Quinn and I had been getting along pretty well before this happened. We'd gone hiking together a couple of times in the mountains at this site. We'd been talking more, too. Talking about music. Talking about relationships. But after this incident about my "productivity," I am not in the mood to hang with Geoff much anymore. I start hiking with the COLT guys and spend a lot more time with them.

A few days later at the OP, there's a little FIST party in progress. One more Saturday night. The sun is going down, and in the distance you can see the sparkling lights of both Syria and Turkey. A fine backdrop for the festivities. Quinn, SSG Gardner, Reid— they don't hang out with us much. Which makes the gathering even better.

A bonfire crackles. There's chicken (purchased from a Yezidi eager for U.S. currency) cooking in goat butter and Mrs. Dash. I don't eat meat, but it's smelling really good. Also: I shouldn't say it, but someone's got vodka in cans from the locals. I'm offered a swig or three.

Why not? It stings going down and has an odor like turpentine. Probably tastes like turpentine, though I can't say, never having tried turpentine. Mixed with Gatorade the vodka's okay, though it's got one hell of a kick. Certainly beats teetotaling after so many months.

"Hey, Boobs," Hodgson says. He never quits calling me this after that first day. "My wife tells me she's taking my paycheck and buying herself fake boobs for when I get home. What do you think of that?"

All the FISTers tell me Hodgson is one scary redneck none of them would ever want to fight. They tell me Hodgson, the youngest of four brothers, had to learn early how to hold his own. They tell me about the time Hodgson beat the shit out of Travis. Knocked Travis's head into a big van door that almost cut his ear off. No one exactly sure what Travis said to Hodgson to deserve this.

"Your wife *needs* boobs, man," someone says. "I've seen your wife."

"Says who?" Hodgson's had a head start on the canned vodka. Unclear how long he's been downing shots. "What's wrong with my wife's boobs? Anyway, I was planning on a new gun with the extra money I'm getting here. Fuck if she thinks she can get cosmetic surgery with it. I like her the way she is. I like her small boobs."

"Hey. Look at me." It's Matt Crowther, another FISTer, rotating his groin obscenely against a Humvee. "I'm fucking a tire just thinking about Hodgson's wife's new boobs."

"Better than humping that sheep," Travis says. "What were you thinking about then? That was too much."

"Hey, that sheep was hot." Matt looks my way, right hand on his crotch.

"Hey. Keep passing that can around!"

"What gets you hot?" It's Matt to me.

"Small dicks. Unmanly men." I look around. "You guys."

"Screw you, hatchet wound."

This talk gives me a nasty shiver.

"Fuck off, peanut prick."

That gets a small guffaw from Hodgson.

"At least with blue medicated foot powder on my nuts," Matt opines, "it's real cool down there when the breeze blows through."

None of them wears underwear, and their pants are ripped in the groin from never changing clothes for weeks on end. None of them knows how to sew.

"Listen now," Travis says. "What's the difference between a hooker and an onion?"

"Ah, that's my joke," I complain, passing the can to him. "No one ever cried when they cut a hooker. Hey. What's the first thing a woman does when she gets back from a battered women's shelter?"

None of them know.

"The dishes, if she's smart."

The alcohol makes the night hazy.

It's easy to judge our adolescent behavior, harder to realize how hard it is to pass the time. Understand: There is *nothing* for us to do.

This is a listening post/operations post (LP/OP). Our Prophet team is the LP; we run twenty-four-hour operations with a four-person team. That means each of us works six hours a day. This gets broken down into two three-hour shifts. We are doing our mission, which is intercept and direction-find on enemy communications. The rest of the time we just sit there. Meanwhile the FISTers watch the border. What I see them do is take notes on the number of vehicles that drive down the road across from Syria. From what I can gather, their main concern is watching for smugglers.

Basically, though, there is nothing to do. We are so desperate to find things to fill the time, we make up games kids in grade school would consider beneath them. Case in point: The FISTers throw rocks at one another and at me. For fun. They aim at my breasts. It's a game. They chuck stones at one another's groins. That's a big game. A major activity. The objective? Get a stone into those small aforementioned rips in a guy's pair of pants. Believe me, it is not easy. With practice, however, it *can* be done.

One day, not the night of the party, someone finds a beetle and decides to chuck it at Matt. The beetle actually gets into the hole in his pants. And clamps down on his penis. Matt panics, screeching like a little girl.

Our life on the mountain.

Other days we take hikes. The mountains are stunning, and hiking does qualify as exercise.

Out hiking, the guys develop more time-wasting activities. More stupid soldier tricks.

"You would *never* jump off that ledge."

"Say I won't?"

"You won't."

"Say I won't?"

"You won't."

Then you have to do it.

"You wouldn't throw a rock at Kayla's boobs now, would you?"

"Say I won't?"

"You won't."

"Say I won't?"

And they keep this up until someone does.

This foolishness eases its way into common parlance until it also works the other way around: You set up what you're going to do by introducing it yourself.

"Say I won't pop off a few rounds at that rock over there?"

"You won't."

"Say I won't?"

"You won't."

And then you do. In other words it isn't a dare so much as an idea you have, and then you provoke someone else to provoke you into doing it.

Juvenile? You bet it is. We're writing the book on juvenile.

One time Hodgson pops off a few rounds, then laughs.

"Say I won't set the mountain on fire with a tracer round?"

Too late. Hodgson does fire a tracer round that does hit a patch of dry grass that obligingly springs into flames. It's such a happy coincidence, Matt grabs his camera to photograph the mountain burning down.

"Holy shit!" It's Hodgson, incredulous at his dumb luck. "I set the side of the mountain on fire!"

Matt's taking pictures while the rest of us, gear bouncing on our backs, run down to snuff out the flames. Seems like I spend too much time in Iraq putting out friendly fires.

Speaking of which.

There's the time the FISTers' platoon sergeant—whom they *like,* by the way—visits the mountain site. Their leadership makes these periodic visits, checking in to see what's up and to resupply food and water. Sometimes he's there overnight; sometimes he stays for a few days. Anyway, this one time their platoon sergeant is making the final ascent to the site. Maybe he's still a hundred meters off when someone suggests: "Say I won't fire a round down there just to get Kelly's attention?"

This is *beyond* wrong, even though the round is not close to him. Nothing personal, of course. Just another "Say I won't?"

Kelly could often be an asshole. A real cocksucker. He really got into the canned vodka and Gatorade. He'd been deployed to Bosnia, Kosovo, Afghanistan, and now Iraq. Like Lieutenant Samuels, Kelly had been part of Operation Anaconda in the mountains of Afghanistan, and even when I got to know him better, he never really wanted to talk about it. It was like a scale with soldiers. Those of us who'd been to Iraq had difficulty dealing with civilians when we got home; we tended to feel more comfortable with other soldiers who'd been deployed. Same thing with Anaconda: Many of them had little to say to those of us who'd only known deployment in Iraq. It just didn't count in the same way. The only difference with Kelly is that he acted out more than most. He got pretty angry, I think. And pretty drunk a lot of the time.

On the other hand he and I shared a lot of musical tastes. So that was a bond of sorts. So we'd talk about music, ideas, politics, books—things like that. We would have interesting conversations even though at the same time Kelly could be a real jackass. Literally, he'd say to me: "Fix me some eggs, bitch." And I'd fix him eggs. Because I'm retarded. Or nice. Or whatever.

Meeting Shane Kelly I was reminded how much women like assholes. How much I tended to like assholes over the years. How much a lot of women like men like Kelly—possibly because they believe that they deserve being treated badly.

The pop psychology theory goes: Women are drawn to men who are like their fathers. So if your father is moody, cold, and emotionally distant, women may tend to be drawn to men who are like that. Again with the pop psychology, you think that if you can win the love of a man like that, you are symbolically winning the love of the father that you never felt you really got. After I meet Shane Kelly, I begin sometimes to analyze myself in this way. But it also has very little to do with him; historically I've dated a lot of guys who treated me like shit.

At some point I think I really figure Kelly out. He will treat you like shit until you've proved that you can be trusted. He has walls just as I do, except that his are pretty thick, probably thicker than mine. So I see rather quickly that a lot of his talk has been just talk. And that he is not in fact a real asshole. That his asshole behavior toward me was a defense mechanism to protect himself from the possibility of pain.

It takes awhile, and it really doesn't happen until much later, but I begin to feel that I understand Shane. I learn a little about his fucked-up childhood; no dad, Mom raises the family by herself and has a predictably hard time. (At least until she remarries; Shane's stepdad is a wonderful man.) To this day Shane has had almost no contact at all with his father. Even later, when the shit really goes down, his father does nothing. Makes no effort to be in touch. And I know that this affects him. To be in a combat zone and your father does not send you even a damned postcard saying: "Hope you live." That has to have an emotional effect on him.

From what I understand, Shane has had a difficult military career. He's gotten in trouble a lot.

Not all his friends see Shane the way I do. Some of his friends tell me: "He doesn't treat you well enough. You can do better than that. You deserve better than that." Because Shane likes to talk like he's bad. He likes to mouth off. He likes to get drunk in bars and stir things up. Feel sorry for himself. So he ends up yelling at Army wives, calling them fat fucks or whatever. Blacks out and forgets how he got himself home.

Yeah, so his friends sometimes tell me I deserve better.

Things do get out of hand. Like one of the nights we drink canned vodka. A night Kelly happens not to be around.

"I gotta piss." It's Hodgson, but when he tries to stand up, he stumbles down again.

"Let me help you," says Matt, watching Hodgson sway. Hodgson doesn't object.

Well, sir, we were completely drunk on vodka purchased from the locals, and then . . . um . . . Hodgson slipped and fell off the mountain—

A difficult thing to explain to the wife. Or to the higher-ups.

So Matt braces Hodgson around the shoulders, and both of them move behind the truck. Shortly we hear them stumbling back.

"Just push me into her, man," Hodgson is whispering loud to Matt. "Push me into her."

"No way." Matt: Always sober. He never drinks at the mountain site, saying later that it was just too spooky. "Not happening. You do not want to do that."

"Just push me, man. Just push me into her."

"Push yourself, man. I'll have nothing to do with this."

They come back together, and Matt sits. Hodgson pretend-stumbles toward me. Before I can react, his hands are up, cupping my tits and squeezing. Hard.

"Mmm." His eyes are closed as he absorbs the sensation, while I shove him away.

"Whatever, dude," I say, slapping his hands. "Stupid redneck."

He's smiling.

"Thank you, Boobs," he mumbles.

"You're one sorry drunk bastard."

"Mmm." Now he's lost and stumbling again, his final ounce of strength consumed by the grope. Done for the night.

"Assholes." I generalize it. "All you guys."

"Ah, come on now. Don't get mad. We're like kittens. Stroke us. Make us purr."

"Let's play a game," Travis says. "Truth or dare."

"Not tonight."

"Some other night?"

"Whatever. I'm going to bed."

"Can we come with?"

"Why don't you jerk each other off? Isn't that what you usually do?"

Matt turns to Travis. "Wanna try?"

I'm gone before I hear an answer.

Sergeant Quinn gets set to go. His time is done. He's been accepted into the Army's Green-to-Gold program. They plan to pay for him to attend college; he'll owe them several more years of his life—but as an officer. The bottom line is: He's heading home.

We'd been strained since Quinn got in my face about my "productivity." I wouldn't go out of my way to spend time with him, but it wasn't a really big deal. When we interacted in the vehicle, I still talked to him. Even after the incident when he criticized my work, Quinn continued to sit and talk with me when I was on shift. He kept me company. So we'd talk about all sorts of things during the three hours of my daytime shift. (I wonder if it offended him that I never stayed with him when *he* was on shift.)

"Listen," he says. "When I spoke to Sergeant Gardner about—"

"Forget it."

"No, I wanted to—"

"*Forget it.*" I pause for a moment. "But there's one thing I want to ask you."

"Yes?"

I confront Quinn right before he leaves.

"Why the hell won't the guys in our platoon ever talk to me anymore?" I ask. "Down at the airfield. What the fuck's going on? Why do they act like they all hate me?"

And Quinn tells me because he knows he won't have to deal with the consequences.

"They think you're a big whore," Quinn says, looking away. "They think you're a slut. And they don't want to have anything to do with you. Because they think you're a slut."

"I don't get it."

"Listen," Quinn says. "I think I know what this is all about. Remember? Right before we deployed? You were having sex with Connelly, right? The guys think that makes you a big slut."

This makes zero sense to me. And I am getting very angry about it.

"Connelly was the only guy I ever fucked at Fort Campbell before we deployed," I say to Quinn. "From when I got there in July until we left, he was the only one. So what the hell . . ."

Then I put it together. The only thing I can think is that I tried briefly dating this guy while I had been at Campbell. But it hadn't worked out. I'd told the guy I was messed up in the head because I'd just gotten divorced.

"I'm not in a place where I can give you an emotional connection," I told this guy. "At all."

And the guy said: "That's fine."

So we were just dating. We never even had sex.

Then at a party at Sergeant Biddle's house, I got really drunk and fucked Connelly.

So this other guy I'm dating, his feelings got hurt, and he got upset about it. For three days. And then he got over it. And we remained friends. We are still friends today.

But the guys in my platoon acted all pissed off. They decided I was a slut or a whore, that I cheated on the guy I was dating. They probably did not even know I never slept with this other guy. They just assumed that if a man and a woman are together, they must be having sex.

So they decided to make this big bullshit judgment on me. And it was really painful. Because I had gone through a situation in high school when I definitely fucked too many guys. I admit that. I'm not proud of it. I got treated horribly. People said vicious things about me when I was in high school. People called me a slut all the time. People were very cruel, and it was tough. I'd been sexually assaulted when I was thirteen—that definitely messed with my sense of control over my own body and my ability to make choices about my own sexuality. But that's over half my lifetime ago by now. And I spent a lot of those years trying to get over feeling crappy for things I'd done when I was a kid.

Now here I am in Iraq being made to feel crappy all over again for things I did *not* do at Fort Campbell. Because at Fort Campbell I was basically responsible. I was basically good. And here these guys are treating me like I'm some dirty slut. It is very upsetting. It brings back a lot of unpleasant memories.

"Yeah," Quinn says, taking it all in.

"And Connelly? He was fucking some sixteen-year-old girl while he was seeing me. But *I'm* the big whore?"

"I know," Quinn says.

"So there's nothing wrong with him, right? He can fuck this sixteen-year-old and fuck me or fuck any other girl he wants at the same time—and there's nothing wrong with him, right?"

"Yeah," Quinn says.

"But if I even *talk* to one guy while I'm fucking another guy, I'm this fucking dirty whore?"

"Yeah," Quinn says.

"Damn them," I say. "They're just jealous because they never got any fucking ass. I think they're just afraid of women. They never get any action, so I'm the slut? Assholes!"

"Time for me to go," Quinn says. "I just thought you should know."

"Yeah," I say.

We hug. It's the one time we ever have any physical contact in all the time I've known him.

I should be glad Quinn's leaving, but I'm not. I feel disappointed. As much of a snot as Quinn sometimes was, I still know I'll miss him.

We went through combat together. Quinn brought me Gatorade when he found out I'd watched a guy die. It was a minor thing, but it meant something to me.

And I'd been able to admit my self-doubts to Quinn. That's not easy for me. I'd opened up to Quinn, and he'd been okay with it. He'd been okay with me. He told me I was a good person, which sounds cheesy but meant a lot to me at the time.

With Lauren gone, Quinn was the only member of my team

with whom I could actually be vulnerable. The only remaining member of my team with whom I had any sort of emotional bond or relationship at all. And now he was going.

The FISTers tried to make up for Hodgson groping me by procuring more food than I could possibly imagine. The halal meals my unit *claimed* it could not find in-country, the FISTers began to get me by the case.

But that was not all. Somehow they procured lots of everything: cases of shelf-stable milk, boxes of cereal, cases of fruit, boxes of banana chips, reams of Nutri-Grain bars, packages of chocolate milk, boxes of condiments, packets of peanut butter and jelly, shelf-stable bread. We're talking *tons* of food. I was not stuck sucking on MREs any longer, watching my entire body fat evaporate. Add all this to the wonderful stuff I got every day from the Yezidis, and I was over my involuntary weight-loss program.

Every morning we called in a report of our supplies. Fuel, ammo, everything we had. And this one morning I got to the report on our food supply.

I said: "We've got a whole shitload of food and water."

"What? Sorry. That won't do."

"Look," I said into the radio. "It's a whole shitload."

"I say again: We need a *count*."

"Okay. Wait one."

So I went and counted. And counted. And counted. And came back to the radio.

"We're got ten cases of . . ." And I ran it down. Every last bit of it.

"Yeah," the guy said when I was finally done. "Roger that. You called it. That is a whole *shitload* of food and water."

I came to adore the mountain site. Up there for six weeks. The best six weeks of the war for me. I told myself someday I'd find my way back, if possible.

Late in June we got pulled from our Shangri-la back to 3rd Brigade for inventories.

Jasu came for a last visit, looking severely bummed.

"I'll miss you," he said.

"Yeah," I said. "Me too. I'll miss you, too."

"One favor?"

"What?"

He pointed to a stack of empty cardboard boxes.

"Cardboard?" I asked. "What about it?"

"For my house," he said, sounding hopeful.

The last time we saw them, Jasu and his donkey were hauling away as many cardboard boxes as possible.

For a floor. For his house.

FREE MARKET

WE MOVED TO a second site on the other side of the same mountain. I was now the only person left on the team that had been there from the beginning. It felt awkward, the constantly shifting personnel.

The only thing that kept me going was the COLT team that relocated with us to this new site. This time, however, we were colocated with others, and the absence of relative privacy sucked. There was a far more crowded scene up there, with probably twenty soldiers around all the time. There was a ground surveillance radar team. There were four retransmission teams spread out about a hundred meters away across the road from us, and they were okay. But there was not a whole lot for them to do, either. Their equipment picked up a signal and retransmitted it so the signal could go farther; once they had it in place they didn't actually have to do anything for the equipment to work. Unless it stopped working. All that was left for the team to do was sit back and let the radios do their thing. They were not pushing buttons for it to operate; it happened automatically.

Efforts were made to make friends. Do the sociable thing. But I didn't really feel into it. I got invitations to cross the road to play cards or watch a VCD, but more often than not I declined. I don't know why. At the first mountain site I guess I got used to being more alone—or alone with the FISTers, and I was not as eager now to reach out.

Let me explain something about the FISTers.

Maybe it sounds like they were jerks who hated girls and liked to talk us down. And I would say to that: They were, but they weren't.

In the real world, guys bond through competition. They play football games. They play video games. They verbally spar. They throw rocks at one another. Guys like to try and establish a hierarchy. They jockey for who's on top.

Now, I can play that game. I tried to play it with Staff Sergeant Gardner, and he was probably better at it than I am. I can play it with guys who value intelligence. But I can only sort of play it with guys like the FISTers. It's not the same with them.

The FISTers would talk trash with me to bond with me.

They wouldn't talk trash with me if they didn't like me. If we weren't friends. Put it this way: They would never have insulted me all the time if I had been only a stranger to them.

Matt and I wrestled. This was definitely a guy thing to do. But we tussled on the mountain.

And the FISTers would yell out: "Hey Matt, you got beat up by a girl!"

Matt would yell back: "No, I didn't! I won!"

The FISTers also always gave me credit when I deserved credit. They would always tell me: "You're really smart. You're smarter than we are."

And I'd give them credit, too. I would tell them: "Sure, I've read more books than you guys. I can speak Arabic. But I couldn't fix my truck if my life depended on it. I know nothing about engines. I would never be able to understand your equipment. You are all smarter than I am about how to make things work."

Being around these guys and military personnel in general had given me a whole new appreciation for nonintellectual skills. These were people with manual skills. They knew how to use their hands. They were not afraid to get sweaty or dirty. And I respected them for it.

Tensions at this site only arose when one of the retrans teams informed our squad leader that we'd have to pull guard shift with them and watch the road. The retrans guys periodically started up the truck so the battery didn't die. But that was really it. Plus pull guard.

We, on the other hand, had to *work* on our shifts. And we were on shift twenty-four hours a day. For us pulling guard meant ninety minutes more shift time a day, on top of our regular shifts. It was a minor gripe, but under the circumstances it took on much bigger importance. Our team had been in-country now for nearly six months working seven days a week running ops twenty-four hours a day. No break. No vacation. No time away from the people, the mission, anything. No such thing as a *weekend*. And so it was the small shit that began to drive us crazy. And this request to pull guard meant even less sleep than we were already getting.

At this point we'd lost Sergeant Quinn, so the three of us each worked two four-hour shifts a day. My shifts for a long time were 10:00 A.M. to 2:00 P.M. and 10:00 P.M. to 2:00 A.M. So I might sleep from 2:30 in the morning (since it always took a while to wind down after a shift) until the sun would hit me and wake me up around 8:00 A.M. That meant between five and six hours of sleep a day, which never felt like enough.

I coped with existence mainly by getting away on hikes. Rock climbing with my M-4 was not easy— it totally threw off my balance. But I did it, and it was great to get away with one or more of the FISTers for a few hours. I tended to go hiking with Matt. But I also hiked occasionally with Travis. I went hiking with Rivers once, and also Bill, our civilian linguist. Technically, at least according to those at higher levels, this walking away from base was probably not permitted, but on-site no one challenged us. So we'd go, wandering wherever. We carried handheld radios, and we were always in range of communication. It felt like a good thing to become more familiar with the area.

Mainly if we came across locals, the locals were Yezidis. I continued to be overwhelmed by their amazing generosity.

Their Arabic was not great, and whatever Kurdish we spoke was limited to a few basic phrases, so conversations tended toward the most common of denominators. And after a time there was a remarkable degree of repetition in these little talks with the Yezidis we met.

On one hike we came to a small Yezidi dwelling in the mountains, and the men practically pulled us over to sit down with them.

Matt and Bill and I sat awkwardly around on the ground while the men watched us, and one prepared tea. These were very poor farming people. They grew pomegranates and grapes and some vegetables. The men told us that they stayed there in the summer months; in the winter they lived in the village below with their families.

Then this one local with a handlebar mustache placed three glasses before us, and there weren't enough glasses to go around. So we drank tea while they sat there. They offered us grapes. And then he got out a raw onion that he chopped into quarters, and laid the pieces out for us. He then sprinkled some coarsely ground salt on a plate, and also set down a large piece of flat bread.

We looked at one another, and then down at the raw onion slices. And then again at one another.

"Eat," the man said in Arabic.

I said, "It's a raw onion."

"Eat. Eat." The man was not understanding our hesitation.

"It's a raw onion," I repeated.

"Yes. You dip it in the salt and eat it with bread."

The guys were really not sure about this.

"You're kidding me?" one of them said.

"No. Eat it."

So we ate it to be polite. And it wasn't that bad, though it was nothing I would serve as an appetizer back home.

Then, as always, I had the obligatory conversation I had with all the Yezidis. No matter what, no matter when, it was always the same conversation, and it went something like this:

"We are Yezidis," the Yezidi man began.

"Yes." I had heard this before, and knew precisely where it was heading. "Yes. I know. You are Yezidis."

"Do you know of the Yezidis in America?"

"No," I would be feeling weary already. "No. Nobody in America has heard of the Yezidis."

"Will you tell the Americans about us?"

"Yes. I will do my best."

"We are *not* Muslims."

"I know. I got it. You're *not* Muslims. You're Yezidis."

"We are like Jews. And we are like Christians. But we are *not* like Muslims."

"Yes. I know." Yes, everyone here told me the same thing. "Yes, I've got it."

"We love Americans because you hate Muslims. And we hate Muslims, too. So that's why we love Americans. And we want America to stay here forever. You—or Israel. To protect us from the Muslims. Because they cut down our fig trees and stole our women."

"Okay." I did not want to start a debate here or an argument, but I wanted to be clear. "We don't hate Muslims," I began. "That's really . . . um . . . not the point. We don't hate any religion. And we're here so that you can have a democracy. And so you can have freedom. And in a democracy everybody gets to help decide how to run the government and how to run the country. And even the Yezidis can help. You can participate in the new government under a democracy. Because you're going to have freedom. That's why we're here, to help establish freedom and democracy. And then we're going to *leave*."

"No, no." He waved away this speech, as if it was foolish or irrelevant. And he spoke now as if to someone who was a trifle dense. "No. It will never work. This would never happen. Americans have to stay here *forever*." He paused. "Or Israel."

"Israel is never going to come." Now it was my turn to make a point that seemed too obvious to mention. "Let me tell you. Israel will never be here. They will never be in Iraq. They will never establish anything here. I promise you. They are not coming."

Somehow these conversations were on a tape loop, and it began again at the beginning.

"We are like Christians. We are like Jews. We hate the Muslims. *Like you*."

"No. We *don't* hate the Muslims—"

"Will you please tell Mr. Bush about the Yezidis?"

I guess the thinking here was that I was not getting it. So they might as well go right to the top. Get the president involved, since this soldier was not grasping the issues.

"I don't know him." I said this as politely as I could.

"Will you write him a letter? Will you call him? Will you tell Mr. Bush? Does Mr. Bush know about the Yezidis?"

"I do not know what Mr. Bush knows about the Yezidis."

"Tell Mr. Bush. Tell Mr. Bush about the Yezidi people. Because we are good people."

"Yes, you are. You are good people. You're generous and kind and friendly people. You give me food all the time. You're very nice. You're very kind. I love the Yezidis."

"Tell Mr. Bush."

"Yeah. All right. Yes. I am going to write Mr. Bush a letter and tell him how great you are."

"Thank you. Thank you."

After our little picnic, we took pictures of the men and their donkey. Then this guy with the handlebar mustache—he was about fifty years old—led us back up the mountain. And he scampered up the mountain in plastic sandals like a goddamn gazelle. Here we were, thinking we're bad-ass Army soldiers, but we couldn't keep up.

And the very next time I met a Yezidi, I had almost the identical conversation all over again. Word for word.

One day these random young people just showed up at our site.

"Hey," they called out to us.

"Hey." What the fuck was going on?

One kid was from Chicago, and started talking to Matt about

growing up in Illinois. He was thinking about possibly attending college in Matt's hometown. But Matt was trying to dissuade him.

"Nah," Matt told this one American teenager. "I wouldn't go there. You can't watch your cornhole that much."

Turned out these kids were volunteers from some Christian group, and they'd all come there to assist the Iraqis.

So we pulled out a bunch of MREs and served lunch for these American kids. But they were having trouble eating out of the pouches like we did. Luckily we happened to have some paper plates; that worked. And the soldiers began to explain how to make the MREs.

We were stoked. We hadn't seen real people in forever.

Matt got all cute.

"Oh, let me help you with that. Let me get that for you."

The kids had come up our way to see the Yezidi shrine. Check out all the great sites of Iraq.

Here's a trash pile! Here's a destroyed tank! There's another rabid dog!

We had the only healthy grown dog in Iraq. The FISTers named her Rak Hammer. She'd been beaten a lot and hated Iraqis. She'd been adopted and then left at the site by the Pathfinders, and when they rolled out, she stayed with the fire support team.

It was a violation of General Order No. 1 to keep pets or mascots. Pets were specifically outlawed—like porn and liquor. But almost everyone we knew in Iraq had a pet of some kind. I knew people who had a cat, a hedgehog, a falcon, and lots of people who had dogs.

Packs of wild dogs roam Iraq, and some are rabid. In Mosul

soldiers would even go on dog-eradication projects and shoot dogs. This was hard for a lot of soldiers to do.

Dogs in Iraq that soldiers adopted often hated the locals with a deep and abiding passion. The locals tended to throw rocks at dogs. And beat them. While we fed them and were friendly to them. So our dog made a big ruckus when locals approached. Which proved convenient. She also became very protective of her territory and kept all the other local dogs away from us. She became fiercely loyal because we treated her well.

We also had a little puppy. One day I was told an older dog killed the puppy—which was an unpleasant thing. (Though I learned more than a year later that it was Sergeant Kelly who accidentally killed the puppy. He'd thrown it up into the air, and it fell hard onto the rocks below. It was maimed, so he killed it.)

Our pets were extremely important for morale. Our dogs became a pretty big part of our lives. I took a lot of pictures of our damned dog.

The Army puts out an informal policy against physical contact. Even though the Army is one of the few environments in the States in which men can touch each other and it's okay. Guys pat each other on the ass all the time in the Army. It's called a "good game." Guys can also half hug each other; not front hug, but a little side shoulder hug. That's perfectly manly and acceptable. If two men in civilian clothes hugged like this it might be considered gay. But Army guys can do it whenever they want—because they're Army. Real tough guys.

But physical contact was more or less something I did not have during my deployment. Guys were extra careful not to touch me. As a female I was not really a part of the "good game."

So having pets around was important for this reason: Here was a creature I could touch and love.

The Yezidi shrine at this mountain site was a small rock building with objects dangling from the ceiling. There were little alcoves in the shrine where locals placed offerings and worshipped. People came and left money that anyone else could take, if someone else came who needed it more. Or people took the money to use toward the upkeep of the shrine itself. And inside the shrine there was another door to a smaller room that I never entered or saw. No one exactly explained the purpose of the shrine, but we sometimes heard accusations from local Muslims that the Yezidis were *devil worshippers.* The dangling objects appeared to have more to do with the rays of the sun, but nothing was made clear.

One day a father came to worship with his several children, and the oldest daughter in the family appeared mesmerized by me.

She was excited to see a female American because she could talk to me. It was not appropriate for her to speak to the men, but she was permitted to speak to me. And it was the first time I encountered a young local woman with whom I could spend some time talking.

She didn't know how old she was, since the locals didn't have a real way to record birthdays, but she estimated that she was about sixteen.

Our conversations were extremely stilted, given her near-absence of Arabic and my difficulty making myself understood as a result.

Her name was Leila, and we became friendly, if not friends.

She returned to the shrine with her family three or four more times while I was there, and we began to exchange gifts.

The mother never joined her family on this pilgrimage.

I noticed that all the girls in the family had tattoos on their faces, but none more than Leila. Small dots on her chin, her forehead, and the sides of her face.

I tried to ask what these dots on her face meant, but there was too much of a language barrier. The only thing I could ascertain was that the girls seemed to receive more of these tattoos as they grew up; Leila's youngest sister had no markings on her face, but her other sisters had one, two, and four as they got older. But whether the dots were religious or cultural, I never learned.

At another time in Iraq, when we were among the Bedouin people, I noticed from a distance that the women appeared to have tattooed writing on their feet. But again I never learned what it meant; I also never got close enough to the Bedouin women to read the tattoos. I was always very curious.

Besides my general interest in the locals, and my desire to get to know what the civilians were like, it was just great to see a girl. This was such a male environment otherwise. And even though our conversations were hobbled by our mutual inability to make ourselves easily understood, there was just a sense of *relief*. For me. And, I began to suspect, for Leila as well.

Jimmy the Ice Man has arrived. Are we glad to see him!

No one knows his real name, or how he first found out we are up here, but everyone calls him Jimmy the Ice Man. The "Ice Man" part is easy: Jimmy brings us slabs of ice he buys down in the village. Jimmy is probably Kurdish or maybe Yezidi; we don't know that, either. We also don't know where "Jimmy" came from; probably some smart-ass soldier's sense of humor that stuck. Anyway, Jimmy is an awesome guy who has quickly and efficiently mastered the skills of the marketplace. We respect this about him. We respect how quickly he has found a market, and how he knows immediately how to exploit it.

The arrangement goes something like this: First Jimmy hires a taxi for the whole day for five dollars. He then loads the taxi with consumer goods—anything and everything he thinks he can sell to a captive American military audience stuck out in the god-forsaken wilderness with little to do and absolutely nothing on which to spend its money. Jimmy starts with the essentials. There's the ice, of course. By this point in the summer we are talking temperatures of a hundred degrees most days, even in the mountains. The ice is very nice, especially when combined with the cases of soda Jimmy hauls to us in his rented taxi. It's a great combination. Buy the ice, and buy the soda to chill on the ice. Prices are reasonable, given that Jimmy is sole vendor for our AO (area of operations). We fully recognize that Jimmy is pulling in a huge profit margin, but we respect and admire his ingenuity. Big slabs of ice about two or three feet long and six inches across that he'd pick up for a quarter. And he'd charge us three dollars. An amazing mark-up on all the same stuff we could get way cheaper at base does not appear unreasonable to us under the circumstances.

"Hey, Jimmy! You got that shit we talked about last time!"

From this basic plan of action, Jimmy gets ambitious. Branches out. He begins to take orders. Anything he can get his hands on, he will happily serve as mule. He wants his customers happy, and he works the crowd to make sure folks are satisfied with the service.

This means lots of business. Soldiers wanting just about anything you can imagine. Cigarettes, gifts for girlfriends or wives, knives, lighters, soccer jerseys, propane tanks, prayer beads—you name it. (Personally, I buy a lot of scarves.) Most of it is junk, but we purchase it. Happy to keep Jimmy happy. Happy to have something, anything, to distract us from the routineness of our routine.

The local kids have been bringing us food almost every day since we got to this new site. All sorts of good stuff. Two kinds of eggplants (green and purple), green peppers, tomatoes, cucumbers, potatoes, onions, eggs—it's their offering to us. Their welcome to the American liberators. They have no sense of what their food should cost, so they start asking for small change. Maybe a dollar. No big deal. We meet their monetary demands with a chuckle.

As Jimmy continues his trips up the mountain with a taxiload of goodies, though, the children grow bolder. Wanting more money for their product. And then they begin to jack up the prices. Two dollars for a bag of vegetables. Then three dollars. Five dollars. And upward. Testing out what the market will bear.

Some of the guys get pissed. They start saying things you'd rather not hear them say. But it's not like we all don't have similar thoughts at one time or another. "Get these fucking locals away from me" or "I'm tired of them asking me for water" or "I'm tired of them asking me for money" or "I don't want to deal with these fucking people." And you understand this attitude after a while. After all these kids are *always* underfoot. Always wanting something. And am I really going to fork over five bucks for some damned eggplants the size of my fist?

Finally we refuse to deal with them, and the situation normalizes. Someone speaks to the kids. Settles them down. Still, you can't help but take note of how *fast* the free market has taken root out here in the Kurdish mountains.

Jimmy the Ice Man is a real character. I love this guy. And he provides some memorable moments.

Like the time he brings us Osama bin lighters. Picture this. A butane lighter with the image of Osama bin Laden and the Twin Towers in New York City. And there's a plane flying into the Twin Towers. And a little red light. When you press down, the light glows red. It's an instant classic. Every soldier wants one. It is gruesome and morbid, but it also reminds us of where we are—and why. (Or at least what our fearless leaders wanted us to think about why we are here; we all knew there was no connection between the war in Iraq and 9/11. We talked about it all the time.) Or how about the lighter shaped like a heart? And it has the faces of both George W. Bush and Saddam Hussein. And the top of the lighter is a fighter plane. Very strange. (Made in China. What's up with that?)

I loved this about Jimmy. That he does this. Capitalism in its purest form.

Sometimes, though, Jimmy's entrepreneurial spirit goes a little too far, and we have to set some boundaries. Or at least I do.

"No, Jimmy," I'm telling him for the umpteenth time. "I do not need *dresses*. I do not need *skirts*."

"Skirts for you," Jimmy says in surprisingly good English, pushing a stack of fabrics closer to make sure I am not misunderstanding that this is a special deal he wishes to make. "No one else. You."

"No, Jimmy," I say. "Thank you for . . . um . . . your interest. Thank you. But no."

"But who else?" He smiles. But he is also disappointed; I can tell. "Who else will wear such things here?" He gestures to all the guys at this site. I am the only woman.

"I don't know," I say. *But I haven't asked you to bring me clothes!*

"Look, Jimmy," I try to explain. "Thank you for your interest. And the effort. But I am not allowed to wear anything but my uniform." I point to my uniform. I try to make *this* the point, as if I too am disappointed that I am not going to be able to model these clothes which are, in fact, beyond hideous. Their bright array of mismatched colors defies easy characterization.

Jimmy is not easily dissuaded. He relents, but then next time he taxis up to us, he tries again. Same dresses. Same skirts.

On another occasion Jimmy wants to know how much we make as soldiers here in Iraq, working for the U.S. military. This is not a simple matter to explain to a man who must consider the fifty dollars he might make on a good day selling ice and soda to twenty Americans in the Sinjar Mountains a small fortune. So I try to make it make sense in a way I hope he can grasp.

"Two thousand dollars a month," I begin, and I see his eyes grow large with wonder. "But—but there are lots of costs involved."

"Costs?"

"Expenses. Back home. We have many things for which we must continue to pay. Even though we are living here. Like, for example, I own a house in America. And I have a mortgage. That's six hundred dollars a month right there. For the next thirty years. And I own a new car. That's three hundred dollars a month for the next five years."

Jimmy is quiet, calculating these expenses. And it's all true: I *am* underpaid. Soldiers of my rank and below with dependents qualify for food stamps. But I'm hardly done.

"And there are other things. Heat for the winter. And electricity. And home insurance and car insurance."

Jimmy is looking increasingly somber, studying me carefully as I itemize the costs of an ordinary American life.

"I just want you to understand—it's expensive." I'm on a roll. I'm almost convincing myself. "We make a lot of money—by the standards here. But—it's expensive. And there's more—"

"Food, telephone—" he interrupts.

"Yes, yes," I say. He gets it.

"Take it, please."

He is holding a can of soda out to me.

"For you. Please. *No cost.* Free soda. It's on me."

Jimmy the Ice Man, whose impoverished people have suffered for centuries at the hands of one oppressor or another, has taken pity on my small salary.

He insists, pressing the soda gently into my hands.

LOSING IT

TRAVIS AND RIVERS found this lost kitten in the shrine. They decided it might be cool to torment it. Capture it. Swing it around by the scruff of its neck like some stuffed animal. They saw that their actions upset me. And so they decided to kill the kitten. Nothing else to do.

"Hey, Kayla. What a pretty pussy, don't you think?"

"Let the damned cat go, Rivers."

"What for?" It was Rivers, the guy I didn't know too well.

"Say I won't toss this little pussy off a cliff?" That was Travis, tormenting me to relieve the boredom.

Rivers in mock astonishment: "You won't."

"Say I won't?"

Both of them playing for my benefit—which I hated. I did not want to see an innocent creature thrown to its death.

I moved to stop them, but Travis skipped out of reach.

"Hey. Say I won't smash this little pussy's head with a rock?"

"Fuck you, jackass!" I moved to stop him.

I grabbed the kitten and held it safe.

What then?

There was a local at the shrine. He had been watching us, and now I approached him.

We exchanged greetings in Arabic, and I explained things.

"Those are bad soldiers up there who want to kill this small cat. Please carry it away from here and—"

"Take it?"

"Yes, please."

"Okay."

And we exchanged farewells.

That same night Travis lost it. Matt found me to tell me just as I was getting off shift.

"He's all curled up. Like a baby. Completely freaked out. Crying and punching himself. Walking around, mumbling bullshit to himself. I try to talk to him, but he won't talk to me. Maybe you—"

"There's nothing to say, Matt. He was a total dickhead today."

"Sure," Matt said, soothingly. "Sure, I know. Yeah. That's right. But maybe you could—I don't know—just talk to him. Anything."

I went. But Travis was even worse than I imagined.

"Hey."

"Get the *fuck* away."

"Listen, if you want to talk or anything, I'll—"

"*Bitch.*"

"I just wondered if—"

Travis kept freaking out. A complete loss of control. Nothing held back. I don't know that I'd ever seen anything like this before. It was like some episode. A psychotic break. There was nothing I could do to make any difference.

I hung around for a while, just to keep an eye on him. But eventually Rivers showed up and I went back to bed.

"Hey."

"Hey."

"Back there last night with Travis," Rivers said. "That was cool. Trying to help and all. That was cool."

"He's a friend," I said. "He was having a bad night. I thought maybe I could help snap him out of it."

"Uh-huh. I tried, too. After you went to sleep. Same bad luck. The guy was unreachable. Rough night."

"Yeah."

"Listen," Rivers said, looking at me hard. "You know Travis tells me you're some kind of kinky slut."

"The fuck he does?" I blurted, my shock tinged with outrage.

Rivers studied me a moment longer.

"Nah," he said, slapping my thighs. "Nah. He never said that. I'm just bullshitting you. That's bullshit. He never said that."

I looked at him as if he was an asshole. Which maybe he was.

"Listen." Rivers was this slightly overweight guy who swaggered like a stud. No doubt covering for his own deep insecurities, I thought. Not my type. At all. "Seriously, though. I'm having this question about my girlfriend. Whether to make her my fiancée."

"Yeah?"

"Yeah."

He showed me this Polaroid. A washed-out blonde, her face a bit blurry.

"Nice," I said, politely. "Pretty."

"Yeah," he said, taking the photo back. "And I was wondering if maybe you thought that was, like, I don't know. You know." He laughed, trying to act cute.

"My opinion?" I hardly knew this guy. But I definitely did not find him cute.

"Well," he started again. "It's like this." He scratched his armpit, looking around. "Like I've had sex with sixty-eight women. And I always wanted to make it to seventy before I married. So if I marry this girl, you know, I'll never make my dream." He smiled. "Like I'd be two short."

"Yeah?"

"Yeah. I'd be two short of fucking seventy girls."

"Yeah?" I wondered why there was suddenly no one else around. And why this guy was telling me this. Though that part I could already guess.

"Well, um, it's like this." He looked at me dead-on. "Do you want to be number sixty-nine?"

I burst out laughing.

"Uh-huh, right," I said. This was too ridiculous. "Sure thing. I'll *definitely* be number sixty-nine, Rivers. Right now. Right here. Would that work for you?"

And now he was laughing too.

"Ha-ha-ha. Sure thing. Absolutely, Kayla. Let's do it in the *hajjis*' shrine."

And we were both laughing, because I was not in the least bit interested in this dude. Frankly I found it hard to imagine who would be.

Hajjis. One of the several words we routinely used to describe the Iraqi people.

The *hajj* is one of the five pillars of Islam. It refers to the pilgrimage to Mecca. Therefore, technically, a *hajji* is one who has gone on the *hajj*. But soldiers called the locals *hajjis* regardless of an Iraqi's religion or ethnicity and oblivious to whether or not this particular local had traveled to Mecca. That was completely irrelevant.

It was no different from the nasty words American soldiers have used throughout our history to describe our enemies in war. The first thing any soldier did in a combat situation was learn to dehumanize the enemy. In prior wars we called them *nips* or *chinks* or *gooks* or *krauts* or *slopes*. In Iraq we called them *hajjis*, but we also called them *sadiqis*—which means "my friends"—or *habibis*—"my darlings." (Soldiers seldom had any idea what these Arabic words meant.) We called them *towelheads. Ragheads. Camel jockeys. The fucking locals.* Words that ensured that we didn't see our enemy as people—as somebody's father or son or brother or uncle.

Later that same week this lieutenant showed up and ordered us to put up concertina wire everywhere. He discussed the possibility of booby traps and the need for all of us to dig in. Adopt fighting positions.

It made no sense at all unless the goal was to lose the hearts and minds of the people. To make them stop thinking of us as *liberators* and start thinking of us as *occupiers*.

But we unfurled the rolls of c-wire, stacking them two or three high, ripping the crap out of our gloves in the process. We began by restricting access to the Yezidi shrine. We made it so any local driving up had to zigzag through a series of c-wire barriers to get near the shrine. We continued by establishing checkpoints along the road up to our OP. To slow people down. And sometime later still, we ordered people to park their vehicles some distance away, and then walk up to the shrine.

I recognized that this sort of thing made sense from a security standpoint. It made sense because at the Tal Afar airfield there would be a mortar attack sometime later that summer. And later still, a car would be driven straight at a guard point in Tal Afar. Things like this did begin to occur later that summer in the area we were in. At this time, though, things were still good. The locals loved us. The Yezidi people adored us. You had to wonder if the subsequent souring of relations with the locals was connected to the escalation in our security. Whether when you cut people's access off to their religious shrines and began to treat them like criminals, they then maybe started to act like criminals?

At least *I* had to wonder this.

On the other hand we were extremely close to the Syrian border. And there was no reason not to think that someone might get the smart idea to attack us. We were a very weakly guarded American location. It would be the easiest thing in the world for someone to take us out. But on a gut level this fortification of our OP struck most of us as simply absurd. The fortification of our site encouraged us to hole up, and it encouraged the locals to minimize their contact with us. We moved dutifully to establish fighting positions that would block potential fire coming at us and keep the enemy from seeing us clearly.

However, we didn't have a lot of materials to make our fighting positions. We had rocks. Lots and lots of rocks. That was it. So our fighting positions involved piling rocks into a kind of enclosure where we might comfortably take cover.

The locals, who built their homes and their walls and everything else by stacking rocks on top of one another, saw us in our little rock-piling project.

They watched us, intrigued.

"No, no. Please. Let us help you."

"This is a military precaution," we explained. "To protect us. From attack."

"Yes. Yes. But please. Let us assist. We know how to do this *better.*"

So we agreed. What else were we going to do? And so the locals built our fighting positions for us.

To help us protect ourselves. From them.

In late July I was lucky enough to be allowed to visit Zoe at her site in Mosul, at 2nd Brigade's BSA (brigade support area), for a few days of R & R. They lived in buildings there, with indoor toilets and running water. There was a pizza place available, and a store with ice cream and other snacks. It was great to get to spend some time with my friend and a few days off work.

While I was there, we learned that Saddam Hussein's two sons—Uday and Qusay—had been killed by Special Forces in Mosul.

The Army moved quickly to establish roadblocks throughout the city. Locals were picked up in sweeps for interrogations on any and all kinds of charges. Maybe they were carrying a pistol—even though in Iraq *every* man carried a weapon almost all the time. Maybe they were carrying more money than a soldier thought they should. Basically any guy we wanted to pick up for questioning was picked up for questioning. Some of the detainees were brought to the BSA and thrown in a pen.

There was a sudden need for anyone fluent in Arabic. So I

was asked: "Will you assist in prescreening?" This was my time off. My first real time off in six months, but I volunteered to do Human Intelligence (HUMINT). Not my job. Not my responsibility. But of course I agreed to help.

I was asked to collect basic file information on people. Name. Date of birth. Occupation. Real straightforward stuff. We knew—and the detainees knew that we knew—that no one there had Intel value. No one had anything to do with Uday or Qusay. Just ordinary locals unlucky to be at the wrong place at the wrong time. They knew they were all going to get released by the end of the night. Which was what happened. Everyone got released.

But the job demanded that we treat everyone the same. That we treat everyone suspiciously—as possibly the one asshole here who *did* support terrorism or whatever. Until we knew who they were, we assumed this guy might be the bad guy. We didn't start from a position of presuming innocence. Quite the opposite. That was the routine, and we followed it.

So this one guy came in, drunk and disorderly.

"What is your name?" I asked in Arabic.

No answer.

"Do you speak English?" I asked again in Arabic.

He shook his head.

A few minutes later he started to curse me in English.

"Why did you lie when you said you spoke no English?" I asked in English.

He shrugged and smiled. He knew exactly what I was saying, and I was getting pissed off.

All the other detainees were moving through the process, answering our questions, and heading back out onto the streets of Mosul. But as the evening went on, this one guy was not going anywhere. Periodically he cursed us out in either Arabic or English, announcing that he had no plans to cooperate with anyone. So it was a question: What were we going to do with him?

"Listen." I attempted a good-cop routine at some point, seeing if it might make this problem go away. "Would you like a cigarette?"

I held a cigarette out to him. I wanted nothing more than to get this guy to cooperate so we could release him. Get him off our hands.

"No, no," he said, drunkenly distressed. "I have my own cigarettes." And he jutted his chin down toward his shirt pocket on his right side. "Just there."

His hands were zip-tied behind his back. He was requesting that I reach into his pockets for him.

I began to get angry again, and he saw this.

"My cigarettes," he said, sneering at me. Goading me. "Mine are *good* cigarettes."

Then I lost it.

"*Fuck* you!" I said. "I'm trying to be nice by offering you a cigarette. But if you don't want my cigarette, you can screw yourself. You won't have any cigarette."

I put my cigarette in my mouth. And I smoked it.

He whined for almost an hour. At some point I felt like whacking his damned skull—anything to make him shut up.

I found myself yelling. I found myself calling this jerk every insulting name I knew. It was just me and this one other soldier, and he was yelling at the guy, too. It was making me even angrier that the guy knew we couldn't touch him—or he was so drunk that he didn't care if we did.

I don't even want to repeat what I said; it sickens me now to think about it.

I grabbed a broom handle and banged it loud on some pipe attached to the wall.

"Rise and fucking shine, you asshole!"

Yet yelling at this guy did also feel perversely good. Because it was not something I was allowed to do. No one does this in our society; we don't just decide we can *scream* at random people who have their hands tied and who have no power to resist.

I don't like to admit it, but I enjoyed having power over this guy.

He was drunk, and at some point all he wanted was to sleep. His energy burned away and there was nothing left. He nodded off.

Sleep deprivation is an accepted and widely used tactic in these situations. Especially in a room where you have complete control over the environment.

I was not going to let this fucking guy fall asleep. He was unhappy about this, and he let us hear about it. But his obvious weariness fueled my pleasure in making him unhappy.

I was uncomfortable with these feelings of pleasure at his discomfort, but I still had them. It did occur to me that I was seeing a part of myself I would never have seen otherwise.

Not a good part.

For months afterward, I think about this episode, minor though it really was. I wonder if my own creepy sense of pleasure at my power over this man had anything to do with being a woman in this situation—the rarity of that enormous power over the fate of another human being. But maybe it has nothing to do with being

female. I've talked to a number of people—both guys and girls—
who did these sorts of interrogations of detainees for months.
People who relished their sense of power. They *loved* doing this
job, though I've come to wonder what it must be like (maybe
especially for a guy) to come back from doing this work for six
months and live again with a wife and a small child. What kind of
readjustment is that? What kind of psychological damage does
this kind of work do? How long does it take to recover from a situation where he gets used to being suspicious of everyone and
where he uses threats and intimidation to get what he wants?
And then comes home to a wife and a three-year-old?

All of us, guys and girls, were in a situation in Iraq where we
were powerless much of the time. Powerless to change what we
did. Powerless to go home. Powerless to make any real decisions
about how we were living our lives while deployed. And then we
found ourselves in this situation where we had all this power over
another person.

And suddenly we could do whatever the fuck we wanted to
them.

Returning to the mountain site after those few days in Mosul, I
get off shift one night in the middle of the night. It's maybe two
in the morning, and I'm not at all sleepy yet. So I head over to
the COLT OP to visit with Matt. I know what times their shifts are
supposed to be running, and I know that Matt comes on shift
right around now. I figure we can hang out until I'm ready to
crash.

It's dark, not pitch black, but really dark. So I have to get in
close before I can see who it is.

"Hey, where's Matt?"

It's Rivers.

"Oh," he smiles. "I didn't wake him up for his shift."

I'm looking around. "That's weird, huh?"

"No problem," he says. "It's no problem."

I'm thinking I'm not going to let Rivers run me off. And being a girl, I'm also not going to be rude and leave. *Okay, 'bye! I wasn't here to see you anyway!*

"Yeah," I say hesitantly. "It's no problem."

So I stand there awkwardly. Rivers and I make small talk.

Things happen fast after that.

It's dark, but not so dark that I can't decipher at some point that Rivers's pants are open. That he's got one hand on his penis. And then suddenly, he's also got one hand on my arm.

He's pulling me pretty firmly toward him, maneuvering my hand toward his crotch.

"What the *fuck*—"

I pull back hard, but Rivers is strong. He's still grabbing my arm, preventing me from leaving.

"*No*," I say. "No, no, no, no, no. Let me go. *Let me the fuck go.*"

"What?" He is genuinely puzzled sounding. "Nobody has to know. We don't have to tell *anybody*."

"Dude," I'm saying as calmly as I can, while still trying to wrest my arm free of him. "I'm *not* interested. I don't want to do this."

And my mind is spinning, seeking some angle that might throw this guy off.

"Dude, what about your girlfriend? Your fiancée? You know, she's a real pretty girl. I mean, shouldn't you be thinking about her?"

"She doesn't matter. And besides, nobody would know."

So I am getting upset. I know I'm tougher now than I was

when I was thirteen, and I do have my *weapon*—but this is *intimidating*. To have this guy physically restraining me. At least on some level, I know I can yell, and Matt would probably wake up. But still . . .

The *shame* of being in a position where you might have to do that. Yell for help. Like some damn damsel in distress. Knowing that you would have to explain what just happened here.

But eventually Rivers drops his grip on my arm. He lets me go.

I leave and head back to my vehicle.

I go to sleep that night, thinking: I am going to have to report this.

The next morning I'm writing in my journal about the incident with Rivers when he appears.

"Listen, Kayla," he says, all sheepish. Looking anywhere but at me. "I apologize. I was totally out of line back there. I hope there are no hard feelings. It was dumb, and it was wrong. So I hope you can, you know, accept my apology on this."

And just like that, he's gone again.

This throws me even more. I have all this righteous anger built up. And—*wham!* An apology? It feels like cheating. Like: This guy steps *way* over the line, and now he gets to be able to have it all just go away. Because now he's *sorry?*

But I'm thinking: He did apologize. Maybe he understood. Maybe he gets it. So I do not bring up the Rivers incident with anyone right away.

For one thing I have to assume that if it comes right down to it, the guys would all back him. As somebody on their team, in their unit, in their MOS.

One of the boys.

If I am to force this issue—if I am to ask them to be loyal to Rivers or be loyal to me—what might happen? I have to imagine which way that would go. This sucks.

As much as the Army would like to tell us that it's not true, girls who file EO (equal opportunity) complaints are treated badly. Even if your chain of command encourages females to file sexual harassment claims—to stand up about these kinds of incidents—in reality, they are discouraged. Technically, if you read the EO regulations, you can file an EO complaint in the Army if you are offended by just about anything. Like somebody telling a dirty joke. If it offends you, you can file a complaint about it.

Needless to say guys do not like girls who file EO complaints. They will talk shit about them. They will not want to be around them more than is absolutely necessary.

Even *girls* don't like girls who file EO complaints—they don't want to rock the boat. Girls don't want to be perceived as filing a frivolous complaint. There's still the assumption that girls lie about harassment to get what they want—to advance their careers or to punish somebody they dislike.

So it's very risky. You don't want to be perceived as overreacting.

But what Rivers did was not like telling a dirty joke. I can and will put up with a lot. I *do* put up with a lot. I am very understanding about a lot of male behavior. I know these guys are under tremendous pressure. They are in a rough environment. They are away from their lover, their family, and everything they know—for a long time. So am I, and I know it isn't easy on any of us. And I don't want to pursue an investigation and risk ruining someone's career under these circumstances. Plus, to be honest, I am afraid that if I do file a complaint, Rivers would tell on me for drinking alcohol. Turn it around. Get me in trouble if I get him in trouble.

You hear all kinds of stories. I hear this one story about some girls in the Navy who came forward about being raped. Then *they* got into trouble because they were drinking when it happened. And they were underage. And so they're the ones who ended up getting punished. Though this only came out because they had come forward about being sexually assaulted. Which is the bigger crime? But that's what happened.

But the more I think about what Rivers did, the more it bothers me.

I finally speak to Staff Sergeant Kelly.

"Look. If something happens with one of the guys in your unit that I think is really inappropriate, do you think I should tell one of you about it? Like you or Sergeant First Class Jakubiak?"

"Yes," Kelly says. He doesn't push me to explain. "You should definitely talk to someone about it."

At this point I still have no idea how this would be handled. I have no idea whether this is something their unit is going to take seriously. But I do soon afterward speak with SFC Jakubiak and explain what happened. I ask that none of this be considered a formal complaint. There is an entire system in the Army set up to file formal complaints. There are military personnel whose job is to handle complaints like this. But I do not want to ruin this guy's career over what I imagine may be an isolated incident in his life.

So I leave the matter for his unit to handle internally. To talk to him or deal with him as they see fit, but for me not to go on record.

And Rivers is pulled off the mountain sometime after this.

Reassigned. I do not know whether there is any connection to what I said or not.

So I feel somewhat good about this, but also not so good at the same time. When you decide to allow people to handle things informally, you never know the result. You don't see somebody get demoted. You don't know if someone yells at him. You don't know if he gets talked to. You don't know if anything is done at all. That's what you give up when you decide to trust somebody else to handle things informally.

The story didn't end there, however. Not exactly.

At a later point, possibly a month after Rivers was reassigned, some other fire support guy I'd never met before came up to the mountain for a brief period of time. He was filling a slot while someone else in the unit was on leave. This guy let me know pretty fast that he was friends with Rivers.

Soon enough he found me so we could have a little chat.

"Hey," he said, all fake smiles. "Let me ask you about something."

And I was thinking, This is about Travis or something like that. His bad night. The breakdown and so forth. I don't know why this is what I thought, but I did.

"No, that's not going to happen," I said. "I don't want to talk about it."

"Come on, now. Don't be shy."

"Look. I don't know you. And I don't really want to talk about anything with you."

But he hounded me a little.

"No," he said. "I *really* have to ask you this."

So I stopped and turned back to listen.

"What?"

He just launched in.

"Rivers tells me that you came over here in the middle of the night one night. He says you said: 'Oh, please let me suck your dick. I want to suck your dick so bad.' And that he said: 'Oh, no. I have a girlfriend, and I love her so much.' And that you said: 'Oh, that's so sad 'cause I want to suck your dick so bad.' And he said: 'No, no. We can't.' And that you were *very* disappointed. *Very* upset."

I wanted to kill the motherfucker for talking shit about me like this. I wanted to kill him because I let him off without a complaint.

It felt like such a betrayal. It makes no sense, I know, but I felt like the COLT guys let me down. Like somehow they were *all* responsible. I had trouble dealing with them for a long while after that.

Everything shifted sometime that August, like water once simmering coming to a boil. You could feel the heat in everyone's mood. We were not in this together any longer. Nasty down the mountain, the insurgency gathered strength day by day. Ugly up here, too.

Like the day some of the guys—tossing a football—told rape jokes. (Are there any jokes about rape that are funny?) My blood—how else to put this?—"froze."

I collapsed. Went into a downward spin. Out of control. Felt the bottom and pushed past it.

After Rivers's friend confronted me, and I withdrew from the COLT guys, things got a little freaky for me. I began to lose it.

I began to experience intrusive images. They were like snapshots. Sudden and disturbing shots of Baghdad on patrol in the spring with Delta Company. The man in pain, bleeding to death in front of me. Or sometimes they were movie clips. A short film in which I watched myself watch him die. And I'm helpless to save him. Utterly powerless to make a difference here. I watch the flies hover. The blood on his legs. The medic. Me running. Attempting to calm the crowd. Like I said, these could be short films, but mainly they were snapshots. A lot of intrusive snapshots.

They happened day or night. And they became difficult for me. I didn't know what it meant. And it was doubly hard because I don't usually have visual memories. My usual memories are stories or words. Not pictures. So these images hit me harder than they might have otherwise. I couldn't make them go away. They didn't come when I was sleeping. When I slept I didn't dream. It was during my waking life that these images intruded.

Did the Rivers incident set this off? Or Rivers's friend? Or that we finally learned that our deployment was going to last a full year? (They kept announcing extensions to our tour—June, then July, then September, until they finally told us it would be March; by that point the news was anticlimactic.)

What was it? Was it my weight loss? I was no longer losing weight, but I was not gaining it back, either. Even with the help of all the Yezidi vegetables, I'd only been able to stabilize my weight.

Was it the guys?

One afternoon Matt approached me.

"What's the deal with you, Williams? You always want to be the center of attention." He was not joking with me now. He was angry. "And by the way, I think you're a whore."

Flipped out on me out of nowhere. And I decided I couldn't

be friends with him because he sulked and pouted and acted hateful because I wouldn't fuck him.

Later that same day Matt apologized.

"About earlier? I'm really sorry about that. I didn't mean it. That was totally wrong of me. I know you're really sensitive about that."

And later still, soon after Matt got moved down from the mountain, he had his own breakdown. Lost it and got really bad. Let himself go. Quit cutting his hair and got all twitchy; talked about how he'd been beating locals at checkpoints. Lost it so bad people got worried enough to think about command referring him for mental health.

But the guys losing it made some kind of sense. Take Matt or Travis. Both of them enlisted at eighteen right out of high school. After their AIT, they went to Korea for a year. Then back to Fort Campbell for a month, and then to Afghanistan for another six months. Then back to the States for six months— interrupted by a one-month rotation at JRTC (joint readiness training center)—and then Iraq for another year. At some point we calculated that both of them had been in the Army for thirty-seven months—Matt was still only twenty-one—and in that time they'd been away from home for thirty-two months. That's intense pressure for anyone to handle.

Me? What's my excuse? I watched some guy die once. Still felt guilt about it. Like I contributed to his death.

And now the guys I considered my friends were treating me like a *girl*. I was tits, a piece of ass, a bitch or a slut or whatever, but never really a *person*.

Bros before hos.

My appetite vanished despite the weight loss. I cried every

day, and felt like I couldn't handle it anymore. The shit was too overwhelming. Everything was. No one asked or cared—or even *noticed*—what the fuck I felt. I withdrew even more. Felt increasingly lethargic. Didn't want to go for hikes. Just wanted to lie down. Read. Sleep. And I felt this powerful desire to be even thinner and thinner. Until I could simply slip away. Disappear.

Eat less and less and less . . .

It was around this time that I contemplated offing myself. It could all be over in a moment. It would be too easy.

UNCEREMONIOUS

FINALLY BACK FROM pulling mission in the mountains, I am feeling useless. That's when there's an awards ceremony at Tal Afar. What's the point of an awards ceremony? It's almost as ridiculous as the mandatory safety briefs we undergo: Is it really important to learn over and over again the hazards of handling fuel? And what good are suicide-prevention courses?

Here we are in Iraq getting pulled from mission every three months to receive a suicide-prevention brief.

"Suicide is a widespread and common problem," the instructor will say. "It is not a sign of weakness. It does not mean that you are a bad person if you are having suicidal thoughts. Sometimes it's a desperate cry for help. Sometimes it's a chemical problem. Sometimes you may notice somebody you know who has been very depressed suddenly get better. But you should remain concerned because that's often when people *do* commit suicide. So it is very important for us to review with you today the warning signs of suicide.

"What are some of the things that you should be looking for and if you see them are potential warning signs for suicide? What are some of the triggers that might lead somebody to consider suicide? Let's review these. Anyone?"

We suck it up, and people start reciting the answers by rote:

"Somebody who starts to give away their possessions."

"Somebody who starts talking about things being over for them."

"Somebody who starts talking about how they can't see any other solution."

"Somebody who talks about having significant family problems."

"Somebody who talks about having serious financial problems."

"Somebody who has just been in trouble or punished by his chain of command."

We watch Army videos during these suicide-prevention briefs.

The videos depict soldiers acting out the warning signs for suicide.

"My father and mother are breaking up. Divorcing. And I can't handle it. I can't stand that there's nothing I can do. I'm feeling so helpless." And so on.

A title tells us that this actor/soldier subsequently kills himself.

Another actor/soldier appears on the screen.

"I never saw it coming. I never imagined that John was so depressed."

An authoritative voice-over cuts in.

"But he should have seen it coming! Notice how John gave away his stereo! And he was clearly collecting pills! He no longer socialized with friends! Friends who should have taken preventive steps to save John—before it was too late!"

Video over, the instructor flips on the lights.

KAYLA WILLIAMS

"If you suspect that someone you know is suicidal, you need to immediately report that person to your chain of command or the chaplain or a mental health personnel. You need to be more concerned about saving their life than saving their pride. You must address this problem. Every one of us must be aware. Everybody must pay attention. It's a tremendous problem."

Easy to say. Harder to do. There is a huge stigma in the military about this topic. We are supposed to be tough. We are supposed to be strong. We are never supposed to exhibit weakness. And suicide is definitely seen as taking the easy way out. It is definitely perceived as a weak response to a difficult situation. (I learned much later that the suicide rate for American soldiers in Iraq in 2003 was unusually high—close to double the Army's rate of 11.1 for each one hundred thousand soldiers in 2002.)

We also receive other quarterly safety briefs. For instance there's the brief on proper methods for handling fuel. (We must wear gloves. We should wear goggles. Be sure to wear the correct safety equipment. And so forth.) And the safe way to handle a generator. There's also the position on sexual harassment or POSH, which we also review on the same days as the safety briefs. We review the two general types of sexual harassment. These are "quid pro quo" and "hostile work environment."

"What does 'quid pro quo' mean? What are the various types of sexual harassment? There's verbal and nonverbal harassment. There's physical harassment. There's threatening somebody with punishment if they don't do what you want sexually. There's rewarding somebody if they do what you want sexually. You have to be really careful and consider everyone's feelings no matter what you're doing. Even putting up posters of girls might offend somebody. If I tell you a dirty joke, and there's somebody sitting over there, and they get offended, I'm wrong for telling that joke."

We also review the reasonable person clause. This means that for something to be sexual harassment, it must be something a reasonable person would consider inappropriate behavior. (None of us ever have any idea who this reasonable person is.)

We review equal opportunity training. ("What is racism? What is sexism? What is racial prejudice? What do these things mean? And how do you see them in your daily lives?") It gets a little bizarre. Imagine a roomful of mainly eighteen- to twenty-two-year-old boys responding to these questions.

"Could someone please give me an example of verbal sexual harassment?"

The instructor is fucking asking for it.

Of course the guys immediately start yelling things out.

My own position is that if there were *real* concern for our safety, they'd get us the hell out of this combat zone. *That* would promote safety. But the Army doesn't think that way. If it thinks at all.

I respected and understood the need for safety briefs. But at some slightly later time, the Army also began to institute various "ethnic themes" for our chow halls in Iraq. For instance, there were displays about Hispanic heritage and African American heritage, and on those days we ate foods from those minority backgrounds: collard greens or fried chicken for African American heritage and fajitas or burritos for Mexican American heritage. Basically, I respected and understood the rationale for these gestures as well. But it also convinced me it was absolutely time for us to go home.

I'm sorry, and I don't mean to sound rude, but if the Army could take time out in Iraq to serve up fried rice to celebrate

Asian American heritage, then it was definitely time for them to send my ass home.

The awards ceremony should have been a thrill. Standing in formation listening to a little speech from our battalion commander about our contribution to the war effort. Getting a medal pinned on. Photographs. Applause. An ARCOM (Army commendation medal) for my service. It should have been great. It should have been exciting.

But it wasn't. I felt pissed off.

My promotion was still fucked up, and it didn't appear that anyone was working to resolve the issue.

And we all noticed in the ceremony that everyone who was a staff sergeant or above was getting a higher honor, the Bronze Star, no matter what they had done. This medal was supposed to be a big deal, but it was looking more political. Some squad leaders put their soldiers in for this medal, while mine did not. Staff Sergeant Moss put me in for the same ARCOM as Lauren, even though Lauren never went out on combat patrol. Meanwhile, people I knew who were never in harm's way—and never led any soldiers—were getting a Bronze Star. It was insulting.

At the same time I am very hesitant to mention this at all because I do not believe that I deserved the honor of a Bronze Star. But neither did I believe that these people deserved it. Awards carelessly given lose their meaning.

To make matters worse, the only two people of my rank who did get Bronze Stars were getting them for doing the identical work I did in Baghdad—going out with the infantry. And they had bulletproof plates in their flak vests.

I mentioned this casually to my new platoon leader, now that

LT Malley had moved up to XO. She told me that those two guys "went above and beyond the linguist job."

Again my head filled with images of a bloodied and screaming man. But I said nothing. She wasn't with us in Baghdad. She had no idea what I did or saw.

Still, the insult of her careless words rankled, and my frustration deepened.

Later that same day, after the ceremony, I cornered our platoon sergeant.

"Look," I said, "it's not about the damn medal. I don't care about the medal."

"You seem upset," he said.

"Upset? If what I did wasn't 'above and beyond,' why should I be receiving an ARCOM? Why should I be receiving anything at all? In fact, you can have the medal. I don't want the ARCOM. And my promotion—I don't want that either. You can shove them both—"

"Calm down," he said. But I'd gotten his attention. "What's going on?"

He was one of those men who didn't notice a complaint until you threw a fit. Then he took notice. But it felt awful that I had to have a temper tantrum to get his attention. I explained the whole situation.

"Listen, we're working on your promotion. I'll see what I can do."

Whatever. (For the record, more than a year later, it still had not been resolved.)

I didn't know Specialist Berenger from a hole in the ground. Never knew her at DLI, where she studied Arabic, too. We were there at different times. Never knew her in-country, either—she had only just arrived about three weeks before. This civilian linguist came to me to ask me a question.

"You know Specialist Berenger?" he asked.

"Can't say that I do."

"She's having some family problems."

"Yeah," I said, chuckling. "Who hasn't? Where I come from, having family problems is the universal sign for human."

"No. I mean, yeah," he stuttered. "Sure." He cleared his throat. "I'm just saying if you find a moment, maybe you could speak to her. Draw her out. Talk to her a little. Find out what's wrong, maybe."

I never asked him why he was asking *me*. Did I look like a camp counselor for troubled teens? I didn't agree to do it. I didn't disagree. To be honest, I didn't think about it one way or the other.

Until I saw her, that is. In the tent. As it happened, we were alone for the moment.

She was not as young as I expected. Or as crazy. In fact, I couldn't for the life of me figure out what the civilian linguist was all worked up about. Was she depressed? Who wasn't? Seemed to me a rational response to an irrational situation.

But she was fidgety. I hate it when girls twirl their hair in their fingers, round and round. Nervous habits make *me* nervous.

I introduced myself. She introduced herself.

We engaged in small talk. She was HUMINT. I'm SIGINT (Signal Intelligence). But we'd had some of the same teachers back in Monterey, and we talked about them for a few minutes. She was a little shy, maybe. A little reserved. But I was thinking about what the civilian linguist said, and so I pursued it.

"My family," I said more or less out of nowhere. "My family is nuts. Just nuts. My mom thinks I'm on vacation here. Sometimes I'm not sure she understands that this is a war. She writes me and asks whether I'm going to get a chance to see the Pyramids. I'm like: Mom, the Pyramids are in Egypt. I'm in Iraq. You know— land of the evil dictator. Weapons of mass destruction. Iraq. I-R-A-Q. *Iraq*. Remember? And she writes me back hoping I'll be safe, and asking me how's the food. Am I eating okay and should she send chocolates. Chocolates? Can you believe it?"

Berenger fiddled with her hair.

"My folks don't know I'm here."

I stopped at that.

"How can that be?" I asked.

"I never told them I deployed. I never told them because I wasn't sure they wanted to know." She paused. "We don't talk too often."

"Damn," I said. "That's rough. Maybe you could send them a note. An e-mail. Put yourselves back in touch. That might be a good thing." Pause. "Under the circumstances and all."

'Yeah," she said, not sounding too convinced. "It's not a good situation, you know?"

"Sure." But I had no idea what she meant. And I didn't know if I should be asking, either.

"Listen," I said. "Families are tough. But they're family. I mean, you might want to let your folks know what's up. That you're here."

Berenger looked at me a moment.

"You know what you said about your mom? That's so incredible, you know? Because I never would have guessed it."

"Why's that?"

"Because you seem so totally together. I wouldn't imagine you had problems."

I looked at her real close for any indication Berenger was mocking me. But no. Not a shred of that. She meant it. Now that's *scary*.

"Yeah," I said. "Sure. But sometimes things aren't exactly what they seem. You know?"

She smiled a sad smile.

"Roger that," she said, noncommittal.

Right then some guys noisily descended on the tent, throwing things onto their cots, acting all loud and disruptive.

"Hey," I said to Berenger. "I go out on mission again tomorrow, but when I get back—"

"Sure, me too," she said. "I head out soon also."

"Let's talk again. I mean, *anytime*. Maybe get some chow together. How's that sound?"

"Sure. That would be good."

It was awkward, but it felt okay. It felt fine. I rummaged through my brain and thought back to the guy who said *talk to her*. Okay, done. And if she wanted more, I'd announced that I could be there for her. What more could I do?

That was it, I guess.

Four days later Berenger was dead. Suicide. A single self-inflicted gunshot wound to the head. That's all it took. I don't know more than that, a suicide not being the sort of thing people wanted to discuss in detail. (This was still more than her family ever learned about the circumstances surrounding her death. When the Army informed Berenger's parents that their daughter was dead, they never asked how it happened. They never asked how she died. And so the Army never told them.)

I did not see this coming. And I wondered: What the fuck is wrong with this place? And thought: What's my problem that I did not see this coming? Should I have done more?

However, that's not the part of the story that gets me every time I think about it now.

So Berenger's dead. And the company organizes a memorial service.

No, let me rephrase that. The company *orders* all soldiers to attend a memorial service.

Actually, let me rephrase that one more time. We are told we have a choice. Attend the memorial service for Berenger or explain to the battalion commander why we don't want to go. No one really wants to attend the memorial service—we didn't really know her and it is depressingly morbid. But we do it. Typical Army. A choice that's no choice at all.

Basically, though we can't say it, we're pissed at Berenger. What gives her the right to do what she did? She's here less than a month—and *pow*. She offs herself. We've been here—most of us—six months or more. Suffered and felt so damned awful for days and weeks at a time, of course we may have considered it. But we didn't do it. And here she comes in, and she gets a little down—and pulls the trigger. And that's the end of that. Why the hell is she getting *recognition* for this? There's a war on. Don't we have anything better to do than memorialize a girl who couldn't take it?

But we do it. We attend. Sitting on folding chairs under the blazing sun in the dust.

A chaplain speaks.

Her platoon sergeant speaks. The first sergeant speaks. The commander speaks.

A girl reads a Bible quote.

By the time our battalion commander stands to speak, this is getting old real fast. It's hot, and we're tired of sitting in the sun listening to a lot of blah-blah-blah about some poor girl no one really knew.

Of course, I'm feeling responsible. Guilty. Berenger saying that I seemed so together should have been my cue. I should have done more. I should have noticed something. Why else put us through all these suicide-prevention briefs? What's the point? I should have forced a conversation. I should have asked a question or two more. Gotten her talking about her shit. Talked to the chain of command or something.

So the BC gets up to speak.

"Specialist Berenger was a good soldier, a good person, and a good friend. She will be missed. We take these moments today to honor her and to mourn her. We recognize the sacrifice she made and the pain she must have felt. We take this time today . . ."

I'm blanking by this point. Wondering when I'll get back out on mission and away from this bullshit. From this place where words matter more than actions. But then the BC cuts off and begins again.

"I would also like to say a few more personal words about what has happened here."

She pauses, and I'm thinking *okay, here we go.* This BC lacks *tact,* this I know from experience. (Like when Lauren returns to Fort Campbell, her husband still grievously ill, the BC blurts out, "Oh, is your husband dead?" That sort of thing.) A good-enough soldier, a decent leader (for the most part). But like I said, she is seriously deficient in tact.

She says: "When I first heard about Specialist Berenger's

death, I was shocked and saddened. But as time passed, I felt another emotion. I was angry. I'm angry at Berenger. She caused this because she never reached out for help. She never went to her chain of command, never went to the chaplain. This is her fault. It should not have come to this."

The memorial service is over. We are stunned. Our disgust at Berenger's action pushed aside by our disgust at our BC. Of course I understood the BC's point. I just think a memorial service is the wrong damn time to say it. It's something you put out to your commanders so they can disseminate it down. If you have a friend that dies of HIV, you may say to other people you know and care about that this should remind everyone to use condoms. But you don't get up at her fucking memorial service and say: "Oh, she brought this on herself by not using condoms." It's tacky. And heartless.

A few days after this, I was working on my Humvee. Checking it and getting it ready to go out again on mission. I was under the hood when I heard a Humvee stop suddenly.

"Specialist Williams!"

I looked up. It was a couple of the guys from Delta Company 1/187, the guys I went with on missions in Baghdad. The man in the passenger seat jumped out and rushed over.

"This is not the proper way to do this. I know that."

I wiped engine grease from my hands. Feeling distracted and sweaty, but glad nonetheless to see these guys.

"The proper way to do what?" I asked.

"We've been looking for you everywhere. In Baghdad. In the mountains. But you're a tough one to catch."

"They keep me busy."

"Yeah, I see that. Listen," their first sergeant said. "I know this is not the proper way to do it. But we wanted you to have this." He held out a recognizable green folder, the kind that holds Army awards. "In recognition of your work with us back in the spring. For service above and beyond. You really deserve it."

It was an Army commendation medal. Just like the one I received from my own unit. But completely different. This one *counted*. It was from the infantry, and they almost never recognize support elements.

I was so touched, felt so proud.

"Thanks—"

"Listen, we're on our way out on mission. Gotta go."

I stood there, grease on my face, feeling better than I had in months.

"Good job, Specialist," he said. And they were gone in a cloud of dust.

LOCKED AND LOADED

WE HEAR ALL the time there's this expectation that as soldiers we should be willing to make sacrifices for our jobs. Put mission first. Even if this means putting the mission above our own personal well-being. But that's what we do. It's what most of us believe we should do.

I could have been medevaced (medically evacuated) to Germany for the foot surgery I needed. I told the doctors that if I did this, I wanted a guarantee I would be sent back to Iraq to finish my tour. But I was told that if I went to Germany, in fact, they would fly me back to the States for surgery. More than likely this would have meant I would not return to Iraq. So I again postponed my surgery, believing that whenever I decided to have it, my tour would end. I'd get sent home. And I was not comfortable with this.

My friends thought I was nuts. People were *trying* to get out. To go home. *I* wanted to go home.

There are certainly lots of ways to fake it. Say you're a homosexual, for instance. That would work—but it's more likely to work if you're a guy because there's a double standard. On paper the rules on homosexuals in the military are written the same.

But in reality most men in the Army—like most men in U.S. society—think that girl-on-girl action is hot, while dudes getting it on is filthy and disgusting. Army guys generally think lesbians rock, since clearly these are chicks just waiting for the right man to come along. What would my first sergeant do if he came across me and another girl getting it on? He'd want pictures. He'd want to join in. He'd want me and this other girl to double-team him right then and there. On the other hand, since most heterosexual men are homophobic and sexist, most straight guys figure gay men will treat them the way they themselves treat women—that is, like sex objects. And this freaks them the fuck out.

What this all means in practical terms is that females are less likely to be chaptered out (that is, forced out) of the Army for being gay than are guys. That's just the way it is.

In any case I had no desire to fake anything. Lauren and I had joked about it all the time while she was still there—we'd finish their war, but when we were done, we'd take some crazy photos and get out. But it was only a joke—in reality, we were both very dedicated. So I fought to stay in Iraq. Morally I believed that staying was the right thing to do.

What was my argument? For one thing, we simply never had enough Arabic linguists in-country as it was. We were constantly low on experienced personnel. We'd already lost a lot of people whose ETS (end term of service—that is, the date they were due to leave the service) had passed after the Army's stop-loss kept them in an entire extra year. When that final stop-loss date approached, the Army had to send them home so that they would get out on time. So these people were all leaving. Also, people could now have a PCS (permanent change of station)—that is, move to another duty station. So we were losing people to

ETS and PCS, and a few random people for other reasons—medical issues, family emergencies, pregnancies, whatever.

I felt strongly that it would be wrong for me to leave. There were people getting killed and people getting seriously injured—people with *real* problems. I didn't feel comfortable getting out of my commitment for what was a relatively minor concern. I would have to be a real jackass to leave my mission because of my foot. I also had developed a deep commitment to my fellow soldiers. My brothers in arms, or whatever cheesy way you want to say it. But it was really true. I wanted to be there for the people I'd served with this whole time.

So instead of surgery, I got the cortisone shots to deal with the pain. It was actually easier to get the shots in Iraq than it had been in America. In the States it was tough to get an appointment. The waiting period could take weeks. In Iraq I headed down to any aid station, explained what was going on, and they gave me a shot right away. It was great, except I ended up getting seven or eight cortisone shots in eight months. Doctors don't recommend more than three shots in a year. But I had to do this just so I could get by.

Finally, however, in late October, I was able to find a doctor who was willing to do the surgery in-country. So I had the surgery. In a tent at D-Rear in Mosul.

This was right around Halloween. As I came out of general anesthetic, I saw cardboard witches and goblins hanging and floating around on strings in the tent. It was a little weird.

Afterward I found out I was going to have problems with my foot for the rest of my life.

Not because of the surgery. The surgery was perfect. It was all the cortisone shots. They'd caused a permanent degradation of the fatty tissue on the ball of my foot. The two toes next to my big toe were going to be numb forever. It was a small thing, I guess, but I would never wear high heels again.

I could deal with it. What was tough was that I was not getting support from the people at D-Rear. Everyone watched me hobble around on crutches, but no one offered to help me. They were total pricks about it. No one even brought me food or water.

So I called my unit at the airfield and asked them to pick me up and bring me back to the airfield. This meant I would travel on a convoy while I was all drugged up in the back of a Humvee over a particular stretch of road where several convoys had been ambushed. I would not have my weapon. I couldn't carry a weapon while I was on narcotics. I would not be able to respond if anything happened. I would not be able to jump and run on crutches. This was all very intimidating, but once we were on the road, the drugs knocked me out. I ended up asleep in the back like a baby for a lot of the trip.

It took close to three weeks before I could handle work again.

Ambush Alley was at the edge of Mosul, right inside the city's gates. On one side of the road there was a group of buildings; on the other side there was a cemetery. As convoys moved through, they got attacked. I don't know why ambushes occurred at this location and not some other location. But they did. Not every ambush resulted in a death. But many resulted in injuries, and sometimes the injuries were serious.

A couple of weeks earlier, a convoy traveling from Mosul to the Tal Afar airfield was hit. It was a coordinated attack—there were one or two rocket-propelled grenades plus small-arms fire and an IED (improvised explosive device) all at once. The bomb in the road involved a propane tank, so there was a lot of fire. A lot of the people who got hurt got hurt with burns. I knew two of the soldiers who were hurt. One was Staff Sergeant Lott from my unit. He received burns and minor cuts—luckily, his injuries were minor enough that he was RTD (return to duty). So he got treated and was released back to us, not medevaced or hospitalized. He earned his Purple Heart all the same (anyone injured by enemy action gets one).

Lott's equipment came back to us, and there was blood on his gear. I helped First Sergeant Duggan, an absolutely amazing leader, wash everything. One of Lott's weapons magazines had been destroyed by shrapnel. We took apart his LBV (load-bearing vest) one clip at a time, so the vest could be washed. We kept the twisted magazine for Lott—as a sort of souvenir.

Staff Sergeant Shane Kelly was the second guy injured. The platoon sergeant for the COLT platoon in the mountains. A guy I was thinking I liked, though we didn't really say much about it before he left for mid-tour leave. Two weeks home. Visiting family. Seeing his daughter. And here he had just flown back into the airport in Mosul where he caught the first convoy back to Tal Afar. Ridiculous timing. Kelly was back in the country for a matter of hours when his convoy got hit. And he was *very* seriously injured. Took shrapnel in the head. Got flown out of the country immediately. To Germany—where they didn't even know if he would survive. He flatlined four times. If this had happened in any previous war, there is no question he would have died. I learned later that soldiers in this war survived at a rate nine times higher than in any prior combat, due to individual body armor— the Kevlar and the flak vest that protected the core organs. And because more of us had been trained in Combat LifeSaver so we could do better, more immediate first aid. And also due to better battlefield technology and rapid medical evacuation.

When the ambushed convoy reached the base, I learned right away that Kelly had been hurt. Only sometime later did I learn how very badly he'd been hurt. And only sometime after that did I learn that he was going to make it. That he was going to be more or less okay.

While traveling among the locals, we always kept our rifles on safe, but whether or not they were locked and loaded could vary by convoy.

Every magazine holds thirty rounds. Thirty bullets. You put the magazine into the magazine well in the bottom of the weapon. However, at that point, the rifle is not ready to fire for two reasons. The first is that the safety is still on. But the second reason is that you don't actually have a round in the chamber. And there are two ways to address this. The first way is to lock the bolt to the rear of the weapon, load the magazine, and then let the bolt ride forward. It will then chamber a round automatically. If the bolt is in the forward position when you load the weapon, you pull the charging handle back, release it, and the bolt picks up a round and chambers the round. Our weapons must have a round in the chamber for them to fire. Different weapons operate in different ways, but our weapons—once you have a round chambered and you fire for the first time—will automatically chamber a second round. And so forth. Therefore you don't actually have to go through this process and chamber each individual round every single time you fire. But you *must* have a round in the chamber to fire that first time.

In Iraq we have three degrees of weapon status: red, yellow, and green. Green means you do not have a round chambered and you do not have your magazine in your magazine well. You do not have a magazine in the weapon at all. The weapon is completely safe. Yellow means you have a magazine in the magazine well, but you do not have a round chambered. Before you can fire the weapon the first time, you would need to chamber a round. And red means you have a round chambered. Depending on the danger of the situation, we were instructed either to keep our weapons at red, yellow, or green.

With the weapon status on red, once you have that round chambered, all you have to do is flip the switch from safe to semi and pull the trigger. Flip, squeeze. It can be extremely fast. It would take you less than a second to start firing. Whereas, if you do not have a round chambered, it would take several more seconds. You are going to have to think about the process harder, and you are not going to be as responsive.

The only time you would have your weapon on green in Iraq would be while you are at a completely secure location. So once we arrive at the Tal Afar airfield or at D-Main or D-Rear, every vehicle in the convoy stops, we get out, drop our magazines, and clear our weapons. We have to aim them at the ground and fire to verify that they're cleared. If there's a click, that's that. The weapon is proved safe. But if someone fires and it discharges accidentally at this point, that person gets in a *lot* of trouble. (An accidental discharge happens a lot more often than you might imagine.)

During actual combat operations in the spring, we are consistently at red. But after combat officially ends, sometime in May or June, and once we move into SASO (sustainment and stability operations), we move to yellow almost all the time while on convoys.

SASO is supposed to be *peacekeeping*. As part of stability and support, you are supposed to be helping people out. Keeping the peace and maintaining order. It's understood that soldiers are going to die during combat; they are *not* supposed to die during SASO. But, as we all know, there have been many more deaths during SASO in Iraq than during actual combat.

So now, by the fall of 2003, as the situation gets worse and worse, we are instructed to place our weapons back to red during convoys.

It's also around this time that we receive new instructions on the ROE (rules of engagement). Actually they have been changing constantly, and it can be difficult to keep up. Like a lot of soldiers, I carry a copy of the ROE card in my Kevlar—though I'm sure it's outdated. The threat level is now high enough, we're told, for yet another escalation. So our instructions on one particular convoy are:

"If you see a guy on the side of the road on a cell phone, point your weapon at him. And if he won't get off the phone, *you can shoot him.* He might be calling in your location to somebody else. So if you think that he is on the phone passing information about your convoy and where it's going, and you feel he's a threat, you are authorized to shoot him."

I cannot believe we're told this. I think it's insane. It's crossing a line to shoot somebody just because he's on the phone. Can you imagine a foreign power coming to the United States and deciding to drive around and shoot your neighbor because he's on his cell phone? Maybe he's out there talking because he can't get a good signal in his house.

I read in *The Zanzibar Chest,* a great book by journalist Aidan

Hartley, how United Nations peacekeeping soldiers in Rwanda and Somalia always had a gun in one hand. And a spoon in the other. Increasingly I feel the U.S. Army is finding itself in a comparable situation in Iraq.

We're here to help you! We're here to help you! Oh, and shoot you— if we feel it's necessary.

It's a terrible position for any soldier on the ground to be in. I don't know if it's a fair position, either, because you are never going to build relationships with the civilian population, or win hearts and minds, when you treat everybody as a threat. It's almost impossible to walk that line.

How to explain this dilemma? If you see someone heading toward you, he could be approaching to offer you information. He could have an explosive device strapped to his waist and be about to kill you. He might want to ask for food. You have to make that call—instantaneously. You have to decide whether or not you will allow this man anywhere near you. You have to decide whether you shoot him where he stands. Or whether you attempt to communicate with him from a distance and tell him to stop. Every car you see driving past you, you have to judge whether or not this could be an attempt to kill you. Or will the driver or passenger wave or completely ignore you? You have to make that judgment call. Every single time. Every time you see any person anywhere close to you.

In truth, every incident that happens is a completely discrete incident, but it's almost impossible to live this way. Basically we all reach a point where we have to assume that everyone is friendly (and respond accordingly), or assume that everyone is a potential enemy (and treat them as such). It simply becomes too overwhelming to play that line at every single moment. To look at each person and make that choice over and over and over again. To ask yourself: Will I give this person food? Or will I point my gun at this person? So we make one choice: We come to assume the worst about everyone. And we stick with it.

Speak to infantry soldiers who have been in tough situations for a long time, and they will say that they treat *everyone* as the enemy. That's how they deal. That's how they survive.

I consider myself a reasonably compassionate person. I speak the language, and I have Arab friends, so I believe I'm better equipped than most soldiers to see these civilians as people. Not simply as *the enemy.* But even for me there are times I am feeling overwhelmed by the situation. God, why can't we just kill everyone—or leave them to fucking kill each other? Because I cannot care any more. I cannot walk this line all the time. It's too hard. I get too angry.

Increasingly many of us are just feeling angry all the time. When we think about the local population now, we're thinking: What are you people doing? We're here to help you! And you're trying to kill us! Are you insane? Do you even *want* peace? Or freedom? Or democracy? Do you want anything? Or do you just want to kill all the time? What's wrong with you?

What is wrong with these people?

For anyone who has anything to do at either D-Main or D-Rear, the convoy leaves the airfield once a day. And then returns to the airfield sometime later that same day. Back and forth, back and forth. Commanders go to meetings. We pick up mail and supplies. People leave for R & R or mid-tour leave. The number of vehicles on any given convoy can vary dramatically. From seven to thirty or more, depending on the day.

On one particular morning I'm on a brigade convoy heading from Tal Afar to Mosul. And the local vehicles traveling with us are moving especially slowly for some reason. We routinely hire local trucks and buses to transport equipment, supplies, or people. And on this day there are quite a number of *hajji* trucks with our convoy. The *hajji* trucks are elaborately painted in colorful patterns, all tricked out with fringes on the windshields and Mercedes symbols on the front. But they are seldom in great shape. So whenever a vehicle breaks down, we have to stop and wait.

The weather is terrible. It's dark and raining, and there's a cold sharp wind that cuts through our uniforms, making everyone miserable.

So our convoy is creeping along through a section of Mosul on this awful day. And I realize that we are approaching Ambush Alley. The same section of Mosul and the same stretch of road where Kelly's convoy was attacked—and where he was seriously injured—only a few weeks before.

So I'm already tense—this road is extremely dangerous.

Did I mention the locals drive like assholes? Or like New York taxi drivers, however you want to look at it. So we're on this divided highway, with two or three lanes in one direction, and the same in the opposite direction. There's a grass divider in the middle. Even if we're driving in the left lane, the locals still like to pass us on the left by driving onto the grass. If we're in the right-hand lane, they still try and pass us on the right by driving onto the shoulder or the berm. Anytime they think we're not moving fast enough, they will attempt to pass us. Then sometimes they'll pass and cut directly in front of our vehicle.

We are all aware how locals who have cut directly in front of military vehicles have also thrown bombs back at those vehicles, or popped up from the trunk and shot at us. Therefore we are well trained never to let anyone cut us off. It is a rule never to let anyone get between your vehicle and the rest of the vehicles in the convoy.

But at the same time, in case there is a roadside bomb, you don't want your vehicle to get caught in the same blast as another vehicle. So you want to keep a certain distance between yourself and other vehicles. Each convoy commander puts out a directive about the desired interval between vehicles on his convoy. Maybe it's a ten-meter interval. Or more. Or less, depending on the convoy and location. In rural areas, a hundred meters is fine. In the city, we often traveled "nut sack to asshole" (as my first sergeant put it), that is, bumper to bumper to prevent locals from squeezing in.

The routine is this: The driver keeps his eyes on the road, looking forward and examining the road for potential roadside bombs. The passengers on the right-hand side focus their attention on their side of the vehicle. Same for the passenger behind the driver on the left-hand side. Each of us has his or her own zone, our own lane or field of fire. And that's what we are trained to focus on.

I am in the rear seat on the left side behind the driver. I don't have a door. The doors on this four-passenger Humvee have been removed. A lot of times, if a vehicle is not up-armored— that is, if it has not been fortified with armor plating and bullet-proof glass (and, at this time, very few Humvees have been up-armored)—the doors are removed to make it easier to jump in and out or to shoot. A door limits your maneuverability and your ability to move your weapon. Canvas doors would do nothing at all to protect us anyway. And they would just slow us down. So the doors are simply removed.

I'm freezing in the cold and rain and wind.

Now I'm noticing this local attempting to pass us. We're driving on the left, and this car is coming up fast on the grass beside us on the left.

It's gloomy and difficult to see, but it's clear that this car is planning to cut in ahead of us. I can tell by the way the driver is glancing back and forth that he is going to cut over.

This is making me nervous. It is also pissing me off. They should know we don't want them to do this. They should know better!

Why would anyone fuck with people who have semiautomatic weapons? Why would anyone do this?

So this vehicle is coming up on us. And coming up closer and closer.

Typically, when you're in the rear of a Humvee and a local is driving up and you don't want them to do whatever they're doing, you gesture with your weapon. Because you are always holding your weapon. Often I would have my weapon resting on my knees, and I might wave at kids with one hand while I'm holding my rifle with my other hand.

Or if I'm on convoy in the back of a cargo Humvee, and I'm looking straight out the back, and a local is moving in between vehicles in the convoy, I might gesture with my weapon at the local and then gesture to another lane. *Hey, you! Get in the other fucking lane! Don't get between us!* And they move. Believe me, they get the point. This method of silent communication with a weapon is very effective.

So I'm gesturing with my weapon at this car moving up next to us. I'm telling them: *Do not cut us off! Back off! DON'T FUCK WITH ME!*

The car is not pulling back. He is not getting the message.

It's tremendously loud with no doors. No one in the Humvee but me sees this car yet. It's my field of fire. It's my call to decide what to do next.

I raise my weapon and point directly into the car. I can feel my adrenaline pumping. I do not know what's going to happen.

I will shoot if this car is beginning to feel like a threat.

My weapon status is red. Always red on convoy now. My safety's on, though I know some soldiers are not bothering with keeping their weapons on safety anymore. But I do. It's still less than a second. Flip, squeeze. After the first round, I can fire at will.

Just then a passenger on my side turns to look for the first time.

It's a little boy. Not more than eight or nine years old. I'm pointing my weapon at a boy who looks exactly like Rick's little brother.

The boy looks at me looking at him.

I lower my rifle and hold it with one hand across my knees. Without thinking, I wave at the boy with my other hand.

And after a moment he waves back.

CROSSING A LINE

In November our team moved once again. This time it was to the large compound at 2nd Brigade's BSA (brigade support area). The compound was a lot more established than it had been in the summer, when I had first come there to visit Zoe. The cage where detainees had been held was a permanent prison now. The prisoners could stay there for a longer time. A whole infrastructure had been built up, and an entire HUMINT platoon—MI who conducted interrogations—was also stationed here now on a permanent basis.

Meanwhile the compound was also getting mortared almost daily, though nothing usually came too close. The enemy's aim was typically terrible. On one occasion, however, the mortar attack was bad—very bad. There were at least a dozen direct hits, and some were so close I heard the rocket's whistle before I heard the explosion.

You never quite got used to it. There was a bug zapper in our room. And every time a bug flew into it and got zapped, I jumped.

And yet in some ways you did get used to it. A mortar hit, and we sat there calculating the distance. *That one doesn't sound too close.*

At the same time, there were EOD teams also blowing things up at certain hours each day. So we began to joke that you'd been in-country too long if the first thing you did when you heard an explosion was look at your watch. You didn't take cover. You didn't grab Kevlar. You checked your watch. Oh, three o'clock. That's EOD. No big deal.

At some point in there, Zoe caught me up on how *her* team leader almost got *her* killed. And how pissed off she'd been about it.

Zoe's near-death experience occurred after she broke her ankle playing basketball. Her foot in a cast, she was running ops when the 2nd Brigade's BSA came under mortar fire. Getting mortared was nothing unusual, but when a blast hit fifty feet away—leaving a crater seven feet in diameter—this freaked her out. Then the radio said take cover inside. Immediately. So Zoe hobbled out of the Humvee, but her team leader appeared out of a building and stopped her.

"What are you doing? Get back in the truck and pull ops!"

He was wearing his flak vest and Kevlar. Zoe had neither.

"We're taking mortar fire!" Zoe shouted at him. "The radio said take cover!"

"No!" her team leader yelled as more mortars hit the base. "The vehicle is sufficient cover! Go back! That's an order!"

Zoe returned to the vehicle. The mortar fire continued. Then her assistant team leader rushed to the vehicle.

"Why are you still out here?" she said in panic. "It came over the radio for everyone to take cover in a building!"

Zoe responded: "Sergeant Watkins told me I had to stay here."

More mortars hit as Zoe and her assistant team leader got on the radio to headquarters. "Is a vehicle sufficient cover during this mortar attack?"

"No," the voice came back. "You *must* be inside a building."

So Zoe now called in again, this time to her platoon leadership. She said: "We are under mortar fire. And we are going to cease operations. And take cover."

"Yes!" the voice came back. "Go inside! What are you doing? Go! Go be safe!"

So Zoe and her assistant team leader shut down the system. And took cover in a building. Where they found her team leader still in his flak vest and Kevlar. *Inside the building.*

Infuriated, Zoe yelled at him. Told him she could never trust his leadership ever again. Never again trust instructions from him. Because he had not taken proper care of his soldier. Because he had chosen to put his own personal safety first. And she planned to report what had happened to her chain of command.

Which she did. To her platoon sergeant and her first sergeant. And Sergeant Watkins received his letter of reprimand. A letter that said he'd been naughty. And that was the end of it.

After I got to 2nd Brigade's BSA in November, Zoe and I were always together. We were together each day all day. When my aunt sent me cross-stitch, Zoe and I cross-stitched together. Something to do with our hands while we talked. The quietly good joy of being able to talk with somebody I loved. Someone who could talk to me about *smart* things. No more throwing rocks and talking about boobs; Zoe and I discussed issues and ideas. Religion, abortion, the death penalty, relationships, our personal development—we talked about everything. We talked about things at a level one might expect in a college classroom, a level that did not occur as often as I might have liked during my time in the military.

Zoe had turned twenty-one in Iraq. And she had grown so much in the three years I'd known her. When we'd first met, Zoe was still practically a girl. Now she was definitely a woman. Someone who had stopped believing in something simply because she'd been taught to believe it. Someone who really thought things through on her own—and believed things because she had thought long and hard about them.

When I reflect on the impact her year in Iraq had on Zoe, I am reminded of a quotation I like. The journalist E. L. Godkin said it: "The sight of a battlefield is one of the most awful lessons in international ethics which a civilized man can receive." So here was Zoe: an intelligent and inquisitive person who suddenly found herself in a place where she saw dead bodies and smelled burning flesh. A place where she experienced both the richness and the destruction of Iraqi culture. And here was Zoe going through all this at a really impressionable age. It would have to result in tremendous personal growth. And in Zoe's case it certainly did.

One day, a HUMINT interrogator approaches me and asks whether I might be willing to assist in interrogations as a female Arabic linguist. I assume he asks because he wishes to interrogate a female prisoner. Or because he simply needs my skills as a linguist. But these assumptions turn out to be wrong.

I'm familiar with the cages. I know about the interrogations. I know we are playing loud rock music day and night to irritate the prisoners. Anything to keep them awake. I know we make prisoners participate in chants of "I love Bush" or "I love America." Anything to piss them off.

When the interrogater and one or two other HUMINT guys coach me on my role for these interrogations, it is not what I expect. Once we get down to the cage area and I cover my nametapes and rank with tape (this is standard practice to prevent retribution), I am told what they will want me to do.

"We are going to bring these guys in. One at a time. Remove their clothes. Strip them naked. Then we will remove the guy's blindfold. And then we want you to say things to humiliate them. Whatever you want. Things to embarrass them. Whatever you can say to humiliate them."

I am surprised by this, but I don't turn around, either. I don't get myself out of there. I want to help—to prevent the kind of thing that has happened to Staff Sergeant Kelly—so I do as I am told.

So I enter the interrogation room. Some HUMINT guys are there along with some other MI guys as guards. There is a civilian interpreter present as well. The sergeant first class in charge of the whole cage is not present.

The prisoner enters the room with a blindfold on and his hands tied behind his back. Things happen like they said they would. They remove his clothes. They position him so he is facing me. When they remove the blindfold, I am the first person he sees.

The civilian interpreter and the interrogator (who also speaks Arabic) mock the prisoner. Mock his manhood. Mock his sexual prowess. Ridicule the size of his genitals. Point to me. Remind him that he is being humiliated in the presence of this blond American female. Anything. Anything that comes to mind.

Degrade the prisoner. Try to break him down. Try to break

his spirit. Occasionally they also ask questions on topics that might have some possible Intel value.

I am watching this, and it is my perception that the Intel value of this prisoner is very limited. However, I am not in a position to judge. I am not in a position to make this assessment. I haven't read the files.

I am prompted to participate. To mock this naked and crying man.

What do I say? What can I say?

"Do you think you can please a woman with that thing?" I ask, gesturing.

I have no aptitude for this work. I prove almost immediately that I am no good at this.

I tell him he had better tell us what we want to know, or we won't stop. But I am almost feeling pity.

What do you say to someone to make them feel like shit? It's just not something I've ever really *practiced* in my personal life. It is not anything I've ever studied how to do. I'm sure there must be plenty of women who would probably know exactly what to say, but I discover that I am actually not one of them.

It is all odd and uncomfortable. But I don't know enough about what it is the HUMINT people do to know whether what I am seeing is what is supposed to happen.

Soldiers flick lit cigarette butts at the prisoner.

It's one thing to make fun of someone and attempt to humiliate him. With words. That's one thing. But flicking lit cigarettes at somebody—like *burning* him—that's illegal.

It's a violation of the Geneva Conventions.

They smack the prisoner across the face.

These actions definitely cross a line.

While I am watching them do these things to this prisoner, I think a lot about Rick. I imagine what it would be like for him in a situation like this. Especially with a woman there to watch. How much it would distress him. The face is not the same, but the prisoner's eyes look a lot like Rick's. The same shape of eyes, the same eye color. The same lashes.

What would it be like for Rick if he ever went home to Palestine and got picked up for any reason by the Israelis and treated this way? What would it be like for him? As I watch, I imagine Rick. I imagine Rick *in this room*.

That becomes about the only thing I think about while everything else is going on. I'm no longer trying to contribute. I'm not insulting the prisoner or trying to mock him. I've fallen silent. But no one notices, because I am still a useful prop. No one seems to mind that I have nothing to say.

When it's over after one more prisoner and a couple of hours, I tell the interrogator that I do not want to do this again.

Then I tell him that what we are doing to the prisoners in these cages is a violation of the Geneva Conventions. (I know this because the Army repeatedly gives us refresher courses on the Geneva Conventions.) I tell him it's illegal to burn prisoners—or smack them.

He does not appear surprised or bothered by what I say.

"Yes," he says. "But you have to know that these people are criminals. This is the only way to deal with them. You know these people only respect strength, power. Under Saddam it was so much worse for them. They'll never listen to us unless we play rough. Besides, the terrorists don't follow the Geneva Conventions—so why should we?"

I say to him: "But you do know that not all these guys are terrorists."

"Sure," he says casually. "Yeah. I know."

"And you know," I add, "that if one of these guys does not walk in here a terrorist, he is going to walk out of here a terrorist."

"Yeah," this NCO says calmly. "Sure. I know that."

After that day I avoid the cages. There's a phone in the office that we can all use for free. To call the States or whatever. I do not go down there to use it often. I don't want to see things that will disturb me. More of the sort of things I've already seen. This building has a courtyard in the middle. When you walk through the area to get to the office phone, you can see into the courtyard. And then you can't help seeing prisoners getting handled roughly—shoved around while blindfolded, forced to do exercises, like the knee bender, for long periods of time.

At a later time the cage where I witnessed these abuses got investigated. A prisoner died in custody there. Another prisoner had a broken jaw. A third prisoner complained to authorities that he had been burned with cigarettes.

So it wasn't only the Abu Ghraib prison near Baghdad where abuses occurred in Iraq at the end of 2003. It was a bigger problem than that.

Later I spoke with one of the officers who had been in charge of a cage in Mosul. He now said that he would conduct interrogations very differently after the revelations of torture at Abu Ghraib. In the fall of 2003, he said, he had definitely been under the impression that just about *any* interrogation procedure was authorized because we were dealing with terrorists. He had been given the firm impression that this had been put out at the highest levels—from George W. Bush and Donald Rumsfeld on down. That the old rules no longer applied because this was a different world. This was a new kind of war.

Later, of course, there would be these huge investigations. All the paperwork would be requested for review. Everything would be gone through again and again. Now the officer told me that if he were ever to return to Iraq, everything would have to be done very differently.

Later, when I was back in the States, I spoke with a HUMINT female who had been present on a routine basis at these interrogations at this compound in Mosul. That had been her job. She had helped to conduct these interrogations almost every day over a period of several months.

This was sometime in late spring of 2004, around the time the Abu Ghraib prisoner-abuse scandal was breaking. I met her at a cookout with mutual friends in Tennessee. Everything was lush and green in Tennessee at that time of year. Verdant. Iraq felt far away.

I mentioned something to her in passing about Abu Ghraib.

Her response was simple:

"I don't see the problem with anything that occurred in those interrogations," she told me. "I don't see a problem with anything those soldiers did."

I was horrified when she said this. I have not been able to have a normal conversation with her since. I still don't even know how to *look* at her.

No one should be allowed to do interrogations every day for as long as our interrogators had been required to do them. It fucks you up in ways we can only guess.

Look at the people who volunteered off the streets to partic-ipate in a famous university study in which they were told to play the roles of prisoners and guards. These participants in this study *knew* they were part of a study. Yet they immediately moved past the line most of us would consider an acceptable response. These participants revealed a remarkable willingness to inflict pain. They showed a tremendous capacity for hurting and tortur-ing other human beings *for no other reason* than that they had been told to do so. And we're talking about ordinary people who knew that they were participating in a research study.

Now make it for real.

Tell these same ordinary people that if they do a good-enough job as interrogators, if they are able to break prisoners down and get intelligence from them, they might be saving the lives of people they know and friends they work with every day. And then observe how these ordinary people respond.

It has been shown time and again that it is not at all unusual for people to cross a line and do what most of us would consider aberrant.

I guess I interpret my own refusal to continue to participate in those interrogations as, in fact, the more unusual response.

However, I did not file a complaint.

I did not go higher.

I did not do anything to stop those interrogations. I did not stand up and say: "This is not okay. It must stop."

I did not do anything like that. All I said was: "I am not going to be a part of it." I did not blow the whistle on anybody.

So how morally culpable am I?

READING *ATLAS SHRUGGED* IN MOSUL

WHEN YOU HAVE a fight-or-flight response, your adrenaline starts pumping. It takes a tremendous amount of control for your mind not to let your body and its hormones do whatever they want. Which is to respond in a physical way to a threat.

At a certain point we all started to hate the fucking locals. The longer we were there, the more difficult things got.

Zoe and I talked about this.

We had both studied the culture. We spoke the language. We understood at least a little about the religion and the history of the region. We had so much more understanding than the average soldier. And even *we* reached the point where we were very close to hating the Iraqi people.

Infantry guys? And not just infantry, but most Army people there?

A lot of Army people said—and seemed to believe—that we should just nuke the region. Nuke the Middle East. And fuck 'em all. They've been trying to kill each other for a thousand years. Kill 'em all.

Let the whole region be glass.

I heard at least twenty people in the Army say this.

Just nuke it.

Me? Being vaguely nonconfrontational (but not really non-confrontational), I tried a whole range of responses.

I said: "Hey, come on, there's innocent women and children here."

And I got back: "Nobody here is innocent. If they're not little killers now, they're gonna grow up to be killers."

So I said: "But you know we're here for the oil, right? And if you nuke Iraq, it'll all be radioactive. And we won't be able to come and get the oil."

And the response was: "Yeah, whatever. Technology will figure it out. They'll figure out a way to be able to do it. It'll be okay."

Understand that these were *not* bad people. These were simply people who were *beyond* frustrated. Beyond angry. Beyond bitter.

Soldiers were put in these impossible situations. For a while, 3rd Brigade's job was propane distribution. They manned points where they passed out propane. These were *soldiers.* Their mission was to fight and win our nation's wars. That is the Army's mission statement. And here were soldiers passing out free tanks of propane to people so they could cook or whatever.

So these soldiers were doing a good thing for people, and then they watched while locals cut in line and shoved little kids out of the way. And sometimes the soldiers reached a breaking point where they just grabbed somebody's empty tank—and chucked it. Just threw it. *If you can't play by the rules, fuck you.*

Whenever I saw prisoners who had been roughed up before they were put in the cage, I never criticized the infantry because they were in extraordinarily stressful situations. These guys were getting shot at all the time. They might have watched their friends die. They're out there in the shit every day. So definitely they responded with more violence. When they arrested somebody, they knocked them around a little. Dealt with them harshly. And I didn't feel like I was in a place to criticize. But if once the prisoners' hands were tied and they were in a secure location, and MI people—or MPs—engaged in that kind of behavior, I did not feel they had any excuse.

You have a higher moral responsibility to treat somebody appropriately when you're a prison guard than when you're an arresting officer. When you are not worried that they might try to kill you. When you are not worried that their family could pour out of a building and shoot you.

Matt told me about these times he was manning Traffic Control Points (TCP). And he injured people. Hit people. Busted out car windows of locals who were behaving inappropriately. And part of it was that he could. He had the power to do it. But part of it was *he was scared.*

And people overreact when they're scared.

It took Matt more than a year before he told me this story about manning a TCP.

"Things would get kind of messy sometimes. We'd string c-wire across the point, and we'd check cars and stuff. There was this one dude who decided to get lippy with this one officer at one point. So the officer made him empty out the entire back of his truck. The dude had all these crates of fruit. And the officer made him empty every piece of fruit off his truck. And so he's pulling off the very last piece, and the officer was like: 'Okay, you can put it all back.' It took this Iraqi four hours to unload and load his truck. Making real sure he wouldn't get an attitude the next time he got to a TCP.

"We were doing twenty-four-hour TCPs when there were reports that Saddam was in the area. Basically we stopped the Iraqis and searched their cars. Then sent them on their way. A few times a car heading toward us would start to turn around. They'd see us and then go back, turning away from the checkpoint. And we opened up with our weapons. Assuming they had something to hide. And might be a threat. Did I ever hit anybody? I don't know. One car, we *had* to have killed some locals. I can't imagine we didn't—we opened up with machine guns. The entire platoon opened up on this one truck. Actually it was pretty funny. There was nothing left of the truck. Another time this other guy I knew killed a local guy and a little kid. Another dude in that car actually lived. I have no idea how he lived, because there were bullet holes everywhere. Good times."

Sometime earlier that fall I spent a month at Range 54 at the base of the mountains outside Sinjar. It was not as secure as the Tal Afar airfield base, but it was relatively secure. There were gates and guards, but it wasn't as built-up as the airfield base. And it was smaller. Range 54 was 2/187's site.

Matt was there as part of a fire support team. By that point I trusted Matt deeply. It was at Range 54 that Matt gave me a metal police baton he had acquired, calling it his "*hajji*-be-good stick."

At Range 54 we worked indoors in a building. And we slept indoors for the first time in many months. There was no hot running water. A shower was a rigged thing that resembled an outhouse. And we also had an outhouse for a toilet. But the outhouse was an improvement because it wasn't a hole in the ground. It did, however, bug me that the guys left their porn regularly in the outhouses—left open to the appropriate page beside a tube of lotion.

One of the FISTers actually confessed to me at some point that it was difficult for him to shit in an outhouse after several months of squatting. He told me: "When I first got back in to the airfield? I'd climb up on the platform of the seat in these outhouses and I'd squat on 'em. 'Cause I couldn't otherwise." Now you have to understand two things about this story: (1) What he said made complete sense to me, and (2) this was a perfectly acceptable topic of conversation by this point in our deployment.

At Range 54 the locals burned our shit for us. Stirred it up with diesel fuel and lit it. For four dollars a day. I assisted with translation to give the locals instructions on what work needed to get done.

That's why Matt gave me the *hajji*-be-good stick. Some of the locals (who drove the buses) slept right behind the building where I slept. Matt didn't trust them. So he wanted to be sure I'd be safe. That's why he gave me the stick to keep under my pillow at night.

At that location I was one of four females out of five hundred people. This was intimidating. And I dealt with it by not making friends with guys there. I became less outgoing, less friendly, less revealing of personal information.

I was already friends with Matt, and I let the other guys assume that because he and I were friends that he *owned* me. I did nothing to correct this assumption. You didn't mess with another guy's girl.

So I got left alone more. I got time to think.

I thought about the mountain time when I was alone mainly with guys I knew and liked. And I thought about the incident with Rivers. It sharpened my focus.

For the longest time I continued to feel so responsible, wondering whether I had encouraged Rivers by being friendly and outgoing. By my willingness to talk about sex with him. By talking about relationships and personal things with guys I didn't know so well. Did I set myself up?

Was it my fault? Was I asking for it?

So I decided to change my behavior. I wasn't so friendly anymore. I kept myself to myself.

I was also coming into a fuller sense of my own abilities and strengths. I was really coming to believe in myself. My confidence, my sense of what I could do, had developed so much that when I was made a team leader—in September 2003—I was really happy. I was thrilled. I felt ready and comfortable moving into a leadership position.

Admittedly my team was me and only one other soldier. By this point in our deployment, there were very few people in my platoon. Our ranks had been seriously reduced due to ETS and PCS. When we left Fort Campbell in January, we had two Prophet teams of four people each in my platoon, a low-level voice intercept (LLVI) team of four people, and a Prophet Control team with six people that did analysis of our data. By this point, there was one two-person Prophet team, one four-man LLVI team, and one three-person Prophet Control team. And that was it.

It was difficult. For one thing we should still have been pulling twenty-four-hour ops. But a team of two soldiers couldn't manage that. We shut down midnight to six.

I was still motivated to get my soldier into shape. He arrived overweight, so I developed a PT program for him. Clearly he had not been responsible for himself, and I went out of my way to find other training opportunities for him.

Since my promotion had not gone through yet, the soldier on my team and I were the same rank. A male friend of mine whose team leader was a girl and also the same rank had already told me that when people came to his site, they would talk to him—not to his team leader. And that would bother him.

He would say: "She's the team leader."

People would say: "Uh-huh. Yeah. Okay." And then keep talking to him. And repeatedly address him as if he were in charge.

He would again say: "No, no. *She's* in charge."

Now the same thing happened to me.

When people came up to our site, they addressed the soldier on my team.

And I had to say, "Excuse me. You know *I'm* in charge. *I'm* the team leader."

Possibly due to my months of solitude, and possibly due to the Rivers incident, I started to pay attention to how females were getting treated. Now there were MKTs (mobile kitchen trailers) at Range 54, so instead of always having MREs, we filed through a line into a shelter and got hot food. Everyone stared at the few women.

And then there was the time I decided to wear mascara to a Bruce Willis concert at Tal Afar. I didn't think about it beforehand. It was a concert. So I put on the mascara, and I honestly did not think anyone would notice.

Everyone noticed.

This guy I knew who *wasn't* at the concert saw me a few weeks later.

"Hey, Kayla, I heard you wore mascara to the Bruce Willis concert."

I could not believe it.

I saw a number of soldiers in my company again, soldiers I had not seen very much since we all left Fort Campbell. And my team was spending a lot more time at the airfield by this time, so there was more time to hang out with the guys in my company. I also saw other MI females in my unit, and we caught up on things. I started hearing gossip from infantry guys about girls. I had no idea how much (if any) of the gossip was true. But I started to hear all kinds of stuff.

"Oh, you're on a Prophet team? Hey, we heard from this guy that we know about this girl on another Prophet Team who sucked his cock in the back of a Humvee."

"You're an MI girl on a Prophet team? Okay. We know about girls like you."

"You know Janice? She's on this other Prophet team? I heard she let a group of guys run a train on her. You know what I mean, right? She pretty much spread her legs while they lined up and took turns. All you girls do that?"

Dammit.

No doubt guys were getting antsy. Bored. By that point the main combat effort was over. Combat really focused our attention. Now we were more settled into locations where we had less movement and fewer missions. So guys started to think a little more about what they weren't getting. At that point we had a little more access to phones. We could occasionally get on the

Internet and check our e-mail. So guys were thinking about home more often. Stuff like that.

So it was around this time that I really began to think about how I was presenting myself to other people.

It was also around this time that I first heard that a female in the Army deployed in Iraq was either a bitch or a slut. That that was the choice we faced.

That was when I began to think: I would rather be a bitch.

And then Staff Sergeant Simmons arrived. When she wasn't busy flirting with infantry guys, she'd take down her long black hair and brush it. And brush it. And brush it. Or whenever a guy walked into our area, she would also take down her hair and brush it. She smoked these long and skinny freakish-smelling cigarettes. Then she'd ash them into half-full water bottles she never capped. After a short while, there were these half-full water bottles with cigarette butts and ashes everywhere.

SSG Simmons outranked me and took over my team. Meeting her, and disliking her, I thought a lot more about how even one horrible female soldier affected how the men saw *all* female soldiers.

Probably some of my initial response to her was territorial. Territorial about my team, my stuff, my job. I probably didn't want to give up my newfound sense of authority and responsibility. After all, I'd signed for all the equipment, and now SSG Simmons came along and wanted to touch things.

When she arrived, I was signed for 1.3 million dollars' worth of equipment. I was signed for our truck. I was signed for three laptops. I was signed for all our equipment. This amounted to nearly two hundred discrete items. Everything had a line item, and it was not easy to keep everything straight. Since this was the fucking Army, every item had its own number and letter. MA711-Charlie? This? I had to learn what every letter and number meant.

When I signed for it from the sergeant before me, he didn't know what everything was. When he signed for it from the sergeant before him, she didn't know what everything was, either. But I had been told that you were not supposed to sign for anything unless you absolutely knew that everything was there. But on the day I started to figure everything out, it got dark, so I said, "Fuck it," and signed for the rest. Then I spent two days laying every single piece of equipment out all over the floor and figuring out what every single item was. Then I put everything related to the solar charging panel into one Baggie, and everything related to something else into another Baggie.

It was a huge pain in the ass.

Now here's SSG Simmons rustling around in my fucking shit. Moving stuff around. No clue what anything is, but feeling free to mess with my organization because she can. Because she's technically in charge now.

She almost immediately pisses everyone off when she decides on her 4:00 A.M. shift to sweep the small building where we live, work, and sleep. We are all still sleeping, and choking clouds of dust wake us up.

For no apparent reason Simmons has laid out a box of books that had been neatly stacked inside a crate. So now all the books are dusty. But that's the least of it.

Our technician says to her: "Please. We have extremely sensitive equipment in here. Do not sweep unless you bag the laptop.

You have to put it inside a plastic bag. To keep the dust from damaging it."

She never does this. She never listens.

"Isn't it great how I did this? Isn't it great how I reorganized everything? It looks so much prettier."

Once Staff Sergeant Simmons announces to Matt that he should bring his infantry friends over to play cards.

She tells him: "Don't worry. I won't bite . . . unless you want me to." (Matt turns her down politely enough to her face, but he tells me later he can't stand that "scary troll bitch.")

SSG Simmons announces to everyone that she's planning to cheat on Simmons, her second husband.

She also never bothers to learn anything about Iraq.

When she first shows up, she asks me: "Can you tell me where we are in the world? What are the neighboring countries? What are the ethnic groups here? What are the religious groups here? Why are we in Iraq? Tell me why we are here."

Not knowing how to respond, I make an attempt at humor: "Oh, ha-ha-ha. No one knows why we're here! You know those weapons of mass destruction—"

"Weapons? Of mass destruction?"

And I think: Oh, my God. She really doesn't know.

So here is this woman in charge of my team in a country where she has been sent to fight and possibly even to die. And she has not bothered to pick up a newspaper or do any basic research. She has no idea what she's doing here.

Staff Sergeant Simmons's cluelessness and lack of motivation crush me.

I am feeling: Enough already with the bad female leadership.

I am starting to feel cursed by God.

———

I leave SSG Simmons and my unit in late October to have my foot surgery in Mosul. Once I've recovered I stay in Tal Afar at the airfield because my team has already left Range 54 on a new mission to work with new equipment. I request to stay at the airfield until I'm off my crutches. Then I rejoin my team at 2nd Brigade's BSA in Mosul, where I stay for the remainder of my deployment.

My time away from SSG Simmons makes nothing better.

In Mosul we get mortared on a regular basis. It is crucial always to tell someone where you are going, how long you plan to be gone, when you plan to return, and so on. That's just common sense. You don't scamper off on your own in a damned combat zone and go do whatever the fuck you please. You tell somebody: "I'm going to chow. I'll be back within an hour."

SSG Simmons does not do this. She makes friends, and she disappears to have visits to watch movies, or whatever. Gone for any number of hours. Without telling any of us where she's going. Or when she's coming back.

A couple of times we're mortared, and the command higher up insists on 100 percent accountability checks. When you verify that everybody in your unit is still alive. And she's just nowhere to be found. If a lower enlisted private did something like that, that person would be in a lot of trouble. But she just slides by.

Things keep getting worse and worse. Staff Sergeant Simmons refuses to learn the equipment. I constantly have to struggle to make sure that the mission is happening. It is an effort all the time. I have to do a lot of things that are supposed to be her responsibility. So I begin to communicate directly with her superior to get the information I need to do my job.

When she learns this, her position is clear.

"You must stop usurping my authority. You are not allowed to have any communication with anybody that does not go directly through me."

It becomes a big problem. SSG Simmons makes it clear that she plans to recommend me for disciplinary action. For insubordination.

My platoon sergeant is very vocal if he believes you are bad at something.

He will tell you: "You're fucked up. You're a shitbag. You are not doing what you are supposed to do. Why don't you know this? What the fuck is the matter with you?"

But he is never vocal about praise.

He will not say to you: "Hey, you're a good soldier. You really know your shit. You're really squared away and you're a good leader."

He does not volunteer positive reinforcement. It's not what he does.

So there's only one way I ever know that he thinks well of me.

When you're a low-ranking enlisted soldier—E-4 or below—you are supposed to get a monthly counseling statement. It tells you what you're doing and what you're supposed to be doing. It's a professional development sort of thing to help you be a better soldier.

Once you become a noncommissioned officer, you get an NCOER—that is, a noncommissioned officer evaluation report. These have to be done yearly or every time you have a change of rater. So every time you get a new boss, your old boss is obligated to do one of these on you. If you get a negative NCOER, it will seriously impact your chances for getting promoted again.

So since Staff Sergeant Simmons is in charge of me, she should be writing an NCOER on me whenever I finally leave her team for my own.

I am quite concerned. So I speak to my platoon sergeant.

"What am I going to do? She's going to give me a bad NCOER—and it's going to mess up my entire Army career."

"No," he tells me. "Don't worry. She will *never* do an NCOER on you. I have made clear to her that you are a team leader and she is a team leader. And that therefore I will rate you. I'm your rater. Not her."

It's a really big deal. He is not going to let her get away with this.

That's the only way I ever know that my platoon sergeant thinks I'm worth a shit.

Finally, sometime around Christmas, things get so bad that SSG Simmons and I end up sitting down together with a lieutenant to mediate our discussion. I want a witness so she cannot claim that I am out of line.

I begin.

"Look, I am not sure that you understand what is going on. And I want to make sure that you are clear on the fact that I am *not* trying to hurt you or your career. I am not trying to usurp your authority. I am trying to help you because you are in charge. If shit is fucked up, it is not me who looks bad. It is you who looks bad. If the mission does not get accomplished, you look bad because you're in charge. Me making sure the mission happens is not me trying to make you look bad. It's me trying to save your ass. It's me trying to make sure that the things you are supposed to accomplish are accomplished *on time* and *to standard.* That's me trying to help you—not me trying to hurt you. I'm trying to talk to you about these things because I feel communication has gotten very poor. And I have to do something because that's not okay. It's not working."

She says: "I really appreciate you coming forward. And making the effort. Taking the initiative. And while we're talking about things, I want to tell you that I feel you don't respect me because you know I don't care about learning anything about the technical side of our job. Or learning anything about our equipment."

This blows my mind.

Well, I want to say. *Yeah.*

But I can't say this, of course. So I just kind of stare at her.

And the lieutenant is staring at her by this point as well. Jaw slightly agape.

Is she honestly saying this to us? As a *defense* for her not knowing her job?

Then she says it again.

"I really am feeling you don't respect me because I don't care about learning about the technical aspects of our job."

And I am looking at her. Searching for words.

"It's important for you to be able to identify the equipment that you are signed for."

She has signed for more than a million dollars' worth of equipment. If it gets lost or broken through an act of negligence—like dropping it in a river or smashing it with a bat or whatever—she is responsible for it. And the Army can take money out of her paycheck.

"Oh," she says, huffily. "So I guess this is going to be the time to just rip on me. And bring up all my faults."

"I . . . " I begin. ". . . don't, um, know . . . how to have this conversation anymore."

———

A month or so later we drive to Kuwait, where we will live in these fifteen-hundred-person warehouses with bunk cots. Just waiting to go back to the States.

There's been this general announcement: *Maintain positive control of your sensitive items.* Like your weapon. You do not lose your fucking weapon. And your night vision goggles are another sensitive item. You must be accountable for them at all times. But people are told to throw their rucksacks onto large baggage trucks to be transported to the warehouses.

When no one is looking, SSG Simmons chucks her NVGs up into the baggage truck with everyone's bags.

Later the people who unpack the trucks find them.

"So whose are these?"

When the commander learns that the NVGs belong to SSG Simmons, she gets severely chastised.

"What are you thinking? What are you doing? What the fuck is wrong with you?"

Simmons sits on her cot and cries. In front of everyone.

And in front of everyone, she blames her crying on PMS. Yet another thing that is absolutely not acceptable in the Army. It encourages men to think what most men think already: that PMS makes girls do incompetent things. Which I prefer to think is not true. Because you still hear lots of stuff like, *Women should never be president because they're too emotional to handle it. What if she got PMS, she'd start a nuclear war!*

People remain concerned about women in leadership roles. So for SSG Simmons to have her breakdown in public does *not* help.

I am horrified. Zoe and I are both horrified.

This woman's incompetence makes all women in the Army look incompetent.

We had a lot of downtime in Iraq. There was plenty of time to read. I probably read two hundred books during my year of deployment.

I started reading Ayn Rand's *Atlas Shrugged* at Range 54. It took me forever to read. I didn't actually finish it until I was at 2nd Brigade in Mosul. Reading *Atlas Shrugged* in Mosul ended up being a very formative experience.

Rand is all about personal responsibility. In a lot of ways she's an intellectual snob. A tremendous elitist. There's a sentiment expressed by a central character in *Atlas Shrugged*. She talks about how she has to struggle *against* other people to get her job done. It's hard enough to do her job, but then she also has to actively fight people who appear to be trying to prevent work from happening. She talks about how frustrating it can be to deal with incompetence. How exhausting and draining it can be.

I identified strongly with this.

Rand's books are also rants against communism. They document all the things that are wrong with communism and how it can ruin people's lives.

And I identified with this as well.

Reading *Atlas Shrugged* in Mosul, I became convinced that the Army was really this vast communist institution in disguise. I don't mean "communist" in the sense of sharing what you have, getting what you need. I don't mean "communist" in the sense of equality for all. Not that utopian bullshit.

I mean real-world communism. The fucked-up kind.

In real-world communism, folks did as little as possible to get as much as possible. They scammed their way up the bureau-cratic ladder. They said to themselves: "There is the hard way, the right way, and the way to get whatever I fucking want without doing anything at all." Door number three, please.

Because so often in the Army, your pay was not related to how hard you worked. That's what I figured out from reading Rand. Because someone else around you was not doing anything—and they were still getting the same amount of money as you. Or more. And if you did work harder, you just ended up feeling like you were getting screwed. In this way the Army encouraged peo-ple to do as little as possible. Of course, not everyone was this way—but it was depressingly common.

This was a powerful revelation because I was realizing how good I was at my job and how hard I worked. And here I was again faced with someone in charge of me who was not good at her job and did not work hard. Here I was stuck with yet another completely incompetent team leader. Feeling this severe frustration.

I began to feel wistfully like it should be permitted to dispose of my team leader. Get her out of my way.

I returned to the Tal Afar airfield for Christmas. To be around people I liked and to get away from Staff Sergeant Simmons. By this point there were trailers at the airfield, and almost everyone was living indoors with heat, which was really nice. It had already started to get cold in November.

By this point they had all these chow halls, courtesy of Halliburton. (By now Halliburton had the contract for building all the chow halls over there. They ended up getting investigated for not meeting their contract—for not providing a certain number of meals to a certain number of soldiers a certain number of times a day. Meanwhile they imported foreign workers to serve us food in these nice shiny buildings. So there were these Pakistani workers at Tal Afar and all these cute little Filipina girls working in Mosul. It was pretty peculiar.)

On Christmas we got a really nice meal. But on the way to the chow hall in the parking lot there were civil affairs and psyop vehicles with mounted speakers. Usually these vehicles would drive through the towns broadcasting warnings or information. Now the Army vehicles were blasting Christmas carols. It was an unreal sight.

On Christmas they showed us a DVD. Shots of people's loved ones back at Fort Campbell holding up signs like HONK, IF YOU SUPPORT OUR TROOPS. And you saw all the cars driving by and honking. You saw children holding up signs like I LOVE MY DADDY. Kids holding up signs that said what unit their dad was in. Everyone waving American flags.

An overweight interpreter named Rob put on a Santa suit. Our first sergeant, our commander, my platoon sergeant, and this guy, Rob, went around and gave everyone a stocking with random Christmasy things like soap and candy.

The videotape and the stockings were surprisingly emotional for me. I started thinking about my own family. About them worrying about me. And missing me.

All this footage of people at home lining the roads and cheering us.

I started to cry, alone in my trailer.

SITUATION NORMAL

WHEN MY TOUR was coming to an end, I got my truck back and had two soldiers under me while we drove all the way from Mosul to Kuwait. We had major mechanical problems with our truck; we had no lights, and our radios were down. At night, I clipped a little flashlight to my sleeve, and when I had to brake, I'd stick my little light out the window so the truck behind me could see me. That was my brake light. The only communication we had was a handheld Motorola with which we could speak with the truck in front of us (that also had a handheld Motorola). The only radios we had were radios we'd purchased with our own money. The entire drive was basically horrible, but once it was over it was great.

At the end there came the moment when we finally saw the berm that separated Iraq from Kuwait. As my first sergeant would say, seeing the berm was a significant emotional event. He liked to say: "There are going to be a lot of significant emotional events for people here." (I also thought of that phrase the day I washed out Lott's bloody gear. The day Berenger died. And I thought of it again then.) It was exactly that—a significant emotional event. We crossed the berm. We survived. We made it out of Iraq alive.

A couple of miles past the berm, we stopped to refuel. And we took off our flak vests. From that point on, we could drive around without those hot fucking things on. That too was a significant emotional event.

Guys were lighting cigars. A lot of people were taking pictures. People were hugging.

We spent the next two or three weeks in Kuwait at an established U.S. Army base. Time to decompress that was very important. We cleaned our trucks and cleaned our equipment. Got everything packed and ready to go on the ships. But we also got to go shopping for souvenirs and wander around and get doughnuts, Chinese food, pizza. Drink near-beer. Use the phone. Check our e-mail. We were able to do pseudo-American things for a little while.

During this time in Kuwait, we were also not allowed to carry around a weapon. I spent nearly the entire time in Kuwait reaching for my carbine no matter where I was. I'd get up from the chow hall in a frantic panic, afraid I'd lost it.

I came home on February 8, 2004. It was snowing lightly at Fort Campbell. It had been almost exactly one year since I'd been here, and it had been snowing when I left. Small sharp flakes that stung the face. I had a surreal moment of feeling like I'd never left; that it had all been a sick dream—or as if, somehow, I had just lost a whole year of my life. There had been this gap in the normal passage of time, and then it fitfully resumed right where it had left off.

The night I got home, I got in touch with Shane Kelly. He had returned to Fort Campbell in January after three months at Walter Reed Army Medical Center. And after that first night, we hung out together all the time.

I was incredibly happy to be back in America. But for the longest time, I did not want to be around non-Army people. And I kept having feelings of wanting to be back there.

When you come home, you spend a lot of time talking about how you want to get back to Iraq. You feel this guilt for not being with your brothers. For not being with *your people*. The people in your unit. You feel like you're still supposed to be there.

You're not done.

I remembered that when I spoke to anybody who took mid-tour leave, they had expressed similar feelings. And now I felt them, too.

There was culture shock.

Everyone in America was fat. Everyone was on some stupid diet. How could a diet encourage you to eat bacon and forbid you to eat bananas? It made no sense to me. I felt like people didn't understand anything. That they were selfish and didn't appreciate what they had.

I came home, and the only things people were interested in were things just beyond my comprehension. Who cared about Jennifer Lopez? How was it that I was watching CNN one morning and there was a story about freaking ducklings being fished out of a damn sewer drain—while the story of soldiers getting killed in Iraq got relegated to this little banner across the bottom of the screen? Ducklings getting pulled out of a sewer. How was this important to our country?

I was not understanding what was going on. I was not grasping anything.

How was I willing to go and die for these fucking people who wear sweatshirts with little kittens on them? Or these people with sequins who bump into me with their carts at the supermarket and then look at me like I'm an asshole?

It's a very strange country we live in.

I felt thoroughly out of place. I felt this jarring sense of *I do not belong here.*

Soon after my return I visited my father and stepmother in North Carolina.

The big talk on their block was the glorified mobile home that was being put in their gated community. The neighbors were up in arms over this. Oh my God! The world is coming to an end! This prefab home does not meet the ideal standards of life in the community!

Everyone was aghast. "What about property values?"

I thought: Who are you people? You people are all *rich.* You have electricity. You have phones. I just came back from a place where people wanted my cardboard boxes for flooring. What the fuck is wrong with you?

My parents were supportive. They were fine.

But everywhere we went, it was always the same.

"This is my daughter. She just got back from Iraq."

"Oh, thank you! Thank you!" And then it was always the same question. "What was it like?"

I understood people were saying this to be nice. But what could I say? What was I supposed to say?

"Well, while I was in Mosul, this sergeant major and his driver got pulled out of their vehicle by a mob and their bodies were literally torn apart. So how's your year been?"

What am I supposed to say?

"Oh, yeah. I watched a guy bleed to death. And I smelled burning shit all the time. It was super."

I didn't know how to deal with people.

My parents' mailman sent me magazines while I was in Iraq. My parents told him that magazines were what I wanted most. So he took it upon himself as his project to collect magazines from all the people on his route. He boxed them up and shipped them to me at his own expense. Sometimes when my parents shipped me things, he just paid for it.

I sent him a thank-you note.

When I got to North Carolina, he stopped by for a visit.

It turned out he was a Vietnam vet.

So I thanked him all over again for the magazines and everything. He told me the letter I sent to him from Iraq thanking him meant more to him than a letter from the president would have meant to him. My letter was just that important and moving to him.

And he told me: "You know, the welcome home that you troops coming back from Iraq are getting is like the recognition we never got. I feel like it's for me too. For me and all Vietnam vets."

He went on about my sacrifice and how important it was that I went to war.

I didn't know how to react to him at all.

Here's a guy who also told me that all but two soldiers in his platoon got killed in Vietnam.

Not one person in my entire company was killed in Iraq. At the time I returned only four hundred American military had died in Iraq. Four hundred soldiers died every week in Vietnam.

I didn't feel like I deserved any of what he told me. At all. I felt like it was wrong. I did not go through anything like what he had gone through.

So for me to think that what I experienced in Iraq was tough or difficult—compared with what this guy went through in Vietnam—felt wrong. Nothing I experienced was as bad as that.

I felt guilty that he treated me so well.

Guilty that he acted like I was so great or did such a great thing.

Like I didn't deserve his praise. It was just awkward.

So you get home and you are supposed to want to be home and you are supposed to be so happy to see your family—and then all you want is to get back to Army people.

I could only handle being home for three or four days.

I ended up fleeing so I didn't have to deal with my own family or civilians. So I went back to Fort Campbell. Where it was easier. Where everyone understood. Where no one asked questions. Where it was easier to talk with other people because they'd been there too. Where you didn't have to explain a lot of things. Back to *people who knew*. It was so much simpler.

I couldn't cope with the rest of it. I didn't want to cope with the rest of it.

At some point I accompanied Shane when he visited his family, and that was also super-awkward. All the attention when his mom told everyone: "This is my son. And he just got back from Iraq."

Even a year after he returned, she still put it the same way.

"This is my son. He just got back from Iraq."

My parents did the same thing for almost a year after I returned.

"No," I'd say. "I did not just get back anymore. It's been awhile."

No more apologies. That's what being in the Army has taught me when all is said and done. I used to be this girl, like so many girls— I mean studies have been done on this, if you don't want to take my word for it—we *qualify* everything we say. This was me: "I kinda think maybe I'd like sorta to do X or Y. I'm not sure. You decide." With a guy I was the same way. Maybe he'd just fucking *lied* to me. And maybe I'd just caught him at it. But it was still me saying: "I'm sorry." Girls do this all the time. I did it all the time.

I also remember clearly that before I went to Iraq, I always made statements that sounded like questions. When I first arrived at Fort Campbell, for instance, I went into my platoon's office and said: "Um, I think we have formation?" (Though of course I *knew* we had formation). And people didn't get up and go to formation. They went and checked. I spoke like that all the time, and it pissed me off at myself. I should have been more assertive. I also should have been less embarrassed about being smart. Less ashamed of my ability to do things well.

When women are good at what they do, they are not characterized as assertive. They are accused of being ballbusters or bitches. This is a struggle that is magnified in the military because it is still such a male environment—a weird little microcosm of society on steroids.

In a combat zone I couldn't be hesitant. I had to be assured. I couldn't just quit. If you decide to quit in a combat zone, you will probably die. I had to keep going. *I had to do it.* And all of a sudden I realized that the mind is incredibly powerful. I *could* do it. I could do almost anything. I could keep going in situations that I certainly imagined before would have broken me. In Iraq I figured out there was no option for me to do anything else but push myself. And keep pushing.

Which I did. Which I've done.

I felt a lot of clarity while I was in Iraq in terms of my personal life. I really felt a sense of what I wanted out of life. And who I was and where I was going. Maybe this was because my lane was so narrow.

Another Army expression: "Stay in your lane." They say it on the firing range. "Watch your lane. Watch your lane only." So you only fire at the targets in your lane. You stay in your lane. And I always thought this was a great Army phrase. (Civilians should use it at work when somebody gets in their business and they have no reason to do so.) Don't try to get involved in things that don't concern you and that you don't know anything about. For instance, I hate it when somebody corrects my soldiers when I am present. If their uniforms are messed up, that's my business. I have either noticed it and plan to deal with it, or I know a reason for it. Whatever it is, it's my business. Nobody else's business. They need to stay in their lane. In general, I think this is good advice in life.

So in Iraq my lane was very narrow. It became very easy to feel like I knew what I was doing and what was going on. Staying alive. Doing my mission. That was my lane.

Now that I was back in the States, everything opened up. I had to check my private e-mail and my work e-mail. I had to know my password for my e-mail and memorize my PIN number for my bank account and my password for my retirement account. My lane was suddenly huge. I had to deal with friends and family and all sorts of personal questions. I had to pick out what color socks I wanted to wear. And I began to feel like a lot of the clarity I felt and the sense of purpose I had in Iraq had really faded.

While I was in Iraq, everything was clear. I wanted to become a journalist. I wanted to go to graduate school and get a master's degree. I wanted to become a Middle East correspondent for National Public Radio. That was what I wanted to do with my life. So I'd apply to Georgetown University—the worst thing they could do was turn me down. There were no fucking explosives if it didn't work out.

Back home, all that clarity of purpose faded almost before I knew it. I wanted it back. I wanted that feeling of solidity and strength again.

Not everything was awful.

The summer I returned I attended this huge outdoor rock festival. We're talking about 150,000 hippies in one place at one time. Hippie central. I assumed if I mentioned what I did for a living people would react very negatively. But I was really intrigued when everybody was supportive. People were like, *Wow, thanks.* Or, *Hey, you guys are doing a great job.* Or like, *That's really cool.* Two people—two hippies—actually asked me about joining the military. Asked me if I would recommend it to them. It blew my fucking mind: It was a different world out there than it used to be even ten years ago. When I used to go to Lollapalooza in the nineties there would not have been that kind of support. I might have said I was a soldier and the response would have been very different. *Why are you selling your soul to the government, blah, blah, blah?* It would never have been, *Hey, wow. You're awesome.*

And certainly here in the communities around Campbell, there were signs up everywhere. WELCOME BACK 101ST! WE SUPPORT OUR TROOPS! It was huge. And it was great. People around Campbell backed the troops in a big, big way. Even if they didn't support the war, they supported the troops.

But there have still been these feelings of depression.

Months after I returned, it still felt weird that I didn't have a weapon with me at all times. There were times when I almost felt like I should go buy a handgun because I didn't have a weapon in my house. What if something happened?

Little things like that felt completely normal to me. Like my reaction to bad drivers. If someone cut me off in traffic here in Tennessee, there was this automatic adrenaline surge. I can't imagine how I might have responded if I had been allowed to carry my M-4 carbine with me off the base. I don't mean to make a joke about it, but I almost think there might be one or two fewer bad drivers out there.

I still swerved to avoid trash in the road. In Iraq it could be an IED. A soda can on the side of the road could be an IED. A grocery bag could be an IED.

I had real trouble sleeping. I rarely had trouble before combat. Now I woke up with my sheets soaking wet. And I never remembered my dreams. I didn't remember my dreams for an entire year after I got back.

My first Fourth of July home was horrible. I freaked every time a firecracker went off in my neighborhood. If I watched the fireworks go up, it didn't bother me too much. But if I was looking away and talking to someone when one went up, I jumped every time.

It's been frustrating. I just want these feelings to go away. I just want to be normal.

Now the feelings come and go. Almost by day or week. Sometimes I feel better, sometimes worse. It remains hard for me to meet new people.

Sometimes now I end up around a bunch of soldiers who were also in Iraq, and we can talk about what it was like. We can bond pretty easily. But when I meet random civilians, I feel like they don't understand things.

Sometimes I feel I have failed horribly. Even here. Even now. With this book. I have somehow failed to express what life in war was like for us.

There are so many things that are still really tough for me to discuss. And I keep trying to put my finger on *why*. Even though we, the troops today, are supported like the Vietnam vets were not—we now know it took lies to get us deployed. (WMDs? What WMDs?) And all the problems that are still going on. People trying to kill us all the fucking time. The conflict that continues of how to deal with being there with a spoon in one hand and a gun in the other. Falluja's a complete disaster. The mess hall in Mosul where Zoe and I ate chow twice a day has now been bombed— more than twenty soldiers were killed and dozens more were injured. Tal Afar has blown up. Since the 101st left, it's been a total mess.

The more we know about what brought about this war in the first place, the harder and harder it gets. It was a year of my life. And what the fuck for? What was it all about? Not having an answer for that makes it hard. Makes it feel dirty. It was hard enough to go. I had enough doubts when I went. I knew even then that at least some of it was bullshit.

It makes it really hard to know that I was over there and lived in privation and filth, risking my life. Away from my family and my home. Seeing death. What Shane went through. The fact that the war was based on lies destroys some of the sense of purpose for me. It degrades some of the goodness of our efforts. Not all of the goodness. Especially when I think about the children I saw, attending schools again in places where they had not been able to do so for more than a generation. They were so happy to go to school. Or when kids saw us and they'd cheer for us. That means there's hope. A future. But otherwise, talking about the war and our reasons for going to war remain difficult for me. For us. For every single one of us.

EPILOGUE

I PARTICIPATE IN a field-training exercise with the Rakkasans on the Back-40, a huge swath of forest far from Fort Campbell's built-up installations and barracks. Several thousand soldiers out in the field for several days. Living and sleeping outdoors. Once again I'm with 1/187, and only a handful of us are female. I don't see another woman for days.

On the Back-40 at Fort Campbell, it is miserably cold and rainy. A few dozen soldiers play the "enemy," or OPFOR (opposing force). As we clear buildings in an "Iraqi village," the OPFOR opens fire. Caught in a firefight, I shoot my weapon. All our guns are rigged with blank adapters that sound real—but nothing comes out of the barrels. (Paintball rounds would have been better, but they jam too easily. And they also can bruise you if you get shot in the face at close range.)

I hang with infantry guys I haven't seen since the real war. I see Delta Co soldiers from that day in Baghdad when the Iraqi man died. They still remember me after so much time, and that means a lot to me. And here I am again. Interpreting as commanders or platoon leaders talk to "locals"—who are played by Iraqi Americans hired for the occasion. The situation may sound totally absurdist to outsiders, but I am happier and more relaxed doing this than I have been in months.

I worry at first about war flashbacks. Horror memories. And a few guys do freak. Overreact to the situation. Rough up the Iraqi Americans. Kneel hard on their heads.

I'm fine. My mind is clear. I feel purposeful again, very competent. It catches me by surprise what a total rush it is. But when it's over, my body also aches. My knees are fucking sore. Thinking: I am getting too old for this shit.

In 2005 I know only a few people who plan to reenlist. And only a handful who plan to make careers out of the Army. Most who are choosing to reenlist will do so once—and then get out. It's no secret: The Army is currently experiencing serious retention problems due to the high operations tempo. We all know that everyone who deploys can expect to deploy again. And most of us don't like it.

Zoe's out of the Army now. She had applied for an early school drop, but the Army lost her paperwork. She was convinced the drop would never go through. Then—suddenly—it did. And she learned that her contract with the Army would end in less than two weeks. Of course she was relieved. But also scared. How was she going to support herself? Getting out so fast meant she would not get monthly paychecks she'd been expecting. And now she had to deal with that. Not to mention everything else. No more life insurance. No more health insurance. No more access to the commissary. She wouldn't be able to go to the cheap mechanics on base if her car broke down. Zoe's now attending college full-time with an idea that she might become a social worker. But she has no clear fix yet on her future.

Matt is currently my housemate. Even though his ETS is August 2005, he is likely to return to Iraq; he may get stop-lossed for a year—or more. He'd like to go to college, but he's a pragmatist. He knows the 101st Airborne Division (Air Assault) is going back; everyone does. Fort Campbell always gets deployed—it's a rapid-deployable unit. That's the whole point of the 101st. It isn't like he can avoid it.

As for Shane Kelly, he also moved into my house sometime in the summer after I returned to Fort Campbell. We're still seeing each other. When I see him with his parents, I realize he's a better son to them than I have been a daughter to my parents. I watch him with his own daughter and see what a great dad he is. It really moves me to watch him with her. I also think he's really tough and smart and sexy. We never say the word *love* to each other, and I don't know what's going to happen. But we're trying to work things out.

Even after several operations, Shane still has shrapnel in his head. His traumatic brain injury causes him severe headaches and wicked depressions. He has trouble with his memory, and the medications have not helped much. At Campbell no one could provide him the care or treatment he really needed. They threw pills at him, but nothing worked. Everything was fucked up. Finally, in the late fall of 2004, he moved back to Walter Reed so he could receive better medical care. But there are still tons of problems; the bureaucracy he has to negotiate to get therapy programs has been horrible. This is a man who almost made the ultimate sacrifice for his country. Now he has to fight for everything. What is going to happen to Shane? Does the Army expect a man with a traumatic brain injury to advocate on his own behalf for the care and treatment he deserves? There are days he can barely get out of bed in the morning, the pain is so intense. Watching how shabbily the Army treats Shane—not to mention so many other seriously wounded veterans of this war—has been the deepest disillusionment for me.

Lauren will go back with the Rakkasans to Iraq for another year. She knows it. She's been promoted to corporal and now has her own team; they gave her a team as soon as they could so it would have more cohesion by the time they're deployed. She's training them now. In the meantime we've become very close friends—sharing an occasional night out and a weekly Sunday brunch. Not long ago, I met her parents for the first time. Afterward Lauren said: "I wish you were coming back with me. I wish we were going back together."

It's so hard. So difficult. I feel guilt about it. I know the mission is not over. I still have the desire to go back. Finish what we started. But I need to move on. I need my life not to be on hold anymore. So it's a terrible conflict for me. I want to be free to do what I please, go where I please, live where I please. I don't want to have to file a mileage waiver form every time I travel more than 250 miles from base. I want to visit Europe. Go to museums in Washington, D.C., and take the train up to New York City. Not live in Clarksville, Tennessee.

But I'm not kidding myself. I know the Army can call me back. It's not over. I'm not really done. When I signed my contract in the spring of 2000, it was five years active and then three more years IRR. Inactive ready reserve. If I'm not stop-lossed, and I do get out of the Army in April 2005, I must still keep them informed of my whereabouts. They need to be able to reach me. I can still get a letter. Telling me to come back.

This does happen. I know a girl with my military occupational specialty on IRR who got the letter to come back. So it's not over. I'm not completely safe until 2008. I could be in graduate school. I could have a job I love. And the letter could come. Tomorrow. Next week. Next month. Next year.

No, it's not over. Not for a long while yet.

ACKNOWLEDGMENTS

I WANT TO thank the wonderful men and women with whom I served—and all who serve today. In particular, I am indebted to the soldiers I worked most closely with, both in MI and combat arms. I was privileged to work alongside amazing people, who have shown me how incredible people can be, both in complexity and in the simplicity of our most basic nature. All you soldiers are better than anyone gives you credit for . . . I could never name all of those who touched me, but I will not forget.

My year in Iraq was difficult—but it would have been nearly impossible for me if it weren't for all the support I got from people back home. To everyone who wrote me and sent me packages, thank you—I cannot properly express the difference it made to get letters and treats so regularly. My parents came through with unconditional support when I needed it most. The rest of my family and my friends kept me in their lives while I was away. And complete strangers made sure that we knew we were not forgotten. My sincerest gratitude goes to all of you.

I want to thank Michael, for coming to me with the idea of this book and working so hard to keep it as accurate as possible.

I also appreciate all the hard work by the people at Norton to make this happen, and our agent for helping us get it published at all. Despite everyone's best efforts, errors are inevitable, and I take full responsibility for those that remain in the book.

There have been a few people who helped me survive the past few years relatively whole. Stephanie, Amber, Justin . . . you have been there for me and been honest with me without fail. Brian, you push me when I need a goad and support me when I need comfort. Thank you most of all—I cannot imagine having done this without you.

UNHOLY WAR

Also by John L. Esposito

Author

The Islamic Threat: Myth or Reality?
Islam: The Straight Path
Women in Muslim Family Law
Islam and Politics
Makers of Contemporary Islam (with John O. Voll)
World Religions Today (with Darrell J. Fasching and Todd Lewis)
Islam and Democracy (with John O. Voll)

Editor

The Oxford Encyclopedia of the Modern Islamic World
The Oxford History of Islam
The Oxford Dictionary of Islam
Political Islam: Revolution, Radicalism, or Reform
Voices of Resurgent Islam
Islam in Asia: Religion, Politics, and Society
The Iranian Revolution: Its Global Impact
Muslims on the Americanization Path?
(with Yvonne Yazbeck Haddad)
Islam, Gender, and Social Change (with Yvonne Yazbeck Haddad)
Religion and Global Order (with Michael Watson)
Islam and Secularism in the Middle East (with Azzam Tamimi)
Muslims and the West: Encounter and Dialogue
(with Zafar Ishaq Ansari)

UNHOLY WAR

Terror in the Name of Islam

John L. Esposito

OXFORD
UNIVERSITY PRESS
2002

OXFORD
UNIVERSITY PRESS

Oxford   New York
Auckland   Bangkok   Buenos Aires   Cape Town   Chennai
Dar es Salaam   Delhi   Hong Kong   Istanbul   Karachi   Kolkata
Kuala Lumpur   Madrid   Melbourne   Mexico City   Mumbai   Nairobi
São Paulo   Shanghai   Singapore   Taipei   Tokyo   Toronto

and an associated company in
Berlin

Library of Congress Cataloging-in-Publication Data
Esposito, John L.
Unholy war : terror in the name of Islam / John L. Esposito.
p. cm.
Includes bibliographical references and index.
ISBN 0-19-515435-5
1. Terrorism—Religious aspects—Islam.
2. Jihad. 3. Islam and world politics.
4. Anti-Americanism. I. Title
HV6431 .E76 2002
322.4'2'0882971—dc21   2001058009

1 3 5 7 9 8 6 4 2
Printed in the United States of America
on acid-free paper

For John and Mary Esposito
in honor of their 87th and 90th birthdays

Contents

Preface

Terror in the Name of Islam

The tragedy of September 11, 2001, brought Americans together as a nation, united in grief and in resolve. At the same time, Americans from every walk of life began asking some hard questions about America, global terrorism, and the Muslim world. More than a decade ago, in the wake of the fall of the Soviet Union and Saddam Hussein's call for a jihad against the West in the 1991 Gulf war, I wrote *The Islamic Threat: Myth or Reality?*, responding to the growing propensity among senior government officials, political commentators, and the media to see a new "evil empire" replacing the communist threat.

Sadly, more than a decade later, the same questions about Islam and the Muslim world are still being asked: Why do they hate us? Why is Islam more militant than other religions? What does the Quran have to say about jihad or holy war? Does the Quran condone this kind of violence and terrorism? Is there a clash of civilizations between the West and the Muslim world? Yet it is now more important than ever that we educate ourselves about Islam and the roots of terrorism.

Master terrorist Osama bin Laden, like other religious extremists, is the product of his upbringing and experiences in life, of the religious world he inherited and which he reinvents for his own purposes. As in the history of every world religion, violent struggles have been a part of Muslim history. Bin Laden and other terrorists exploit the authority of the past (Muhammad, the Quran, and Islamic history) for the religious rationale, precedents, and radical interpreters to justify and inspire their call for a jihad against Muslim governments and the West; they legitimate warfare and terrorism, and they equate their suicide bombings with martyrdom. An understanding of the religious and historical sources for their beliefs, values, tactics, and actions becomes imperative. Have they hijacked Islam for their own unholy purposes, or do they, as they claim, represent a return to the authentic teachings of the faith?

In some sense, bin Laden and al-Qaeda represent a watershed for contemporary Islamic radicalism. Although in the past the Ayatollah Khomeini and other major Islamic activist leaders had called for a broader Islamic revolution, both violent and nonviolent, the focus and impact of most extremist movements from North Africa to Southeast Asia had been at the local or regional level. Osama bin Laden and al-Qaeda represent the next major step, jihad international, that not only declares jihad against governments in the Muslim world and attacks Western representatives and institutions in the region but now makes America and the West a primary target in an unholy war of terrorism.

America's wars of the twentieth century were fought on the soil of other countries. Now, the battle has been brought to our own shores and to the symbols of our economic and political power. The stakes have risen for everyone. The attacks against America on September 11 have rightly been seen as a clarion call to recognize our danger and respond to an enemy that threatens all—all the countries, cultures, and peoples of the world.

The twenty-first century will be dominated by the global encounter of two major and rapidly growing world religions, Christianity and Islam, and by the forces of globalization that will strain relations between the West and the rest. It is not a time for provoking a clash of civilizations or for the self-fulfilling prophecy that such a clash is inevitable. It is rather a time for global engagement and coalition building, for the active promotion of coexistence and cooperation. Amidst pressures to win the global war against terrorism at any cost, how we understand Islam and the Muslim world will affect how we address the causes of terrorism and of anti-Americanism and whether we preserve our American values at home and abroad. We must be able to move beyond political rhetoric, beyond the world of black and white, of unadulterated good versus evil invoked not only by bin Laden and those like him but by his opponents as well.

I have written this book for the vast majority of people in the West, non-Muslims as well as Muslims, whose lives and communities in the twenty-first century are inextricably intertwined. The Muslim world is no longer "out there"; Muslims are our neighbors, colleagues, and fellow citizens, and their religion, like Judaism and Christianity, rejects terrorism. Never before have soft phrases like "building bridges of understanding" been more critical in a war that ultimately cannot be won simply by military power. Understanding and action go hand in hand for Muslims and non-Muslims alike. All of us are challenged to move beyond stereotypes, historic grievances, and religious differences, to recognize our shared values as well as interests, and to move collectively to build our common future.

Of all the books I have written this has been the most difficult, because of the horrific occasion that precipitated it and the range and selection of coverage. As a result, I am especially indebted to those who assisted me and worked under severe time constraints. Natana De Long-Bas is in every sense my senior research assistant. Her work on this project as on others reflected consistent excellence. Her commitment is captured in a picture I have of Natana in labor in the hospital delivery room, working on her research for this book! Juliane Hammer came late to the project but at critical points provided much-needed quick and thorough research. My work has been made infinitely easier due to two remarkable people, Clare Merrill, Assistant Director, and Thomas Jordan, Administrative Assistant, of the Center for Muslim-Christian Understanding at Georgetown, whose intelligence, energy, and results-orientation are invaluable.

I am indebted to several scholars—Ahmed Rashid, Tamara Sonn, James Piscatori, and John O. Voll—who read all or portions of the manuscript, often providing key insights. Cynthia Read, my long-time editor at Oxford, played an especially important role with this book, carefully reviewing each chapter and providing invaluable feedback. The most important person in writing this book was Jean Esposito, my wife, partner, and best friend. While she always managed to balance her own career and interests with substantial involvement in all my books, for this book she was a pivotal force as we determined its structure, contents, and text, and when I was ready to pull the plug, she convinced me to continue. *Unholy War* is in every sense of the words as much her book as mine.

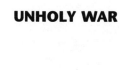

UNHOLY WAR

1

The Making of a Modern Terrorist

Osama bin Laden seems like the last person destined to be a global terrorist. His journey from a life of wealth and privilege, as the scion of a multibillionaire Saudi family with close ties to the king and royal family, to the caves and military training camps of Afghanistan sounds more like the stuff of fiction than reality. What happened to transform a quiet, shy, serious, and wealthy Saudi young man into the world community's most wanted criminal? How are we to understand a man who has been described as "an Islamic zealot, a military genius, a poet, and an impassioned enemy of the United States"?[1]

Osama bin Laden was born in Riyadh, Saudi Arabia, in 1957, the seventeenth (the seventh son) of fifty-two children. His father, Muhammad bin Laden, had come to the Kingdom from South Yemen around 1930 as an illiterate laborer. He started a small construction business and went on to become one of Saudi Arabia's wealthiest construction magnates. He developed ties to the royal family and was awarded exclusive contracts. In the 1950s, Osama's father designed and built the al-Hada road, which permitted Muslims from Yemen to make the pilgrimage to Mecca (*hajj*), one of the five basic religious requirements of Islam, more easily. His company also received a multibillion dollar contract to restore and expand the Grand Mosques of Mecca and Medina, raising his company's prestige throughout the Muslim world and setting the stage for the company's expansion beyond Saudi Arabia. The bin Laden family established a large industrial and financial empire,

the Bin Laden Group, which became one of the largest construction companies in the Middle East.[2] Ironically, given Osama's recent outrage at the Saudi-American alliance and the presence of
American forces in the Kingdom, the Bin Laden Group built many
military support facilities in the Kingdom, including those used
by U.S. forces during the Gulf War.

The relationship between the bin Laden clan and the royal family goes beyond business ties to include friendship and intermar-
riage. The bin Laden sons have attended the same schools as
numerous princes of the royal family in Europe and America and
have studied at and/or given money to some of the best universities, including Harvard, Oxford, and Tufts.[3]

Osama's father was a strong, hard-working, dominating, pious
man who insisted on keeping all of his children in one household
and raised them according to a strict moral and religious code.
The family home was open to many Muslims, especially during
hajj, and Osama was able at an early age to meet Muslim scholars
and leaders of Islamic movements from all over the Islamic world.[4]
Like many in the Arab world, bin Laden's father is said to have felt
passionately about the Palestinian-Israeli conflict. This appears in
an anecdote that has the elder bin Laden seeking to contribute to
the liberation of Palestine. One day, as the story goes, he demanded
that his company's engineers convert two hundred bulldozers into
tanks for the purpose of attacking Israel. Told that the task was
impossible, he decided instead to produce as many sons as possible and convert *them* into fighters. But out of all the bin Laden
sons, Osama became the only fighter.[5]

Information on Osama bin Laden's youth is limited and at times
contradictory. Some maintain that he was a religiously committed young man protected from corruption by his early marriage to
a Syrian girl.[6] Other sources report that, like many wealthy youths
of his time, he visited Beirut in the early 1970s, where he enjoyed
the nightlife and women of this cosmopolitan city, known at that
time as "the Paris of the Middle East."[7] Like most young people,
he would find or begin to define himself at university.

Bin Laden was educated in Medina and Jeddah, earning his degree in public administration in 1981 at Jeddah's King Abdulaziz University, where he studied management and economics. During his studies, he became more and more religiously oriented, influenced by his university experience and unfolding events in Saudi Arabia and the wider Muslim world. Osama's religious worldview was shaped both by Saudi Arabia's deeply conservative Wahhabi interpretation of Islam and by the revolutionary Islam that began to spread in the 1970s. Each of these influences would be formative in the development of his jihadist vision, mission, and strategy.

The Islamic Vision

Islam emphasizes action, performing the will of God. It more closely resembles Judaism with its focus on following the law than Christianity with its emphasis on belief. Muslims are enjoined to act, to struggle (*jihad*) to implement their belief, to lead a good life, to defend religion, to contribute to the development of a just Islamic society throughout the world. The life and experience of the early community provide the model for the spread and defense of Islam through *hijra* and jihad. When Muhammad and his Companions suffered unremitting persecution in Mecca, they emigrated (*hijra*) to Yathrib, later renamed Medina, "the city" of the Prophet. Having regrouped, established, and strengthened the community at Medina, Muhammad then set about the struggle (jihad) to spread and defend God's Word and rule. This pattern of hijra and jihad in the face of adversity, coupled with the concept of the *ummah* (the worldwide Islamic community), which stresses a pan-Islamic unity, has guided Muslims throughout the ages, including bin Laden and many terrorists today.

Jihad and the Creation of Saudi Arabia

Osama bin Laden's worldview was very much influenced by the religious heritage and political climate in Saudi Arabia and the

Arab world in the 1960s and 1970s. Key influences included the environment of Saudi Arabia, a self-styled Islamic state with a rigid, puritanical, Wahhabi brand of Islam, the militant jihad ideology of Egypt's Sayyid Qutb, whose disciples had found refuge and positions in the kingdom, and the devastating Arab defeat in the 1967 Arab-Israeli war.

The kingdom of Saudi Arabia from its earliest beginnings has relied on the blending of religion and political power. Its origins stretch back to the eighteenth century when an Islamic revivalist and theologian, Muhammad ibn Abd al-Wahhab, formed an alliance with a local tribal chief, Muhammad ibn Saud of Dariyya (a town near modern-day Riyadh), to create a religiopolitical movement, Wahhabism. The movement swept across central Arabia, capturing Mecca and Medina and uniting its tribes in what its followers believed was a re-creation of Islam's seventh-century beginnings under the Prophet Muhammad. Athough the movement was crushed by the Ottoman Empire, a descendant of the House of Saud, Abdulaziz ibn Saud (1879–1953), reasserted the family's claims to Arabia and led a religious and political movement that resulted in the establishment of modern-day Saudi Arabia.

The Wahhabi religious vision or brand of Islam, named after Muhammad ibn Abd al-Wahhab, has been a staple of the Saudi government, a source of their religious and political legitimation. It is a strict, puritanical faith that emphasizes literal interpretation of the Quran and *Sunnah* (example) of the Prophet Muhammad and the absolute oneness of God. The Wahhabis denounced other tribes and Muslim communities as polytheists or idolaters. Anything the Wahhabis perceived as un-Islamic behavior constituted unbelief (*kufr*) in their eyes, which must be countered by jihad. Thus jihad or holy war was not simply permissible: to fight the unbelievers and reestablish a true Islamic state was required.

Abdulaziz framed the development of Saudi Arabia using stories and symbols drawn from the life and struggles of Muhammad. He recruited Bedouin tribesmen to join the brotherhood of believers and, like Muhammad's community, engage in a process of hijra and jihad. Like Muhammad and the early community, they emigrated to new settlements where they could live a true Islamic life and be trained religiously and militarily. They combined missionary zeal, military might, and a desire for booty to once again spread Islamic rule in Arabia, waging holy wars approved by their religious leaders. Abdulaziz used the banner of the puritanical Wahhabi to legitimate fighting other Muslim tribal leaders and seizing Mecca and Medina. As in the Christian tradition, death in battle merited martyrdom and eternal bliss in paradise; likewise, as in the Christian Crusades, victory meant not only the triumph of virtue but also the rewards of plunder and booty. Wahhabi history and paradigms were an essential part of Osama bin Laden's religious faith and sense of history, a heritage he would turn to in later life for inspiration and guidance.

During the 1970s many Islamic activists, both Saudi-born and foreigners, were to be found in the Kingdom. Among Osama's teachers at King Abdulaziz University was Dr. Abdullah Azzam, who would later become prominent in Afghanistan. Azzam, a Jordanian member of the Palestinian Muslim Brotherhood and reportedly a founder of Hamas, had strong academic and Islamic activist credentials.[8] Trained at Damascus University in theology, he earned a doctorate in Islamic jurisprudence at Egypt's famed al-Azhar University. Azzam was an advocate of a militant global jihad ideology and culture, seeing it as a duty incumbent on all Muslims. Sometimes described as the Emir of Jihad or Godfather of global jihad, Azzam was a captivating speaker who preached a clear message of militant confrontation and conflict: "Jihad and the rifle alone: no negotiations, no conferences, and no dialogues."[9] Azzam's jihad was global in scope, aimed at recouping the glories and lands of Islam. "This duty will not end with victory in Afghanistan; jihad will remain an individual obligation until all other lands that were Muslim are returned to us so that Islam will reign again: before us lie Palestine, Bokhara, Lebanon, Chad, Eritrea, Somalia, the Philippines, Burma, Southern Yemen, Tashkent and Andalusia [southern Spain]."[10]

Dr. Muhammad Qutb, a famous scholar and activist, was another of Osama's teachers. He was a brother of Sayyid Qutb, a leader of the militant wing of the Muslim Brotherhood who was executed in 1966 when Gamal Abdel Nasser's government crushed and outlawed the Brotherhood. Sayyid Qutb is widely acknowledged as the father of militant jihad, a major influence on the worldview of radical movements across the Muslim world, and venerated as a martyr of contemporary Islamic revivalism. Qutb's writings and ideas provided the religious worldview and discourse for generations of activists, moderate and extremist. For those Muslims who, like bin Laden, were educated in schools and universities with Islamist teachers, Sayyid Qutb was a staple of their Islamic education.

Bin Laden was educated at a time when Islamic movements and religious extremist or jihad movements were on the rise in the broader Muslim world and within Saudi Arabia. The disastrous and humiliating defeat of the Arabs in the 1967 Six-Day Arab-Israeli war, in which the combined forces of Egypt, Syria, and Jordan were beaten within hours by "tiny little Israel," was a major turning point in the history of contemporary Islam. It generated deep soul-searching about what had gone wrong with Islam, the modern failure and impotence of a Muslim world that for centuries after its creation had experienced unparalleled success and power. What came to be called The Disaster was countered in 1973 by a jihad against Israel fought by Anwar Sadat. Its code name was Badr, symbolizing the first great and miraculous victory of the Prophet Muhammad over a superior Meccan army. This was followed by another significant event in the world of Osama bin Laden. The Arab oil embargo, with its crippling impact on the West, gave Muslims a new sense of pride. The Arab world and the heartland of Islam seemed to reemerge as a major economic power after centuries of subservience to European imperialism.

The 1970s also witnessed an increase in the power and visibility of internal Islamic opposition and reform movements. In Egypt the Muslim Brotherhood along with a series of radical groups reemerged as a major oppositional force. Iran's Islamic revolution came as an inspirational rallying cry for Islamic activists across the Muslim world. Saudi Arabia itself was rocked by the seizure of the Grand Mosque in Mecca in 1979 by militants who called for the overthrow of the House of Saud. Many of these militants were well-educated, pious activists who denounced the wealth and corruption of the "infidel" regime and the corrosive impact of the West on religious and social values. They wanted to purify and return to traditional Islam, re-creating a true Islamic state and society. While bin Laden does not seem to have sided with Saudi extremists, he could not help but be strongly affected by the activist mood of the 1970s in Saudi Arabia and beyond.

Jihad in Afghanistan:
The Making of a Holy Warrior

A major turning point in Osama bin Laden's life, the beginning of his journey toward becoming a *mujahid,* or warrior for God, occurred with the 1979 Soviet invasion and occupation of Afghanistan. As bin Laden would later say, "What I lived in two years there, I could not have lived in a hundred years elsewhere."[11] By the 1970s Afghanistan had become overwhelmingly dependent on the Soviet Union's patronage for its survival. Marxist and Maoist parties thrived while Islamist parties and movements were repressed. In July 1973 Prince Muhammad Daud, a former prime minister and cousin of the Afghan King Zahir Shah, overthrew the government, abolished the monarchy, and proclaimed himself president of Afghanistan. Five years later the People's Democratic Party of Afghanistan staged a coup and established a new communist government. This was followed by the direct intervention and occupation of Afghanistan by the Soviet Union in 1979. The occupation galvanized Afghanistan's diverse tribal and religious leaders and movements in a popular jihad. Afghanistan's tribal society had a fragile unity offset by the realities of its multiethnic tribal society comprising Pashtuns, Uzbeks, Tajiks, and Hazaras divided religiously between a Sunni Muslim majority and a minority of

Shii Muslims. Soviet occupation, however, provided a common enemy and mission. The call for a jihad offered a common, though transient as history would prove, Islamic religious identity and source of inspiration. The *mujahidin* holy war to liberate Islam and Afghanistan from Soviet (atheistic) communist occupation would eventually drive out the Soviet military, defeat the Afghan communists, and lead to the establishment of an Islamic state in 1992.[12]

When the anti-Soviet jihad began, bin Laden was among the first to rush to the Afghan refugee camps in Peshawar, Pakistan, to meet with mujahidin leaders, some of whom he had already come to know during hajj gatherings at his home in Saudi Arabia. From 1979 to 1982 he collected funds and materiel for the jihad and made intermittent visits from Saudi Arabia to Pakistan. In 1982 he finally entered Afghanistan, bringing large quantities of construction machinery as well as funding, and becoming a full participant in the Afghan jihad. By 1984 increasing numbers of Arab mujahidin were arriving in Pakistan to join the holy war. Bin Laden responded by establishing a guesthouse in Peshawar for Arabs on their way to the front in Afghanistan. In 1986 Osama became more directly involved in the war, setting up his own camps and commanding Arab mujahidin forces who became known as Arab Afghans in battle. He subsequently created al-Qaeda (the base), to organize and track the channeling of fighters and funds for the Afghan resistance. Six-feet five-inches tall, with a long beard and piercing eyes, the wealthy and powerfully connected bin Laden was well on his way to becoming a poster-boy for the jihad, at first as a hero and later as a global terrorist.

Bin Laden's activities were applauded by the Saudi government, which, along with the United States, had made a heavy commitment to supporting the jihad against the Soviet Union. For America, this was a "good jihad." Ironically, although the United States had been threatened by Iran's revolutionary Islam and the violence and terrorism committed by jihad groups in Egypt, Lebanon, and elsewhere, our government was able to cheer and support Afghanistan's holy warriors, providing considerable funding as well as

Central Intelligence Agency (CIA) advisers. Everyone was in agreement. For Osama bin Laden, as for Saudi Arabia and indeed Muslims worldwide, the Afghan jihad to repel foreigners from Islamic territory was eminently in accord with Islamic doctrine.

Bin Laden proved himself to be a selfless and dedicated mujahid, or holy warrior. Still young, he was more comfortable as an activist than as an ideologue, focused primarily on the jihad in Afghanistan rather than on Muslim international politics and activism. Ahmed Rashid, expert on the Taliban and al-Qaeda, writes of bin Laden:

> Arab Afghans who knew him during the jihad say he was neither intellectual nor articulate about what needed to be done in the Muslim world. In that sense he was neither the Lenin of the Islamic revolution, nor was he the internationalist ideologue of the Islamic revolution such as Che Guevera was to the revolution in the third world. Bin Laden's former associates describe him as deeply impressionable, always in need of mentors, men who knew more about Islam and the modern world than he did.[13]

The Radicalization of a Saudi Elite

How did Osama bin Laden, member of the Saudi elite, mujahid, and hero of the war in Afghanistan, become radicalized? After Soviet troops withdrew from Afghanistan in 1989, bin Laden returned to Saudi Arabia and a job in the family business. Though initially received as a hero, speaking at mosques and to private gatherings, he was soon at loggerheads with the royal family, vociferous in his warning of an impending Iraqi invasion of Kuwait. Saudi Arabia, along with Kuwait and the United States, had for many years, in particular during the Iraq-Iran War, been strong supporters of Saddam Hussein's Iraq, seeing it as a check on the Ayatollah Khomeini's Iran. When Iraq did invade Kuwait in August 1990, bin Laden quickly wrote to King Fahd, offering to bring the Arab Afghan mujahidin to Saudi Arabia to defend the kingdom. Instead, the deafening silence from the palace was shattered by news that American forces were to defend the House of Saud. The admission and stationing of foreign non-Muslim troops in Islam's holy land and their permanent deployment after the Gulf war, bin Laden would later say, transformed his life completely, placing him on a collision course with the Saudi government and the West. He spoke out forcefully against the Saudi alliance with the United States, obtained a *fatwa* (legal opinion) from a senior religious scholar that training was a religious duty, and sent several thousand volunteers to train in Afghanistan.

Like other Arab Afghans who returned to their home countries, in Afghanistan bin Laden had enjoyed the freedom to think and act and to engage in a religious mission to overcome injustice and create an Islamic state and society. In Saudi Arabia he found himself bound within the confines of a regime whose policies and alliances he more and more came to despise as corrupt and un-Islamic. While many of the Arab Afghans who returned to Egypt, Algeria, and elsewhere quickly became involved in radical opposition movements, bin Laden continued to struggle within the system. The government restricted his movement in an attempt to silence him. Finally, in April 1991 he escaped to Afghanistan via Pakistan. When he arrived, however, he found himself not in the Islamic state for which the jihad had been fought but in one mired in the religious and ethnic warfare of its aftermath.

Within a brief period after the Soviet withdrawal, the great Islamic victory had collapsed into interethnic and sectarian warfare, fueled by foreign patrons. The net result was chaos and the devastation of Afghanistan as various warlords vied to set up their own fiefdoms.

Despite the Afghan victory, the jihad had failed to develop a coherent ideology or basis for political unity. The United States walked away from an Afghanistan whose countryside was devastated by a ten-year Soviet occupation that had cost more than one million lives. Mujahidin groups, many of which today make up the Northern Alliance that with U.S. backing fought and defeated the Taliban, represented competing ethnic, tribal, and religious groups. The country was gripped by a civil war that pitted the majority Pashtun population in the south and east against the ethnic minorities of the north—Tajik, Uzbek, Hazara, and Turkmen. The conflict was further compounded by the intervention and competing agendas of outside powers. Pakistan and Saudi Arabia supported Sunni mujahidin groups while Iran backed an alliance of Shii minority organizations. The majority of Afghans found themselves caught in the middle of a prolonged civil war marked by heavy fighting, lawlessness, pillaging, rape, and plunder. Bin Laden was frustrated by his inability to contribute to the resolution of the problems of chaos and lawlessness. In 1992, after several months amidst the inter-mujahidin squabbling and fighting over succession after the collapse of the pro-Soviet regime, bin Laden moved to Sudan.

Sudan and the Entrepreneur-Mujahid

In January 1989, in a coup led by Colonel Omar al-Bashir, the National Islamic Front (NIF) had come to power in Sudan and established an Islamic republic. Bashir had enlisted the help of Hasan al-Turabi, the Sorbonne-educated leader of the NIF, regarded by many as one of the most brilliant and articulate of the Islamic activist leaders of political Islam internationally. Al-Turabi became the ideologue of the regime, holding a number of political positions, including speaker of the parliament. NIF members provided the backbone and infrastructure for the new government. The government, in a relationship that proved mutually beneficial, welcomed bin Laden. Bin Laden found a refuge and invested his wealth in much-needed construction projects as well as farms and other businesses in the fledgling Islamic state. During these years Sudan, with its open borders, was increasingly condemned by America and Europe for its links with revolutionary Iran and for harboring international terrorists and their training camps. In 1993 Sudan was placed on the State Department's list of countries that sponsor terrorism. bin Laden was among those individuals whom U.S. intelligence identified as sponsoring terrorist training camps. Although he denied direct involvement and was never formally indicted, bin Laden voiced his approval for the World Trade Center bombing in 1993 and the killing of U.S. troops in Mogadishu, Somalia. American officials were divided as to whether he provided training and arms to those responsible.

Bin Laden's final break with Saudi Arabia came in 1994 when the Kingdom revoked his citizenship and moved to freeze his assets in Saudi Arabia because of his support for fundamentalist movements. From that point on, bin Laden became more outspoken in his denunciation of the House of Saud. Now pushed to the fringe, he joined with other dissident activists and religious scholars to create the Advice and Reform Committee, founded in Saudi Arabia but forced subsequently to move to London. This political opposition group strongly criticized the Saudi regime but did not overtly advocate violence.

By 1995, a series of events and accusations had catapulted the previously obscure bin Laden to center stage. U.S. intelligence sources claimed that he had established extensive training operations in northern Yemen near the Saudi border.[14] Investigators charged that Ramzi Yousef, the captured mastermind of the World Trade Center bombing, had stayed at a bin Laden–financed guesthouse and had financial links to bin Laden. Bin Laden sent a letter to King Fahd advocating guerrilla attacks to drive the U.S. forces out of the Kingdom. Some charged that he was linked to an unsuccessful assassination attempt in Addis Ababa, in June 1995, against President Hosni Mubarak of Egypt. When five Americans and two Indians were killed in a truck bombing in Riyadh in November 1995, bin Laden denied involvement but praised those who committed the attack.[15] Responding to mounting international pressure, especially from the United States and Saudi Arabia, in May 1996 Sudan expelled bin Laden. Ironically, Sudan offered to extradite him to Saudi Arabia or America; both refused to take him. Though some had urged the United States to take advantage of the tentative overtures that the NIF government was making, the Clinton administration chose otherwise.

Bin Laden fled back to Afghanistan.[16] Shortly after, in June, a large truck bomb tore apart the Khobar Towers, a U.S. military residence in Dhahran, Saudi Arabia, killing nineteen servicemen. Investigators were initially divided between placing the blame with bin Laden or with a militant Saudi Shii organization.[17] Bin Laden praised those behind the Riyadh and Dhahran bombings but denied direct involvement: "I have great respect for the people who did this. What they did is a big honor that I missed participating in."[18] In June 2001 thirteen members of Saudi Hizbollah, a Shiite group from the Eastern province of Saudi Arabia, were indicted in the United States for the Dhahran bombing.

The Taliban and bin Laden

In 1996, Afghanistan witnessed the rise of an improbable militia that would go on to unite 90 percent of the country and declare the Islamic Republic of Afghanistan. After almost eighteen years of Soviet occupation followed by civil war, a seemingly endless cycle of carnage and chaos was abruptly reversed by the astonishing success of a new Islamic movement.

Late in 1994, as if out of nowhere, the predominantly Pashtun Taliban, a band of *madrasa* (seminary) students (*taliban*) who had been living as refugees in Pakistan suddenly appeared. Initially the Taliban were portrayed as having no military background. In fact many of their *mullahs* (religious leaders) and students were veterans of the Afghan-Soviet war who had returned to the madrasas after the departure of the Soviets. Within two years they swept across the country, overwhelming the Northern Alliance of non-Pashtun minorities. Denouncing the contending mujahidin militias, the Taliban claimed the mantle of moral leadership as representatives of the majority of Afghans who were victims of the internecine warfare.

At first the Taliban were hailed as liberators who promised to restore law and order, stability and security, and make the streets safe for ordinary citizens. They disarmed the population, cleaned up corruption and graft, and imposed *Shariah* (Islamic law). Initially, they enjoyed success and popularity as a reform movement. It was not until their capture of Kabul in 1996 that they revealed their intention to rule the country and to impose a strict puritanical form of Islam. With substantial support from Saudi Arabia and Pakistan, by 1998 they had subdued 90 percent of the country and driven the Northern Alliance into a small area of northeast Afghanistan.

The Taliban brand of Islamic radicalism has been significantly influenced by a militant neo-Deobandi movement in Pakistan. Ironically, the Sunni Deobandi began in the Indian subcontinent as a reformist movement. However, its political expression and ideology were transformed within Pakistan's Jamiyyat-i-Ulama-i-Islam (JUI), a religious party with a rigid, militant, anti-American, and anti-non-Muslim culture. Many of the Taliban were trained in the hundreds of JUI madrasas. Often run by semiliterate mullahs, these schools were first set up for Afghan refugees in the Pashtun-dominated areas of Pakistan, along the border with Afghanistan. Many were supported by Saudi funding that brought with it the influence of an ultraconservative Wahhabi Islam. Students received free education, religious, ideological, and military training. The Taliban teachers showed little knowledge or appreciation for their classical Islamic tradition or for currents of Islamic thought in the broader Muslim world today. They espoused a myopic, self-contained, militant worldview in which Islam is used to legitimate their tribal customs and preferences. The classical Islamic belief in jihad as a defense of Islam and the Muslim community against aggression was transformed into a militant jihad culture and worldview that targets unbelievers, including Muslims and non-Muslims alike.

When they came to power, the Taliban turned over many of their training camps to JUI factions, who in turn trained thousands of Pakistani and Arab militants as well as fighters from South and Central Asia and the Arab world in their radical jihad ideology and tactics. Assisted by military support from Pakistan and financial support from the Wahhabi in Saudi Arabia, with JUI mentoring and influenced by Osama bin Laden's evolving radical jihadist political vision, the Taliban promoted their own brand of revolutionary Islam. They imposed their strict Wahhabi-like brand of Islam on Afghan society. They banned women from school and the workplace, required that men wear beards and women *chadors*, banned music, photography, and television, and imposed strict physical punishments on deviators. Their intolerance for any deviation from their brand of Islam expressed itself in the slaughter of many of Afghanistan's Shii minority (10 percent of the population), whom they disdained as heretics, when the Taliban overran Shii areas such as Mazar-e Sharif in northwest Afghanistan.

Many Muslim religious leaders around the world denounced Taliban "Islamic" policies as aberrant. Muslim governments as diverse as Iran and Egypt, along with Western governments and international human rights organizations, condemned Taliban violations of human rights. Despite their control of most of Afghanistan, by the fall of 1998, neither the United Nations nor most of the global community acknowledged their legitimacy. The Taliban government was recognized by only three nations, Saudi Arabia, Pakistan, and the United Arab Emirates.

Nevertheless, bin Laden found the Taliban's Afghanistan a comfortable haven and useful base of operations. The Taliban leader, Mullah Omar, had been quick to offer sanctuary and express his admiration for bin Laden's sacrifices and dedication to jihad. Bin Laden skillfully cultivated and developed his relationship with Mullah Omar and the Taliban, providing financial support, building roads and other construction projects, and sending his Afghan Arabs to fight alongside the Taliban in critical battles.

Bin Laden's entourage and followers grew steadily. He attracted Arab and other Muslim dissidents, many of whom had had to flee their native countries. Among them were several prominent Egyptian radicals: Dr. Ayman al-Zawahiri, a physician and a leader of the banned Islamic Jihad in Egypt; Rifai Taha Musa, leader of Egypt's banned Gamaa Islamiyya; and two sons of Shaykh Omar Abdel Rahman, the blind Egyptian preacher indicted for involvement in the assassination of Anwar Sadat, suspected of involvement in the World Trade Center bombing of 1993, and later found guilty of conspiring to blow up major sites in New York City. Omar Abdel Rahman had visited Afghanistan several times during the war against the Soviets, when he and bin Laden had first met. Of these men, however, the one to wield the most influence over bin Laden would be Dr. Ayman al-Zawahiri.

Ayman al-Zawahiri:
From Medical School to Jihad University

The story of Ayman al-Zawahiri is that of a gifted surgeon who became a leader of an Egyptian terrorist group on the road to becoming Osama bin Laden's confidant, reputed mentor, and successor. Ayman al-Zawahiri was born in 1953 into a prominent and conservative religious family. He grew up in Maadi, an upscale suburb of Cairo inhabited by wealthy Egyptians and foreign diplomats. His grandfathers were the rector of al-Azhar University, the Islamic world's oldest and most prestigious religious school, and president of Cairo University, Egypt's leading modern secular university.

Family and friends remember Ayman as a normal, well-adjusted young man—an intelligent, well-read, polite student who went on to become a physician. However, 1967 had been a defining moment for him as it was for many in the Arab world. After the disastrous Arab defeat in the 1967 Arab-Israeli (Six Day) war and the disillusionment over Arab (secular) nationalism and socialism that followed, al-Zawahiri turned to political Islam. He joined the Muslim Brotherhood when he was only fourteen years old. By 1979, he had embraced a radical option and joined Islamic Jihad, a violent extremist group composed of small clandestine cells. He quickly became one of its leaders and by 1983 was recruiting members, organizing secret cells and underground operations. After the assassination of Anwar Sadat, Zawahiri was arrested along with hundreds of others. Though no direct link to Sadat's death could be established, he was tried and sentenced to three years in prison on charges of possessing weapons. After his 1984 release from prison, where like many others he had been beaten and tortured, he briefly returned to medical practice in a clinic. The political climate in Egypt and his radical past and prison record, however, prompted al-Zawahiri to emigrate and take a position in Saudi Arabia. Within the year he went to Afghanistan, where he worked as a surgeon, treating wounded Afghan and Arab fighters in field hospitals.[19] It was during this time that he met Dr. Abdullah Azzam, the Palestinian Islamist activist who had taught bin Laden at King Abdulaziz University in Jeddah, Saudi Arabia. Azzam had gone to Pakistan to make his contribution to the war in Afghanistan. After a short stint teaching at the Islamic University in Islamabad, Pakistan, he founded the Jihad Service Bureau, whose mission was the recruitment of Saudis and other Arabs through publications and other media. Azzam joined with bin Laden and Zawahiri in recruiting and training Muslims for the jihad against the Soviets. They formed a lasting friendship and alliance in their growing commitment to a global jihad. After the Soviet defeat in 1989, Zawahiri returned to Egypt and to his leadership role in Islamic Jihad.

Zawahiri played an important role during the 1990s, organizing underground operations and integrating former mujahidin into the ranks of Islamic Jihad. The violence and terrorism of Islamic Jihad were met with equal force by Egyptian military and police. Bloody confrontations were accompanied by the arrest, interrogation, torture, and imprisonment of thousands.

In 1992 Zawahiri moved to Sudan with bin Laden, and in 1996 both returned to Afghanistan. From there, al-Zawahiri continued to be involved in the jihad against the Egyptian state. He is believed to have been the mastermind behind terrorist attacks, including the massacre of fifty-eight tourists in Luxor in 1997, for which he was sentenced to death in absentia by an Egyptian court in 1999. He also merged Islamic Jihad with al-Qaeda and worked with Osama bin Laden to plot and execute their global jihad.

Many believed that Zawahiri possessed a deeper theological understanding and more international perspective than bin Laden, and that he was responsible for broadening bin Laden's vista for jihad beyond the Arab world to the wider Muslim world and to a jihad against America and/or the West. Hamid Mir, a Pakistani journalist who interviewed bin Laden, believes that al-Zawahiri also masterminded the September 11, 2001, attacks. Although only religious leaders can legitimately issue fatwas, bin Laden had nevertheless issued a fatwa allowing the killing of innocent people: "to kill Americans and their allies—civilians and military—is an individual duty for every Muslim who can do it in any country in which it is possible to do it." When Mir pressed him on how this was permissible in light of the fact that the Prophet Muhammad forbade Muslims to kill innocent civilians, he noted that bin Laden responded only after consulting with Zawahiri and checking some Islamic sources.[20] Others, however, contend that bin Laden has long had a global animosity toward America and Israel as well as the intellectual and financial means to pursue it, and that it is he who broadened the perspective of Zawahiri, who had spent the bulk of his formative years as a terrorist focused on toppling the regime and establishing an Islamic state in Egypt. Regardless of who influenced whom, the bin Laden and Zawahiri joint venture produced a powerful global ideology and agenda.

Afghanistan and bin Laden's
Declaration of Holy War

Safely entrenched in Afghanistan, Osama bin Laden assumed a more visible and vocal leadership role in international terrorism, calling openly for a jihad against America and its allies. In August 1996 he issued a Declaration of Jihad whose goals were to drive U.S. forces out of the Arabian peninsula, overthrow the Saudi government, and liberate Islam's holy sites of Mecca and Medina, as well as support revolutionary groups around the world. In November, he again repeated his threat to wage holy war against the United States and its allies if Washington did not remove its troops from the Gulf.[21] By 1998, he seemed increasingly comfortable and astute in using the media to propagate his message and garner support in the Muslim world. From that time onward, his media appearances and statements were carefully crafted, emphasizing both his image and message.

In 2000 bin Laden announced the formation of the World Islamic Front for the Jihad Against Jews and Crusaders, an umbrella group of radical movements across the Muslim world, and issued a fatwa stating that it is the duty of all Muslims to kill U.S. citizens and their allies. The title of the organization summed up the man and his view of the world. Muslims were under siege, their lands occupied in a world dominated by their historic enemies, militant Christianity and Judaism. All true Muslims had an obligation to heed the call to a global jihad, a defense of the worldwide Islamic community. Global politics were indeed for bin Laden a competition and jihad, a clash of civilizations between the Muslim world and the West, between Islam and a militant Judeo-Christian conspiracy. Foreign influence and intervention in the Islamic world had once again underscored the traditional division of the world into the land of Islam (*dar al-Islam*) and the land of warfare (*dar al-harb*). Because of Western abuses, the entire world has been divided, he claimed, "into two regions—one of faith where there is no hypocrisy and another of infidelity, from which we hope God will protect us."[22] If bin Laden and al-Qaeda's attempt to mobilize the world of Islam for their jihad further convinced most Muslim and Western governments of the magnitude of the Islamic threat, it also seemed to contribute to bin Laden's attraction for a growing number of Muslims, particularly in the younger generation. Like Ayatollah Khomeini and Saddam Hussein before him, bin Laden seeks legitimacy and the mobilization of the "Muslim street" or general population through identification with many of the perceptions and grievances of mainstream as well as extremist Muslims. He hijacks Islam, using Islamic doctrine and law to legitimate terrorism.

The major issues and themes of bin Laden's message reflect both his Arab roots and a growing awareness of the broader Islamic community. His primary focus was at first the presence of foreign troops in the Arab peninsula, the overthrow of the Saudi regime, and the Palestinian-Israeli conflict. Bin Laden labeled America and Israel as crusaders and Jews and Zionists and condemned the Saudi regime as compliant and corrupt. He then extended his accusations to embrace the death of one million innocent Iraqis due to Western sanctions as well as struggles in Bosnia, Chechnya, and Kashmir.

Bin Laden played to the Muslim sense of historic oppression, occupation, and injustice at the hands of the West. After September 11, he charged, "What the United States tastes today is a very small thing compared to what we have tasted for tens of years. Our nation has been tasting humiliation and contempt for more than 80 years."[23] He paints a world in which Muslims and Islam are under siege:

> America and its allies are massacring us in Palestine, Chechnya, Kashmir, and Iraq. The Muslims have the right to attack America in reprisal. . . . The September 11 attacks were not targeted at women and children. The real targets were America's icons of military and economic power.[24]

The heart of bin Laden's jihad against America starts with his outrage at the injustice in his homeland—the infidel's occupation of sacred territory and its support for a corrupt un-Islamic government: "The call to wage war against America was made because America spearheaded the crusade against the Islamic nation, sending tens of thousands of troops to the land of the two Holy Mosques over and above its meddling in Saudi affairs and its politics, and its support of the oppressive, corrupt, and tyrannical regime that is in control."[25] Refusing to any longer recognize Saudi Arabia by name, bin Laden referred to the sacred territory it "occupies." Interestingly, King Fahd and the House of Saud some years earlier had taken to using the title "Custodian of the Two Holy Sites" of Mecca and Medina because they recognized their vulnerability to Islamic critics who insisted that monarchy is antithetical to Islam.

Bin Laden also connected Western presence in the Gulf with a more international concern: America's complicity in Israeli expansionism, its support for "Jewish and Zionist plans for expansion of what is called Greater Israel."[26] Contrary to what many said in the aftermath of September 11, Palestine is a primary issue for bin Laden. His messages have consistently spoken of Zionist and Jewish offenses against Muslims. His passionate statements on the plight of the Palestinians, who have been living under Israeli military occupation in violation of UN Security Council resolutions for over forty years, graphically describe, capture, and appeal to the outrage of many in the Arab and Muslim world toward Israeli policy and the complicity of the international community:

> For over half a century, Muslims in Palestine have been slaughtered and assaulted and robbed of their honor and of their property. Their houses have been blasted, their crops destroyed. And the strange thing is that any act on their part to avenge themselves or lift the injustice befalling them causes great agitation in the United Nations which hastens to call an emergency meeting only to convict the victim and to censure the wronged and tyrannized whose children have been killed and whose crops have been destroyed and whose farms have been pulverized. . . .[27]

Bin Laden holds the American people, who elect their president and Congress, responsible for Israeli oppression of Palestinians: "their government manufactures arms and gives them to Israel and Israel uses them to massacre Palestinians."[28] He charges that the Jewish lobby has taken America and the West hostage. He calls upon the American people to rise up against their government as they did during the Vietnam war and force it to give up America's anti-Muslim policies and massacre of Muslims. Muslims have the right, indeed the obligation, to defend themselves. He appeals then to the Islamic teaching that jihad in the defense of Islam and to correct an unjust political order is legitimate and required:

> We are carrying out the mission of the prophet, Muhammad (peace be upon him). The mission is to spread the word of God, not to indulge in massacring people. We ourselves are the target of killings, destruction, and atrocities. We are only defending ourselves. This is defensive jihad. We want to defend our people and our land. That is why we say, if we don't get security, the Americans, too, would not get security. This is the simple formula that even an American child can understand. Live and let live.[29]

In bin Laden's view, charges of "terrorism" are specious in a world of immorality and oppression within which ostensible acts of terrorism are sometimes necessary and justified. He paints the modern world in polarities, a world of belief and unbelief, within which the forces of evil, oppression, and injustice assault the forces of good. The Muslim world and Islam are under siege:

> They rob us of our wealth and of our resources and of our oil. Our religion is under attack. They kill and murder our brothers. They compromise our honor and our dignity and dare we utter a single word of protest against the injustice, we are called terrorists.[30]

Like a Muslim jurist, he legalistically distinguishes between "commendable" and "reprehensible" terrorism. To terrify the innocent is unjust; however, terrorizing oppressors is necessary:

> There is no doubt that every state and every civilization and culture has to resort to terrorism under certain circumstances for the purpose of abolishing tyranny and corruption. . . . The

terrorism we practice is of the commendable kind for it is directed at the tyrants, the traitors who commit acts of treason against their own countries and their own faith and their own prophet and their own nation. Terrorizing those and punishing them are necessary measures to straighten things and make them right.[31]

Osama bin Laden plays to a centuries-long tradition of reform in Islam, most of it aimed in the last one hundred years toward the struggle over Muslim oppression by the West. Why do his calls for a defensive jihad resonate as truth for mainstream Muslims as well as for extremists who live today in the Muslim world? This is the question we will examine in the next chapter.

2

Jihad and the Struggle for Islam

If you were watching a television special on *jihad*, with four Muslim speakers, you might well hear four different responses to the question: "What is jihad?" One might say that jihad is striving to lead a good Muslim life, praying and fasting regularly, being an attentive spouse and parent. Another might identify jihad as working hard to spread the message of Islam. For a third, it might be supporting the struggle of oppressed Muslim peoples in Palestine, Kashmir, Chechnya, or Kosovo. And for the final speaker, as for Osama bin Laden, jihad could mean working to overthrow governments in the Muslim world and attacking America. However different these interpretations are, all testify to the centrality of jihad for Muslims today. Jihad is a defining concept or belief in Islam, a key element in what it means to be a believer and follower of God's Will.

In the late twentieth and twenty-first centuries the word jihad has gained remarkable currency. It is used by resistance, liberation, and terrorist movements alike to legitimate their cause and motivate their followers. The Afghan mujahidin, the Taliban and the Northern Alliance, have waged a jihad in Afghanistan against foreign powers and among themselves; Muslims in Kashmir, Chechnya, Dagestan, the southern Philippines, Bosnia, and Kosovo have fashioned their struggles as jihads; Hizbollah, Hamas, and Islamic Jihad Palestine have characterized war with Israel as a jihad; Algeria's Armed Islamic Group has engaged in a jihad of terror against the government there, and Osama bin Laden has waged a global jihad against Muslim governments and the West.

The importance of jihad is rooted in the Quran's command to struggle (the literal meaning of the word jihad) in the path of God and in the example of the Prophet Muhammad and his early Companions. These are fundamentals of Muslim belief and practice. Jihad is a concept with multiple meanings, used and abused throughout Islamic history. Although jihad has always been an important part of the Islamic tradition, in recent years some Muslims have maintained that it is a universal religious obligation for all true Muslims to join the jihad to promote a global Islamic revolution.

Many Muslims today believe that the conditions of their world require a jihad. They look around them and see a world dominated by corrupt authoritarian governments and a wealthy elite, a minority concerned solely with its own economic prosperity, rather than national development, a world awash in Western culture and values in dress, music, television, and movies. Western governments are perceived as propping up oppressive regimes and exploiting the region's human and natural resources, robbing Muslims of their culture and their options to be governed according to their own choice and to live in a more just society. Many believe that the restoration of Muslim power and prosperity requires a return to Islam, the creation of more Islamically oriented states and societies. Some Muslims, a radicalized minority, combine militancy with messianic visions to inspire and mobilize an army of God whose jihad they believe will liberate Muslims at home and abroad.

If jihad has so many meanings, how are they to be understood? Which interpretations are correct? Which of the meanings promote positive improvements and reforms, and which have been exploited to justify extremism and terrorism? These questions are not new—they have been debated by Muslims throughout the ages.

The history of the Muslim community from Muhammad to the present can be read within the framework of what the Quran teaches about jihad. The Quranic teachings have been of essential significance to Muslim self-understanding, piety, mobilization, expansion, and defense. Jihad as struggle pertains to the difficulty and complexity of living a good life: struggling against the evil in oneself in order to be virtuous and moral, making a serious effort to do good works and to help to reform society. Depending on the circumstances in which one lives, it also can mean fighting injustice and oppression, spreading and defending Islam, and creating a just society through preaching, teaching and, if necessary, armed struggle or holy war.

The two broad meanings of jihad, nonviolent and violent, are contrasted in a well-known prophetic tradition. It is said that when Muhammad returned from battle he told his followers, "We return from the lesser jihad to the greater jihad." The greater jihad is the more difficult and more important struggle against one's ego, selfishness, greed, and evil.

Understanding the various ways in which jihad has been interpreted throughout Muslim history will enable us to distinguish between extremist organizations on the one hand and the majority of Muslims on the other.

When Osama bin Laden or the leaders of other terrorist groups speak today, like all Muslims they often consciously or unconsciously use the past to legitimate their agenda and tactics. They place themselves under the mantle of the Prophet. They also link their militant jihadist worldviews to famous earlier interpretations of jihad, for example, that of the prominent medieval theologian and legal scholar Ibn Taymiyya or that of Sayyid Qutb, the godfather of modern revolutionary Islam. Are they simply appropriating a tradition of holy war or are they reinventing their tradition to support their self-declared unholy wars of violence and terrorism?

The struggle for the soul of Islam going on today is the product of a rich and complex history. From the very beginning, jihad was used both by those in power and by those who challenged that power, by insiders and by outsiders. Early Muslim history provides the clearest antecedents and paradigms for what is going on today. And so to understand jihad, we must begin with the Prophet Muhammad and the Quran.

Muhammad's Jihad

Islam and the Quran, like all the great world religions and their scriptures, offer a universal message, a discourse that can speak to all times and places. Believers in every age and situation find teachings, principles, and values that give them meaning and guidance. Jews can look to the Hebrew Bible to find stories of Joshua and King David spreading and defending their faith and community by warfare, as well as passages that extol the virtues of peace. Christians look to a tradition that can support pacifism but also a just-war theory that legitimates warfare. Similarly, the Quran and the Sunnah, or prophetic example, provide a theology for peace, for living in a world of diverse nations and peoples. They also provide guidelines on how to fight the enemy as well as how to fight against corruption and oppression. As we shall see, the challenge in Islamic history has been to draw a careful line between self-defense and aggression, resistance and rebellion, reform and terrorism.

The world in which Islam emerged in the seventh century was a rough neighborhood where war was the natural state. Arabia and the city of Mecca, in which Muhammad lived and received God's revelation, were beset by tribal raids and cycles of vengeance and vendetta. The broader Near East, in which Arabia was located, was itself divided between two warring superpowers of the day, the Byzantine (Eastern Roman) and the Persian (Sasanian) Empires. Each had competed against the other for world dominion.

Seventh-century Arabia was critically located along the profitable trade routes of the Orient. As a result it was subject to the rivalry and interventions of its powerful imperial neighbors. The rise and spread of Islam was caught in both the local politics and fighting of Arabia and the imperial warfare of the Near East. Muhammad's preaching would add to this mix and would itself become a source of conflict.

Muhammad's reformist message posed an unwelcome challenge to the religious and political establishment, the priests, tribal leaders, and businessmen of the community. The new religious mes-

sage that Muhammad preached, like that of Amos and other biblical prophets before him, denounced the status quo and called for
social justice for the poor and the most vulnerable in society—
women, children, and orphans. Muhammad and the Quran condemned Arabian polytheism and put a spotlight on Meccan society's
unbridled materialism, avarice, and corruption, a condition of ignorance and unbelief called *jahiliyyah*. This is a very important
term, rich in meaning, that has been reappropriated and reinterpreted by fundamentalists today to describe and condemn Western society.

Muhammad's prophetic call summoned the people to strive and
struggle (jihad) to reform their communities and to live a good
life based on religious belief and not loyalty to their tribe. His
insistence that each person was personally accountable not to tribal
customary law but to an overriding divine law shook the very foundations of Arabian society. Muhammad's newly claimed status and
authority as God's messenger and his entreaties to believers to take
action against social corruption threatened the authority of powerful elites. Muhammad proclaimed a sweeping program of religious and social reform that affected religious belief and practices,
business contracts and practices, male-female and family relations.
The Quran rejected Arabian polytheism and insisted that there
was only one true God. It denounced the corrupt practices of many
merchants and the exploitation of orphans and their inheritance
rights. It condemned infanticide, spoke of the religious equality
of men and women, and expanded the marriage and inheritance
rights of women. To uphold this deeply challenging message and
mission, Muhammad and his followers would have to fight, wage
jihad, to stay alive.

The example of the original Islamic community has deep significance for reformers as the only model to be emulated. Sayyid
Qutb, writing in the mid-twentieth century, echoes those who came
before and after him and testifies to the continuing power of the
first Islamic community to inspire Muslims in all ages:

At one time this Message [the Quran] created a generation—the generation of the Companions of the Prophet (may God be pleased with them) without comparison in the history of Islam, even in the entire history of man. After this, no other generation of this calibre was ever again to be found.[1]

Hijra and Jihad: Response to Persecution and Conflict

The first decade of Muhammad's preaching met with resistance and persecution and produced limited results. The community remained small and under constant pressure. The experience of Muhammad's nascent community would provide the model for later generations, a guide for responding to persecution and rejection, to threats to the faith, to the security and survival of the community. The twin ideals of *hijra* (which means to emigrate from a hostile un-Islamic jahiliyyah environment) and jihad were established. Faced with ever-increasing threats and persecution, in 622 C.E. Muhammad and his followers moved (hijra) from Mecca to Medina, approximately 250 miles away, where he established the first Islamic community or city-state. The central significance given to this move can be seen in the fact that the Muslim calendar begins with the year of the hijra and the creation of the Islamic community, rather than earlier dates such as the year Muhammad was born or the year in which he received his first revelation from God.

Moving from the traditional safety of one's tribe and kinsmen in warring Arabia to form alliances with alien tribes based on a broader Islamic ideal and a collective surrender to the will of God was another of Muhammad's revolutionary concepts—one fraught with danger and potential strife. Therefore, it follows that what many refer to as "defensive jihad" appears in the earliest Quranic verses, revealed shortly after the hijra to Medina when Muhammad and his followers knew they would be forced to fight for their lives: "Leave is given to those who fight because they were wronged—surely God is able to help them—who were expelled

from their homes wrongfully for saying, 'Our Lord is God'" (22:39).
The defensive nature of jihad is reinforced in 2:190—"And fight
in the way of God with those who fight you, but aggress not: God
loves not the aggressors." Both mainstream and extremist movements and "holy warriors" like Osama bin Laden, who emigrated
from Saudi Arabia to establish his movement and community with
its training bases in Afghanistan, have selectively used the pattern
of hijra and jihad for their own purposes.

Jihad for Defense and Expansion

From 622 C.E. until his death ten years later, Muhammad very successfully consolidated his power in Medina and united the feud-
ing tribes of Arabia. At critical points throughout these years
Muhammad received revelations from God that provided guidelines for the jihad. As the Muslim community grew, questions
quickly emerged about who had religious and political authority,
how to handle rebellion and civil war, what was proper behavior
during times of war and peace, how to rationalize and legitimize
expansion and conquest, violence and resistance. Answers to these
questions were developed by referring to Quranic injunctions. The
Quran provides detailed guidelines and regulations regarding the
conduct of war: who is to fight and who is exempted (48:17, 9:91),
when hostilities must cease (2:192), how prisoners should be treated
(47:4). Verses such as Quran 2:294 emphasize proportionality in
warfare: "whoever transgresses against you, respond in kind." Other
verses provide a strong mandate for making peace: "If your enemy
inclines toward peace then you too should seek peace and put
your trust in God" (8:61), and "Had Allah wished, He would have
made them dominate you and so if they leave you alone and do
not fight you and offer you peace, then Allah allows you no way
against them" (4:90). From the earliest times it was forbidden to
kill noncombatants as well as women and children and monks
and rabbis, who were given the promise of immunity unless they
had taken part in the fighting. The Prophet's example (and Islamic

law) also provide answers to questions about how the Muslim community should act. Stories about how the Prophet behaved are preserved in narrative traditions or *hadith*. They have been and continue to be used throughout the world to provide guidance for Muslim decisions and behavior.

Under the leadership of Muhammad and then his early successors, the Islamic community spread rapidly, creating a vast empire greater than Rome at its zenith and stretching from North Africa to India. Muslim armies—motivated both by economic rewards from the conquest of richer, more developed societies and by religious zeal, the promise of reward in heaven—successfully overran the Byzantine and Persian Empires, which had become exhausted from endless warring with each other.

The religious rationale (as distinct from the practical political and economic motives) for conquest and expansion was not to force conversion to Islam upon other faiths who had their own prophets and revelations—the Quran states clearly, "There is no compulsion in religion" (2:256)—but rather to spread its righteous order so that ignorance and unbelief could be replaced by just societies throughout the world. The religious justification made for a jihad to propagate the faith is connected to Islam's universal mission to spread the word of God and the just reign of God's will for all humanity: "So let there be a body among you who may call to the good, enjoin what is esteemed and forbid what is odious. They are those who will be successful" (3:104); and, "Of all the communities raised among men you are the best, enjoining the good, forbidding the wrong, and believing in God" (3:110).

Martyrs who sacrifice their lives to establish Islamic ideals or to defend those ideals hold a special place in Islam. The Quran has many passages that support the notion of martyrdom and that comfort those left behind. For example, "Were you to be killed or to die in the way of God, forgiveness and mercy from God are far better than what they amass" (3:157); and, "Never think that those who are killed in the way of God are dead. They are alive with their Lord, well provided for" (3:169). Both Sunni and Shii traditions value and esteem martyrdom in their beliefs and devotions. Sunni Islam has historically valorized martyrdom through veneration of the struggles (jihads) of the early community with the Meccan Arabs and within their jahiliyyah culture of unbelief, while Shii Islam celebrates annually the martyrdom of its early leaders who fought to reinstate the true values of Islam into their society.

Hadith literature also provides many affirmations of the rewards for those who die for Islam. Muslim tradition teaches that martyrs are distinguished from others in life after death in several ways: their self-sacrifice and meritorious act render them free of sin and therefore they are not subject to the post-mortem interrogation of the angels Nakir and Munkar; they bypass "purgatory" and proceed to one of the highest locations in heaven near the Throne of God; as a result of their purity, they are buried in the clothes in which they died and do not need to be washed before burial.

With the growth, expansion, and development of the Islamic community, concern about the power and lifestyles of rulers and the need to expound more fully and clearly what the Quran said about the "straight path of Islam" resulted in the emergence of religious scholars (*ulama*, the learned). The ulama developed the *Shariah*, Islamic law, seen as the ideal blueprint for Muslim life.

Over the ages, Islamic law and jurists became the primary authorities for the meanings of jihad, when to declare and when to restrict jihad. While Muslim rulers declared and conducted the jihad, legal experts, known as *muftis*, provided *fatwas* (legal opinions) that could be used either to legitimate or to challenge the legitimacy of a jihad, a practice that continues up to the present day. For example, during the Gulf war, Muslim rulers obtained fatwas to legitimate their participation in the American-led coalition against Saddam Hussein's declared jihad, and Saudi Arabia obtained a fatwa to legitimate the presence of non-Muslim American troops in the Kingdom.

Islamic law stipulates that it is a Muslim's duty to wage war not only against those who attack Muslim territory, but also against polytheists, apostates, and People of the Book (at first restricted to

Jews and Christians but later extended to Zoroastrians and other faiths) who refuse Muslim rule. Muslims gave these people two choices: conversion or submission to Muslim rule with the right to retain their religion and pay a poll tax (a common practice applied to outsiders, within and outside of Arabia). If they refused both of these options, they were subject to war. Muslim jurists saw jihad as a requirement in a world divided between what they called the *dar al-Islam* (land of Islam) and the *dar al-harb* (land of war). The Muslim community was required to engage in the struggle to expand the dar al-Islam throughout the world so that all of humankind would have the opportunity to live within a just political and social order. One school of law, the Shafii, posited a third category, the land of treaty (*dar al-sulh*), a territory that has concluded a truce with a Muslim government.

Other Quranic verses, sometimes referred to as the "sword verses," are quoted selectively to legitimate unconditional warfare against unbelievers and were used by jurists to justify great expansion. The argument, developed during the period under the early caliphs, a time when the ulama enjoyed royal patronage, was that the sword verses abrogated all the earlier verses that limited jihad to a defensive war: "When the sacred months have passed, slay the idolaters wherever you find them, and take them, and confine them, and lie in wait for them at every place of ambush" (9:5). Yet the full intent of this verse, if it is used in isolation, can be overlooked. It is followed by: "But if they repent and fulfill their devotional obligations and pay the *zakat* [tax for alms] then let them go their way for God is forgiving and kind"(9:5). Although this verse has been used to justify offensive jihad, it has traditionally been read as a call for peaceful relations unless there is interference with the freedom of Muslims. The same is true of the following: "Fight those who believe not in God nor the Last Day, Nor hold that forbidden which hath been forbidden by God and His Apostle, Nor hold the religion of truth (even if they are) of the People of the Book, Until they pay the tax with willing submission, and feel themselves subdued" (9:29).

Jihad: Sectarianism and Terrorism in Early Islam

From its beginnings the faith, unity, and very survival of the Islamic community were threatened by civil war, sectarianism, violence, assassination of its leaders, and terrorism. Disorder (*fitnah*) was and remains a primary political and social evil. The Quran and the example of the Prophet's community or state at Medina linked Islam with politics and society in the struggle (jihad) to implement God's will and to create a just social order. Islam was riven by deep divisions and conflicts revolving around leadership and authority. The community divided into two major and often competing branches, Sunni and Shii.

Although Islam is the second largest religion in the world, many in the West knew nothing about it until Iran's Islamic revolution catapulted Islam into the consciousness of the world. It is ironic that the West's contemporary encounter with Islam began with the actions of Islam's Shii minority, who make up only 15 percent of the Muslim community. Throughout the 1980s, the Western nations' primary experience of Islam was with the Ayatollah Khomeini's brand of radical Islamic fundamentalism. Fears of its export throughout the Muslim world dominated the corridors of power and media headlines.

In the United States, Shii Islam is identified primarily with the militancy, anti-Americanism, and terrorism of the Iranian revolution and of Hizbollah in Lebanon. This has obscured the richness of the Shii religious tradition and spirituality, its diverse branches and differing experiences of and attitudes toward war and peace. Shiism is a faith born out of the experience of oppression and tyranny. It is the official religion of empires and states in North Africa as well as in Iran and Oman. It has fought jihads of liberation and of expansion and conquest. In modern times, its leaders have included a seminary-trained revolutionary like Ayatollah Khomeini and the cosmopolitan, urbane Harvard-trained Agha Khan, who uses his community's wealth for major educational and social welfare projects around the world. The road traveled by

Shii from their origins to the present reveals a rich legacy able to provide support for both reformers and revolutionaries.

The origins of Shii Islam go back to the death of Islam's charismatic prophetic leader in 632 C.E. The community was plunged into a crisis over who would succeed Muhammad. Should the successor be the most pious Muslim or a direct descendant of the Prophet? The seeds of dissent in the Islamic community were planted when the companions of the Prophet moved quickly to select Abu Bakr, Muhammad's father-in-law, an early convert and well-respected member of the community, as the Prophet's first successor or *caliph*. The caliph was to be the political leader of the community. Although not a prophet, a caliph enjoyed a certain religious prestige and authority as head of the community. He led the Friday congregational prayer, and his name was mentioned in the prayer. As the protector of Islam, the caliph led the jihad and was to govern the community by the Shariah (Islamic law). Those who accepted the choice of Abu Bakr, the majority of the community, became known as Sunnis (followers of the *Sunnah*, or example of the Prophet).

This transition of leadership set in motion a sequence of events that led to division, rebellion, and historic conflict. A minority of the community, the Shii (meaning the party or followers of Ali), took strong exception to the selection of Abu Bakr. They believed that before his death Muhammad had designated the senior male of his family, Ali, the Prophet's cousin and son-in-law, to be leader, or *Imam*, of the community. Ali was eventually chosen as the fourth in a succession of caliphs, but his Shii followers suffered Ali's assassination after five years of rule (656–661) and then the subsequent massacre of Ali's son, the brave and charismatic Hussein, as he and his army battled to try to regain power and reinstate the true values of Islam. Hussein and his forces were defeated by the army of the caliph Yazid in 680 C.E. The death or martyrdom of Hussein in the Battle of Karbala became a defining symbol for Shii Muslims of the profound injustice of the world. It inspired and motivated Shii jihads against what they considered the un-Islamic

Umayyad and Abbasid dynasties, whose caliphs they regarded as illegitimate.

During this time the Shii community itself split into two major branches, Twelvers and Seveners, over the issue of leadership. The numerical designation of each branch stems from the death or disappearance of their Imam and thus the disruption of succession. Shii theology resolved the problem of the Imam's absence with the doctrine of the "hidden Imam" who will return as a messianic figure, the Mahdi, at the end of the world to usher in a perfect Islamic society in which truth and justice will prevail.

Shii history and religious symbolism has been used in every age to bring about reform. In the twentieth century modern Shii religious leaders reinterpreted the memory of Hussein's martyrdom to mobilize support for revolutionary movements. Portraying the Shah of Iran as the new Yazid, the Umayyad general responsible for the massacre at Karbala, the Ayatollah Khomeini called for a revolution to overthrow their un-Islamic leader. Khomeini also appealed to Shii in Sunni-dominated Iraq, Saudi Arabia, Bahrain, and Kuwait to rise up against oppressive regimes and claim their rightful inheritance. With Iranian backing, Lebanon's Shii Hizbollah (Party of God), which had come into being in response to the Israeli invasion of Lebanon, declared jihad against Israel and its American "patron."

Sunni and Shii Conceptions of Jihad

Despite their historic differences and their ongoing conflicts today, Sunni and Shii both have the same overall conception of jihad as a struggle in the path of God, and both distinguish between the greater jihad, the personal, spiritual struggle, and the lesser, warfare form of jihad. They see jihad as a religious duty incumbent on individuals and the Islamic community to defend life, land, or faith and to prevent invasion or guarantee the freedom to spread the faith. However, they differ with regard to who can declare a jihad. For Sunnis, the caliph, with the support of the ulama (religious scholars), had the religious and political authority to declare a jihad. Shii view this power as having been unjustly taken from the true successors to Muhammad, the Imams. However, in the absence of their Imam, only a defensive jihad was considered permissible. This problem was resolved as some ulama claimed that all legitimate forms of jihad were defensive and therefore able to be waged in the Imam's absence. This rationale led Iran's Ayatollah Khomeini as well as Lebanon's Hizbollah to declare jihad.

Jihad in the Creation of a Worldwide *Ummah*

Sunni and Shii share a common faith rooted in the Quran and Muhammad and belong to the same global Islamic community. Like a family, the members of the *ummah*, or worldwide community of believers, may be very different. They may have bitter family feuds but nevertheless are bound together by a bond that continues to survive in Muslim faith and religious imagination. Like tribal or ethnic communities and nation states, they often pull together when faced by a common external threat but then fall back into intrareligious conflict. Thus, many Sunni Muslims identified with, celebrated, and were inspired by Iran's Islamic revolution, which Khomeini was careful to proclaim an Islamic (not simply a Shii) revolution. However, this bond dissolved when Khomeini attempted to rally the Shii of southern Iraq in the Iran-Iraq war. In this instance, the effects of nationalism and centuries-old Persian–Arab rivalries prevailed, and Iraqi Shii fought for their country.

The concept of the ummah developed as the first Muslim community at Medina quickly expanded and established its hegemony over central Arabia under Muhammad's guidance. Through military action and astute diplomatic initiatives, the tribes of Arabia were united in an Arab commonwealth with a common faith, ideology, centralized authority, and law. For the first time, an effective means had been found to end tribal vendettas, to inspire, unite, and replace tribal allegiance with a common religious bond. As the Quran commanded, Muslims were a community of believers, in a special covenant with God that transcended all other allegiances. They were to realize their obligation to strive (jihad), to submit (*islam*) to God, and to spread their faith both as individuals and as a community.

Islam's transnational dimension was expressed through the existence of empires and sultanates from the seventh to the eighteenth century as Islam became the global power and civilization of its day. The breakup of Muslim empires, the fragmentation of the Muslim world by European colonialism, and the creation of modern nation states in the twentieth century reduced the concept of the ummah to a more distant ideal. In the twentieth century, the resurgence of Islam and the spread of international communications have reinforced and reinvigorated Muslim awareness and identification with the worldwide Islamic community. The influential activist and ideologue Sayyid Qutb describes an ummah that reflects an international perception today:

> In this great Islamic society Arabs, Persians, Syrians, Egyptians, Moroccans, Turks, Chinese, Indians, Romans, Greeks, Indonesians, Africans were gathered together—in short, peoples of all nations and all races. Their various characteristics were united, and with mutual cooperation, harmony and unity they took part in the construction of the Islamic community and Islamic culture. This marvellous civilisation was not an "Arabic civilisation," even for a single day; it was purely an "Islamic civilisation." It was never a "nationality" but always a "community of belief."[2]

Consciousness of the ummah has been reinforced in the past few decades by world events, greatly assisted by media coverage. Muslim sentiment, support, and engagement were triggered by the jihad against the Soviet occupation of Afghanistan, in which thousands of Muslims from the Arab world and beyond came to fight. The Iranian revolution had a similar impact. The creation of international Arab and Muslim newspapers and media, such as the television station al-Jazeera, with daily coverage from embattled Muslim frontiers, as well as CNN, the BBC, and the Internet have brought the many struggles, or jihads, of Muslim communities in Palestine and Afghanistan, Bosnia, Iraq, Chechnya, and Kashmir into the living rooms and everyday consciousness of Muslims around the world.

The creation and proliferation of Muslim organizations world-wide that sought to change the circumstances in which they lived intensified the language of jihad to fire up the determination needed in their struggle for reform. However, as we shall see, who can declare a jihad and what constitutes a legitimate defensive jihad as opposed to an aggressive unholy war of aggression would, like beauty, be determined by the eye of the beholder/believer. Jihad would remain a powerful defining concept for ideologues seeking, in times of crisis, to use their tradition to return power, peace, and social justice to their communities. How did Islam and jihad get redefined for use in the twentieth century? Who was responsible for the creation and spread of these ideas? To begin to answer these questions we must again visit a distant past.

Historical Sources of Revolutionary Jihad

TERROR AND JIHAD IN THE NAME OF GOD

The world of early Islam, like many Muslim societies today, expe-rienced the terror of religious extremist movements. The Kharijites and the Assassins represent early examples of the way in which dissent could turn to unholy war in the name of Islam. As we shall see in the next chapter, traces of the Kharijites' militant piety and fundamentalist worldview are found in Saudi Arabia's Wahhabi movement and in radical twentieth-century movements like Egypt's Islamic Jihad and bin Laden's al-Qaeda.

The Kharijites (from *kharaja*, to go out or exit) were followers of Ali, who broke away because they believed Ali guilty of compromis-ing God's will by agreeing to arbitration to settle a long, drawn-out war. After breaking with Ali (whom they eventually assassinated), the Kharijites established their own separate community, based on their vision of a true charismatic society strictly following the Quran and the Sunnah. They adopted the prophetic model of hijra and a radical, militant form of jihad. First they withdrew to live in their own community and then from their encampments waged war against their enemies in the name of God.

The Kharijites believed that the Quranic mandate to "command the good and forbid evil" must be applied literally, rigorously, and without qualification or exception. Their world was divided neatly between belief and unbelief, Muslims (followers of God) and non-Muslims (enemies of God), peace and warfare. Any action that did not conform rigorously to the letter of the law constituted a grave or mortal sin. Sinners were guilty of unbelief and thus excommunicated (*takfir*, exclusion for unbelief). Grave sinners were not just seen as religious backsliders but apostates, guilty of treason and meriting death unless they repented.

The Kharijites viewed other Muslims who did not accept their uncompromising viewpoint as infidels or idolaters, and thus the enemies of God. They held the egalitarian belief that the caliph should be selected by popular consent, but they insisted that a caliph could only hold office as long as he was thoroughly upright and sinless. His fall from this state constituted a grave sin. It rendered him an apostate from Islam, outside the protection of its laws, who must be deposed and killed.

Believing that they were God's army fighting a jihad against the forces of evil, they considered that the end justified the means. Violence, guerrilla warfare, and revolution were not only legitimate but also obligatory in the battle against the sinners who ignored God's will and sovereignty. This mentality has been replicated in modern times by Islamic Jihad, the assassins of Egypt's President Anwar Sadat, Osama bin Laden, and other extremists who have called for the overthrow of "un-Islamic" Muslim rulers and for jihad against the West.

Historically, the Kharijites remained on the margins or outside of Islamic orthodoxy, politically and religiously. The same fate of marginalization awaited the Assassins, as it would later radical movements.

The notorious Assassins, a Shii offshoot, were driven by a messianic vision. They lived apart in secret communities from which they would emerge to strike at unbelievers and were guided by a series of grand masters, who ruled from the mountain fortress of Alamut in northern Persia. Each grand master became known as the Old Man of the Mountain. The Assassins' jihad against the Abbasid dynasty terrorized Abbasid princes, generals, and ulama whom they murdered in the name of the hidden Imam.[3] They struck such terror in the hearts of their Muslim and Crusader enemies that their exploits in Persia and Syria earned them a name and memory in history long after they were overrun and the Mongols executed their last grand master in 1256.

IDEOLOGUES AND MOVEMENTS OF
REVOLUTIONARY JIHAD

It is therefore necessary—in the way of the Islamic movement—that in the early stages of our training and education we should remove ourselves from all influences of the Jahiliyyah in which we live and from which we derive benefits. We must return to that pure source from which those people derived their guidance . . . which is free from any mixing or pollution. . . . From it we must also derive our concepts of life, our principles of government, politics, economics and all other aspects of life.[4]

This statement by Sayyid Qutb illustrates the extent to which Muslims rely heavily on the past for meaning and guidance in the present. Many non-Muslims might be prepared to understand a believer's return to the Quran and Sunnah of the Prophet Muhammad for guidance, but they would be astonished to learn the extent to which the ideas of medieval and pre-modern theologians and movements directly impact the world of Islam today. Both modern reformers and radical extremists draw (often selectively) on the teachings and examples of early Islamic revivalist thinkers and activist movements to justify their contemporary jihads, their holy and unholy wars.

Islam possesses a long tradition of religious revivalism and social reform starting with the prophet-reformer Muhammad himself and the struggle of the early Islamic community to improve their jahiliyyah world. In every age, the glaring disparities (real or perceived) between God's will and the state of the world inspired religious reformers (*mujaddids*) and movements who called Muslims to follow Islam more faithfully and to reform their society.

For pious believers, political fragmentation and economic and social decline must be evidence of a departure from the straight path of Islam. The heart and soul of renewal require a process of purification and return to the pristine teachings of Islam. Based on a tradition of the Prophet, "God will send to this ummah [community] at the beginning of each century those who will renew its faith," Sunni Islam developed the belief that revitalization would be necessary in every age.[5] The clear disjunction between public life and the Islamic ideal contributed to the popular expectation of a future messianic figure, the Mahdi (the guided one), who would come to deliver the community from oppression by the forces of evil and restore true Islam and the reign of justice on earth. As we have seen, Shii Islam developed its own messianic variant, a belief in the awaited return of the Hidden Imam as the Mahdi. This belief was expressed popularly in the twentieth century when followers of Ayatollah Khomeini took to calling him "Imam Khomeini." Although Khomeini himself never claimed the title Imam, he never publicly discouraged others from doing so. Many Shii who did not follow Khomeini were scandalized by this practice.

Throughout the ages, in times of division and decline religious scholars and movements have risen up to call the community back to its fundamental message and mission. Several prominent examples will give us an idea of the continuing power of the past in the minds of Islamic activists today. Among the most significant reformers for today are the medieval intellectual-activist Taqi al-Din Ahmad ibn Taymiyya and the leaders of the great jihad movements of the eighteenth century. Their teachings and actions are part of a revivalist legacy from which contemporary Islamic movements, both mainstream and extremist, have drawn heavily.

IBN TAYMIYYAH

Perhaps no medieval scholar-activist has had more influence on radical Islamic ideology than Ibn Taymiyya (1268–1328). A scholar of Islamic law and theology as well as a political figure, he was a major conservative voice who in the modern period is quoted by liberals, conservatives, and extremists alike. Described by some as the spiritual father of (Sunni) revolutionary Islam, others regard him as "the model for revivalists and vigilantes, for fundamentalist reformers, and other apostles of moral rearmament."[6] Though he was addressing the problems of his society in the thirteenth century, his ideas influenced and have been appropriated by Saudi Arabia's eighteenth-century Wahhabi movement, Egypt's modern activist ideologue Sayyid Qutb, Islamic Jihad's Muhammad al-Farag, and contemporary extremists like Osama bin Laden.

Ibn Taymiyya lived during one of the most disruptive periods of Islamic history, which had seen the fall of Baghdad and the conquest of the Abbasid Empire in 1258 by the Mongols. The empire's defeat represented the impossible—the apparent conquest of the caliphate and of Islam. Ibn Taymiyya's family was forced to flee to Damascus; his painful experience as a refugee colored his attitude toward the conqueror Mongols throughout his life. A professor of Hanbali law, the most conservative of the four Sunni schools of law, he balanced the life of a religious scholar with political activism. Like many mujaddids who have followed him, his writing and preaching earned him persecution and imprisonment in Egypt and Syria.[7] Combining ideas and action, his belief in the interconnectedness of religion, state, and society has exerted both conscious and unconscious influence on eighteenth-century and twentieth-century revivalism.

Ibn Taymiyya called on a rigorous, literalist interpretation of the sacred sources (the Quran and Sunnah, and the example of

the early Muslim community) for the crucially needed Islamic renewal and reform of his society. These sources constituted his yardstick for orthodoxy. Like many who came after him, he regarded
the community at Medina as the model for an Islamic state. His
goal was the purification of Islam. A return to the pristine purity
of the period of Muhammad and the First Four Righteous Caliphs,
he believed, was necessary to restore the Islamic community's past
power and greatness. He distinguished sharply between Islam and
non-Islam (the dar al-Islam and the dar al-harb), the lands of belief and unbelief. In contrast to his vision of a close relationship
between religion and the state, he made a sharp distinction between religion and culture. Although a pious Sufi (a practitioner
of Islamic mysticism), he denounced as superstition the popular
practices of his day such as saint worship and the veneration of
Sufi shrines and tombs.

Ibn Taymiyya's ire was especially directed at the Mongols. Despite their conversion to Islam, the Mongols had been locked in a
jihad with the Muslim Mamluk rulers of Egypt. Because the Mongols
continued to follow the Yasa code of laws of Genghis Khan instead
of the Islamic law, Shariah, for Ibn Taymiyya they were no better
than the polytheists of the pre-Islamic jahiliyyah. He issued a fatwa
that labeled them as unbelievers (*kafirs*) who were thus excommunicated (takfir). His fatwa regarding the Mongols established a pre-
cedent: despite their claim to be Muslims, their failure to implement
Shariah rendered the Mongols apostates and hence the lawful object of jihad. Muslim citizens thus had the right, indeed duty, to
revolt against them, to wage jihad.

Later generations, from the Wahhabi movement to modern
Egypt's Sayyid Qutb, Islamic Jihad, the assassins of Anwar Sadat,
and Osama bin Laden, would use the logic in Ibn Taymiyya's fatwa
on the Mongols to call for a jihad against "un-Islamic" Muslim
rulers and elites and against the West. Applying the emotive pre-
Islamic term jahiliyyah to societies infiltrated by tribal or Western
culture, they would draw a rigid distinction between true belief
and unbelief, level the charge of unbelief, proclaim excommunication, and call for a jihad.

EIGHTEENTH-CENTURY JIHAD MOVEMENTS

The global emergence of eighteenth-century revivalist movements holds the key to understanding the mindset of reformers and extremists today. The world of Islam in the eighteenth century experienced an Islamic revivalist wave that, as is happening again today, swept across the Muslim world, from Africa to Asia. In contrast to prior periods when Islamic revivalism occurred in a specific empire or region, eighteenth-century movements extended from modern-day Sudan, Libya, and Nigeria, across the Arabian peninsula and the Indian subcontinent to Southeast Asia.

For our purposes, we will focus on the ideas of the Wahhabi movement in Arabia, a prominent example of eighteenth-century Islamic revivalism, which had a profound impact on Arabia and the development of Saudi Arabia. Perhaps most important, it continues to be a significant force in the Islamic world, informing both mainstream and extremist movements from Afghanistan and Central Asia to Europe and America.

Muhammad ibn Abd al-Wahhab (1703–1791) studied Islamic law and theology in Mecca and Medina and took Ibn Taymiyya as his exemplar. Disillusioned by the spiritual decline and moral laxity of his society, he denounced popular beliefs and practices as idolatry and jahiliyyah, rejected much of the medieval law of the ulama (religious scholars) as innovation (*bida*) or heresy, and called for a fresh interpretation of Islam that returned to its revealed sources.

Central to al-Wahhab's theology and movement was the doctrine of God's unity (*tawhid*), an absolute monotheism reflected in the Wahhabi's self-designation as "unitarians" (*muwahiddun*)— those who uphold the unity of God. Citing the tradition that Muhammad had destroyed the pantheon of gods in his Meccan shrine, the Wahhabi forces set out to destroy "idolatrous" shrines, tombstones, and sacred objects. They spared neither the sacred tombs of Muhammad and his Companions in Mecca and Medina nor the Shiite pilgrimage site at Karbala (in modern Iraq) that housed the tomb of Hussein. The destruction of this venerated site has never been forgotten by Shii Muslims and has contributed to the historic antipathy between the Wahhabi of Saudi Arabia and Shii Islam in both Saudi Arabia and Iran. Centuries later, many would point to Wahhabi-inspired iconoclasm and religious fanaticism as the source behind the Taliban's wanton destruction of Buddhist monuments in Afghanistan, an action condemned by Muslim leaders worldwide.

Muhammad ibn Abd al-Wahhab joined religious zeal with military might and allied with Muhammad ibn Saud, a local tribal chief, to form a religiopolitical movement. Ibn Saud used Wahhabism as a religious ideal to legitimate his jihad to subdue and unite the tribes of Arabia, converting them to this puritanical version of Islam. Like the Kharijites, the Wahhabi viewed all Muslims who resisted as unbelievers (who could be fought and killed). They were therefore to be subdued in the name of Islamic egalitarianism. In the early nineteenth century Muhammad Ali of Egypt defeated the Saudis, but the Wahhabi movement and the House of Saud proved resilient. In the early twentieth century, Abdulaziz ibn Saud recaptured Riyadh. With the *Ikhwan* (brotherhood), a nontribal military, he once again united the tribes of Arabia, restored the Saudi kingdom, and spread the Wahhabi movement. The kingdom melded the political and religious; it was led by a succession of kings from the House of Saud with the close support of the religious establishment, many of whom are descendants of al-Wahhab, since they had married into the royal family.

The House of Saud's appeal to Wahhabi Islam for legitimacy has also been used against it by dissidents. As discussed in the next chapter, in November 1979 militants seized the Grand Mosque in Mecca, accused the royal family of compromising their Wahhabi faith, and called for the overthrow of the House of Saud. Again in the 1990s and the aftermath of the Gulf war, the Saudi government had to move forcefully to arrest and silence independent, nongovernment ulama in Mecca, Medina, and Riyadh who were calling for greater political participation and accountability and denouncing religious deviance and corruption.

Internationally, the Saudis, both government-sponsored organizations and wealthy individuals, have exported a puritanical and at times militant version of Wahhabi Islam to other countries and communities in the Muslim world and the West. They have offered development aid, built mosques and other institutions, funded and distributed religious tracts, and commissioned imams and religious scholars. They exported their Wahhabi ideology and provided financial support to Afghanistan, Pakistan, the Central Asian republics, China, Africa, Southeast Asia, the United States, and Europe. Wealthy businessmen in Saudi Arabia, both members of the establishment and outsiders such as Osama bin Laden, have provided financial support to extremist groups who follow a militant fundamentalist brand of Islam with its jihad culture.

Trailblazers of the Islamic Revolution

Western historians have marveled at the speed with which Islam took root and grew. Muslim tradition had always viewed the remarkable spread of Islam as a miraculous proof and historic validation of the truth of the Quran and Islam's claims and as a sign of God's guidance. But European colonialism from the eighteenth to the first half of the twentieth century and the subsequent failure of many modern Muslim states posed a serious challenge to this belief. Some Muslims came to believe that Islam had lost its relevance, and many others concluded that Western dominance and Muslim dependency were the result of unfaithfulness and departure from the path of Islam. This was a powerful argument that encouraged holy warriors to struggle (jihad) to bring the ummah back to the straight path. Muslim responses to European colonialism precipitated a new debate about the meaning of jihad.

As discussed in the next chapter, Islamic modernists and movements like the Muslim Brotherhood of Egypt and Pakistan's Jamaat-i-Islami (Islamic Society) worked to combine religious reform and political mobilization. Islamic activist organizations framed their struggle in a call for a jihad against British imperialism and corrupt Muslim rulers.

Volumes have been written on the ideologues who inspire contemporary activists and terrorists. While a comprehensive discussion is impossible here, three key intellectual-activists—Hasan al-Banna, Mawlana Mawdudi, and Sayyid Qutb—have been so influential in creating the vision of modern Islamic reform that they warrant our attention. It is almost impossible to exaggerate the direct and indirect impact and influence of these three men. Their writings have been published and distributed throughout the Muslim world. Their ideas have been disseminated in short pamphlets and audiocassettes. The leadership of most major Islamic movements, mainstream and extremist, nonviolent and violent alike, has been influenced by their ideas on Islam, Islamic revolution, jihad, and modern Western society. Their recasting of Islam as a comprehensive ideology to address the conditions of modern Muslims produced a reinterpretation of Islamic belief that has been so widely used, it has been integrated unconsciously into the religious discourse of Muslims throughout the world who would normally disassociate themselves from Islamic movements.

When Hasan al-Banna (1906–1949) established the Egyptian Muslim Brotherhood and Mawlana Mawdudi (1903–1979) created the Jamaat-i-Islami in Pakistan, few in the West or in their own societies took serious notice. Both al-Banna and Mawdudi recognized that change would be slow to come. Expecting rejection and persecution, their focus was to train future generations. They were very successful in achieving their goal.

Sayyid Qutb (1906–1966) built upon and radicalized the ideas of al-Banna and Mawdudi. Qutb created an ideological legacy that incorporated all the major historical forms of jihad, from the reforms of Muhammad to the extremes of the Kharijites and the Assassins. Within a few short decades, the ideas of al-Banna's Muslim Brotherhood and Mawdudi's Jamaat-i-Islami, often viewed through the prism of Qutb's more radicalized interpretation, became the primary models for new activist organizations across the Muslim world.

Though part of a centuries-old revivalist tradition, all three men were modern in their responses. They were neofundamentalist in the sense that they returned to the sources or fundamentals of Islam. But they reinterpreted Islamic sources in response to the challenges of the modern world. This is apparent in their teachings, organization, strategy, tactics, and use of modern science and technology. Indeed, many Islamic activists are the product of modern educations, leaders in professional associations of physicians, engineers, lawyers, journalists, university professors, and students.

HASAN AL-BANNA AND MAWLANA MAWDUDI

The Brotherhood and the Jamaat were established in 1928 and 1941 respectively, both within Muslim societies in crisis. Hasan al-Banna, a teacher, and Mawlana Mawdudi, a journalist, were pious, educated men with traditional Islamic religious backgrounds and a knowledge of Western thought. Both placed primary blame for the ills of their society and the decline of the Muslim world upon European imperialism and westernized Muslim elites. Like revivalists of old, they initially called for moral and social reform but soon also became embroiled in political activism and opposition.

For Hasan al-Banna the failure of liberal nationalism in Egypt was reflected in the creation of Israel and the consequent displacement of millions of Palestinians as well as continued British occupation, massive unemployment, poverty, and corruption. He rejected the preference for the spiritual jihad (greater Jihad) over a military (lesser jihad) one. Since Muslim lands had been invaded, he said, it was incumbent on all Muslims to repel their invaders just as it was an Islamic imperative for Muslims to oppose rulers who blocked the establishment of Islamic governments.

For Mawdudi, the decline of Muslim rule in South Asia and the dismemberment of the Ottoman Empire were the products of British and French colonialism. Muslim identity and unity were threatened by the rise of Hindu secular nationalism and the imposition of modern nationalism, a foreign Western ideology whose purpose was to weaken and divide the Muslim world by replacing the universal pan-Islamic ideal of the equality and solidarity of all Muslims with an identity based upon language, tribe, or ethnicity.

Though inspired by the past, in particular the eighteenth-century revivalist movements, al-Banna and Mawdudi did not retreat to it but responded to modern society. They were just as critical of the failure of the religious establishment's conservatism as they were of secular Muslim elites' Western-oriented reformist visions. Although they were influenced by Islamic modernist reformers, who had attempted to bridge the gap between tradition and modernity, they nevertheless believed that Islamic modernism tended to westernize Islam, to recast Islam in light of Western standards and solutions to the challenge of modernity. Though antiwesternization, they were not against scientific and technological modernization. They both stressed the self-sufficiency of Islam, not the ulama's irrelevant medieval Islamic vision but a new interpretation and application of Islam's revealed sources that addressed the political, economic, and cultural challenges of modernity.

Both al-Banna and Mawdudi proclaimed Islam the clear alternative to the ills and shortcomings of Marxism and Western capitalism. As al-Banna declared, "Until recently, writers, intellectuals, scholars, and governments glorified the principles of European civilization, gave themselves a Western tint, and adopted a European style and manner; today on the contrary, the wind has changed, and reserve and distrust have taken their place. Voices are raised proclaiming the necessity for a return to the principles, teachings and ways of Islam . . . for initiating the reconciliation of modern life with these principles, as a prelude to final 'Islamization.'"[8] Despite differences, Hasan al-Banna and Mawlana Mawdudi shared a common ideological worldview which would come to inspire and inform the struggle (jihad) of later Islamic movements. The following represents the main points of the worldview that the two men shared:

1. Islam is a total, all-encompassing way of life that guides each person and his or her community and political life.
2. The Quran, God's revelation, and the Sunnah of the Prophet and the early Muslim community are the foundations of Muslim life, providing the models that guide daily actions.

3. Islamic law (Shariah) provides the ideal and blueprint for a modern Muslim society not dependent on Western models.

4. Departure from Islam and reliance on the West are the causes for Muslim decline. A return to the straight path of Islam will restore the identity, pride, success, power, and wealth of the Islamic community in this life and merit eternal reward in the next.

5. Science and technology must be harnessed and used. This must be achieved within an Islamic context, not by dependence on foreign Western cultures, to avoid the westernization and secularization of society.

6. Jihad, to strive or struggle, both personally and in community, in ideas and in action to implement Islamic reform and revolution, is the means to bring about a successful Islamization of society and the world.

Both men posited a struggle (jihad) between the forces of God and Satan, good and evil, darkness or ignorance (jahiliyyah) and light. Each envisioned his organization as a vanguard, a righteous community that would serve as a dynamic nucleus for true Islamic reformation within the broader society. Though they were quick to denounce imperialism and the threat of Western culture, they nevertheless realized (as do many Islamic organizations today) that the Muslim predicament was first and foremost a Muslim problem. Rebuilding the community and redressing the balance of power between Islam and the West must begin with a call (*dawah*) to all Muslims to return and reappropriate their faith in its fullness or totality of vision.

Dawah has two meanings: an invitation to non-Muslims to convert to Islam and the call to those who were born Muslim to be better Muslims. The Brotherhood and the Jamaat emphasized the latter, calling on Muslims to renew their faith and practice in order to bring about a social revolution, the re-Islamization of the individual and society. The Brotherhood and Jamaat disseminated their message through schools, mosques, publications, student organizations, professional associations, and social services that combined religious commitment, modern learning and technology, and social and political activism.

The jihad (struggle) that became a central concept in describing the process of self-transformation and political activism, both against European colonialism and later against corrupt, un-Islamic Muslim states, was primarily one of reform, not violent revolution. Yet, it did include the defense of the Muslim community and of Islam against colonialism and injustice. As a youth, Hasan al-Banna was impressed by an abortive revolt against British occupation: "Despite my preoccupation with Sufism and worship, I believed that duty to country is an inescapable obligation—a holy war."[9] The conclusion he drew as a thirteen-year-old regarding the relationship of religion to politics would become a foundation stone for the Muslim Brotherhood, from its domestic political opposition in Egypt to its involvement in the war in Palestine.

Despite criticism of Western models of development, al-Banna accepted, though he qualified and Islamized, notions of patriotism, nationalism, and parliamentary democracy. He accepted Egypt's constitutional government, but criticized the extent to which its laws deviated from Islamic norms regarding alcohol, gambling, prostitution, and usury.[10]

Mawdudi's early rejection of nationalism and democracy as un-Islamic was influenced more by his opposition to westernization and secularization than by religion. He would later come to accept both with qualifications, and the Jamaat would participate in elections and serve in government. Mawdudi's prolific writing on Islam, translated into many Muslim languages, has had a global impact. His writing on jihad, in both its defensive and corrective roles, would have unforeseen consequences.

Mawdudi's conception of "what jihad really is" starts with his argument that jihad has become so difficult for Muslims and non-Muslims to understand because of two major misconceptions. First of all, Islam, he said, is not a religion in the sense of "a hodge podge of some beliefs, prayers and rituals."[11] Rather, "it is a comprehensive system that tends to annihilate all tyrannical and evil systems in the world and enforce its own program . . . in the interests of mankind."[12] Secondly, Muslims are not a nation in the conventional sense of the term because Islam urges "mankind as a whole to bring about revolution and reform."[13] Therefore, Islam is "a revolutionary concept and ideology which seeks to change and revolutionise the world social order and reshape it according to its own concept and ideals."[14] And so Mawdudi sees Muslims as an international party organized to implement Islam's revolutionary program, and jihad as the term that denotes the utmost struggle to bring about an Islamic revolution.[15] Mawdudi stresses that jihad is not a war between nations for selfish or material ends, but a "struggle for the Cause of Allah," that is devoid of all selfish motives such as "gaining wealth and splendour, name and fame, or any personal glory or elevation" and "should be directed to achieve the one and the only end, i.e., the establishment of a just and equitable social order for humanity as a whole."[16] For Mawdudi, jihad is both offensive and defensive at one and the same time, offensive because the opposing principles and ideology (not the land of the opponents) must be assaulted, and defensive because Muslims must retain power in order to implement their new ideology.[17] Mawdudi's position on the nature of jihad would be elaborated on by others including the Muslim Brotherhood's Sayyid Qutb, the ideologue of Islamic revolution in the Sunni world, and the Ayatollah Khomeini in Shii Iran.

While both al-Banna and Mawdudi sought to work within the system, the growth of their organizations and condemnation of rulers and regimes brought them into conflict with governments. After World War II, the Brotherhood stepped up their opposition to the British occupation and the Egyptian government's policies. In 1948 a Brotherhood member assassinated the prime minister; in 1949 Hasan al-Banna was assassinated by members of the secret police.[18]

Mawdudi and the Jamaat found themselves at loggerheads with the government on many occasions but were nevertheless able to continue to function. Indeed, at one point, although Mawdudi had been sentenced to death, his conviction was overturned. Although Pakistan was ruled by military regimes, state repression was always far less than in Egypt and much of the Arab world and its court system more independent. Thus, the Jamaat remained an opposition able to function within the system. By contrast, the repression of the Muslim Brotherhood under Egypt's Gamal Abdel Nasser would lead to the emergence and growth of radical jihad organizations.

SAYYID QUTB: GODFATHER AND MARTYR OF ISLAMIC RADICALISM

It would be difficult to overestimate the role played by Sayyid Qutb in the reassertion of militant jihad. He was a godfather to Muslim extremist movements around the globe. In many ways, his journey from educated intellectual, government official, and admirer of the West to militant activist who condemned both the Egyptian and American governments and defended the legitimacy of militant jihad has influenced and inspired many militants, from the assassins of Anwar Sadat to the followers of Osama bin Laden and al-Qaeda.

Just as the interpretations of Hasan al-Banna and Mawlana Mawdudi were conditioned responses to the political and social realities of their times, so too Sayyid Qutb's Islam grew out of the militant confrontation between the repressive Egyptian state and the Brotherhood in the late 1950s and 1960s. Increasingly radicalized by Gamal Abdel Nasser's suppression of the Brotherhood, Qutb transformed the ideology of al-Banna and Mawdudi into a rejectionist revolutionary call to arms. Like al-Banna, he would be remembered as a martyr of the Islamic revival.

Qutb, like al-Banna, had a modern education. He studied at Dar al-Ulum, a college set up by reformers to train teachers in a modern curriculum. He became a great admirer of the West and Western literature. After graduation, he became an official in the Ministry of Public Instruction, as well as a poet and literary critic.

A devout Muslim who had memorized the Quran as a child, he began to write on Islam and the Egyptian state. In 1948, he published *Islam and Social Justice*, in which he argued that Islam possessed its own social teachings and that Islamic socialism avoided both the pitfalls of Christianity's separation of religion and society and those of Communism's atheism.

In the late 1940s Qutb visited the United States. This proved to be a turning point in his life, transforming an admirer into a severe critic of the West. His experiences in America produced a culture shock that made him more religious and convinced him of the moral decadence of the West. He was appalled by its materialism, sexual permissiveness and promiscuity, free use and abuse of alcohol, and its racism, which he directly experienced because of his dark skin. His views on America are summarized in his influential tract, *Milestones*:

> Look at this capitalism with its monopolies, its usury . . . at this individual freedom, devoid of human sympathy and responsibility for relatives except under force of law; at this materialistic attitude which deadens the spirit; at this behaviour, like animals, which you call "free mixing of the sexes"; at this vulgarity which you call "emancipation of women"; at this evil and fanatic racial discrimination.[19]

Qutb's stay in America coincided with the establishment of Israel as a state guaranteed by the United States and the beginning of the Cold War between the U.S. and USSR, during which Egypt, under Nasser, aligned itself with Russia and secular nationalism, moving even farther away from the prospect of establishing an Islamic state. In addition, Qutb felt betrayed in America when he saw what he considered to be anti-Arab and pro-Jewish coverage in the newspapers and movies that fostered contempt for Arabs and Muslims. As a final blow, during these years in America, Hasan al-Banna was assassinated and the Muslim Brotherhood was significantly weakened. Shortly after his return to Egypt, Qutb joined the Muslim Brotherhood.

Qutb quickly emerged as a major voice in the Brotherhood and as its most influential ideologue amidst the growing confrontation with a repressive Egyptian regime. Imprisoned and tortured for alleged involvement in a failed attempt to assassinate Nasser, he became increasingly militant and radicalized. While in prison, Qutb witnessed a massacre in which twenty-five members of the Muslim Brotherhood were killed and close to fifty were injured, an experience that strengthened his conviction that the Egyptian government was un-Islamic and jahiliyyah and must be overthrown.

Qutb was an incredibly prolific author, publishing over forty books, many translated into Persian and English and still widely distributed. "Qutb's fiery style provoked great emotions of dignity, solidarity, unity, universality and . . . could uplift the reader to the greatness of Islam. His style was also capable of stimulating through his criticism, profound anger and revulsion."[20] During ten years of imprisonment in the equivalent of a concentration camp, Qutb developed a revolutionary vision captured in *Milestones,* which was used as evidence against him and led to his being sentenced to death. The power of his writings was recognized in the fact that anyone in Egypt who owned a copy of *Milestones* could be arrested and charged with sedition. Qutb took many of the core concepts of al-Banna and Mawdudi, reshaped and sharpened them to exhort Muslims to radical action. His ideas reverberate loudly today in the radical rhetoric of revolutionaries from Khomeini to bin Laden.

Qutb developed prescriptions for belief and action that would help Islamic movements in the Muslim world to function within repressive, anti-Islamic governments and societies. As he explains:

It is necessary to revive that Muslim community . . . which is crushed under the weight of those false laws and customs which are not even remotely related to the Islamic teachings, and which in spite of all this, calls itself the "world of Islam."[21]

Like Ibn Taymiyya before him, he sharply divides Muslim societies into two diametrically opposed camps, the forces of good and of evil, those committed to the rule of God and those opposed, the party of God and the party of Satan. There was no middle ground:

> . . . the callers to Islam should not have any superficial doubts in their hearts concerning the nature of Jahiliyyah and the nature of Islam and the characteristics of Dar-ul-Harb and of Dar-ul-Islam for through these doubts many are led to confusion. Indeed, there is no Islam in a land where Islam is not dominant and where its Shariah is not established; and that place is not Dar-ul-Islam where Islam's way of life and its laws are not practised.[22]

Strongly influenced by Mawdudi, Qutb emphasized the need to develop a special group of true Muslims within this corrupt and faithless society:

> How is it possible to start the task of reviving Islam? . . . there should be a vanguard which sets out with this determination and then keeps walking on the path, marching through the vast ocean of Jahiliyyah which has encompassed the entire world . . . and I have written Milestones for this vanguard which I consider to be a waiting reality about to be materialized.[23]

The Islamic movement (*haraka*), the true Muslims, would create a righteous minority adrift in a sea of ignorance and unbelief, akin to the un-Islamic society in which Muhammad was born. Their models for training would be what Qutb considered to be the first unique generation of Muslims whose instruction came solely from one pure source, the Quran. "From it we must also derive our concepts of life, our principles of government, politics, economics and all other aspects of life"[24] because "our foremost objective is to change the practices of this society . . . to change the jahili system at its very roots—this system which is fundamentally at variance with Islam and which, with the help of force and oppression is keeping us from living the sort of life which is demanded by our Creator."[25] Qutb used the classical designation for pre-Islamic Arabian

society, jahiliyyah—a period of ignorance—to paint and condemn
all modern societies as un-Islamic and anti-Islamic:

> We must free ourselves from the clutches of jahili society, jahili
> concepts, jahili traditions and jahili leadership. Our mission is
> not to compromise . . . nor can we be loyal to it . . . we will not
> change our own values and concepts . . . to make a bargain with
> this jahili society. Never! We and it are on different roads, and if
> we take even one step in its company, we will lose our goal en-
> tirely and lose our way as well.[26]

Sayyid Qutb's teachings recast the world into black and white
polarities. There were no shades of gray. Since the creation of an
Islamic government was a divine commandment, he argued, it was
not an alternative to be worked toward. Rather, it was an imperative that Muslims must strive to implement or impose immediately:

> There is only one place on earth which can be called the home
> of Islam (Dar-ul-Islam), and it is that place where the Islamic
> state is established and the Shariah is the authority and God's
> limits are observed and where all the Muslims administer the
> affairs of the state with mutual consultation. The rest of the
> world is the home of hostility (Dar-ul-Harb).[27]

Given the authoritarian and repressive nature of the Egyptian
government and many other governments in the Muslim world,
Qutb concluded that change from within the system was futile
and that Islam was on the brink of disaster. Jihad was the only
way to implement the new Islamic order.

For Qutb, jihad, as armed struggle in the defense of Islam against
the injustice and oppression of anti-Islamic governments and the
neocolonialism of the West and the East (Soviet Union), was incumbent upon all Muslims. There could be no middle ground.
Mirroring the Kharijites, Qutb taught that those Muslims who refused to participate were to be counted among the enemies of God,

apostates who were excommunicated (takfir) and who should be fought and killed along with the other enemies of God. Many radical extremist groups formed decades after Qutb's death have kept his vision alive in their ideologies and tactics.

Like Hasan al-Banna and Mawlana Mawdudi, Qutb regarded the West as the historic enemy of Islam and Muslims as demonstrated by the Crusades, European colonialism, and the Cold War. The Western threat was political, economic, and religiocultural. Equally insidious were the elites of the Muslim world who rule and govern according to foreign Western secular principles and values that threaten the faith, identity, and values of their own Islamic societies. Going beyond al-Banna and Mawdudi, Qutb denounced governments and Western secular-oriented elites as atheists against whom all true believers must wage holy war.

Qutb's revolutionary antiestablishment rhetoric can be heard distinctly in this call to jihad by Iran's Ayatollah Khomeini:

> Give the people Islam, then, for Islam is the school of jihad, the religion of struggle; let them amend themselves and transform themselves into a powerful force, so that they may overthrow the tyrannical regime imperialism has imposed on us and set up an Islamic government. . . . If certain heads of state of Muslim countries . . . permit foreigners to expand their influence . . . they automatically forfeit their posts. . . . Furthermore, it is a duty of the Muslims to punish them by any means possible.[28]

The two options for an Islamic revolution, evolution, a process of revolutionary change from below, and violent revolution, the use of violence and terrorism to overthrow established ("un-Islamic") governments, have remained the twin paths of contemporary Islamic movements. Both types of movement began to spring up and spread like wildfire across the Muslim world in the 1970s. The quiet that seemed assured after Gamal Abdel Nasser's apparent neutralization of the Muslim Brotherhood in the late 1960s was shattered by the proliferation of radical groups during the rule of his successor, Anwar Sadat.

Armies of God: the Vengeance of Militant Jihad

Sayyid Qutb's revolutionary ideology bore fruit across the Middle East amidst the worsening living conditions experienced by the majority of Arabs following the failures of the 1967 Arab-Israeli war. Numerous radical organizations in Egypt, Lebanon, and Palestine waged jihad against incumbent governments and the West. By the mid-1970s, the stability and security of Egyptian government and society were threatened by a number of secret Islamic revolutionary organizations; among them, Muhammad's Youth (sometimes referred to as the Islamic Liberation Organization), Jamaat al-Muslimin (Society of Muslims), more popularly known as Takfir wal Hijra (Excommunication and Flight), Salvation from Hell, Gamaa Islamiyya (Islamic Group), and Jamaat al-Jihad or Islamic Jihad. In contrast to mainstream groups like the Egyptian Brotherhood, which rejected Qutb-inspired extremism and pursued a nonviolent path of social and political activism, these clandestine groups espoused violence and terrorism to disrupt and destabilize society politically and economically and sought to overthrow the government.

Their common goal was the creation of a true Islamic society under a restored caliphate. A clear and at times chilling articulation of the new jihadist culture and its indebtedness to the past can be found in the writing of Muhammad al-Farag, a member of the radical organization Islamic Jihad, who articulated its ideology in *The Neglected Duty*. Farag drew heavily from al-Banna, Mawdudi, and especially Ibn Taymiyya and Sayyid Qutb. He takes the ideas of Ibn Taymiyya and Qutb with respect to jihad and pushes their application to its radical conclusion regarding the condition of the Muslim world and Egypt in particular.

Farag believed that the decline of Muslim societies was made possible by those who had lulled the community into believing that jihad was nonviolent; the restoration of the Muslim world to the straight path of Islam hinged on reclaiming the true meaning of jihad, the forgotten or neglected requirement of Islam. Farag maintained that jihad was the sixth pillar of Islam, forgotten or obscured by the majority of ulama and Muslims:

Jihad . . . for God's cause [in the way of Allah], in spite of its importance for the future of religion, has been neglected by the ulama . . . of this age. . . . There is no doubt that the idols of this world can only disappear through the power of the sword.[29]

As in the time of Muhammad, Farag maintained, this was the task of a minority, a vanguard who must be prepared to fight against unbelief and apostasy, prepared to suffer and die for their faith. Looking at the state of the ummah, and especially Muslim governments, he concluded unbelief and apostasy were endemic diseases:

The Rulers of this age are in apostasy from Islam. They were raised at the tables of imperialism, be it Crusaderism, or Communism, or Zionism. They carry nothing from Islam but their names, even though they pray and fast and claim to be Muslim.[30]

The punishment for their apostasy is loss of all rights, including their right to life. Given the authoritarian and corrupt nature of regimes and their societies, a true Islamic state could not be established through nonviolence but only through radical surgery, militant jihad, and the overthrow of apostate rulers.

We have to establish the Rule of God's Religion in our own country first, and to make the Word of God supreme. . . . There is no doubt that the first battlefield for jihad is the extermination of these infidel leaders and to replace them by a complete Islamic Order.[31]

Islamic Jihad and Farag saw the bulk of Egyptian society as basically good Muslims who were caught between the land of Islam or peace and the land of war, living in un-Islamic states, governed by un-Islamic laws and nominal Muslims. Holy war against Egypt's "atheist" state and ruler was both necessary and justified, an obligation for all true believers. The creation of an Islamic state required the eradication of Western law and implementation of Islamic law and the toppling of regimes through armed revolution:

This state is ruled by heathen laws despite the fact that the majority of its people are Muslims. These laws were formulated by infidels who compelled Muslims to abide by them. And because they deserted jihad, Muslims today live in subjugation, humiliation, division and fragmentation. . . . the aim of our group is to rise up to establish an Islamic state and restore Islam to this nation. . . . The means to this end is to fight against heretical rulers and to eradicate the despots who are no more than human beings who have not yet found those who are able to suppress them with the order of God Almighty.[32]

Muhammad Farag's *Neglected Duty* and Islamic Jihad's ideological worldview were but another stage in the spread of Islamic radicalism's jihad across the Muslim world, promulgating the rationale for extremist movements and the growth of networks that would later, as a result of the jihad in Afghanistan, become a global jihad. Their narrow, extremist interpretation of Islam and jihad was one side in the struggle within Islam between extremist and moderate Muslims, and it demonstrated yet again the ability of religious scriptures and tradition to be interpreted, reinterpreted, and misinterpreted.

The Struggle for the Meaning of Jihad

As this review of the development of jihad in response to challenges through the ages amply illustrates, there is no single doctrine of jihad that has always and everywhere existed or been universally accepted. Muslim understanding of what is required by the Quran and the practice of the Prophet regarding jihad has changed over time. The doctrine of jihad is not the product of a single authoritative individual or organization's interpretation. It is rather the product of diverse individuals and authorities interpreting and applying the principles of sacred texts in specific historical and political contexts.

JIHAD IN WARFARE

Jihad is often simply translated as and equated with aggressive holy war. For many in the West, it has come to symbolize Islam as a religion of violence and fanaticism. Religious extremists and terrorists reinforce this belief as they freely declare jihad to justify attacks against and murders of all who disagree with them. In fact, as we have seen, Muslims throughout the ages have discussed and debated and disagreed about the meaning of jihad, its defensive and expansionist, legitimate and illegitimate forms. Terrorists can attempt to hijack Islam and the doctrine of jihad, but that is no more legitimate than Christian and Jewish extremists committing their acts of terrorism in their own unholy wars in the name of Christianity or Judaism. Therefore, looking at what Islamic history, law, and tradition have to say about jihad and warfare becomes critical both in trying to understand the mind of a bin Laden and in forging future relations between Islam and the West.

Quranic passages referring to jihad as armed struggle fall into two broad categories: defensive, those that emphasize fighting against aggression, and offensive or expansionist, a more general command to fight against all unbelievers and spread the message and public order or Pax Islamica of Islam.

Muslims are urged to fight with great commitment so that victory will come and battle will end: "If you meet them in battle, inflict on them such a defeat as would be a lesson for those who come after them, and that they may be warned" (8:57). However, as is noted in the following passage, if they propose peace, then the fighting must end: "But if they are inclined to peace, make peace with them, and have trust in God for he hears all and knows everything" (8:61).

Many modern reformers, defending Islam against charges that it is a violent religion and sensitive to Western criticisms that violence is endemic to Islam, have emphasized that jihad is only justified for defense and have rejected earlier attempts to abrogate Quranic verses that emphasize defensive jihad by the "sword verses." Prominent modern Shii scholars such as Ayatollahs Mahmoud Taleqani and Murtaza Mutahhari argue that jihad is the defense of one's life, faith, property, and the integrity of the Muslim ummah. However, Mutahhari and others have interpreted defense broadly to include resistance to oppression not only in one's society but also against oppression anywhere, defense of the oppressed of the earth. In commenting on the Quranic dictum, "There is no compulsion in religion" (2:256), and that therefore wars aimed solely at the spread of Islam by force are not allowed, they also maintain that religious oppression must be resisted whether it is in a Muslim or non-Muslim society.[33]

As with other religious traditions whose controversies must also be understood within their historical contexts, Muslim disagreement over the use of jihad through the ages has been deeply influenced by social and political contexts. The right or obligation to wage jihad against religious, political, or social oppression has gained widespread usage in recent decades in order to justify holy and unholy wars. Khomeini used it to call on Muslims throughout the world, especially in the Gulf, to rise up against un-Islamic rulers. It was a means of legitimating Iran's export of revolution to Lebanon and elsewhere. The Shii of Lebanon experienced both violent and nonviolent expressions of jihad. Imam Musa Sadr was a tall, striking, charismatic Iranian-born religious leader, educated in Qom, the religious center associated with the Ayatollah Khomeini and sometimes referred to as "the Vatican." Musa Sadr moved to Lebanon and in the 1970s led a major social movement, the Movement for the Dispossessed, to protest and demand Muslim equity within Lebanon's Maronite Christian–dominated society. The radical organization Hizbollah emerged in the early 1980s as a resistance movement, inspired by Khomeini and supported by Iran, in reaction to the Israeli invasion and occupation of Lebanon.

Sunni Muslims have been equally drawn to this use of jihad. Hamas in Palestine defines itself, and justifies its jihad, as a resistance movement to Israeli occupation and oppression. Terrorist groups from Egypt to the southern Philippines have also used political and religious oppression as an excuse for their violent jihads.

While the Chinese and Indian governments repress the Uighurs and Kashmiris respectively, Islamic opposition groups press what they regard to be a jihad against oppressive states that have threatened their autonomy and independence. Chechens have harnessed their Islamic identity and called for jihad to resist Russia's reoccupation, and Islamic movements in several Central Asian republics have waged jihad against authoritarian rulers. Even Osama bin Laden has found it useful to claim that his jihad is to overthrow the oppressive and corrupt Saudi regime and prevent the infidel U.S. force from occupying Saudi Arabia, the land of Muhammad.

If some feel a need to justify all jihads as defensive, others do not. Thus, Muslims who insist that the defense of Islam is the only justification for jihad, and that all of the wars in the early days of Islam were defensive, have been criticized by others who believe that the restriction of jihad to defensive wars alone is a product of European colonialism and an unwarranted accommodation to the West.

JIHAD FOR CONVERSION

The common Western image is that Islam is a religion of the sword, that Muslims are required to use every means, including force and warfare, to spread and impose their faith. This issue like others is subject to a spectrum of opinions. While most Muslim scholars have agreed that it is never justified to wage jihad against non-Muslims simply because of their faith or to convert them, some bluntly state, as Ibn Khaldun, an acclaimed medieval Muslim historian, did: "In the Muslim community, holy war is a religious duty, because of the universalism of the Muslim mission and (the obligation to) convert everybody to Islam either by persuasion or by force."[34] Other medieval authors, like their Christian counterparts, went even further, teaching that the purpose of jihad is to rid the earth of unbelievers.

Because of the Islamic vision of the inseparability of religion and politics, oppression and injustice came to be equated with unbelief. However, although jurists and commentators on the Quran often failed to distinguish disbelief from political injustice, they did not sanction jihad merely on grounds of difference in belief. Many modern Muslim thinkers have distinguished disbelief from persecution or injustice and hold that unbelief alone is not a sufficient condition for waging war. The famous twentieth-century Egyptian jurist Mahmud Shaltut, former rector of Egypt's al-Azhar University, an internationally recognized seat of Islamic authority, argued that the Quranic verses that command fighting against the unbelievers are not referring to a jihad against all unbelievers as such but rather to unbelievers who had assailed the Muslim mission.

Even Sayyid Qutb rejected forced conversions, believing instead that a successful jihad included the possibility of conversion as a likely result once people were free to choose:

> It is not the intention of Islam to force its beliefs on people, but Islam is not merely "belief." . . . Islam is a declaration of the freedom of man from servitude to other men. Thus it strives . . . to abolish all those systems and governments which are based on the rule of man over men and the servitude of one human being to another. When Islam releases people from this political pressure and presents to them its spiritual message, appealing to their reason, it gives them complete freedom to accept or not to accept its beliefs. However, this freedom does not mean that they can make their desires their gods or that they can choose to remain in the servitude of other human beings, making some men lords over others.[35]

Contemporary scholars utilize Quranic passages to demonstrate Islam's acceptance of a diversity of religious beliefs and laws.[36] For example, "Surely the believers, the Jews, the Sabians and the Christians—whoever believes in God and the Last Day and does good deeds—They shall receive their reward from their Lord. They shall have nothing to fear and they shall not grieve" (5:69 and 2:62).

Jihad and Martyrdom:
The Ultimate Profession of Faith

If you are killed in the cause of God or you die, the forgiveness and mercy of God are better than all that you amass. And if you die or are killed, even so it is to God that you will return (3:157– 158).

To die for one's faith is the highest form of witness to God, according to the Quran. Like the Greek word martyr, which simply means witness, as in witness to your faith, the Arabic Quranic word for martyr, *shahid*, means witness. Martyrdom comes from the same root as the Muslim profession of faith (*shahada*) or witness that "There is no God but God and Muhammad is the Prophet of God." When jihad is invoked to urge Muslims to take part in wars against nonbelievers, its main motivator is the belief that someone who is killed on the battlefield, called a shahid, will go directly to Paradise.

With the severe dislocations experienced in much of the Muslim world from the eighteenth century to the present, a new understanding of martyrdom has been born. Martyrdom was a powerful theme in the Iran-Iraq war where both Sunni Iraqis and Shii Iranians relied on the promise of martyrdom to motivate their soldiers. Since the late twentieth century, the term martyrdom has been used broadly by Muslims around the world for all of those who die for their faith or in the defense of Muslim territory in "just" causes in Palestine, Iran, Egypt, and Lebanon as well as Azerbaijan, Bosnia, Chechnya, Kashmir, and the southern Philippines.

Shii Islam has a particularly powerful martyrdom tradition and legacy, starting with the martyrdom of the Prophet's grandson Hussein, which became the paradigm for Shii theology and spirituality. This tragic event is ritually reenacted annually in Shii communities. It has expressed itself in the special place given to visiting the graves of the martyrs, and mourning and emulating the suffering of Hussein and his companions with prayer, weeping, and self-flagellation—a ritual analogous to the commemoration of the passion and death of Jesus Christ. In postrevolutionary Iran, the tradition is reflected in the creation of martyr cemeteries for those who died in the Iran-Iraq war and for the revolution's clergy and supporters who were murdered or assassinated by opposition forces.

In some ways, we have come full circle since 1979–1980. However little Westerners knew about Islam, many were then able to distinguish between two major jihads, Khomeini's Islamic revolution with its threat to the West and the mujahidin's jihad to liberate Afghanistan. The United States government judged the jihad, whether it was a holy or unholy war, and its warriors, whether they were extremists or liberators, by their goals and conduct—by whether they were fighting America's Cold War adversary or an ally, the Shah of Iran. But things were never that simple. Understanding the dynamics of Muslim politics today and the dangers and threats that now exist requires a fuller understanding both of jihad itself and of how the United States got to the point where it is now number one on the hit list of Muslim terrorists.

Wherever one turns, the image and words of Osama bin Laden seem to embody jihad. He stands before us with a Quran in one hand and a Kalashnikov in the other, surrounded by his band of religious zealots. However, bin Laden is symptomatic of a broader phenomenon. His disappearance from the scene will not eliminate the danger of global Islamic terrorism.

We have seen the power that the legacy of the past, faith and tradition, holds for Muslims and the key figures or ideologues whose ideas and examples still live today in the minds and faith of many believers. They provide the multitude of meanings of jihad that individuals and movements draw on when they use the tradition of jihad to renew themselves and their communities today. How has this multifaceted concept of jihad been translated into action by Islamic organizations? What are their motivations, missions, strategies, and tactics? We turn now to the reality, the holy and unholy wars that represent reality for the twentieth and twenty-first centuries.

The Armies of God

November 20, 1979, was a day that Muslims around the world had awaited, the dawn of Islam's fifteenth century. At 5:30 A.M. as over forty thousand worshippers prayed the dawn prayer in the Grand Mosque in Mecca, the largest Islamic shrine in the world, their sacred space and time were shattered by the profane. Shots reverberated through the massive courtyard and a young man fell dead. A powerful force of armed militants, not only Saudis but also Egyptians, Kuwaitis, Bangladeshis, Yemenis, and Iraqis, pushed their way into the praying crowd and declared that the long-awaited Mahdi had arrived.

The more than three hundred members of this militant band and their families were led by Juhaiman al-Utaiba, the brother-in-law of the self-declared Mahdi, who had come to cleanse Islam before the end of the world. Juhaiman and his followers had been bitter critics of the Saudi government, its alliance with the West, and its disruptive modernization programs. They called for the overthrow of the sinful and unjust Saudi regime, the establishment of a true Islamic state, the eradication of Western cultural influences, and the end of oil exports to America.[1] The militants barricaded themselves in the mosque and held out against government forces for five days before being forced to retreat to the cellars and tunnels below the mosque where they remained for another nine days.

The Saudi government debated long and hard about how to best respond to this very delicate situation. The use of arms or fighting in the mosque is strictly forbidden. It had been unthinkable that Muslims would violate the sanctuary. Juhaiman's choice of the Grand Mosque was a fatal strategic error. Whatever its symbolic value, the group's action shocked and offended many, who were horrified by the shedding of blood in the shrine holding the *Kaaba*, the stone marking the center of Islam, the direction to which Muslims worldwide turn to pray. However legitimate their grievances, their actions were *haram*, forbidden and thus illegitimate. After initially hesitating, the king finally obtained a *fatwa* from Shaykh Abdul-Aziz Bin Baz, head of the government's Council of Ulama and the most powerful religious leader in the kingdom. Bin Baz approved the use of force within the Grand Mosque. The siege was finally ended after two weeks. Its leaders, whom the government had ridiculed as *Khawarj* (like the Kharijites, the first significant Islamic extremist movement, they had seceded and turned on their ruler), were either killed in the battle that ensued or captured and later executed.

The charismatic Juhaiman al-Utaiba had studied at Medina University, which was founded by members of the Egyptian Muslim Brotherhood who had fled Nasser's Egypt. He had also attended lectures by Bin Baz, who was known as a very learned but extremely conservative scholar. Juhaiman had left the university with a group of followers in 1974 and began to preach fiery sermons and build his new organization. In 1978, he and a large group of his followers were arrested for distributing his pamphlets calling for opposition to the House of Saud and condemning their corruption and un-Islamic lifestyles. Few in the West took note of the fact that the militants who invaded the Grand Mosque to protest against the Saudi regime and Western influences were not only Saudis but also members of Islamic activist groups in Egypt, Kuwait, the Indian subcontinent, Yemen, and Iraq.

To Western observers, this affair was baffling. An Islamic group was attempting to overthrow the government of Saudi Arabia, an Islamic state and protector of Islam's holiest sites, in the name of Islam? The House of Saud was being judged and condemned as corrupt and un-Islamic by the very Islamic yardstick that it used to legitimate itself.

This incident brought together militants from many countries. It was a precursor of changes that would become apparent in the Soviet-Afghan war, the globalization of jihad movements with holy warriors drawn from many parts of the *ummah* coming to the "defense of Islam." No one imagined then that the government of Saudi Arabia and Saudi dissidents would in the next few years become so intimately connected with the globalization of *jihad* and its tragic terrorist trajectory.

Twenty years later Osama bin Laden and al-Qaeda's declaration of war against America would bring together many elements from Muslim history (militant jihad, eighteenth-century revivalists, Wahhabi Islam, and condemnation of Western alliances with autocratic Muslim leaders) and add another dimension, the greatly enhanced power that globalization affords to terrorist groups— the ability to harness religion and modern technology to strike anywhere, anytime, and anyplace. This dark side of globalization now strengthens the threat of Islamic radicalism to our stability and security and forces us to recognize that the growing threat of terrorism in the name of Islam is part of a much bigger picture.

The terrorists responsible for the atrocities of September 11, 2001, are the radical fringe of a broad-based Islamic jihad that began in the late twentieth century. Islam's power and the idealistic concepts of jihad have been "spun" to become the primary idiom of Muslim politics, used by rulers and ruled, by reformers, political opposition, and terrorists.

Many violent radicals justify the horrors they commit by reciting a litany of deeply felt Muslim grievances against the West. Historic memories of the Crusades and European colonialism, the creation of Israel, the Cold War, and American neocolonialism— all the actions of a militant Christian West—get superimposed upon current events: the second Palestinian intifada, the presence of American troops in the Gulf, the devastating impact of sanctions on Iraqi children, jihads of resistance and liberation in Kashmir and Chechnya. These memories feed resentment, ignite new anger, and deepen anti-Americanism, not just among terrorists but also in the broader Muslim world. A climate of suspicion and animosity toward the West is reflected in the common use of words like Christian Crusaders, neocolonialism, and Zionist expansionism. And it is strikingly illustrated by the unfounded rumors that swept across the Arab and Muslim world, Europe, and America that the WTC attacks were perpetrated by Mossad and that four thousand Jews who work in the WTC did not show up for work on September 11 due to a tip from Israeli security.[2]

From the Crusades to Western Imperialism

The Crusades and European colonialism have had a universal and lasting impact on the Muslim imagination. I used to joke about an event whose significance is clearer to me now. I was at a national professional conference on the modern Muslim world. We were running late. The panel chair, to assure that there would be enough time for this nervous young professor to participate, asked his colleagues to skip the first part of their papers denouncing the Crusades and European colonialism for their long-lasting negative legacy. At the time, it seemed merely humorous. Today, some twenty-five years later, it has proven enduringly revealing.

For many in the West, the Crusades for the liberation of Jerusalem were a shining moment of religious fervor in the defense of Christianity. Western sports teams, marketing firms, and media have long used images of Crusaders as brave and powerful warriors, lofty symbols of self-sacrifice, honor, and valor. Few of us know or remember that Pope Urban called for the Crusades for political rather than his ostensible religious reasons or that, on balance, the Crusaders ultimately were the losers not the victors. The significance of the Crusades is less a case of what actually happened than what the stories taught us to believe. Each community looks back with memories of its commitment to defend its faith and to heroic tales of bravery and chivalry in struggling against "the infidel." Both Muslims and Christians saw the other as determined to conquer, convert, or eradicate the other, and thus as an enemy of God. For Westerners, Islam is a religion of the sword, of holy war or jihad. For Muslims, Christianity is the religion of the Crusades and hegemonic ambitions. The last segment of a BBC series on Islam, which covered colonialism and postcolonialism, gave support to this belief in its title, "The Final Crusade."

President George W. Bush's use of the word crusade in a speech about the war against terrorism, and the protests and apologies that followed, highlighted the distance between Muslim and Western historical memories. Muslims wondered, Would American soldiers entering Afghanistan become the first step in a broader, militant agenda? Would America repeat European colonialism and attempt to infiltrate, dominate, and ultimately redraw the map of the Middle East once again?

No one who has traveled in or studied the Muslim world can be oblivious to the tendency of many to attribute their past and current problems in large part to the second traumatic event affecting Islam and the West, the legacy of European colonialism. Again, their memories are different from ours. Many of us have forgotten what the twentieth-century map of the Muslim world reveals. The names of regions (the Middle East) and countries as well as the boundaries and rulers of countries were created by European colonial powers. Those who would understand the state and state of mind of the Muslim world today should start by examining the extent of foreign dominance and Muslim subordination to Europe in the recent past: the French in North, West, and Equatorial Africa, and the Levant (Lebanon and Syria); the British in Palestine, Transjordan (now Jordan), Iraq, the Arabian Gulf, and the Indian subcontinent; and in Southeast Asia, the British in Malaya (Malaysia, Singapore, and Brunei) and the Dutch in Indonesia.

The Ayatollah Khomeini spoke dramatically of the depth of Western penetration and extent of its threat to Muslim societies:

> The foul claws of imperialism have clutched at the heart of the
> lands of the people of the Quran, with our national wealth and
> resources being devoured by imperialism . . . with the poison-
> ous culture of imperialism penetrating to the depths our towns
> and villages throughout the Muslim world, displacing the cul-
> ture of the Quran.[3]

European colonialism reversed a pattern of Muslim rule and
expansion that had existed from the time of the Prophet. As the
balance of power and leadership shifted to Europe, much of the
once dominant Islamic civilization found itself either directly ruled
or dominated by the Christian West, threatened by crown and
cross. Many Europeans believed that modernity was evidence of
the inherent superiority of Christianity as a religion and culture.
Britain spoke of the "white man's burden" and France of its "mission to civilize" to justify European imperialism as they colonized
much of Africa, the Middle East, South and Southeast Asia.

Europe's threat to Muslim identity and autonomy raised profound religious as well as political questions for many in the Muslim world: What had gone wrong? Why had Muslims fallen
behind? Why had Muslim fortunes been so thoroughly reversed?
Was it Muslims who had failed Islam or Islam that had failed Muslims? How were Muslims to respond? More than a century later,
these same questions and issues remain. Combined with a Muslim belief that their societies must be reformed in every age, they
make a combustible mixture that readily ignites into the flame of
desire for a new world and the will to take radical action to make
this vision of reform a reality.

From Hijra and Jihad to
Modernization and Islamic Reform

Four Muslim responses to colonialism form the foundations for
much of what we see today: resistance and warfare, withdrawal
and noncooperation, secularism and Westernization, and Islamic

modernism. Resisters sought to follow the example of the Prophet: emigration (*hijra*) out of a territory no longer under Muslim rule and jihad, fighting to defend the faith and lands of Islam. Emigration for large numbers of people was impractical, however, and holy war against Europe's overwhelming military strength was doomed to defeat. For many religious leaders, the practical alternative was simply to refuse to deal with the new colonial masters, to shun their company, schools, and institutions.

Others thought their survival depended on following Europe's lead. The Egyptian modernist Taha Husayn (1889–1973) exmplified this position. A brilliant student, born blind, he attended al-Azhar University for ten years but then went on to the Egyptian University in Cairo followed by four years of study in France. He became a dominant and at times controversial figure in intellectual and academic circles. His book *The Future of Culture in Egypt* (1938) epitomized the orientation of many emerging elites who advocated a liberal secular reform program in emulation of the West. Many judged Islam as either the cause of decline or incapable of meeting the needs of modern life. They therefore advocated a modernization program that borrowed heavily from Western models of political, social, and legal change.

Taha Husayn aligned Islam with Christianity and maintained that Egypt's modern renaissance was based on Europe:

> The essence and source of Islam are the essence and source of Christianity. So far has the European ideal become our ideal that we now measure the material progress of all individuals and groups by the amount of borrowing from Europe.[4]

Muslim rulers in the Ottoman Empire, Egypt, and Iran had been quick to climb onto what they hoped would be a bullet-train to modernization. Scholars and students were sent to Europe, new universities and centers were created at home. Muslims studied languages, science, and politics, translated and published Western works. New westernized elites accepted a secular outlook that restricted religion to personal life and turned to Europe to "modern-ize" their Muslim societies. The traditional Islamic ideology that had for centuries given legitimacy to Muslim societies was slowly altered as imported secular models from the West took over.

In Muslim society, this trend toward westernization created a growing social split. Modern secular schools functioning along-side traditional religious institutions produced two classes of Mus-lims living side by side but developing different worldviews and prospects for the future: a modern, westernized, elite minority and a more traditional, Islamically oriented majority. In a very real sense, there was a clash of cultures, one of skills and values as well as of power and privilege. This division has remained a major cause of the crisis of identity and resurgence of religion in many Muslim societies.

A fourth response to the challenge of the West, Islamic mod-ernism, tried to bridge the gap between Islamic traditionalists and secular reformers. Islamic modernism, like much of the Muslim response to the West today, displayed an ambivalent love-hate at-titude toward the so-called Success of the West. They admired Eu-rope for its strength, technology, and ideals of freedom, justice, and equality but rejected its colonialist goals and policies. Mod-ernists wanted to develop an Islamically based rationale for edu-cational, legal, political, and social reform in order to promote a renaissance for their community and a first step to national inde-pendence and power.

Islamic modernism was both a success and a failure: it reawakened a sense of past power and glory, argued the compatibility of Islam with modern reform, and distinguished between Western ideas and technology and Western imperialism. Reformers offered an Islamic alternative to either rejecting or uncritically assimilating the West. Their ideas and values became part of Muslim discourse and mainstream Muslim thought. However, the modernist intel-lectual movement did not produce organizations to pass on, de-velop and implement their ideas in a sustained manner. Some disciples of the great modernist thinkers turned to a more secular path. Most important, Islamic reformism was not sufficiently integrated into the curricula of religious schools (*madrasas*) and the training of religious scholars and leaders. As late as the 1970s and 1980s, Muslim and non-Muslim scholars writing about Islam and modernity or Islamic reformism would commonly point to Muhammad Abduh who died in 1905 and Muhammad Iqbal who died in 1938. While their role and legacy are important, the fact that they had been dead for decades seemed a tacit commentary on the failure of Islamic modernism to inspire new leaders and take hold within the broader community. Today the term "*salafi*," which had once been used to refer to Muhammad Abduh's Islamic modernist movement with its emphasis on Islam and rational modernism, is instead applied to some of the most extreme, anti-Western groups.

Islam and the Modern State

After World War II, the success of independence movements in over-throwing European rule and the creation of modern Muslim states brought pride and high expectations for a strong and prosperous future. Nation building in the Muslim world with its artificially drawn borders superficially uniting peoples with diverse centuries-old identities and allegiances was a fragile process that bore the seeds for later crises of identity, legitimacy, power, and authority.

When we ask today why much of the Muslim world remains politically unstable or underdeveloped, we need to remember that most modern Muslim states are only several decades old, carved out by the now-departed European powers.

The fragility of new nation-states was demonstrated time and again. In South Asia, for example, the British divided the Indian subcontinent into India and the new Islamic Republic of Pakistan. Kashmir was a state with a Muslim majority but led by an Indian maharaja who acceded to Indian rule, an arrangement that has been contested by Pakistan ever since. The majority of territory, the 54,000 square miles of Jammu Kashmir, was taken by India while Pakistan ruled a smaller parcel of 32,000 square miles, Azad Kashmir.

The creation of India and Pakistan resulted in communal war-fare that left millions dead. Tens of thousands of Hindus and Mus-lims were forced to emigrate, Hindus to India and Muslims to Pakistan. Pakistan proved equally fragile. East Pakistan (later Bangla-desh) and West Pakistan were separated by 1,000 miles of Indian territory. The difficulty of establishing a strong sense of nationalism in countries with such enormous ethnic, tribal, linguistic, and cul-tural diversity can be deduced from the fact that in both India and Pakistan the vast majority of the citizens in each country could not speak their national language (Hindi and Urdu respectively). The bloody results of colonial map making and nation creation were evident yet again in the brutal 1971 Pakistan civil war which led to the creation of Bangladesh, and in the bloody ethnic clashes that have threatened the stability of Pakistan to the present day. In Kash-mir, the creation of a Muslim majority state within India resulted in wars between India and Pakistan in 1947 and 1965. Since 1987, Kashmiri separatists have been locked in a struggle against India's rule that has brought as many as 750,000 Indian troops to Kash-mir to carry out a brutal war. To the present day, Kashmir contin-ues to be a major incendiary issue in relations between India and Pakistan.

In the Middle East, the French created modern Lebanon by tak-ing some portions of Syria, while Britain set the borders and rulers for Iraq and Kuwait. These arbitrary borders fed ethnic, regional, and religious conflicts that have threatened national unity or sta-bility in numerous countries. The Lebanese Civil War (1975–1990) pitted Christian and Muslim militias against each other and also resulted in Syria's intervention and occupation. Iraq's 1990 inva-sion of Kuwait was justified by Saddam Hussein's claim on Ku-waiti territory. In the post–Gulf war period, Saddam Hussein's savage repression of Shii and Kurds reflected the artificiality and fragility of the Iraqi nation, a cobbled-together state led by a Sunni ruler with a long history of repressing Iraq's majority Shii popula-tion in the south and its (Sunni) Kurds in the north. Both Saddam's actions and the initial reluctance of the first (George H.) Bush administration to intervene were based on fears of Iraq's breakup or "Lebanization." Other countries, like Transjordan (Jordan), were totally new British creations. A popular story has Winston Churchill spending a lazy Sunday hunched over a map, smoking a good cigar, while drawing the boundary lines for his new "country" of Jordan.

Often the claims and legitimacy of rulers were equally artificial. The Hashimite family of Arabia provides an interesting example. The British created Transjordan and Iraq as states to be ruled by the Hashimite family. Prince Abdullah from Arabia was made emir (prince) of Transjordan. (He later upgraded to king of Jordan.) Abdullah's brother, Faisal, whose rule in Syria had been ended quickly by French intervention, was then made king of Iraq by Britain! And the most volatile example of European nation building in the Middle East remains the creation of Israel amidst competing and still-unresolved religious, nationalist, and territorial claims which resulted in the bitter legacy of the Arab-Israeli wars.

By the mid-twentieth century, most of the Muslim world had achieved political independence. Most rulers, even in those countries where Islam played an important role, had chosen the more Western-influenced secular path. Nevertheless, looking across the Muslim world, you could see three models for new states: Islamic, secular, and Muslim.

Saudi Arabia was a self declared Islamic state. The monarchy of the House of Saud legitimated its domestic and foreign policies by claiming to govern and be governed by the Quran and Islamic law. At the other end of the spectrum, Turkey, the only remnant of the Ottoman Empire, opted for a secular state and severely restricted religion to personal life. Turkey under the leadership and direction of Mustafa Kemal (popularly known as Ataturk, Father of the Turks, d. 1938) embarked on a comprehensive process of Turkification, westernization, and secularization.

Most Muslim countries fell into a middle position. Creating modern states modeled on Western paradigms, they superficially injected Islamic provisions into constitutions requiring that the head of state be a Muslim or that Islamic law be recognized as "a" source of law even when it was not, in reality, recognized at all. These governments sought to control religion by incorporating schools, courts, and mosques into their ministries of education, law, and religious affairs. In some Muslim countries, languages for government, the courts, and universities were European. Individuals and institutions were "modern" to the degree that they were Western—in language and dress, manners and values, architecture and infrastructure.

Few questioned the accepted wisdom that modernization meant the progressive westernization and secularization of society. A modern education was the surest ticket to responsible positions in government, business, the professions, and academia. Close international ties were forged between the governments, the military, oil companies, and banks of the Muslim world and the West and set the stage for decades of educational and technical exchanges as well as political, economic, and military alliances. The United States, lacking the negative baggage of colonial powers, enjoyed a certain pride of place. It became a magnet for diplomats, bureaucrats, military, and security forces who received university and professional education there, and a haven for many who escaped poverty or persecution under authoritarian regimes. It seemed reasonable to expect that every day in every way westernization and secularization were making things better and better. How wrong that expectation turned out to be!

During the 1950s and 1960s widespread dissatisfaction with the track record of Western-inspired liberal nationalism took its toll. Monarchs and governments tumbled from power and new governments emerged in Egypt, Libya, Syria, Sudan, Iraq, and Algeria. All were based on some form of Arab nationalism/socialism with its populist appeals to Arab-Islamic roots, stress on Arab unity, criticism of the failures of liberal nationalism and the West, and promise of far-reaching social reforms. At the same time, the Muslim Brotherhood attracted tens of thousands of members in Egypt and Sudan as well as Syria, Jordan, and Palestine. Both Arab nationalism/socialism and the Brotherhood were populist movements that captured the imaginations, hopes, and aspirations of many in the Arab world and beyond. Muslim governments and societies continued to rely heavily on the West but now tilted more to the Soviet Union. Initially, Arab nationalist leaders such as Egypt's Gamal Abdel Nasser and his admirers such as Sudan's Jafar al-Numeiry and Libya's Muammar Qaddafi seemed to be in the driver's seat, controlling, marginalizing, or repressing Islamic activism. By the 1970s, however, Arab nationalism/socialism was discredited by the disastrous Arab defeat in the 1967 Arab-Israeli war, the failure of economic policies, and government corruption. In response, governments in all three countries were forced to turn to Islam to buttress their legitimacy and deal with rising Islamic reform and opposition movements.

Back to the Future: The Islamic Resurgence

Iran's Islamic revolution of 1978–1979 abruptly detoured the march toward Western modernization. Leading modernizing governments in Iran, Egypt, and Lebanon seemed to be experiencing the revenge of God. They were not alone. Islamic revivalism produced a wave of fundamentalist movements from Egypt, Sudan, and Iran to Pakistan, Afghanistan, and Malaysia.

The causes of the resurgence vary by country and region, but there are common threads: widespread feelings of failure and loss of identity in many Muslim societies, as well as failed political systems and economies. Overcrowded cities with insufficient social support systems, high unemployment rates, government corruption, a growing gap between rich and poor, and the breakdown of traditional religious and social values plagued many nations. Israel's crushing victory over the combined forces of Egypt, Jordan, and Syria in the 1967 Arab-Israeli Six-Day war symbolized the depth of Arab and Muslim impotence and the failure of modern nation-states in the Muslim world. Israel seized major pieces of territory, including the Sinai peninsula and Gaza Strip from Egypt, the Golan Heights from Syria, and the West Bank and East

Jerusalem from Jordan. The loss of Jerusalem, the third holiest city of Islam, which embraces major Muslim holy sites, the Dome of the Rock and the al-Aqsa Mosque, was particularly devastating to Muslims around the world, making Palestine and the liberation of Jerusalem an Islamic, not just an Arab or Palestinian, issue.

The year 1967 proved a turning point for many in the Muslim world who blamed Western political and economic models for their moral decline and spiritual malaise. Disillusionment with the West and in particular with the United States, its pro-Israel policy, and its support for authoritarian rulers like Iran's shah fed anti-Western feelings. Muslim religious leaders and activists believed their message had been vindicated, maintaining that the failures and troubles of Muslims were a result of turning away from God's revealed path and relying on the West. From the 1970s onward, religious revivalism and the role of Islamic movements became a major force in Muslim politics.

Building the Armies for God

Modern Islamic movements have been the driving force behind the resurgence of Islam. As discussed in the previous chapter, Muslims have a rich legacy of traditions that call upon them to reform their societies in every age. Given the vision of early Islamic power and success and then its decline for several centuries, it is not surprising to see a proliferation of Islamic movements in the twenty-first century striving to create a better world. Nonviolent revolutionary change from below and violent revolution to overthrow established un-Islamic governments have remained the twin paths of contemporary Islamic movements. Both seemed to spring up in the 1970s and spread like wildfire across the Muslim world.

The two pioneer Islamic movements described earlier, Egypt's Muslim Brotherhood and Pakistan's Jamaat-i-Islami, spread to Sudan, Jordan, and the Gulf, Bangladesh, India, and Kashmir and inspired a proliferation of similar movements across the world.

While all have been committed to a jihad to transform Muslim societies, their formation, development, strategy, and tactics have reflected the diverse political, economic, and social environments in which they arose. The direction of that jihad, whether it followed a nonviolent or violent path, has often been influenced as much by governments as by Islamic organizations. A majority of Muslim reform organizations have operated above ground, working within their societies; a radicalized militant minority has engaged in a violent jihad to seize power or attack Muslim governments, America, Europe, and Israel.

As Osama bin Laden and al-Qaeda have reminded us, what happens "over there" does in fact have an impact here in the United States and elsewhere in the West. Countries such as Afghanistan, Egypt, Israel/Palestine, and Algeria have proven fertile ground in which the seeds of violence and terrorism have thrived. No country better demonstrates the many faces of political Islam, violent and nonviolent, domestic and international, than Egypt. The birthplace of the Brotherhood, of its paths of political participation and violent revolutionary jihad, Egyptian society has produced a long list of reformers and terrorists, the progeny of Hasan al-Banna and Sayyid Qutb, extending from Muhammad Farag, the ideologue for Islamic Jihad, the assassins of Anwar Sadat to Dr. Ayman al-Zawahiri and other al-Qaeda leaders of the jihad against America.

Egypt and the Rage for God

"I have killed Pharaoh and I do not fear death"
Khalid Islambuli, the assassin of Anwar Sadat

Egypt has long been a leader in the Arab and Muslim world, a long-time ally of the United States. It is a major destination for foreign tourists who are fascinated by its pyramids, pharaohs, and mummies. Egypt's marketing image and major tourist sites that feature ancient Egyptian history, however, have long masked its deep Islamic identity, character, and culture.

The most modern and modernizing of countries, politically, culturally and religiously, Egypt has also been the most prominent site of both Islamic reform and radical extremism. Egypt's Islamic movements have spanned the spectrum from the modernists in the late-nineteenth and twentieth centuries to recent extremist groups such as Takfir wal Hijra, Islamic Jihad, and Gamaa Islamiyya who have terrorized Egyptian society, inspired Osama bin Laden, and became part of his al-Qaeda network. The Egyptian experience offers a full-blown example of political Islam from its pioneers to its mainstream and terrorist fringes today and reflects the ironic fact that some of the most developed countries in the Middle East have experienced and been victims of significant violence and terrorism. What can we learn about the nature of political Islam and the role of violence and acts of terror? What is the legacy of Egypt's movements for global terrorism in the twenty-first century? Recent history will help to answer these questions.

THE BELIEVER-PRESIDENT AND JIHAD

When Anwar Sadat succeeded Gamal Abdel Nasser as president of Egypt, he faced a formidable task. He replaced an enormously popular charismatic leader, influential not only in Egypt but also throughout the Arab world. In some Arab countries, you might see more pictures of Nasser than of the local president. At first Sadat's portrait was hung next to Nasser's to bolster his legitimacy. Later, however, to escape living in Nasser's shadow, Sadat shifted gears and made strong appeals to Islam. Sadat wished to distance himself from Nasser's party, his failed socialist ideology, policies, and allies, and to define his own path and policies.

Sadat assumed the title the Believer-President, an allusion to the Islamic caliph's title Commander of the Faithful. He began and ended his speeches with verses from the Quran. TV broadcasts frequently featured him in a mosque, cameras zeroing in on his prominent prayer mark, a callous caused by touching the forehead to the ground in prayer. Sadat encouraged the growth of Islamic student associations on campus and was able to gain enough control over the shaykh (rector) and leading religious scholars at al-Azhar University to be able to count on their support for the Egyptian-Israeli peace treaty. This treaty won him great praise in the West and a Nobel Peace Prize. However, despite generous aid from the United States following the Camp David Accords in 1978–1979, the standard of living for most Egyptians continued its steady decline, and the Palestinians, always the symbol of the success or failure of Arab leadership, remained stateless and persecuted under military occupation.

It soon became clear to Sadat that appealing to Islam was a two-edged sword. Using strict Islamic criteria, activists judged Sadat to be a hypocrite and traitor for his relations with the West, his failure to implement the Shariah as the official law of Egypt, and his liberal family-law reforms, which critics, who saw them as Western rather than Islamically inspired, sarcastically dubbed "Jihan's laws" after Sadat's half-British wife.

By the mid-1970s, the quiet achieved by Nasser's 1960s suppression of the Muslim Brotherhood was gone. New members who were attracted to emerging organizations included those who had believed in westernization and modernization, but who were now disaffected by the continuing economic decline. They included the majority of the unemployed younger generation as well as former secularists. The Muslim Brotherhood was back and so were new extremists, secret revolutionary groups like Muhammad's Youth, Takfir wal Hijra (Excommunication and Flight), and Islamic Jihad promoting their jihad of violence and terrorism. They seized buildings, kidnapped and executed government officials, and tried to assassinate Sadat and declare an Islamic republic.

In a nationwide crackdown, the government arrested 620 militants; 454 were tried by special military courts and imprisoned. The leaders of Muhammad's Youth and Takfir were executed. Many militants went underground only to reemerge as new groups, the Army of God (Jund Allah) and Islamic Jihad (Jamaat al-Jihad, or Holy War Society).

Increasingly, Sadat responded to all of his Islamic critics, mainstream and radical alike, with a heavy hand. He warned: "Those who wish to practice Islam can go to the mosque and those who wish to engage in politics may do it through legal institutions."[5] The government tried to imprison all opposition, gain control of all mosques, and ban Islamic student associations. Sadat also moved to silence others: intellectuals, journalists, lawyers, university professors, former cabinet ministers who had criticized his policies. When food riots shook Cairo in January 1977, Sadat blamed Marxists and Leftists, and continued to arrest any opposition. While he was being praised in the West as a progressive Muslim leader, for many in Egypt Sadat's new economic open-door policy just meant greater Western (especially American) economic involvement. It meant lining the pockets of multinational companies and Egyptian elites, not solving basic economic and social problems:

> How can the peasant, the hardworking Egyptian fellah, maintain his dignity when, after sweating in the hot sun all day long, he has to stand in line to receive a frozen American chicken? . . . As he sits in the evening with the family to watch the television that his son has purchased from the fruits of labor in Saudi Arabia, the intrigues of J.R. Ewing and Sue Ellen on Dallas strip him of what is left of his legitimacy as a culture bearer in his own culture. Between programs, he is told in English that he should be drinking Schweppes or in dubbed Arabic that he should use deodorant, and that all his problems are caused by having too many children—a total package of imported ideas.[6]

The September 1978 Camp David Accords were viewed by Arabs and Muslims at home and abroad as an opportunistic capitulation to Israel and its American patron. Sadat's foreign minister resigned, and protest demonstrations throughout Egypt denounced the accords as a treasonous act of an "unbeliever." Only Egypt seemed to benefit from the accords, as Israel eventually withdrew from the Sinai, and Egypt got massive aid from the United States as a reward for signing. However, Israel's occupation of Palestinian territories on the West Bank and Gaza, as well as of Syria's Golan Heights, remained in place. Al-Azhar's endorsement of the peace agreement was seen as simply reconfirmation that it had become a puppet of the government. Although the Muslim Brotherhood initially responded cautiously, by March 1979 it had called for a holy war against Israel.

In early September 1981, faced with mounting discontent and opposition, in a sensational move the government launched a massive dragnet, arresting more than 1,500 people. Secular and Islamic opposition publications were banned. Those imprisoned represented the entire political spectrum, from extreme right to extreme left, Muslim Brothers and militants, as well as Marxists, Muslims, and Copts, young and old, journalists, writers, professors, and other professionals. They included Dr. Nawal Saadawi, the prominent Egyptian author, feminist, and former cabinet minister. In a television address, Sadat maintained that he was saving Egypt from political and religious "sedition." Many believed that politically he had signed his "death warrant"; tragically, this prediction would prove to be literally true.[7] Like the shah of Iran when faced with mounting opposition, Sadat became more autocratic and increasingly identified the Egyptian state with his own personality and will. As Saad Eddin Ibrahim has noted,

> Sadatinization of Egypt was expressed in almost every song on radio and television. . . . Two processes were at work: a Sadatanization of Egypt on the one hand and a deification of Sadat on the other—the rebirth of the Egyptian pharaoh.[8]

Despite the growing tensions in Egyptian society, few expected what happened on October 6, 1981. Anwar Sadat, adorned in his gold-braided uniform sat amidst two thousand dignitaries from all over the world viewing a weapons display that commemorated the "success" of the 1973 war. As they shielded their eyes from the blazing sun, they watched fighter-plane aerobatics above and a slow-moving procession of artillery trucks below. Suddenly, four gunmen, appearing from behind the trucks, fired their automatic rifles and threw their grenades at the reviewing stand. The Believer-President, struck by at least five bullets as well as shrapnel, died almost immediately. Sadat was assassinated by members of Jamaat al-Jihad or Islamic Jihad, the organization that developed from an abortive coup staged by Muhammad's Youth. Their leader, a military officer, cried out, "I am Khalid Islambuli. I have killed Pharoah and I do not fear death!" Years later Khalid's brother, Mohammed Islambuli, would surface with Osama bin Laden in Afghanistan. Sadat's state funeral was attended by a host of celebrities, presidents, and politicians from Europe and America. However, Arab leaders were prominently missing, and the people of Egypt did not mourn for their Believer-President.

ISLAMIC JIHAD

The Egyptian Islamic Jihad has had a long track record of violence and terrorism. Its well-educated members have come from the presidential guard and military intelligence and include civil servants, radio and television workers, university students, and professors. They were recruited from religious societies and Quran study groups. Their social centers provided students with free books and tutoring and families with much-needed food, clothing, and housing.

The mission of Islamic Jihad was to create a true Islamic state and society in Egypt. This was to be the first step in achieving their long-term goal: a single Muslim government under a true Islamic caliphate. They have rationalized their holy war against Egypt's "atheist" state and rulers as required, the obligation of all true believers.

Islamic Jihad's war is waged against all nonbelievers, Muslim and non-Muslim alike. Extremist groups like Jihad reject Islam's traditional tolerance of the protected communities of Jews and Christians, People of the Book (*dhimmi*). Like Osama bin Laden, they see Jews and Christians as part of a historic battle or Crusade connected with European colonialism and Zionism, and they regard Israel as a Trojan horse of the West, a fifth column within Muslim societies.[9] Once people have been condemned as unbelievers who must be subject to the sword, they forfeit their right to life, security, and property. Shaykh Omar Abdel Rahman, spiritual adviser to Islamic Jihad and Gamaa Islamiyya, issued a fatwa sanctioning the killing and plundering of Christians in Luxor in 1997 because they were anti-Muslim. This outlook has been passed on to other groups in the Arab and Muslim world who believe that international conspiracies, Jewish Zionism, the Christian West, and atheistic communism all intend to divide the Muslim world and destroy Islam. In public protests they chant: "Holy war against lackeys—Jews, Christians, and Atheists" and "No to America! and No to Israel!"

After Sadat's assassination, Islamic Jihad regrouped and declared jihad against the new government of Hosni Mubarak. They reemerged in the 1990s along with Gamaa Islamiyya to threaten the security of Egyptian society. Dr. Ayman al-Zawahiri returned from the Afghan jihad and brought many other Arab Afghans with him and right into the Jihad organization. Egyptians had made up a large proportion of the foreigners fighting the Soviets. They returned to Egypt with new ideas, extensive *mujahidin* credentials, and the taste of victory against overwhelming odds. They brought Egypt's Islamic Jihad and Gamaa Islamiyya a new ideological dimension, transforming the more limited nationalist agenda to create an Islamic state in Egypt into a commitment to wage global jihad.

Islamic Jihad's activities reflected their rage and their agenda. In 1990, five Jihad members were arrested for killing the speaker of the National Assembly. Jihad members who unsuccessfully attempted to assassinate the interior minister and the prime minister in 1993 were believed to be behind the 1995 assassination attempt on President Mubarak in Addis Ababa, the bombing of the Egyptian embassy in Islamabad, and the slaughter of fifty-eight tourists at Luxor in 1997—a crime for which al-Zawahiri was sentenced to death *in absentia*. Jihad's spiritual adviser, Omar Abdel Rahman, was exiled to the United States, but continued to influ-

ence Jihad as well as Gamaa Islamiyya. He was implicated in the
1993 World Trade Center bombing and imprisoned for participation in a conspiracy to commit other bombings in America. Jihad
split into two wings, one loyal to Abboud al-Zamour, one of the
original founders, and the other, Vanguards of Conquest or the
New Jihad Group led by bin Laden protégé al-Zawahiri, who would
merge his group with al-Qaeda.

The Gamaa Islamiyya (Islamic Group) began during the Sadat
era as student Islamic groups active on university campuses and has
evolved into a terrorist network. It became an umbrella organization for violent extremists' clandestine cells active in Cairo, Alexan-
dria, and Upper Egypt. It attracted younger, less-educated followers
from more desperate conditions of poverty and unemployment who
espoused a more radical ideology and engaged in more random acts
of violence to destabilize the government politically and economically. They attacked tourists, a major source of Egypt's foreign rev-
enue, bombed and burned government buildings and banks, as well
as theaters and video and book stores that popularized Western culture. The Gamaa especially targeted Christians, bombing and burning churches and homes, robbing, beating, and murdering Christian
Egyptians. The Gamaa's other targets included columnist Farag Foda,
who was killed in 1992, and Egypt's Nobel laureate writer Naguib
Mahfuz, who in 1994 was stabbed in order to silence and intimidate outspoken critics of fundamentalists.

A DUAL REVOLUTION:
MAINSTREAM AND MILITANT JIHAD

During the Mubarak years extremists and government security
forces and police have been locked in an all-out unholy war in
which both sides use deadly force and terrorism against their enemy. The struggle has cost more than one thousand lives and led
to charges by human rights organizations, international media,
and political experts that the effort to capture and eradicate extremists has degenerated into indiscriminate state repression. More
than twenty thousand Islamists have been imprisoned, many de-

tained without charge and subjected to torture. Extralegal military courts that exclude the right of appeal were created; laws were enacted to restrict freedom of the press, take control of mosques, and prevent elected Islamists from leading professional associations.

Like other authoritarian regimes in the Middle East, the Mubarak government seized the opportunity to use its war against terrorism to silence both extremists and mainstream legal opposition, not only those movements that have carried out violent attacks, but one, namely the Muslim Brotherhood, that had become dominant in university faculties, labor and professional associations, and many municipalities.[10]

By 2000 the Mubarak government's strategy had clearly paid off. Imprisoned leaders of Gamaa Islamiyya had declared a unilateral cease-fire; the government released thousands of detainees. Islamic Jihad in Egypt, significantly weakened, many of its leaders imprisoned or in exile, soon followed suit. But Islamic Jihad abroad, in particular Ayman al-Zawahiri and Islamic Jihad leaders in Afghanistan, rejected the ceasefire and continue their global jihad.

MAINSTREAM FUNDAMENTALISM AND THE STATE

Despite the apparent success of the Mubarak government in containing Islamic radicalism, it is not responding successfully to the declining standard of living, high unemployment, and decreased freedom and democratic rights. As a consequence, Islamic revivalism has had a significant impact on mainstream Egyptian society. Egyptian society has itself become more Islamized at the grassroots level. New Islamic trends are seen in new educated religious leaders who have mass followings from middle- and upper-class audiences. Physicians, journalists, lawyers, political scientists, men and women write and speak out on issues of Islamic reform such as pluralism, women's rights, and social justice. Islamic belief, symbols, and values inform the government, courts, professions, dress, and values of society (modern as well as traditional sectors) *countering* the expectations of secular modernization theory and the policies of the Mubarak government.

The Muslim Brotherhood exemplifies the quiet social revolution that has been taking place in Egypt's cities and towns. Islamic activism has become institutionalized. Islamic schools, clinics, hospitals, and social services, as well as Islamic banks and publishing houses, are part of mainstream society, an alternative set of social institutions and services. They present an indirect indictment of the government's failure to respond to people's needs. The performance of Islamists at the polls has been equally impressive. Prevented by law from participating as a legal political party, the Muslim Brotherhood formed coalitions and alliances and emerged as the leading opposition in those parliamentary elections in which they participated.

The story of Egypt, an ally of the United States, is one of the many examples of how political and economic conditions coupled with repression spawn militant opposition movements that misuse Islam to motivate and legitimate violence and terrorism.

The Jihad in Palestine: Hamas

> If someone confiscated your land, demolished your home, built settlements to prevent you from coming back, killed your children and blocked you from going to work, wouldn't you want to fight for your country?[11]

Major Islamic movements arise in response to failures and crises in their societies and to vacuums in effective leadership. Nowhere has this been more dramatically visible than in Israel/Palestine. The late 1980s produced two militant Islamic responses to the failures of the Israeli and Palestinian leadership—Hamas and Islamic Jihad. Hamas, though always a minority, has proven the more effective, harnessing religion with political and social activism, and increasingly using acts of terrorism in the escalating violence and terror of the Palestinian-Israeli conflict.

Hamas is an offshoot of the Palestinian Muslim Brotherhood. It was created in 1987 during the Palestinian uprising (*intifada*) against Israeli occupation and rule in Gaza and the West Bank. The Brotherhood's support had dwindled, especially among the younger generation, after the Arab defeat in the 1967 Arab-Israeli war. Its apolitical path, focused on running schools, youth camps, and social welfare services, did not address the core causes of the continued disenfranchisement of the Palestinians and so fell short of the desperate mood of the times. Leaving the Brotherhood on the periphery, the majority of Palestinians turned to Yasser Arafat's Fatah and the Palestinian Liberation Organization (PLO), the coalition of Palestinian groups of which Fatah is a member.

However, when the intifada erupted in 1987, the Brotherhood moved quickly, taking advantage of Arafat's failures and the outpouring of frustration and rage against Israel to establish its relevance during the uprising. The Brotherhood created Hamas, ("fervor"), an acronym for the Islamic Resistance Movement; Hamas quickly took on a life and mission of its own, assuming a major leadership position during the intifada. Filling a vacuum, it provided a militant Islamic alternative to the secular nationalism of the PLO. Because of the Brotherhood's size, broad-based activities, and influence, Hamas became the principal alternative to the PLO.

From the beginning, Hamas's struggle to end the Israeli occupation was conducted as a jihad, a multifaceted struggle of political action, social welfare, and militant resistance, including acts of violence and terrorism. Hamas combined its religious message with social reform, which attracted the older generation, and with resistance and jihad, which spoke to the frustrations and fury of Palestinian youth. Hamas's success overshadowed the Brotherhood and challenged Yasser Arafat and the PLO's leadership in the struggle.

Hamas, like other Islamic movements, is engaged in a process of *dawah* (the call to become better Muslims) and jihad (the call to fight against oppression). The predicament of the Palestinian people, the hegemony of Israel, is attributed to loss of faith and departure from the straight path of Islam. Hamas calls all Muslims to give up their secular culture and lifestyles and return to religious observance: prayer, fasting, Islamic dress, moral and social values to re-create a proper Islamic society so that Muslim society can again become strong and wage a successful jihad to liberate Palestine from Israeli control.

As its charter states, Hamas "found itself at a time when Islam disappeared from life. Thus, rules were broken, concepts were vilified, values changed and evil people took control; oppression and darkness prevailed, cowards became tigers; homelands were invaded, people were scattered . . . when Islam is absent from the arena, everything changes."[12] From this perspective, Israel's occupation is seen as a punishment from God for deviations from Islam. Thus, independence, civil and political rights, dignity, and development will all be achieved only by a return to Islam, a re-Islamization of Palestinian Muslim society.

Hamas views the Muslim claim to the land of Palestine as religiously anchored and immutable: "The Islamic Resistance Movement believes that the land of Palestine has been an Islamic *Waqf* [religious endowment] throughout the generations and until the day of resurrection. . . . this waqf will endure as long as heaven and earth last." Islam is combined with Palestinian and Arab nationalism in Hamas's mission; Hamas's jihad is the defense of Palestine, a complementary combination of political and military activities, incumbent on all Muslims to liberate Palestine from Israeli occupation: "Nothing is loftier or deeper in nationalism than waging jihad against the enemy and confronting him when he sets foot on the land of the Muslims. . . . When our enemies usurp some lands, jihad becomes a duty on all Muslims."[13]

The PLO charter, on the other hand, identifies the enemy as Zionism, the European Jewish movement to create the state of Israel, which disregarded the rights of Palestinians whose land was needed to establish the state. The PLO goal is a secular state with equal rights for all citizens, Muslims and Christians (a significant minority of the Palestinian population). In contrast, Hamas rejects the distinction between Judaism and Zionism, seeing the Palestinian-Israeli conflict in religious terms as a confrontation between Islam and Judaism as represented by the religious state of Israel. In the words of Hamas's leader Mahmoud Zahar: "They [the Jews] made their religion their nation and state. . . . They have declared war on Islam, closed mosques and massacred defenseless worshippers at al-Aqsa and in Hebron. They are the Muslim-killers and under these circumstances we are obliged by our religion to defend ourselves."[14]

Like Takfir wal Hijra and Islamic Jihad as well as Osama bin Laden's al-Qaeda, Hamas sees the Palestinian-Israeli conflict as the most recent iteration of an age-old struggle between Islam and Judaism, dating back to the Jews' rejection of Muhammad and Islam in the seventh century.[15] Like many Muslim groups it draws on Western anti-Semitic literature, especially *The Protocols of the Learned Elders of Zion*, an apocryphal book that describes a fictitious Jewish conspiracy to destroy Christian civilization and establish Jewish hegemony, to bolster its indictment. Thus, for Hamas the Palestinian struggle is a jihad in the fullest militant sense of the term, a holy war between Muslims and Jews based on conflicting religious and territorial claims.

MEMBERSHIP AND ACTIVITIES

Hamas was founded by Shaykh Ahmad Yassin, the charismatic paraplegic leader of the Palestinian Muslim Brotherhood. Its leadership has included religious officials (*imams*), but most members are professionals and technocrats trained in medicine, engineering, science, or business. Members are recruited from a network of mosques, schools, and charitable institutions into this religious, social, political, and military movement. The combination of political and social activism with guerrilla warfare earned the financial and moral support of many Palestinians and others in the broader Arab and Muslim world. Its extensive network of community and charitable projects and programs—kindergartens, schools, scholarships, support for students studying abroad, libraries, social and sports clubs, and other social welfare services—was a primary reason for its popularity and following.

Hamas has engaged in political education, mobilization, and protest, challenging the legitimacy and platform of the PLO, claiming to offer a more authentic and equitable Islamic alternative. Political forums, pamphlets, and cassettes, as well as mass demonstrations and strikes, have been effective political instruments for them. Of course, their popularity and support, their ability to get votes from the majority depend on progress or, more correctly, lack of progress, in the peace process. When relations between Israel and the Palestinians deteriorate, the popularity of Hamas candidates in municipal, professional associations, chambers of commerce, and university student elections soars because the dominant PLO is blamed for continued failure. Hamas, in this sense, benefits from the continuing deadlock between the Palestinians and Israelis. Those two powers are blamed for the continued humiliation of the Palestinian people and frustration of their desire for political and civil rights. Hamas promises to get tough with Israel in order to achieve Palestinian rights: that is the purpose of its militant and terrorist acts.

NATIONALIST MOVEMENT OF RESISTANCE OR TERRORIST ORGANIZATION?

Whatever the accomplishments of Hamas as a social and political movement, only its violent activities are known in the West. Members of Hamas participated in the everyday confrontations with Israeli forces during the intifada. The Qassem Brigade, a specialized military wing fully operational by 1992, engaged in well-planned guerrilla warfare against Israeli military and police. Qassem's members worked in small clandestine cells. Their identity was unknown to the majority of Hamas members and they functioned with relative autonomy.

When Israel and the United States condemned Hamas as a terrorist organization, Hamas leaders responded by saying that the use of violence is both legitimate resistance and retaliation that was restricted to political and military targets in the occupied territories. Their actions were a response to Israel's occupation and its use of unrestrained violence and terror against Palestinians. This position changed dramatically after the 1993 Oslo Accords and in response to two events in Israel and the West Bank and Gaza.

On February 25, 1994, a Jewish settler named Baruch Goldstein walked into the Mosque of the Patriarch in Hebron, opened fire, and killed 29 Muslim worshippers during their Friday congregational prayer. In response, Hamas introduced a new type of warfare, the suicide bombers. Their attacks increased exponentially. Promising swift revenge for the Hebron massacre, the Qassem Brigade undertook five operations within Israel itself in Galilee, Jerusalem, and Tel Aviv. The most deadly took place on October 19, 1994, in the heart of Tel Aviv with the bombing of a bus that killed 23 and injured nearly 50 people. The Israeli assassination of Yahya Ayash, a suicide-bomb maker, resulted in another series of retaliatory suicide-bomb attacks. Peace negotiations in July 1997 were again disrupted when suicide bombers killed 13 and wounded more than 150 in a Jerusalem market.

What drives young Muslims to become suicide bombers? Many Palestinians have seen generations grow up in refugee camps or under Israeli occupation since the creation of Israel in 1948. Their sense of oppression and victimhood has been compounded as the promise of the Oslo Accords evaporated, like those of Camp David, under Yasser Arafat's Palestinian National Authority. The increased use of force under the Ariel Sharon government sparked the second intifada, which began in September 2000. Growing up oppressed and under siege, facing a future with little hope, high unemployment, and endemic poverty can produce an anger and desire for revenge against those responsible. Just as among inner city youth in the United States, some of those young people lose all hope. For others, religion holds the answer. For a small minority, suicide bombing seems a proud and powerful response.

Completely out of their league militarily when compared to Israel, these militant Palestinians boast of their new and most effective deadly weapon. As student posters at universities in the West Bank and Gaza declare: "Israel has nuclear bombs, we have human bombs."[16] Suicide is forbidden in Islam, but militant Palestinians do not see this as suicide. It is self-sacrifice for the cause of Palestinian freedom. The simplicity of the act enables an otherwise impotent individual to slip into a crowd unnoticed and then with a simple detonation wreak horrendous carnage. The use of concepts like jihad and martyrdom to justify suicide bombing provides a powerful incentive: the prospect of being a glorified hero in this life and enjoying Paradise in the next.

Suicide bombing has taken the conflict beyond the military and into the streets; Hamas has struck an unparalleled sense of vulnerability and terror into Israeli society. Because it is so effective, its use has escalated along with the Sharon government's escalation of violence, bombings, missile attacks, and assassination of Palestinian leaders. While the Palestinians are no match for Israel in numbers or weapons, Dr. Abdel Aziz Rantisi, a senior Hamas leader, believes such attacks ensure that "Israelis will have no stability and no security until the occupation ends. Suicide bombers are Israel's future."[17]

The new tactics of suicides and slaughter of civilians opened deep political cleavages within Hamas and summoned both support and condemnation on religious grounds in the broader Muslim world. Some Hamas leaders say targeting civilians is counterproductive; "The truth is that it did a lot of damage to Islam's image in the West. . . . Any time you kill civilians that happens."[18] Others countered that Hamas was responding legitimately to Israel's war against Palestinian civilians, its "illegal occupation" of the West Bank and Gaza, and its "barbaric treatment" of Palestinians.[19] Shaykh Yassin, founder of Hamas, and many other Palestinian religious leaders have argued that suicide bombing is necessary and justified. Other international Islamic leaders have been divided in opinion. Shaykh Tantawi, the grand *mufti* of Egypt, defends it, while Shaykh al-Sheikh, the grand *mufti* of Saudi Arabia, has condemned all suicide bombing as un-Islamic.

The attempt to distinguish between the political and the military wings of Hamas, especially when it comes to suicide bombings and terrorism, has been contentious. Critics reject the distinction as disingenuous. Both the Clinton and George W. Bush administrations have placed Hamas on their lists of terrorist organizations and outlawed all contributions to Hamas by Americans or American-based organizations, refusing to acknowledge any distinction between its social welfare and humanitarian work and its militia.

Unlike extremist organizations like bin Laden's al-Qaeda, the history of Hamas, like that of many other Islamic movements, demonstrated an ability to balance ideology and a pragmatic activism that responds to political and social realities. At no time has this been clearer than in the post-Oslo years, when Hamas was challenged on many fronts. Although the PLO's leadership of Palestinians had been seriously questioned since the 1980s, the Oslo Accords demonstrated that Yasser Arafat and the PLO had negotiated with Israel in the name of the Palestine people and thus had obtained official recognition as leaders of the Palestinian people. Hamas, the most viable option to the PLO, was caught off guard by the quietly and privately negotiated settlement. Its continued opposition to Arafat and the accords and its call to continue the Palestinian struggle against Israel now put it at odds not only with Israel but also with the PLO and the newly established Palestinian National Authority (PNA). Prior to the accords, the PLO and Hamas both had been dismissed as terrorist organizations. With the "rehabilitation" and legitimation of Yasser Arafat and the PLO by the international community, Arafat the "terrorist" now became Arafat the statesman. In contrast, Hamas became the common enemy of Israel and the PLO, the primary obstacle to peace, and roundly denounced as extremist and terrorist.

The post-Oslo period saw growing divisions within Hamas. Younger militants, especially in the Qassem Brigade, were convinced the Oslo Accords would fail to bring Palestinian independence, just as Sadat's Camp David Accords had. They believed they were just another ruse by Israel who would find an excuse to abandon them and blame the Palestinians. Rather than a process, they wanted the occupation ended completely and immediately. Unlike the PLO, which had accepted the legitimacy of the state of Israel within its pre-1967 boundaries in accordance with UN Security Council resolutions and international law, Hamas never ac-

cepted the legitimacy of the state of Israel. They therefore wanted
to step up the armed struggle against Israeli occupation and continue the intifada. Hamas boycotted the Palestinian National Authority elections, and the main political wing grappled with the
fact that nonparticipation in elections would further marginalize
them. Some wanted to form a political party to assure that Hamas's
voice was a presence in the PNA government and Palestinian politics. Hamas founder Shaykh Yassin, in a series of letters from prison,
reflected on these choices and cautiously opted for participation.

    Yassin's pragmatism was embraced by the general Hamas lead-
ership, who accepted Arafat's election as president of the PNA and
disassociated themselves from militants whose radical rejection
has led to continued armed struggle. While rejecting the accords,
a majority adapted to the political realities, renouncing violence
and engaging in direct participation in politics. A small minority
continues to espouse violence and terrorism to liberate the whole
of Palestine.

Algeria: The Army vs. the Army of God

While for many in the West the 1980s were dominated by fears
that "Islam" would come to power through revolutions or the violent overthrow of governments by clandestine groups, Algeria saw
their Islamists succeed through the ballot box. But this initial Islamist political success gave birth to a spiral of violence and
counterviolence that has threatened the very fabric of Algerian
society. Following bloody antigovernment riots in October 1988,
the Algerian government, long regarded as the most monolithic,
single-party political system in the Arab world, felt constrained to
hold multiparty elections that included the Islamic Salvation Front
(FIS), North Africa's first legal Islamic political party. Islamic opposition parties had flourished when Algerian state-socialism failed
to resolve its social and economic problems.

    The FIS, with a national organization and an effective mosque
and social welfare network, emerged as one of the strongest opposition parties. Its support included small-business owners and pros-

perous merchants, civil servants, university professors, physicians, lawyers, and other professionals. They constituted a new and different elite, with modern educations but a more Islamic orientation, looking for a national identity that reflected Algeria's religious and cultural heritage and a government that responded more effectively to the country's political, economic, and moral failures. Other support came from the unemployed, socially marginalized youth, called the "hittists" (those who lean against the walls), who had become fixtures on the streets and in the alleyways.

In the June 1990 municipal elections, the first multiparty election since independence from France in 1962, the FIS scored a stunning victory, capturing 54 percent of the vote, while the FLN ruling party garnered 34 percent. Even after arresting the FIS leaders and gerrymandering to redraw districts more favorably, the FLN failed to prevent an even more surprising electoral victory by the FIS in the June 1997 parliamentary elections. Amidst euphoric celebrations of Islamists within Algeria and across the Muslim world, the Algerian military intervened, forced the resignation of the President, arrested FIS leaders, imprisoned more than 10,000 in desert camps, outlawed the FIS, and seized its assets.

Threatened by the performance of the FIS, the Algerian military tightened their control on power and moved quickly to repress any significant legal opposition or political alternative through arrests and trials before special military courts, trials that were denounced by international human rights organizations. Having driven FIS leaders into exile or underground, the Algerian military had set in motion a cycle of violence and counterviolence. Originally moderate, nonviolent FIS members whose leaders had been imprisoned or exiled became an FIS militia, the AIS (Islamic Salvation Army). The result was a protracted civil war. The majority of Algerians were caught in the middle, victims of terror between a faction of hard-line military and security forces (the *éradicateurs*), who rejected dialogue and would only be justified by the eradication of Islamism, and the equally uncompromising Armed Islamic Group (GIA, Groupe Islamique Armé). The GIA, a radical extremist movement, emerged after the repression of the

FIS; its members included Arab Afghans, men who had returned from the jihad in Afghanistan, and it became one of the many currents within the FIS.[20] The military's intervention, abrogation of the FIS victory, and suppression of the FIS radicalized these battle-seasoned Afghan veterans and triggered their militant jihad. The failure of the FIS's aborted electoral victory had global implications: it was used by jihad groups against more moderate voices to argue that participation in elections is a useless strategy. They pointed to this as yet another example that even if Islamic parties prevailed in elections, authoritarian "un-Islamic" states, with support from their Western allies, would block them from coming to power peacefully.

The hard-liners prevailed in 1995 when the government refused to participate in or to recognize a summit of Algeria's major secular and Islamist leaders and political parties sponsored by the St. Egidio Catholic community in Rome. The parties' fourteen-point agreement, approved by the United States and France, a close ally of Algeria, was rejected by the military as a capitulation to the Islamists.

By the late 1990s, the number of fatalities from this protracted struggle had risen to 100,000. In 1997 and 1999, new parliamentary and presidential elections were held and a cease-fire was called between the government and the AIS, the military wing of the FIS. Parliamentary elections were marred by criticisms from UN observers and charges of massive fraud by losing parties as President (formerly General) Liamine Zeroual's National Democratic Rally won 156 of 380 seats. Although the FIS was prohibited from participating, two other Islamic parties, the Movement for Society and Peace and the Renaissance Party, won 69 and 38 seats respectively. Presidential elections in April 1999 were flawed by the last-minute withdrawal of all six opposition presidential candidates, who charged that the military had rigged the elections in favor of Abdelaziz Bouteflika, who received less than 30 percent of the votes cast by the less than 25 percent of registered voters.[21]

While the military-backed government remains in control, conditions for national reconciliation and stability remain fragile. The

military continues to dominate if not control the political process, and the GIA continues its bloody jihad. Bouteflika has maintained his refusal to lift the eight-year ban on the FIS and has
done very little to significantly strengthen civil society. Algeria
continues to be plagued by severe longstanding economic and
social problems: an official unemployment rate of 30 percent (some
put it at 50 percent), an acute housing shortage, an unresolved
national and cultural identity crisis, and a "gap between a tiny
minority of superrich and the overwhelming majority of the people
impoverished by rising prices and cuts in social benefits."[22]

The electoral performances of Islamic movements defied the
conventional wisdom that Islamists would be rejected at the polls.
Ironically, the successes of Islamic movements within the democratic process were viewed as an even more dangerous threat than
armed revolution. While many world leaders were on guard against
"other Irans," the FIS victory in Algeria raised the specter of an
Islamic movement coming to power through ballots, not bullets.
Yet, as one Algerian expert noted:

> There is now a preponderance of evidence from Algeria's last six
> years to indicate that the human suffering, environmental dev-
> astation and potential regional destabilization have been infinitely
> greater than they could have been under any imaginable scenario
> involving an Islamist regime coming to power through universal
> suffrage. It is hard to dispute that the fundamental source of con-
> flict is a denial of popular legitimacy. To portray it as cultural or
> ideological, secular or fundamentalist, is misleading and plays
> into the hands of extremists and anti-democrats alike. What is at
> stake is an increase or decrease of power and privilege.[23]

The Wahhabi Threat

Although originally associated with Saudi Arabia, Wahhabi Islam
or Wahhabism has come to be used popularly, although inaccu-
rately, as a blanket term for Islamic fundamentalism, religious

extremism, and radicalism. For this reason, some prefer the terms Salafi or Salafiyyah movement. This has the advantage of both reflecting the activists' claim to be returning to the pristine Islam of Muhammad and the first generation of Muslims (*salafi*, or pious ancestors) and of indicating, more accurately, that this ultraconservative, rigid, and exclusivist worldview is common to many groups and organizations. Saudi Arabia's Wahhabi Islam is but one strand. Ultimately, both Wahhabi and Salafi can be misleading, as they are used as umbrella terms that incorporate diverse ideologies and movements, medieval and modern, nonviolent and violent.

Since the late-twentieth century, the term Wahhabi has been applied to militant movements that have taken up arms against existing governments. This particular labeling is not all that new. In nineteenth-century colonial India, the British labeled indigenous, anti-imperialist, Islamic revivalist movements, Wahhabi. In recent years, Wahhabi Islam has been identified not only with the Taliban and Osama bin Laden's al-Qaeda but also with Islamic opposition movements in other areas, in particular Russia, the Caucasus, Chechnya, Dagestan, and Central Asia.

First and foremost, Wahhabi describes Saudi Arabia's ultraconservative, puritanical brand of Islam: literalist, rigid, and exclusivist. Presenting their version of Islam as the pristine, pure, unadulterated message, the Wahhabi seek to impose their strict beliefs and interpretations, which are not commonly shared by other Sunni or by Shii Muslims throughout the Muslim world.

The Wahhabi vision went international in the 1960s in response to the threat posed by Arab nationalism and socialism. It was fueled by petrodollars, especially the wealth from skyrocketing revenues after the 1973 oil embargo. Saudi Arabia and other monarchies were threatened in particular by Nasserism and in general by radical Arab socialist governments that came to power promising a social revolution for the masses and condemning conservative Arab monarchies. Under the leadership of Prince (later King) Faisal, the Saudis championed a pan-Islamic policy against Nasser's "secular, socialist" pan-Arabism with its ties to "atheistic communism" in the Soviet Union and Eastern Europe. Saudi Arabia asserted its global Islamic leadership as custodian of Islam's two holiest sites and made common cause with other Muslim governments in the struggle against Nasser and his disciple, Libya's Muammar Qaddafi.

Saudi Arabia created state-financed international Islamic organizations to promote its Wahhabi-based, pan-Islamic vision and ideology. Established in 1962, the World Islamic League vigorously engaged in an energetic international dawah, preaching and propagating Wahhabi Islam to other Muslims (as well as non-Muslims), financing the building of mosques, schools, libraries, hospitals, and clinics. It trained and supported imams for mosques, distributed tens of millions of Saudi-approved translations of the Quran and religious literature. Other Gulf countries like Kuwait and the United Arab Emirates followed suit.

The Jeddah-based Organization of the Islamic Conference (OIC) was created in 1969 to promote Islamic solidarity among member states, to safeguard the holy sites of Mecca and Medina, and to support the "struggle" in Palestine and the "struggle" of all Muslim people. In the 1970s, the OIC created the Islamic Development Bank to promote the development of an Islamic banking system and finance development projects in Muslim countries. Through such organizations, the Saudi government and many wealthy Saudi businessmen have exported Wahhabi Islam to the rest of the Muslim world as well as to Europe and America.

The Saudi government also developed close ties with major Islamic movements such as the Muslim Brotherhood and the Jamaat-i-Islami. Despite significant differences, they shared a religious vision based on a return to the fundamentals of Islam and an antipathy to common enemies—Nasserism, secularism, and communism. Saudi Arabia gave asylum to Muslim Brothers such as Muhammad Qutb, the brother of Sayyid Qutb, who fled Nasser's suppression of the Brotherhood in the mid-1960s. The Saudi government and other Gulf countries provided significant funding for Islamic movements and conferences. Petrodollars became a major enabling mechanism for the movements to internationalize and spread organizationally, to translate the writings of al-Banna, Qutb, Mawdudi, and later to produce audiotapes to be distributed around the world, creating an international Islamist discourse. In addition, many Islamists from other countries, well educated and possessing needed professional and technical skills, were employed in the Gulf and could send funds back to their homelands to support mainstream and clandestine movements. Saudi funding to Islamic groups worldwide accelerated dramatically after the Iranian revolution, in order to counter the challenge from Iran's alternative revolutionary Islamic system. Iran's call and support for a global (Sunni and Shii) Islamic revolution and its funding of Shii groups in the Middle East and South Asia to counter Saudi influence threatened Saudi Arabia's Islamic leadership.

Saudi initiatives produced a rapid growth of Islamist groups and the dissemination of their worldview and fundamentalist interpretation of Islam in many countries. The Islamists' informal alliance with the Saudis and their acceptance of refuge or patronage was in fact a marriage of convenience, since many regarded the monarchy to be an un-Islamic form of government and were critical of the un-Islamic behavior and corruption of many royals.

Many of those benefiting from Saudi largesse learned that it came with a hefty price tag, the purification or eradication of local belief, practice, and culture. Particular targets for purification are Sufism and Shiism. Much as Saudi armies destroyed major Shii shrines in the nineteenth century, Saudi aid agencies have been responsible for the destruction or reconstruction of many historic mosques, libraries, Quran schools, and cemeteries in Bosnia and Kosovo because their Ottoman architecture, decorations, frescoes, and tombstones did not conform to Wahhabi iconoclastic aesthetics that regard statues, tombstones, or artwork with human representations as idolatry and polytheism. To the extent that the Taliban reflected this puritanical, militant mentality—seen in their strict ban on television and music, their insistence on the veiling and public segregation of women, their use of religious police to enforce Islamic behavior, and their destruction of Buddhist monuments—they have been labeled Wahhabi. However, Saudi and Taliban strict controls on some modern technology such as the Internet or satellite dishes have often been driven less by religious concerns than by security concerns. They certainly cannot represent a complete rejection of modern technology; Islam has not proven to be an obstacle in their use of other modern communications technology, weapons, and transport.

The influence of Wahhabi Islam on the Taliban was cultivated and reinforced through the madrasa system of Islamic schools and seminaries, many of which were set up in Pakistan after the Soviet-Afghan war. Pakistan's madrasa system has for many decades enjoyed substantial funding from Saudi Arabia and the Gulf, an important reason why the number of madrasas in Pakistan has grown from 147 in 1947 to more than 9,000 today. In the 1970s, Saudi Arabia was worried about the influence of the Left in Pakistan, epitomized by Prime Minister Zulfiqar Ali Bhutto, a Berkeley- and Oxford-trained secular socialist. However, when Bhutto needed to rebuild Pakistan after the 1971 civil war in which East Pakistan broke away to become Bangladesh, he turned to the oil-rich Arab states, appealing to their common Islamic heritage. In exchange for funding from the Gulf, Bhutto recast his socialism as Islamic socialism, introduced Islamic laws, and supported Islamic institutions and projects. The growth of madrasas increased exponentially during the rule of Bhutto's successor, General Zia ul-Haq, who seized power using the name of Islam to overthrow, try, and execute Bhutto and implement an Islamic system of government. Zia provided generous patronage to the *ulama* and embarked on an ambitious expansion of the madrasa system with generous assistance from Saudi Arabia and other Gulf states.

After the Afghan war, madrasas continued to thrive both as part of Saudi Arabia's ongoing export of its ideology and as a means to create a strong Sunni wall against Iran's export of its revolution. Governments, their religious agencies, and wealthy members of the business community pumped in large amounts of money to build and support madrasas. In Pakistan, a country of some 150

million with a nearly two-thirds illiteracy rate and an annual average per capita income of $450, the madrasas provided much-needed
shelter along with free education for millions of Afghans who found
refuge there as well as for Pakistanis whose state (secular) educational system had collapsed due to lack of funding.

Pakistan's Deobandi established hundreds of madrasas. The
Deobandi movement began in India in the nineteenth century as a
reformist movement that attempted to harmonize traditional or
classical Islam with modern life. Pakistan's Deobandi, however, have
increasingly espoused a more rigid and militant conservatism, forging close ideological and political ties with Saudi Arabia and with
its Wahhabi ulama. Most of Pakistan's mainstream madrasas offer a
sound classical Islamic education supplemented by a modern curriculum. Deobandi madrasas, however, are often run by religious
teachers with little knowledge of or appreciation for classical Islam
and whose chief task was promoting a militant jihadist vision and
culture. The Deobandi vision became jihadist and global in scope,
intolerant of competing or alternative Sunni beliefs, and fanatically
anti-Shii. Their madrasas trained Taliban and tens of thousands of
Pakistanis, many who went off to fight the jihad in Afghanistan.
Others became religious leaders and teachers. Some estimate that as
many as 80,000 to 100,000 Pakistanis trained in Pakistan's madrasas
and fought in Afghanistan between 1994 and 1999.[24]

The Deobandi are represented by a major religious political party
that has been active since the creation of Pakistan, the Jamiyyat-i-
Ulama-i-Islam (JUI). In 1996 the Taliban turned over training camps
for the education and training of Pakistanis and Arab militants to
JUI partisans; in July 1999, the JUI issued death threats to all Ameri-
cans in Pakistan if Pakistan extradited bin Laden to the United
States.[25] Two radical JUI offshoots, Sipah-Sahaba Pakistan (Pakistan's
Army of the Companions of the Prophet) and Lashkar-e-Jhangvi
(Jhangvi's Army), became notorious for their acts of violence and
terrorism, including the slaughter of hundreds of Shii. When
Pakistan's president Nawaz Sharif cracked down on their organi-
zations after two alleged attempts to assassinate him, their leaders

fled to asylum in Kabul. The Taliban-JUI alliance for many years benefited from significant support from Saudi Arabia and from the intelligence agency of Pakistan (the ISI).

THE WAHHABI THREAT IN
RUSSIA AND CENTRAL ASIA

While the primary use of the name Wahhabi designates Saudi Arabia's ultraconservative Islam, Wahhabi's second and more overtly political meaning is Islamic extremism, radicalism, and terrorism, with a direct connection to the Taliban and bin Laden. This usage is exploited by many governments, including those of Russia and the Central Asian republics. Governments find the label "Wahhabi" especially useful because it implies a foreign source for indigenous problems and equates their political opposition with an "Islamic threat." Local conditions and grievances (failed economies, corruption, and self-interested power holders), and local opponents (especially the younger generation who want to replace or overthrow the old, corrupt systems) are placed under the "Wahhabi Threat" umbrella and are thereby more easily dismissed or ignored.

The blanket use of Wahhabi to describe militant jihad groups obscures more than it enlightens. Organizations and movements are branded as Wahhabi because they possess common "family resemblances" such as ultraconservative, literalist, puritanical, and exclusivist religious doctrines. However, many of these movements, as well as Osama bin Laden, actually owe more to the militant ideology of Sayyid Qutb or Egyptian radical groups such as Islamic Jihad, Takfir wal Hijra, and Gamaa Islamiyya than to Saudi Arabia's Wahhabi tradition, which by and large is religiously and politically conservative rather than revolutionary. That said, Saudi policies of supporting Wahhabi-oriented schools worldwide have resulted in unintended consequences as witnessed by the Taliban–bin Laden alliance and jihadi madrasas.

Despite Soviet domination and anti-Islam policies in Central Asia, Islam remains a core component of individual and community identity and an important part of religious and cultural life.

Following the breakup of the Soviet Union, Islam has been integral to the process of nation building in post-independence Central Asia, contributing to the development of new national identities, value systems, guidelines for social and political life, and new relations with the Muslim world.

The attitude of Central Asia's post-independence ruling elite toward Islam has fluctuated since 1992. At first, governments coopted Islam and Islamic symbols as a component of national identity. However, as soon as Islam emerged as a potent political force, countries like Uzbekistan and Tajikistan moved from cooptation to repression, resulting in a devastating civil war in Tajikistan and repression and armed conflict in Uzbekistan.

Like many other parts of the Muslim world, Central Asia has in fact in recent years faced a religious revival that has affected both faith and politics. The post-independence boom in the building of mosques, schools, and libraries, the distribution of Qurans and other Islamic materials, and the activities of missionaries from other Muslim countries like Saudi Arabia, the Gulf, Pakistan, and Turkey have brought greater piety, religious divisions and conflicts, and Islamic political activism and opposition movements.

Militant groups have been especially active in Uzbekistan and Tajikistan, whose governments have been the most repressive. Most began as protest and opposition movements against governments led by former communist officials. Among the more prominent has been the Islamic Renaissance Party (IRP) in Tajikistan, the first populist Islamic movement in Central Asia, bringing together a cross-section of religious leaders, professionals, and disaffected youth to oppose communist rule. It emphasized spiritual renewal and political and economic independence. Hizb al-Tahrir al-Islami (The Islamic Liberation Party) is an import from the Middle East, with roots in Jordan and Saudi Arabia. Its global goal has been the establishment of an Islamic caliphate. Having entered Central Asia in the mid-1990s, it has worked to spread its influence first in the Farghona Valley, which border both Tajikistan and Uzbekistan, and then throughout Central Asia.

The most feared militant group is the Islamic Movement of Uzbekistan (IMU), which has operated in Uzbekistan, Tajikistan and Kyrgyzstan. In late September 2001, the United States government declared the IMU both a foreign terrorist organization and an al-Qaeda member, reiterating the previous administration's designation of September 2000. Although the IMU grew as an opposition movement in Uzbekistan, widespread repression under President Islam Karimov's government led to violent confrontations in the 1990s. IMU leaders found refuge with and support from the Taliban and Osama bin Laden in Afghanistan. Like many other militant groups, they began as opposition within their home countries and only went to Afghanistan when in need of help and training or to set up their own training camps. Many obtained training and fought with the Taliban but then returned home to continue their domestic jihad. In 1997, after several police officers were killed in Namangan, Uzbekistan, the government arrested hundreds on charges of belonging to extremist groups.

The IMU was blamed (as were all opposition groups initially) for bombing attacks in February 1999, part of an alleged assassination attempt against President Karimov of Uzbekistan which led to a bloody crackdown. The IMU struck back with a number of highly visible attacks including kidnappings of Japanese and Americans. By the late 1990s, its ranks had been swelled with fighters from Central Asia, Chechnya, and Pakistan, reflecting the growing global jihad culture. Blocked in Uzbekistan, IMU leaders shifted their activities to Kyrgyzstan in August 1999, taking control of some areas in southern Kyrgyzstan that border Uzbekistan and Tajikistan. In November 2001, its legendary leader Juma Namangani was reported killed in heavy fighting near the northern Afghan city of Kunduz.

It is not easy to assess the presence, growth and vitality of religious extremist groups in Central Asia and the northern Caucasus. Hard data are difficult to come by because of the groups' clandestine nature but even more because of the tendencies of regimes to exaggerate terrorist groups' presence and threat.

All major conflicts or opposition movements tend to be interpreted as an Islamic threat to Russia and Central Asia via Afghanistan. The alleged Taliban-Wahhabi fundamentalist threat was the
basis for a pact among Russia, Uzbekistan, and Tajikistan in 1998,
designed to prevent Islam from destabilizing the region.
Uzbekistan's president Islam Karimov referred to "the threat which
is coming to us from the south . . . a threat of aggressive fundamentalism, aggressive extremism, and above all Wahhabism."[26]
President Karimov's sweeping definition of fundamentalism as
religion that interferes in politics means that mere involvement
in politics, without any commitment to violence and terrorism,
constitutes fundamentalism. Karimov has presented himself as the
protector of Uzbekistan from Islamic fundamentalism's threat to
and spread in Central Asia. Equating fundamentalism with radicalism is so pervasive that even those Russian and Central Asian
observers who strive to present a balanced account tend to define
any Muslim opposition to government as Islamic radicalism. Russian president Vladimir Putin provided a vivid example of the exploitation of the rhetoric of "Islamic threat" when he used the
specter of Wahhabi fundamentalism and Taliban-trained mujahidin
in the Caucasus to justify launching a war to reassert Russian authority over Chechnya. A veteran human rights activist who visited Grozny, the capital of Chechnya, early in the war disputed
the charges, dismissing official Russian accounts as a "monstrous
lie" and was equally dismissive of the claims that three hundred
Afghan mujahidin fought fiercely against the Russian troops in
Grozny. Visiting all the places in Grozny where the Russian government claimed there were Afghan mujahidin, he found no evidence of their presence.

Chechnya's president Aslan Maskhadov also used the threat of
Wahhabism to crack down on domestic political opposition. In
an October 1998 speech before the Congress of the Chechen People,
President Maskhadov repudiated Wahhabism as an unwelcome
import preached in Chechnya by foreigners, alien to Chechnya's
traditional Islam, and responsible for acts of violence.

The actual size and threat of radical Wahhabi-inspired movements is hotly contested and difficult to verify. Russian and Central Asian governments charge that Wahhabis trained at bases in countries such as Afghanistan, Pakistan, and Sudan infiltrate mosques, Islamic teaching centers, and charitable organizations to indoctrinate and recruit. Wahhabi-inspired groups are accused of waging a jihad of violence and terrorism, suicide bombings, and attacks on marketplaces, schools, offices, and places of worship that result in civilian casualties, and of using drug money to finance terrorist campaigns. Drug traffic is believed to have financed the developing global terrorist networks, the purchase of weapons and supplies, and the creation of social welfare organizations under the guise of mainstream Islamic activism.

Religious leaders in countries that claim Wahhabi influence often criticize Wahhabism for challenging their religious authority and rejecting traditional and local Islamic beliefs and practices. They say Wahhabism breaks one of the cardinal rules of warfare in Islam—that Muslims should not fight other Muslims. The Wahhabi, their critics charge, get around this by dividing the world strictly into believers and nonbelievers who must be fought.

Although governments have clearly exaggerated the threat for their own purposes, Wahhabi religious ideology has found fertile soil in societies where economic development is poor and moral and political decay are rampant. Its claim that returning to a purer, more moral way of life will restore law and order can be very attractive to those suffering from chronic poverty and political repression. The Wahhabi compare very favorably in educational levels to local religious leaders in Central Asia; Soviet policy and persecution had a devastating impact on the recruitment and training of Islamic scholars. The younger generation, struggling in authoritarian states with a scarcity of jobs and housing, is attracted to Wahhabism as a means to reject the status quo (the Soviet-era communist elite culture) in favor of an apparently more indigenous source of identity, nationalism, and values. Prosperous merchants and others are sometimes attracted by the Wahhabi emphasis on law and traditional morality against individualism, liberalism, and mass culture.

The powerful symbolism and revolutionary meaning of jihad dominates modern Muslim politics to an extent unparalleled in history. Islamic movements and organizations have become primary vehicles for its spread and implementation. If many thought that Iran's revolution was a singular event, succeeding decades have demonstrated the force and pervasiveness of an Islamic activism that has moved from the periphery to the center of Muslim societies. Islamic experiments in Egypt, Palestine, Algeria. and Central Asia have also revealed the many faces and voices of political Islam and the diverse understandings of jihad. Peaceful or violent, all share a common commitment to an Islamic revolution, a jihad or struggle to implement an Islamic order or government.

The "armies of God" have passed through several stages, becoming ever more global in outreach. Initially, most groups focused on their own countries. They were primarily Egyptian, Algerian, or Tunisian movements. The Afghan jihad against Soviet occupation marked a turning point as Muslims in record numbers traveled to Afghanistan to join in the jihad against oppression of Muslims. The experience and success of that jihad created a new, more global jihad sentiment and culture embodied in Arab Afghans—Arabs and other Muslims who had fought in Afghanistan—and in a sense of solidarity, which subsequently brought Muslims from various parts of the world to participate in jihads in Bosnia, Kosovo, Kashmir, Central Asia, and Chechnya. Some few have become mercenaries in the more radicalized efforts not just to defend Muslims against oppression, but to overthrow world powers believed responsible for their suffering, through terrorist strategies. Jihad today has thus become the evocative symbol and rallying cry for mobilization in holy and unholy wars, in wars of resistance and liberation as well as in global terrorism.

Jihads expressing a "Rage for God" have increased and have spread. From Algeria and Egypt to Afghanistan and Central Asia, governments, often authoritarian, found themselves under siege in the 1990s. Afghanistan and Pakistan became primary centers for the globalization of jihad and the culture of jihad through networks of madrasas and training camps. The Taliban and al-Qaeda provided refuge and training for militants, many of whom have had to flee their home countries, from Egypt, Algeria, Yemen, Saudi Arabia, Malaysia, Thailand, the Philippines, Uzbekistan, Tajikistan, Kyrgyzstan, Chechnya, as well as Uighurs from the Xinjiang province in China. A hitherto little-noted part of the world spawned a Taliban–al-Qaeda alliance that became the base for a network of organizations and cells from across the Muslim world that hijacked Islam, indiscriminately slaughtering non-Muslims and Muslims alike.

September 11, 2001, marked a turning point, signaling the ability of terrorists to land a devastating strike on its primary international target, the United States, at home. In the mid-1990s both Paris and New York had been attacked by terrorists. North American and European countries had been monitoring terrorists and potential terrorist groups. However, few had anticipated so massive an attack, a diabolical act that carried out bin Laden's declaration of war and marked the global expansion of al-Qaeda's unholy war of terror to the West.

Having routed the Taliban and al-Qaeda in Afghanistan, where do we go from here? September 11 has resurrected old questions, giving them a new urgency: Is there a clash of civilizations between Islam and the West? Why do they hate us? Is there a direct connection between Islam, anti-Americanism, and global terrorism? Are Islam and modernity incompatible? We now turn to these and other issues that will determine all of our futures.

4

Where Do We Go from Here?

In the aftermath of September 11, 2001, as we ask, Why did this happen?, government officials, pundits, and experts bombard us with a litany of certitudes: bin Laden and al-Qaeda are religious fanatics; this is proof positive of a clash of civilizations between Islam and the West; the terrorists hate our American way of life— our power, prosperity, and freedoms; Islam is incompatible with modernity and democracy; violence and terrorism are integral to Muslim belief and practice; we are now facing a global jihad against the West.

Making Sense of Islam and the Muslim World

Several decades ago, a Muslim ambassador to the United Nations wrote a short book, *Islam: The Misunderstood Religion*. At that time, given the invisibility of Muslims on the American landscape and in our educational curriculum, the author's choice of title seemed appropriate. Today, we know more, but much of our knowledge has been gained through headline events, from the Iranian Revolution to September 11. When the Iranian Revolution occurred in 1978, despite the fact that Islam was the second largest of the world's religions, encompassing more than fifty countries, during the hostage crisis the *Today Show* coanchor found it necessary to interrupt his reading of the news to give Americans a brief background on Islam. It was very brief: Islam is the second largest world religion; it has a scripture called the Quran and a prophet named

Muhammad. This most basic information was deemed necessary for viewers in one of the world's most advanced and educated nations! At the same time, most Americans would have expected that any educated person in the world would recognize the terms Judaism, Christianity, and Bible and the names Moses and Jesus.

Our knowledge of the Islam of the vast majority of Muslims and its connection to the Judeo-Christian tradition remains minimal or nonexistent. While Christians today have been raised to appreciate family resemblances with Judaism and to speak of a Judeo-Christian tradition, at best Islam has been presented as a foreign, non-Western religion, often grouped with Hinduism and Buddhism. The fact that Islam, like Judaism and Christianity, has its origins in the Middle East, that it represents belief in heaven, hell, and the Day of Judgment, and venerates prophets from the Old and New Testaments including Abraham, Moses, and Jesus is unknown to the vast majority of non-Muslims.

How many Jews and Christians know that they join Muslims as "Children of Abraham," that Muslims believe that they are the religious descendants of Ismail, the first-born son of Abraham and his servant Hagar? How many know that the Quran acknowledges, "We believe what you believe, your God and our God is one" (29:46)? Yet, while Yahweh is generally known to be the Hebrew name for the God of the Bible, Allah is often still regarded as the proper name of an alien God rather than the Arabic word for God, used by Arab Christians as well as Muslims when they pray.

Christians have come to know and value their Jewish neighbors because of decades of living together and the active efforts of many to establish linkages, in particular an awareness of a shared religious heritage, a Judeo-Christian tradition, and the scourge of anti-Semitism which culminated in the Holocaust. Muslims have gone from the unknown "other" or the product of oriental stereotypes of Arabian Nights—sheiks and harems and flying carpets—to masked, armed hijackers and hostage takers. While many in the United States have come to appreciate the historic persecution and victimhood of Jews and understand the creation of Israel, American textbooks and media in past years had precious little to say about the Palestinian side of the story: the Israeli occupation of Palestine, the hundreds of thousands of refugees and generations raised in refugee camps, strangers in their homeland. The Palestinian-Israeli conflict is a tragedy for two peoples with mutual claims, entitlement, and histories of suffering, violence, and terrorism.

Despite increased coverage and awareness of Islam, the necessity of responding to Osama bin Laden and al-Qaeda forced many policymakers, commentators, the media, and the general public to realize how little they really knew about a major religion and strategic part of the world. As one Senate leader confessed, "I know a lot about many things but nothing about Islam and the Muslim world—and neither do most of my colleagues!" While many are sincere in their desire to know more, others epitomize the saying: "My mind's made up, don't confuse me with the facts!" At one level, it is easy to portray September 11 as the latest phase in a historic battle between Islam and the West, as militant Islam has now gone global. However, this dangerous oversimplification mimics the distorted, polarized worldview and message of the bin Ladens of the world. If we start out by presuming that the other is completely different, we can find whatever we are looking for.

As we move forward in the twenty-first century, a key reality to keep in mind is that Islam is the second largest and fastest growing religion not only out there, but also in Europe and America. Improving our understanding of the faith of our fellow citizens and neighbors will require that we look at Muslims with new eyes and judge Islam by the totality and teachings of the faith, not just the beliefs and actions of a radical few.

An important first step is to guard against judging Islam by a double standard. When we approach Judaism or Christianity or understand our own faith, we operate differently. We interpret the violent, bloody texts in the Bible in their historical contexts. We explain the history of violence, slaughter, and imperialism in the name of Judaism or Christianity in terms of the times and context, or we condemn such acts as aberrations or extremist. The

Christianity that inspired Archbishop Desmond Tutu and many others in the struggle against apartheid in South Africa has also been claimed as the religion of Afrikaaners, the faith of American slave owners and their pastors on the one hand and Martin Luther King, Jr., on the other. The Judaism of members of the Jewish Defense League or of the young assassin of Yitzak Rabin is the transcendent, transforming faith of the prophets of Israel and countless pious Jews through the ages. Most people readily recognize distinctions between those who are true examples of faith and those who hijack the faith, as well as between the mainstream and extremists on the fringe.

Looking to the future, as we become more familiar with Islam as a major world religion and the soon-to-be second largest faith in America, the idea of a Judeo-Christian-Islamic religious tradition will become more internalized. We will recognize that each faith represents shared beliefs and values as well as distinctive differences. Points of conflict are one part of the story but so are religious and cultural cooperation and co-existence, past and present. Theological similarities and competing interests put Christianity and Islam, the West and the Muslim world on an early collision course. Both of these major world religions had a universal message and mission, the belief that their covenant with God was the final and complete fulfillment of God's earlier revelation to a previous community that had gone astray. We don't often remember that while Christendom experienced Islam's expansion as a threat to its hegemony, Islam proved more tolerant and provided greater religious freedom for Jews and indigenous Christians, and it eliminated the persecution of heretics for which imperial Christianity was noted:

> By an exquisite irony, Islam reduced the status of Christians to that which the Christians had earlier thrust upon the Jews, with one difference. The reduction in Christian status was merely juridical; it was unaccompanied by either systematic persecution or a bloodlust; and generally, though not everywhere and at all times, unmarred by vexatious behavior.[1]

As it becomes more commonplace to work with Muslim colleagues and live with Muslim neighbors, it will be even more important to know about events in our history that have been overlooked. Many do not know that the development of imperial Islam and Jewish-Christian-Islamic coexistence produced a rich Islamic civilization and a religious and cultural synthesis and exchange. With significant assistance from Christian and Jewish subjects, Muslims collected the great books of science, medicine, and philosophy from the West and the East and translated them into Arabic from Greek, Latin, Persian, Coptic, Syriac, and Sanskrit. The age of translation was followed by a period of great creativity as a new generation of Muslim thinkers and scientists made their own contributions to learning: in philosophy, medicine, chemistry, astronomy, algebra, optics, art, and architecture. Then the cultural traffic pattern was again reversed when Europeans, emerging from the Dark Ages, turned to Muslim centers of learning to regain their lost heritage and to learn from Muslim advances. These historical dynamics should be kept in mind when we are tempted to view Islam and Muslims as aliens with whom we have nothing in common.

Muslims are now in a position similar to other ethnic and religious groups in their relationship to modernity. In the not too distant past, many non-WASP (White Anglo-Saxon Protestant) immigrants to America (Irish, Italian, Polish, etc.) were viewed as the other and not accepted as equals. My friends and I grew up very conscious that Catholic ethnics were seen as laborers but hardly material for Ivy League schools and corporate leadership. Years later, after I had endured a dinner party of Italian jokes and speculation that one of our prosperous neighbors must be mafia, a friend said to me, "Remember John, to them, you're not Italian, you have a Ph.D."

Those who believe that Arab or Muslim culture is inherently incompatible with modernization need to reflect on Western attitudes toward non-Western societies in the recent past. Only a few decades ago, if you received a gift that was stamped "made in Japan" you knew you had an inferior product, a cheap imitation of goods from Paris, London, or New York. Westerners all knew that the Japanese as well as other Asian civilizations or cultures were somehow Third World, that they lacked Western knowledge, creativity, or work ethic. History now tells a different story. Today, Lexus competes head to head with Mercedes and Jaguar, and Toyota and Honda outsell American brand-name cars.

Religions like societies change and develop. Similarly, civilizations are not monolithic and static. New ideas began in one civilization—Chinese, European, or Islamic—and then spread, were appropriated, and further developed by others. Science, technology, philosophy, and morality ultimately have no fixed boundaries. They are not the preserve of any single people, civilization, or religion. Today, in a reverse process, we see the transfer of science and technology and the spread of modern notions of democratization and pluralism from the West to the Muslim world and beyond. Globalization has also resulted in collaborative efforts in modern science. Increasing numbers of Muslims are trained in the sciences, many in the best universities of America and Europe, and work in the West or in the Muslim world with multinational corporations.

To ask whether Islam is compatible with Western civilization is to ignore past and present exchanges and cross-fertilizations. It also privileges Western civilization as the universal norm and implies that civilizations are mutually exclusive and diametrically opposed. In fact civilizations and cultures overlap; they have similarities and differences. What are the essentials of Western civilization—reason, individualism, science, democracy, human rights, pluralism, secularism, capitalism? However different and diverse, most Muslims, like most people on this planet, rely on reason, science, and technology, desire greater political participation and freedom, and seek economic advancement and prosperity. At the same time, like conservative Christians and Jews, many Muslims believe that religion is under siege from secular liberalism first and foremost within their own societies.

Historically, over many decades, Christianity and Judaism made their own accommodations with modernity. The process produced further divisions and differences among them: liberal, fundamentalist, and evangelical Protestantism; orthodox, conservative, reform, and reconstructionist Judaism; orthodox or traditionalist and liberal Catholics. Catholicism was for some time a distant third to Protestantism and Judaism in dealing with modernity. Until the second Vatican Council in the 1960s, pontiffs had condemned much of modernity—including modern biblical criticism, democracy, pluralism, and women's rights. Despite change, all of the children of Abraham continue to struggle with modernity. The global resurgence of religion is driven by a desire of many well-educated believers of different faiths to rethink and reevaluate the relationship of religion to modernity. Many question the excesses of modernity, trying to reassert a faith and values that limit the unbridled use of science and technology, the sexual freedoms that weaken family life, the emphasis on individual rights rather than on responsibilities, or the accumulation and maldistribution of wealth.

Muslims struggle with many of the same questions and issues of modernity faced by the West but with distinctive differences. They have not had the luxury of time, the centuries the West had had to develop and accommodate modernity. Despite the violence we see today, however, the Muslim encounter with modernity has occurred without anywhere near the West's high cost of bloody wars (for example, the French and American revolutions, the American Civil War, and the wars of the Reformation). Furthermore, many Muslim countries face serious political and economic handicaps. The Muslim world's dominance by the West and marginalization as a world power, which has challenged Islam's relevance to modern life, and its lack of control over the forces of development have been daunting barriers to progress. When in power, Muslim empires were open and pluralistic in engaging foreign cultures and civilizations. When in charge of the process, there was little fear of loss of identity, faith, and pride. In defeat, Muslims faced questions of identity as well as faith: Does being modern mean our only option is to talk, dress, think, live and act like them? How would Americans or Europeans respond if modernization and globalization meant domination by Japan, politically, economically, militarily, linguistically, and culturally? The closest example we have in the West is perhaps the wrenching adjustment former European empires like England and France have had to make to American international ascendance .

Religion, Modernization, and Development

Modernization or development theory in the mid twentieth century could be summarized by the adage: "Every day in every way, things are and will continue to get more and more modern and secular," which meant better and better. It was taken for granted that modernizing meant the progressive westernization and secularization of a society: politically, economically, legally, and educationally.[2] The choice faced by developing countries such as those in the Muslim world seemed to be between the polar dichotomies of tradition and modernity, Mecca and mechanization. Christianity encountered the same secularizing trends. Theologians spoke of demythologizing the scriptures, of a secular gospel for the modern age, of the triumph of the secular city (as opposed to Augustine's City of God), and of a "death of God theology."[3] Religious faith was at best supposed to be a private matter. In academia, the degree of one's intellectual sophistication and objectivity was judged according to a secular liberalism and relativism that seemed antithetical to religion. In politics, while church or synagogue membership was recognized as useful, most candidates avoided discussing their faith or religious issues in public.

The global resurgence of religion in the late twentieth century has led presidents, corporate leaders, and athletes to do a wide turnaround, freely discussing their faith and morality in the media. Congressional prayer breakfasts and prayer groups of athletes, lawyers, and physicians are commonplace. A few decades ago, it was important for a president to have a church to attend on major holidays but not to profess his faith in public. Now presidents from Jimmy Carter to George Walker Bush publicly profess that they are "born again," and presidential and congressional candidates make no secret of their religious beliefs or the fact that some are clergy. In the 2000 presidential campaign, George W. Bush comfortably cited Jesus as his hero, and Senator Joseph Lieberman, an orthodox Jew, frequently appealed to God in his speeches.

Moreover, the global religious resurgence has been especially evident in international politics. Religion, nationalism, and ethnicity have proven to be enduring sources of identity and conflict from Somalia and Rwanda to Lebanon, Bosnia, Kosovo, Kashmir, India, and Sri Lanka.

These changes in the public profile of religion have challenged and discredited the secular expectations of modernization models. The prominent sociologist of religion Peter L. Berger, a key figure in articulating secularization theory, has also changed his mind, declaring that "a whole body of literature by historians and social scientists loosely labeled 'secularization theory' is essentially mistaken."[4] Indeed, much is now made of a "desecularization of society" as religion is recognized as an increasingly key factor in domestic, transnational, and international relations.

An Inevitable Clash of Civilizations?

In a controversial 1993 article, "The Clash of Civilizations?," Samuel P. Huntington warned that a "clash of civilizations will dominate global politics"[5] and precipitated a heated worldwide debate among scholars, political leaders, commentators, and the media. Many in the Muslim world saw this important American academic and opinion maker, who had also held a prominent position in government, as articulating what they always thought was the West's attitude toward Islam. If some academics and government officials were quick to distance themselves from Huntington's position, the sales of his subsequent book, its translation into many languages, and the sheer number of international conferences and publications that addressed the question demonstrated that there was "a market for clash." The attacks of September 11 and the global threat of Osama bin Laden and al-Qaeda have resurrected a knee-jerk response of "the clash of civilizations" for an easy answer to the question, Why do they hate us?

Huntington, like many others today, played into old stereotypes by characterizing Islam and the West as age-old enemies—"Conflict along the fault line between Western and Islamic civilizations has been going on for 1300 years"[6]—and by citing Islam's resistance to secular Western models as necessarily hostile to human rights and progress—"Western ideas of individualism, liberalism, constitutionalism, human rights, equality, liberty, the rule of law, democracy, free markets, the separation of church and state, often have little resonance in Islamic [and other] . . . cultures." [7]

In his 1997 follow-up book, Huntington concluded that "Islam's borders are bloody and so are its innards."[8] His blanket condemnation went beyond Islamic fundamentalism to Islam itself: "The underlying problem for the West is not Islamic fundamentalism. It is Islam, a different civilization whose people are convinced of the superiority of their culture, and are obsessed with the inferiority of their power."[9] Though Huntington has now significantly refined his position, September 11 unleashed new, updated versions as many found it more expedient to fall back on convenient stereotypes of a monolithic Islam and historic clash of civilizations rather than to examine the complex causes of terrorism.

Ironically, the clash of cultures appears as evident with reference to our allies in the Muslim world as with our enemies. Whatever the common economic and political interests, primarily centered on oil, the contrasts between Saudi Arabia and the United States are stark. The religious and cultural traditions of America's long-time ally—religiously puritanical and exclusivist worldview, sexually segregated society, lack of political parties and elections, punishment of theft by amputation, prohibition of building churches or practicing Christianity—as well as the fact that bin Laden and so many of the hijackers of September 11 were Saudi, indicate that we live in two different worlds. Similarly, the declared war of religious extremists and terrorists against entrenched

Muslim governments and the West—all in the name of Islam—
seems to underscore the incompatibility of Islam and democracy.
However, while the actions of extremist groups and of authoritarian governments, religious and nonreligious, reinforce this perception of a cultural clash, the facts on the ground present a more
complex picture.

Neither the Muslim world nor the West is monolithic. Common sources of identity (language, faith, history, culture) yield
when national or regional interests are at stake. While some Muslims have achieved a transient unity in the face of a common enemy, as in the Iranian Revolution, their solidarity quickly dissipates
once danger subsides and competing interests again prevail. The
evidence that there is no monolithic Islam is abundant. The inability of Arab nationalism/socialism, Saudi Arabia's pan-Islam, or
Iran's Islamic Republic revolution to unite and mobilize the Arab
and Muslim worlds, the competition and conflict between countries like Egypt, Libya, Sudan, and Saudi Arabia, the disintegration
of the Arab (Iraq and the Gulf states) coalition against Iran after
the Iran-Iraq war, and the subsequent Iraqi invasion of Kuwait
and divisions in the Muslim world evident in the 1991 Gulf war
are but a few examples. As James Piscatori observed, "The problem
with assuming a unified response is that it conceals the reality of
. . . entrenched national differences and national interests among
Muslims."[10] The failure of Osama bin Laden , like Saddam Hussein
and Khomeini before him, to effectively mobilize the Islamic world
in his unholy war, despite his global terrorist network, is a reminder
that Muslims, like every global religious community, are indeed
diverse. Moreover, as Islamic history makes abundantly clear, mainstream Islam, in law and theology as well as in practice, in the end
has always rejected or marginalized extremists and terrorists from
the Kharijites and Assassins to contemporary radical movements
such as al-Qaeda.

In responding to the attacks of September 11, some charged that
the clash of civilizations revolved around conflict with our modern
Western way of life, with, for example, democracy, women's rights,

and capitalism. In fact, capitalism exists in the Muslim world both in home-grown forms as well as Western-inspired versions. The issue for many in the Muslim world is not capitalism but the dangers of Western economic hegemony and its side effects. In fact, Islam does not have any problem with many of the essentials of Western capitalism. It is important to recall that Muhammad's early followers included prosperous merchants. He himself engaged in financial and commercial transactions to make a living. The Quran, *hadith* (traditions about what the Prophet said and did), and Muslim historical experience affirm the right to private property and trade and commerce. As Maxime Rodinson, a French scholar and Marxist, wrote in his *Islam and Capitalism*: "Economic activity, the search for profit, trade, and consequently, production for the market, are looked upon with no less favor by Muslim tradition than by the Koran itself."[11] Mosques throughout the world, such as the Umayyad mosque in Damascus and the magnificent mosques of old Cairo and Teheran, are often adjoined by magnificent bazaars. Traders and businessmen were among the most successful sectors in society and were responsible for the spread of their faith.

Perhaps the best response to those who ask whether Islam and capitalism are compatible is to look at the lives of the millions of Muslims who live and work in our midst in America and Europe. Many have come here to enjoy freedom and the opportunities offered by our economic and political systems. Like other religious and ethnic minorities before them, they too struggle with issues of identity and assimilation but not with their desire to enjoy the best that we represent.

Another frequently cited issue, used to demonstrate a civilizational clash, is Islam's treatment of women. If there is one image used to depict Islam and Muslims, it is that of oppressed, gender-segregated women, covered by the veil. Rather than considering that women's status might be caused by the continued strength of patriarchy, Islam is presumed to be particularly misogynist. Gender in Islam remains a highly charged issue today at the popular level and among scholars and religious leaders. If some blame Islam for the oppression of women, others see it as a beacon of light and reform. Still others insist that the status and role of women in Muslim societies should be attributed primarily to socioeconomic forces rather than to religious belief. The explanations are as diverse as the Muslim world itself.[12] Thus, charting the progress or regression of women, whether under secular or religious governments, is a tricky task. Often we compare our "ideal" to selected "realities" in other religions and cultures, overlooking the diversity that exists within them.

For several decades women in Muslim societies have been part of the dialectics of change, an erratic, vacillating, and contradictory process that creates many anomalies. In Egypt, long regarded as one of the most modernizing of Muslim states, women cannot serve as judges, and yet in Morocco more than 20 percent of judges are women. Women in Egypt and Malaysia have access to the best education and hold responsible professional positions in virtually every sector. Yet, like women in most Muslim societies, they need a male family member's permission to travel. Women in Saudi Arabia own much of the real estate in Riyadh and Jeddah, can own businesses but cannot drive a car, are sexually segregated, and restricted to "appropriate" professions. In nearby Kuwait, women function in society, hold responsible positions in many areas, but have not been able to get the vote. In Iran, where they must wear the chador in public, women constitute the majority in universities, hold professional positions, serve in Parliament, and there is a female vice president in the Islamic republic. Though Pakistani women can vote, serve as ambassadors and as prime minister, they, particularly the poor and powerless, also suffer under Islamic laws enacted by General Zia ul-Haq and still in force. In Afghanistan, the Taliban in the name of Islam forced professional women to give up their jobs and prohibited girls from attending school.

Critics charge that fundamentalists, religious extremists, want to drive modern Muslim societies back to a medieval past. Feminist organizations from Algeria to Malaysia warn that Islamist power-sharing would reverse the educational and social gains of the post-independence period, remove women from public life, and again restrict their roles solely to that of wife and mother.

For those who wish to implement a more Islamic order, reforms affecting women and the family provide a quick fix, legitimated in religious tradition and easy to apply. Affirming the centrality of the family in Islam is both an act of piety and of political expediency. The Muslim family has long been regarded as the nucleus of the Islamic community, its identity, piety, and strength. Women as wives and mothers have played a pivotal role in the upbringing, education, and training of their families. If westernized reforms seemed to threaten the identity and values of family life, reestablishing its Islamic roots through the Islamization of the family can become the panacea. Formulating and implementing an Islamic state or returning to the use of Islamic law (*Shariah*) in politics, business, and economics has proved difficult, and so many activists have found it easier to focus on women and the family.

Viewed as culture bearers, women have been put at the center of the wars of religious and cultural identity being fought in many Muslim countries today. Sometimes they are agents of change but often they are the victims. Throughout the twentieth century, regimes have used women's bodies to prove their modern orientation and identity. Reza Shah Pahlavi in Iran, Attaturk in Turkey, and Bourghiba in Tunisia banned or discouraged veiling and encouraged Western dress as a sign of modernity. The abolition of the veil in 1936 by Reza Shah Pahlavi has often been celebrated as a major step toward women's emancipation. However, this reform chiefly benefited upper-class elite women. For many middle- and lower-class Iranian women, the forcible removal of the veil was traumatic. In addition, despite the shah's modernizing symbols, the regime did not substantially change patriarchal values and attitudes (its own or those of the religious establishment): "I felt no matter what class they belonged to, women were considered as dolls and objects by their male colleagues."[13]

If many associate the veil with the oppression of women, others regard veiling as an authentic practice that preserves the dignity, freedom, and modesty of women, enabling them to act and to be treated in terms of who they are and not how they look. Since the 1970s, a significant number of modern women from Cairo to Jakarta have turned or returned to wearing Islamic dress. Often this is a voluntary movement led by young, urban, middle-class women, who are well educated and work in every sector of society. In many cases, the process is distinctly modern, with new fashions and styles encompassing new understandings of the status and role of women. Such women are not passive victims of male-imposed mores but active agents for change. Some who wear Islamic dress believe that they are better able to function as active, self-directed, independent subjects, commanding respect, acknowledged and treated as persons rather than (sex) objects. Islamic dress is also used as a sign of protest and liberation. It has developed political overtones, becoming a source of national pride as well as resistance to Western (cultural as well as political) dominance and to authoritarian regimes.

A new source of women's empowerment today has become active participation in the mosque and use of Islam's tradition to reclaim their rights in Islam. Reformers today emphasize that just as women during the time of the Prophet prayed in the mosque, so too today they actively exercise that right. In the centuries after the death of Muhammad, women played a small but significant role as transmitters of hadith (prophetic traditions) and in the development of Sufism (Islamic mysticism). Gradually, however, women's religious role and practice, particularly their access to education and the mosque, were severely restricted. Male religious scholars cited a variety of reasons, from moral degeneration in society to women's bringing temptation and social discord, to restrict both their presence in public life and their access to education and the mosque.[14]

Today, in many Muslim countries and communities, particularly those that have been regarded as among the more modernized, such as Egypt, Jordan, Malaysia, and in the United States, women lead and participate in Quran study and recitation groups as well as in mosque-based educational and social services. In countries such as Iran, women serve as prayer leaders (imams) for congregational prayers; however, they are only permitted to lead groups of women. Female reformers look to early Islam for examples of women noted for their learning, leadership, and piety to strengthen the rationales for women's contemporary role in public activities. Strong, public female figures during the Prophet's time include Khadija, Muhammad's first wife of twenty-five years, who owned her own business, in which Muhammad had been employed, and played a formative and significant role in the birth of the Muslim community. After Khadija's death, Muhammad's wife Aisha was very prominent as a major source of religious knowledge, an authority in history, medicine, and rhetoric.[15]

Though patriarchy, legitimated in the past by religion, remains very much alive as an ideology and value system, in many Muslim countries it is progressively challenged by women in the name of religion as well as for economic realities. Rather than breaking with tradition, female reformers argue that their religious activism today reclaims an ideal forgotten by later generations. As a result of this new approach, increasing numbers of women have an alternative model that enables them to broaden their expectations both inside and outside the home.

Voices of Reform and Dialogue

Because acts of violence and terrorism grab the headlines, we seem to know a lot more about Islamic advocates of a "clash," the militant jihadists, than about those who are working toward a peaceful revolution and civilizational dialogue. Today, Islam's encounter with the West and the need for Islamic reform are being addressed by intellectuals, religious leaders, and activists alike. Like the Islamic modernist movements in the late nineteenth and early twentieth centuries and later the Islamic (fundamentalist) movements of the Muslim Brotherhood and the Jamaat-i-Islami, today's Islamically oriented intellectuals and activists continue the process of Islamic modernization and reform. However, today's reformers represent a creative new stage in that they not only reformulate Islam conceptually but also implement their ideas through their positions in government and the public arena.

Three remarkable examples reflect the diverse voices of Islamic reform and civilizational dialogue that can be heard from the Middle East to Asia.[16] Active as intellectuals and politicians, Anwar Ibrahim, former deputy prime minister of Malaysia, Mohammad Khatami, president of the Islamic Republic of Iran, and Abdurrahman Wahid, former president of Indonesia, have played important roles in defining the terms for an intercivilizational dialogue, rather than a clash of civilizations. At the same time, each takes a position that is uniquely different from the West's, reflective of his own culture and political environment. Though all three object to concepts of development that presume the desirability of Western secularization for Muslim societies, they recognize the strengths and weaknesses of Western-style modernity. Thus, they advocate an active two-way dialogue among civilizations, especially between Islam and the West.

ANWAR IBRAHIM: GLOBAL *CONVIVENCIA*

When Anwar Ibrahim, sometimes called "Malaysia's own Islamic zealot," joined the government of Prime Minister Mahathir Mohammed in 1980, he stunned friends and foes alike.[17] Nevertheless, he showed that he could succeed in both worlds, rapidly evolving from a charismatic opposition leader to deputy prime minister and finance minister. Ibrahim worked effectively with diverse political forces and navigated Malaysia's complex multireligious (Muslim, Christian, Hindu, Buddhist) and multiethnic (Malay, Chinese, Indian) society. He had impressed many at home and abroad with his ability to bridge religions and cultures and to work effectively to achieve common goals. He had earned the reputation of "an unabashed globalist well suited to the modern world of markets and media"[18] and a "liberal."[19] Eighteen years later, he would be tried and convicted on politically inspired charges, an action condemned internationally by many political and religious leaders and human rights organizations. He remains, although in prison, a significant voice on issues of sociopolitical and economic development, advocating pluralism in multireligious societies and intercivilizational dialogue as the only alternative to a deadly clash of civilizations.

A pragmatic man of politics as well as of faith, Ibrahim argued that both Marxist and Western models of secular materialism had failed. "Marxism . . . severs man from his moorings in faith. . . . There was no place for ethics, morality or spirituality,"[20] and the West also rejects "any reference to moral and ethical considerations. Cultural preservation is regarded as retrogressive in the march for development."[21]

In contrast to more conservative Islamist groups that called for a return Islamic law, Ibrahim said,

[Southeast Asian Muslims] would rather strive to improve the welfare of the women and children in their midst than spend their days elaborately defining the nature and institutions of the ideal Islamic state. They do not believe it makes one less a Muslim to promote economic growth, to master the information revolution and to demand justice for women.[22]

Anwar Ibrahim's Islam is a dynamic, developing tradition that responds to diverse times and places. He rejected the conservative imitation (*taqlid*) of the past in favor of independent analysis and reinterpretation (*ijtihad*), believing that Islam is "a pragmatic religion whose real strength and dynamism was in its ongoing revitalization. . . ."[23] A strong proponent of East-West dialogue, he believes Islam is also inclusive, and as in the past, so too today Islam should be open to all cultures.

Pluralism and tolerance based upon mutual respect and understanding are cornerstones of Anwar Ibrahim's vision of a civilizational dialogue or *convivencia*, that has deep roots in medieval Islamic history. *Convivencia* (living together) alludes to the spirit of Roger II's twelfth-century Sicily and Muslim rule in the Iberian Peninsula in centers like Toledo, Cordoba, and Granada. In Iberia, Christians, Muslims, and Jews lived together in a context of social intercourse and cultural exchange. It was a time of prosperity and achievement; the arts, literature, poetry, astronomy, and medicine flourished. Many Christians became known as Mozarabs because of the extent to which they adopted elements of Arab dress, culture, and language, including Arabic names. Some Christian scholars wrote in Arabic instead of Latin.

Ibrahim finds the roots of *convivencia* supported both in Islamic history and in the Quran, as illustrated by the verse, "Oh mankind! Verily we have created you all from a male and a female, and have made you into nations and tribes that you may come to know one another" (49:13).[24]

Convivencia, for Ibrahim, is an Islamic form of pluralism, a vision quite different from the typical Islamist programs that make a place for non-Muslims in a traditionally conceived Islamic society. It is based on the primacy of social and economic justice and equality, recognized as fundamental to other religions as well as Islam. This pluralist vision is the foundation for his call for civilizational dialogue:

> For us, the divine imperative as expressed in the Qur'an is unambiguous. Humanity has been created to form tribes, races and nations, whose differences in physical characteristics, languages and modes of thought are but the means for the purpose of *lita'arafu*—"getting to know one another."[25]

Ibrahim appreciated the urgency of diffusing global confrontations, stressing that *convivencia* is a necessity for progress. However, it must be an encounter among equals.[26] Old Western imperialist attitudes of their "civilizing mission" as well as fundamentalist rejections of the enemy West threaten human survival.

MOHAMMAD KHATAMI:
DIALOGUE OF CIVILIZATIONS

For more than twenty years America and Iran were locked in a cycle of "mutual satanization." Memories of the Iranian revolution, American diplomats held hostage, Iran's ambitious attempts to export its revolution, and Ayatollah Khomeini's *fatwa* condemning to death British author Salman Rushdie for his book *The Satanic Verses* made Iran the epitome of an Islamic global threat.

In August 1997, eighteen years after the Iranian revolution had stunned the world, the newly elected president of the Islamic Republic surprised the international community in his inaugural address. Mohammad Khatami called for a dialogue of civilizations, "in our world, dialogue among civilizations is an absolute imperative."[27] The president of a country that America labeled terrorist became one of the major advocates for a new policy debate within Iran and within the global community about the clash of civilizations.

The new climate was dramatically conveyed to the world in a televised CNN interview with Christiane Amanpour in which Khatami surprised many by stating that Western civilization and the United States were worthy of respect, citing in particular the experience of the Pilgrims at Plymouth as an important event in affirming religious freedom, and the importance of the example of Abraham Lincoln.[28]

Khatami articulated a distinctive alternative approach to relations between Islam and the West. The old-fashioned jihad–clash-of-civilizations perspective offered stark alternatives of victory or defeat. Khatami's vision combined a nonmilitant jihadist defense of Islamic identity and values with a call for civilizational dialogue by which all societies could benefit through the exchange of information and ideas.[29]

Khatami's model for dialogue does not preclude strong criticism of Western policies, especially those of the United States. Speaking of a flawed U.S. policy of domination, Khatami denounced America's use of sanctions against Iran and others. America, he said, attempts to "impose their own domestic law on the world . . . [but the] world will not tolerate a master any more—not only will we not tolerate a master, neither will the world."[30] Thus, Khatami combines strong affirmation of Iran's principles and critique of U.S. policy with an emphatic advocacy of the dialogue of civilizations and of improved Iranian-U.S. relations in particular.

Mohammad Khatami's dialogue of civilizations is an alternative both to the old militant jihadist rhetoric and to uncritical
dependence on the West (what some have termed "westoxication").
In contrast to the hard-line position of Ayatollah Ali Khamenei,
Khomeini's successor as Supreme Guide of the Islamic republic,
Khatami boldly asserts that Islamic reform, open to a dynamic
interaction with Western civilization, must build a bridge between
tradition and modernity:

> We must concede that the incompatibility of modern civiliza-
> tion with our tradition-bound civilization is one of the most
> important causes of the crisis in our society. What is to be done?
> Should we insist on remaining immersed in our tradition, or
> should we melt fully into Western civilization? Or is there an-
> other way of removing this contradiction?[31]

Khatami's vision of the history and development of civilizations is dynamic; civilizations constantly change and evolve. The
West is the latest,

> but not the ultimate human civilization, which like all other
> human artifacts, is tentative and susceptible to decay. . . . Civi-
> lizations change and there is no such thing as an ultimate and
> eternal civilization.[32]

Khatami believes that at the beginning of the twenty-first century the need is for the creation of a new civilization. However, his
call for dialogue must be seen within the context of his particular
worldview, which differs from that of many in America and Europe. Many in the West assume that dialogue with the West means
that eventually non-Western peoples will see the advantages of Western civilization and become more westernized. This would be a complete misunderstanding of Khatami's vision of dialogue, which is
not a passive policy of accommodation but a competitive strategy
for strengthening and transforming Islamic civilization. It tran-

scends a militant vision of jihad and offers a way to avoid destructive conflict. Dialogue with the West is an important way of strengthening Islam. Khatami's vision holds out the hope that, as the West evolves and possibly declines, Islam will regain its position as the leading progressive world civilization.

In the continued encounter of Islam and the West in the twenty-first century, Khatami's dialogue of civilizations reflects a significant perspective very different from that of both Western analysts such as Samuel Huntington and old-style Islamic advocates of militant jihad such as Sayyid Qutb and, more recently, Osama bin Laden.

ABDURRAHMAN WAHID:
COSMOPOLITAN ISLAM AND GLOBAL DIVERSITY

In October 1999, Abdurrahman Wahid, leader of the Nahdatul Ulama, (Renaissance of Religious Scholars), the biggest (35 million members) Islamic organization in the world's largest Muslim country, became the first elected president in Indonesia's history.[33] Nahdatul Ulama (NU) is a predominantly conservative, rural-based sociocultural organization founded in 1926 to defend the interests of traditional Islam and counter the threat of modernism. Wahid, however, is best described as a modern, urban, liberal Muslim intellectual. As a religious leader and social and political reformer, he has staunchly opposed those who would reassert Islam's role in politics and has warned of the dangers of Islamic fundamentalism.

Bridging the worlds of traditional Islam and modern thought, Wahid espouses a reformist intellectual synthesis and social agenda that distinguishes between unchanging religious doctrines or laws and those that can be altered to accommodate social change. Wahid is among a generation of reformers who advocate a progressive Islam, one that is inclusive, democratic, pluralistic, and tolerant. Wahid advocates a cosmopolitan Islam, the product of creative reinterpretation or reformulation, responsive to the demands of modern life and reflecting Indonesian Islam's diverse religious and ethnic history and communities.

Wahid believes that contemporary Muslims are at a critical cross-road. Two choices or paths confront them: to pursue a traditional, static legal-formalistic Islam or to reclaim and refashion a more dynamic cosmopolitan, universal, pluralistic worldview.[34] In contrast to many "fundamentalists" today, he rejects the notion that Islam should form the basis for the nation-state's political or legal system,[35] a notion he characterizes as a Middle Eastern tradition, alien to Indonesia.[36] Indonesian Muslims should apply a moderate, tolerant brand of Islam to their daily lives in a society where "a Muslim and a non-Muslim are the same," a state in which religion and politics are separate.[37] Rejecting legal-formalism or fundamentalism as an aberration and a major obstacle to Islamic reform and to Islam's response to global change,[38] Wahid has spent his life promoting the development of a multifaceted Muslim identity and a dynamic Islamic tradition capable of responding to the realities of modern life. Its cornerstones are free will and the right of all Muslims, both laity and religious scholars (*ulama*) to "perpetual reinterpretation" *(ijtihad)* of the Quran and tradition of the Prophet in light of "everchanging human situations."[39]

Wahid's cosmopolitan Islam is pluralistic and global, affirming the diversity of peoples and civilizations. The challenge for contemporary Muslims is to articulate and preserve an authentic identity informed by their Islamic heritage but open to the cosmopolitan realities of a global environment. It is based on a recognition of universal basic rights, respect for other faiths, ideologies, and cultures, and open to the best that modern science and technology have to offer.[40]

A political realist who recognized the needs to create national unity in the face of communalism, to establish the rule of law, and to develop viable economic frameworks for the equitable distribution of wealth, Wahid also put his finger on a major cause of violence and terrorism in Muslim countries. Most governments in the Muslim world rely on sociopolitical engineering, authoritarianism, political suppression, and violence to impose their vision. Wahid maintains that governments close their eyes to a fundamental issue of development when they reduce national problems solely to political and socioeconomic and technical factors. The failure to address the relationship of faith to national identity and to institution building contributes to instability and risks "massive social explosions."[41] Governments that rely on social control rather than consultation, that employ violence and repression, create a climate that contributes to radicalization and violence against the state. Wahid has astutely identified the heart of the struggle in Islam today. Movements are faced with two options, "the choice of following either a radical approach or a gradual response in their struggle for social justice, equal treatment before the law and freedom of expression."[42]

Anwar Ibrahim, Mohammad Khatami, and Abdurrahman Wahid are but three of many voices for Islamic reform. They demonstrate that there is no essentialist or monolithic Islam or Muslim society. All may share a common faith, at times articulate an Islamically inspired worldview, and use Islam as a source of legitimacy and mobilization. Still, their visions, goals, and strategies are shaped as much by diverse political and cultural contexts as by faith. They challenge those who see the world of the early twenty-first century in polarities, either confrontation and conflict or dialogue and cooperation, to appreciate the limitations and failures of old paradigms and to develop new paradigms for governance and policy that are sensitive to the importance of religion and culture.

Finally, in an increasingly global society, defining Islam and the Muslim world monolithically becomes more difficult as clear boundaries between Islam and the West evaporate. Not only are Muslim countries, societies, and institutions deeply involved with non-Muslim societies and communities but, more important, Islam is so present in America and Europe that Muslims have become part of the fabric of Western societies, as citizens, professionals, and neighbors. Many Muslims are third- and fourth-generation citizens in Western societies, no more and no less American or European than Jews, Christians, and Hindus. And yet, one of the questions we constantly hear is, Can they be democratic?

Islam and Democracy

The most glaring difference between the Muslim world and the
West today is the contrast between authoritarian and democratically elected governments. Authoritarianism has been the norm
not the exception in Muslim politics, cutting across the political
and ideological spectrum. The track record of governments both
non-Islamist (Algeria, Tunisia, and Egypt) and Islamist (Afghanistan, Sudan, and Iran) reveals a culture of authoritarianism that is
incapable of tolerating any significant opposition.

Those already convinced about how different "they" are—that
Islam is incompatible with modernization and that the mixing of
religion and politics is an explosive formula for violent extremism
and terrorism and an inevitable clash of civilizations—have solid
examples to buttress their arguments. In theory, Islam and democratic or parliamentary forms of government are not incompatible. In actual practice, the results have been mixed, with strikingly
contradictory experiences. Khomeini's Iran, Afghanistan's Taliban,
Sudan's Islamic government have provided damning examples of
political oppression, sexual discrimination, domestic and international violence and terrorism.

The case of Iran, the longest-lasting experiment in creating a
modern Islamic system, demonstrates the changing dynamic relationship between religion and sociopolitical realities. During its
first decade, the Islamic republic remained authoritarian, with strict
and narrow limitations on political participation. However, the
political system has experienced a push from both above and below along the democratization path. President Khatami's emphasis on the importance of civil society, democratization, and the
rule of law has been a response to societal pressure, especially from
women and the younger generation who make up a significant
number of Iranian voters. However, given the ongoing struggle
between reformers and a more hard-line conservative political and
religious establishment led by Ayatollah Ali Khamenei, the out-
come remains uncertain.

Why the glaring absence of democratic governments? As we have seen, the Muslim world is dealing with a legacy that created a powerful culture of authoritarianism still deeply entrenched in many countries. It is perpetuated today by rulers who inherited or seized power: from the unelected kings and emirs of Saudi Arabia, Jordan, Morocco, and Kuwait to the military and ex-military presidents of Sudan, Pakistan, Egypt, Libya, and Iraq. So too, political authoritarianism, whether religious or secular, has often been the norm, not only in the Islamic governments of Iran, Sudan, Pakistan, Afghanistan, and Saudi Arabia but also in the more secular governments of Tunisia, Egypt, Syria, Algeria, and Indonesia, where the situation has changed with the fall of Suharto and democratic elections but remains precarious.

Most Muslim countries remain security (*mukhabarat*) states whose rulers are focused on retaining their power and privilege at any cost through strong military and security forces. Many rulers have been "reelected" in government-controlled elections in which they garner 95 to 99.91 percent of the vote. Political parties and trade unions are nonexistent or severely restricted, elections are often rigged, and the culture and institutions of civil society are weak. Democratic elections have occurred in a number of countries (Turkey, Pakistan, Malaysia, Bangladesh, Jordan, Morocco, and Egypt) but most remain limited or guided democracies at best. Turkey and Pakistan have experienced military intervention and rule. Jordan and Morocco are monarchies. The recent succession of Syria's Bashir Assad after the death of his father, Hafez al-Assad, and the apparent grooming of Saddam Hussein's son in Iraq portend a new nondemocratic paradigm. The modern Muslim experience supports the impression that Islam and democracy are incompatible.[43]

Many say that Islam and democracy do not mix because traditional Islamic institutions such as the caliphate preclude significant popular political participation and democratic institutions. Yet, the history of religions demonstrates that religious traditions, like political ideologies such as democracy and communism, are capable of multiple interpretations and relations to the state. Modern reforms transformed European monarchies and principalities, whose rule had been religiously justified by divine right, into modern Western democratic states. Moreover, democracy itself has meant different things to different peoples at different times, from ancient Greece to modern Europe, from direct to indirect democracy, from majority rule to majority vote.[44] Judaism and Christianity, once supportive of political absolutism and divine right monarchies, have been reinterpreted to accommodate the democratic ideal. As a result, many Jews and Christians now believe that modern democracy is rooted in the Judeo-Christian tradition or at least not in conflict with their religion.

Islam throughout history has proven dynamic and diverse. It adapted to support the movement from the city-state of Medina to empires and sultanates, was able to encompass diverse schools of theology, law, and philosophy as well as different Sunni and Shii branches, and has been used to support both extremism and conservative orthodoxy. Islam continues today to lend itself to multiple interpretations of government; it is used to support limited democracy and dictatorship, republicanism, and monarchy. Like other religions, Islam possesses intellectual and ideological resources that can provide the justification for a wide range of governing models from absolute monarchy to democracy. In recent years, the democracy debate has intensified.

Experts and policymakers who worry that Islamic movements will use electoral politics to "hijack democracy" often fail to show equal concern that few current rulers in the region have been democratically elected and that many who speak of democracy only believe in "risk-free democracy." They permit political participation and liberalization as long there is no risk of a strong opposition (secular or religious) or a potential loss of power. Failure to appreciate that the issue of the hijacking of democracy is a two-way street was reflected in the responses (awkward silence or support) of many western governments and experts for the Algerian military's intervention and their abrogation of the results of the democratic electoral process, the Turkish military's suppression of the Islamic Refah party, and the growing authoritarianism of the Mubarak government in Egypt.

Democrats and Dissidents

A diversity of voices, some harmonious and others strident, discuss and debate political participation. Secularists argue for the separation of religion and the state. Rejectionists (both moderate and militant Muslims) maintain that Islam's forms of governance do not conform to democracy. King Fahd of Saudi Arabia, a longtime ally of the West, says that "the democratic system prevalent in the world is not appropriate in this region. . . . The election system has no place in the Islamic creed, which calls for a government of advice and consultation and for the shepherd's openness to his flock, and holds the ruler fully responsible before his people."[45] Extremists agree, condemning any form of democracy as *haram* (forbidden), an idolatrous threat to God's rule and divine sovereignty. Their unholy wars to topple governments aim to impose an authoritarian Islamic rule. Conservatives often argue that popular sovereignty contradicts the sovereignty of God, with the result that the alternative has often been some form of monarchy.

Reformers reinterpret key traditional Islamic concepts and institutions: consultation (*shura*) of rulers with those ruled, consensus (*ijma*) of the community, reinterpretation (*ijtihad*), and legal principles such as the public welfare (*maslaha*) of society to develop Islamic forms of parliamentary governance, representative elections, and religious reform. Just as it was appropriate in the past for Muhammad's senior Companions to constitute a consultative assembly (*majlis al-shura*) and to select or elect his successor (*caliph*) through a process of consultation, Muslims now reinterpret and extend this notion to the creation of modern forms of political participation, parliamentary government, and the direct or indirect election of heads of state.

Some advocates of Islamic democracy argue that the doctrine of the oneness of God (*tawhid*) or monotheism requires some form of democratic system. "No Muslim questions the sovereignty of

God or the rule of Shariah, Islamic Law. However, most Muslims do (and did) have misgivings about any claims by one person that he is sovereign. The sovereignty of one man contradicts the sovereignty of God, for all men are equal in front of God. . . . Blind obedience to one-man rule is contrary to Islam."[46]

The Tunisian Islamist leader of the Renaissance Party and political exile Rashid Ghannoushi provided an early example of a growing democratic trend: "If by democracy is meant the liberal model of government prevailing in the West, a system under which the people freely choose their representatives and leaders, in which there is an alternation of power, as well as all freedoms and human rights for the public, then Muslims will find nothing in their religion to oppose democracy, and it is not in their interests to do so."[47]

However, reformist efforts toward political liberalization, electoral politics, and democratization in the Muslim world do not imply uncritical acceptance of Western democratic forms. Most accommodationists would agree that it is important for Muslims not to uncritically copy what the West has done, emphasizing that there are different forms that legitimate democracy can take. Iran's president Mohammad Khatami, in a television interview in June 2001 before his country's presidential elections, noted that "the existing democracies do not necessarily follow one formula or aspect. It is possible that a democracy may lead to a liberal system. It is possible that democracy may lead to a socialist system. Or it may be a democracy with the inclusion of religious norms in the government. We have accepted the third option." Khatami presents a view common among the advocates of Islamic democracy that "today world democracies are suffering from a major vacuum which is the vacuum of spirituality,"[48] and that Islam can provide the framework for combining democracy with spirituality and religious government.

Grass-Roots Democratization

The most pervasive and vibrant example of the push from below for greater democratization and power sharing is the growing presence and implementation of Islam in civil society, in nongovern-mental institutions and associations (NGOs). The development of a strong civil society is a critical ingredient for building demo-cratic institutions. It incorporates and inculcates the principles and values of power sharing: greater political participation, represen-tation, self-determination, government accountability, the rule of law, and social justice.

Although for much of the 1980s revolutionary Iran and extremist movements provided the dominant note, the late 1980s and 1990s revealed the many faces of Islamic social and political activism. Islamic movements and associations became part and parcel of mainstream institutional forces in civil society. Islamic activist organizations and NGOs created networks of mosques, hospitals, clinics, day-care centers, youth clubs, legal aid societies, foreign language schools, banks, drug rehabilitation programs, insurance companies, and publishing houses. They fill a void and thus serve, in some countries, as an implicit indictment of the government's ability to provide adequate services, in particular for the nonelite sectors of society. Their services provide an alternative to expen-sive private institutions and overcrowded public facilities. At the same time, they reinforce a sense of community identity as well as spiritual and moral renewal.

Though many Islamic associations and NGOs are nonpolitical and nonviolent, others like Lebanon's Hizbollah and Hamas in Palestine have combined extensive and effective educational and social services with political action and militant jihad. Their vio-lent confrontations with Israel and acts of terrorism have led two successive American presidential administrations to designate Hamas and Hizbollah as terrorist organizations and to shut down several American Muslim organizations charged with channeling funds to them. At the same time, Hizbollah provides an instruc-tive example of the extent to which Islamic movements are shaped not simply by a religious impulse but by political contexts. Hiz-bollah was primarily a militant Shii response to Israel's invasion and occupation of Lebanon and the Lebanese Civil War. With the end of the civil war, Hizbollah put down its arms in the north, became a political party, and won seats in Parliament. However, it kept up its militant resistance to Israeli occupation of Southern Lebanon, fighting Israeli forces until Israel's withdrawal from Lebanon. Though Hizbollah remains on some countries' list of terrorist states (including the lists of the United States and Israel), it functions today within mainstream Lebanese society, combining politics with a vast network of educational and social services.

Many Islamic movements in recent years have eschewed violence and terrorism. Alongside the terrorist trail of unholy wars, there exists a democratic track record of Islamically oriented candidates who have been elected president of Indonesia, prime minister of Turkey, deputy prime minister of Malaysia, speakers of parliaments in Indonesia, Iran, Jordan, and Sudan, cabinet ministers and parliamentarians in Egypt, Algeria, Sudan, Kuwait, Pakistan, Jordan, Yemen, Malaysia, Indonesia, Turkey, and Lebanon. The performance of Islamist groups in national and municipal elections defied the predictions of those who had insisted that Islamic movements were unrepresentative and would not attract voters.

An Islamic Democratic Threat?

The wide participation of religiously motivated Muslims (political and apolitical) in Islamic professional associations and other private voluntary organizations has led to the gradual Islamization of society from below, increasingly evident throughout much of the Muslim world. Ironically, the nonviolent participation and apparent strength of Islamists in mainstream society has led to more stringent limits on political liberalization and democratization in the 1990s.

Authoritarian governments and secular elites who fear any significant opposition as a potential challenge to their power and privilege have raised the specter of fanatic fundamentalism and terrorism, charging that radical Islamists were out to hijack democracy, to come to power through ballots as well as bullets. The Algerian military seized power, imprisoned Islamists, and denied them their electoral victory. Tunisia and Egypt backed away from their commitment to open elections and instead crushed (Tunisia) or curtailed (Egypt) mainstream, nonviolent Islamist participation, making little distinction between treatment of moderates, who operated aboveground and within the system, and violent revolutionary extremists. Yielding to pressures from its powerful military, Turkey's government forced Prime Minister Ecmettin Erbakan to resign and subsequently outlawed his Welfare Party. A new, more broad-based Islamic party, Virtue, was created only to have Turkey's Parliament refuse to seat a woman parliamentarian who insisted on wearing a headscarf; finally the party itself was banned.

At best the attitude of many rulers may be characterized, in the words of one Western diplomat, as an openness to "risk-free democracy" or, as another put it, "democracy without dissent." Openness to government-controlled and -dominated change—yes; openness to a change of government that would bring to power Islamic activists (or for that matter *to any opposition party*)—no. Recent years have shown that, at best, opposition parties and groups, whether secular or religious, are tolerated only as long as they remain relatively weak or under government control and do not threaten the regime or ruling party at the ballot box. However, questions remain. Can the ills of societies be reduced to a single cause or blamed on "fundamentalist fanatics"? Are the activities of a radical minority a convenient excuse for the failure of many governments to build strong and equitable modern states? Does this perceived threat support authoritarian, military or security governments, whose nonelected rulers' primary wish is to perpetuate their own power?

The issue of democratization, like that of authoritarianism, in Muslim societies is not primarily one of religion but of history and political and economic development. Centuries of European colonial rule followed by decades of authoritarian governments have created and perpetuated conditions that are not conducive to democratization. One-man or one-party governments, limited political participation, restricted freedom of speech and of the press, government control of politics, economic, social, educational development, and of the media produce authoritarian political cultures and values. The absence or weakness of civil society (nongovern-mental institutions and associations) contributes to the inevita-bility that many governments in the Muslim world will follow one of two paths, religious or secular authoritarianism. Despite the odds, however, democratization has increasingly become an issue in Muslim politics.

The political and economic realities of many states continue to foster alienation, opposition, and radicalism or extremism. De-spite the growing desire for greater political participation and gov-ernment accountability, authoritarian governments with limited political participation and freedoms remain the norm in many countries. Regarding the future role of Islam in Muslim politics, the comment of one expert on Egypt is equally relevant to other states: "Egypt's rulers can expect to see an Islam that faithfully reflects the skill or folly of their own statecraft."[49]

Democracy is an integral part of modern Islamic political thought and practice, accepted in many Muslim countries as a litmus test by which both the openness of government and the relevance of Islamic groups or other political parties are certified. However, questions about what particular forms democratization might take in diverse Muslim political cultures remain difficult to answer. Muslim political traditions and institutions, like social conditions and class structures, continue to evolve and are critical to the fu-ture of democracy in the Muslim world.

Western governments are challenged to balance longstanding relationships with regimes against the principles and values of self-determination, democratization, and human rights that they claim to stand for and support. Governments in the Muslim world are challenged to promote and strengthen the development of civil society—those institutions, values, and culture that are the foun-dation for true participatory government. They must be willing to allow alternative political voices to function freely in society and express their opinions and dissent through the formation of po-litical parties, private associations, newspapers, and the media. Is-lamic activists and movements are challenged to move beyond slogans to programs. They must become more self-critical in speaking out not only against local government abuses but also against those of Islamic regimes in Sudan, Afghanistan, and until recently Iran, as well as acts of terrorism committed in the name of Islam by extremists. They are challenged to provide an Islamic rationale and policy that would extend to their opposition and to minorities the very principles of pluralism and political participation that they demand for themselves.

All are challenged to recognize that democratization and the building of strong civil societies in the Muslim world are part of a process of experimentation, necessarily accompanied by failure as well as success. The transformation of the West from feudal monarchies to democratic nation-states took time, trial and error. It was accompanied by political and intellectual revolutions that rocked both state and church in a long, drawn-out process, among contending voices and factions with competing visions and interests.

Global Terrorism and Islam

Terrorism has been a worldwide threat, affecting countries as dissimilar as Italy, Germany, Peru, Japan, and Greece, Israel/Palestine, Egypt, Yemen, Iran, Turkey, and Iraq. Terrorists have targeted local populations often in the name of nationalist groups or governments. In recent years, radical groups have combined nationalism, ethnicity, or tribalism with religion and used violence and terrorism to achieve their goals: Serbs in Bosnia, Hindu nationalists in India, Tamil and Sinhalese in Sri Lanka, Jewish fundamentalists in Israel, Christian extremists in the United States. However, the most widespread examples of religious terrorism have occurred in the Muslim world. Al-Qaeda (modern in terms of educational profiles, knowledge and use of modern technology from computers, faxes, the Internet, and cell phones to weapons) represents a new form of terrorism, born of transnationalism and globalization. It is transnational in its identity and recruitment and global in its ideology, strategy, targets, network of organizations, and economic transactions.

Though global terrorism has no single location or source, for the time being it has become associated with Islam and jihad. While

President George W. Bush and other national and religious leaders have distinguished between Islam and terrorism, and many average Americans have proven remarkably supportive of Arab and Muslim colleagues and neighbors, others have not. Although the U.S. administration has remained consistent in its statements, the actions of the attorney general and proposed congressional anti-terrorism legislation, as well as the detention of individuals for indefinite periods without trial or access to evidence, raise deep concerns about the erosion of civil liberties and human rights for Arabs and Muslims, and others as well. The issue goes to the core of what the United States is and stands for, who we are now, and what we might become.

Like all the world's major religious traditions, Islam has its extremist fringe. However, Osama bin Laden 's steady dose of proclamations and threats has assured that Islam, not just extremism or terrorism, receives special treatment. The climate today is one in which questions can be asked and statements can be made about Islam, not simply about the beliefs and actions of extremists, that would not be tolerated if directed at Judaism or Christianity. The danger of this approach is to overlook the fact that militant jihad movements and terrorism are not just the products of warped individuals or religious doctrine, whether mainstream or extremist interpretations, but of political and economic conditions.

Reacting to Terrorism:
American Foreign Policy in the Muslim World

After September 11, the depth of hatred expressed by bin Laden and his al-Qaeda followers along with scenes of some Arabs celebrating in the streets revolted many but also led some to ask, Why do they hate us? The temptation for some government officials and political commentators was to condemn and dismiss, to explain away anti-Americanism as irrationality, ingratitude, jealousy of our success, or hatred for "our way of life." Slogans to the effect that we are in a war between the civilized world and terrorists; a war between fundamentalists who hate Western democracy, capitalism, and freedom; or a war against evil and merchants of death may reflect the rhetoric of some extremists and be emotionally satisfying, but they fail to get at deeper realities and long-term issues. Similarly, belief that overwhelming force has brought a quick victory and proven an effective answer and message to other terrorists or potential terrorists also overlooks real and future threats. Other bin Ladens exist as do the political and economic conditions that they can exploit to recruit new soldiers for their unholy wars.

Osama bin Laden, like the secular Saddam Hussein and the cleric Ayatollah Khomeini before him, cleverly identified specific grievances against Muslim regimes and the United States that are shared across a broad spectrum of Muslims, most of whom are not extremists. He then used religious texts and doctrines to justify his jihad of violence and terrorism. Anti-Americanism is driven not only by the blind hatred of the terrorists but also by a broader-based anger and frustration with American foreign policy among many in Arab and Muslim societies: government officials, diplomats, the military, businessmen, professionals, intellectuals, and journalists. Many enjoy close friendships with their Western counterparts. They have graduated from and send their children to Western schools, vacation and own property in America and Europe, admire many of the principles and values (political participation, accountability, the basic freedoms of speech, thought, and the press). But they also believe that these principles are applied selectively or not at all when it comes to the Muslim world.

Lost in our litany of slogans and easy answers is the recognition that they see more than we see. In recent years, the United States has become less international-minded and more preoccupied with domestic issues. Many members of Congress see no reason to travel abroad; a prominent congressional leader freely quipped that he had been to Europe once and saw no reason to return. Major media networks and newspapers have cut back on the number of foreign bureaus and correspondents; domestic news coverage has expanded at the expense of public awareness of international affairs. By contrast, and unlike in the past, many in the Muslim world are no longer dependent on CNN and the BBC for news of the world.

International Arab and Muslim publications and media provide daily coverage of foreign affairs. Families sit glued to their television sets, watching daily coverage on al-Jazeera, and see in vivid color live news from Palestine/Israel, Iraq, Chechnya, and Kashmir.

Many see the United States' espousal of self-determination, democratization, and human rights as disingenuous in light of its foreign policies. While average Americans might see the latest explosive headline event such as a spectacular terrorist attack in Israel, they are not bombarded daily with images of acts of Israeli violence and brutality, the disproportionate firepower, the number of Palestinian deaths and casualties, the use of American weapons including F-16s and Apache helicopters provided to Israel and used against Palestinians, including civilians, in the occupied territories. America's relationship with Israel has proved to be a lightning rod. While some in the West downplay or deny the significance of the Palestinian issue, surveys continue to verify its importance to Muslims globally. A survey in spring 2001 of five Arab states (Egypt, Saudi Arabia, the United Arab Emirates, Kuwait, and Lebanon) demonstrated that the "majority in all five countries said that the Palestinian issue was the single most important issue to them personally."[50] In a Zogby International poll of American Muslims taken in November and December 2001, 84 percent believed that the United States should support a Palestinian state, 70 percent believed that it should reduce financial support to Israel.[51]

The American government's tough stand (often fully justified) with Yasser Arafat but kid-glove treatment of Israeli Prime Minister Ariel Sharon's aggressive and brutal policies in the West Bank and Gaza, and America's long record of relatively uncritical support of Israel—expressed in its levels of military and economic aid to Israel, its voting record in the United Nations, official statements by American administrations and government officials, and votes by Congress (often opposed by administrations in the past) to move the American embassy from Tel Aviv to Jerusalem in direct contravention of longstanding UN resolutions—are seen by many in the Muslim world as proof of American hypocrisy.

Other critical foreign policy issues include the impact of sanctions on more than a half-million innocent Iraqi children (with little direct effect on Saddam Hussein), and sanctions against Pakistan while failing to hold India and Israel to similar standards for their nuclear programs. The moral will so evident in Kosovo is seen as totally absent in U.S. policy in the Chechnya and Kashmiri conflicts. A native-born American convert to Islam, Ivy League–educated and formerly a government consultant, spoke with a frustration shared by many Muslims: "Every informed Muslim would point to America's bizarre complicity in the genocidal destruction of Chechnya, its tacit support of India's incredibly brutal occupation of Kashmir, its passivity in the ethnic cleansing of Bosnia, and even America's insistence on zero casualties in stopping the ethnic cleansing of Kosovo. These are hot spots in the so-called 'ring of fire' around the edge of the Muslim world, where Muslims are throwing off the shackles of old empires."[52]

To understand the love-hate relationship, the attraction-repulsion toward America that exists in many parts of the world and is widespread in the Muslim world, we must not only know who we think we are and how we view others but try to understand how others might see us. As Paul Kennedy has observed, few of us ask:

[H]ow do we appear to *them,* and what would it be like were our places in the world reversed. . . . Suppose that there existed today a powerful, unified Arab-Muslim state that stretched from Algeria to Turkey and Arabia—as there was 400 years ago, the Ottoman Empire. Suppose this unified Arab-Muslim state had the biggest economy in the world, and the most effective military. Suppose by contrast this United States of ours had split into 12 or 15 countries, with different regimes, some conservative and corrupt. Suppose that the great Arab-Muslim power had its aircraft carriers cruising off our shores, its aircraft flying over our lands, its satellites watching us every day. Suppose that its multinational corporations had reached into North America to extract oil, and paid the corrupt, conservative governments big royalties for that. Suppose that it dominated all international institutions like the Security Council and the IMF. Suppose that there was a special state set up in North America fifty years ago, of a different religion and language to ours, and the giant Arab-Muslim power always gave it support. Suppose the Colossus state was bombarding us with cultural messages, about the status of women, about sexuality, that we found offensive. Suppose it was always urging us to change, to modernize, to go global, to follow its example. Hmm . . . in those conditions, would not many Americans steadily grow to loath that Colossus, wish it harm? And perhaps try to harm it? I think so.[53]

The war against global terrorism should neither become a green light for authoritarian regimes in the Muslim world to further limit the rule of law and civil society or to repress nonviolent opposition, nor justify a gradual erosion of important principles and values at home and abroad. Many governments use the danger of "Islamic fundamentalism" as an excuse for authoritarian responses and policies, labeling all Islamic movements, extremist as well as moderate (whom they characterize as wolves in sheep's clothing), as a threat. Many Muslim and Western governments oppose any Islamic candidates' participation in elections, fearing that they will hijack elections. These fears often obscure the fact that many governments themselves have proven nondemocratic or authoritarian track records.

American, as well as European, responses must remain proportionate, from military strikes and foreign policy to domestic security measures and antiterrorism legislation. A reexamination and, where necessary, reformulation of U.S. foreign policy will be necessary to effectively limit and contain global terrorism. Short-term policies that are necessitated by national interest must be balanced by long-term policies and incentives that pressure our allies to promote a gradual and progressive process of broader political participation and power sharing. Failure to do so will simply perpetuate the culture and values of authoritarianism, secular as well as religious, and feed anti-Americanism. If foreign policy issues are not addressed effectively, they will continue to provide a breeding ground for hatred and radicalism, the rise of extremist movements, and recruits for the bin Ladens of the world.

Globalization of the Jihad

What is distinctive about global jihad today? The Soviet-Afghan war marked a new turning point as jihad went global to a degree never seen in the past. The *mujahidin* holy war drew Muslims from many parts of the world and support from Muslim and non-Muslim countries and sources. In its aftermath, the new global jihad spread as jihad became the common symbol and rallying cry for holy and unholy wars. Most major Muslim struggles were declared a jihad. Afghan Arabs moved on to fight other jihads in their home countries and in Bosnia, Kosovo, and Central Asia. Others stayed on or were trained and recruited in the new jihadi *madrasas* and training camps.

Today, the term jihad has become comprehensive; resistance and liberation struggles and militant jihads, holy and unholy wars, are all declared to be jihads. Jihad is waged at home not only against unjust rulers in the Muslim world but also against a broad spectrum of civilians. Jihad's scope abroad became chillingly clear in the September 11 attacks against both the World Trade Center and the Pentagon, targeting not only governments but also civilians.

Terrorists such as bin Laden and others go beyond classical Islam's criteria for a just jihad and recognize no limits but their own, employing any weapons or means. They reject Islamic law's regulations regarding the goals and means of a valid jihad (that violence must be proportional and that only the necessary amount of force should be used to repel the enemy), that innocent civilians should not be targeted, and that jihad must be declared by the ruler or head of state. Today, individuals and groups, religious and lay, seize the right to declare and legitimate unholy wars in the name of Islam.

On the other hand, Islamic scholars and religious leaders across the Muslim world such as those at the Islamic Research Council at al-Azhar University, regarded by many as the highest moral authority in Islam, have made strong, authoritative declarations against bin Laden's initiatives: "Islam provides clear rules and ethical norms that forbid the killing of non-combatants, as well as women, children, and the elderly, and also forbids the pursuit of the enemy in defeat, the execution of those who surrender, the infliction of harm on prisoners of war, and the destruction of property that is not being used in the hostilities."[54]

Globalization of communications, technology, and travel has heightened a new consciousness of the transnational identity and interconnectedness of the Islamic community (*ummah*) that follows events across the Muslim world on a daily, even hourly basis. They reinforce a sense of solidarity and identification. Regardless of national and cultural identities, most Muslims are not secular; they do self-consciously identify themselves as Muslim. They celebrate or bemoan successes and failures of Muslim struggles for self-determination, freedom from oppression, and economic development across the world, as well as of militant jihads, holy and unholy wars. The dark side of globalization and interconnectedness is that communications and technology support the existence of global terrorist networks in the twenty-first century.

If Western powers need to rethink, reassess foreign policies and their support for authoritarian regimes, mainstream Muslims worldwide will need to more aggressively address the threat to Islam from religious extremists. Their jihad or struggle will be religious, intellectual, spiritual, and moral. But it must be a more rapid and widespread program of Islamic renewal that builds on past reformers but that follows the lead of enlightened religious leaders and intellectuals today more forcefully, and that more effectively engages in a wide-ranging process of reinterpretation *(ijtihad)* and reform. There are formidable obstacles to be overcome—the conservatism of many (though not all) ulama, reform in the training of religious scholars and leaders, the countering of more puritanical exclusivist Wahhabi or Salafi brands of Islam, and the discrediting of militant jihadist ideas and ideologies.

Like the process of modern reform in Judaism and Christianity, questions of leadership and the authority of the past and tradition are critical. Whose Islam? Who leads and decides? Is it rulers, the vast majority of whom are unelected kings, military, and former military? Or elected prime ministers and parliaments? Is it the ulama or clergy, who continue to see themselves as the primary interpreters of Islam, although many are ill prepared to respond creatively to modern realities? Or is it modern educated, Islamically oriented intellectuals and activists? Lacking an effective leadership, will other Osama bin Ladens fill the vacuum?

The second major question is, What Islam? Is Islamic reform simply returning to the past and restoring past doctrines and laws, or is it a reformation or reformulation of Islam to meet the demands of modern life? Some call for an Islamic state based on the reimplementation of classical formulations of Islamic laws. Others argue the need to reinterpret and reformulate law in light of the new realities of contemporary society.

Religious traditions are a combination of text and context—revelation and human interpretation within a specific sociohistorical context. This has gone on for many centuries. All religious traditions demonstrate dynamism and diversity and that is why there are conservative elements as well as modernist or progressive elements in all religions. Judaism and Christianity, the Hebrew Bible and the New Testament have been used to legitimize monarchies and feudalism in the past, and democracy and capitalism, as well as socialism in the present. The Gospels and Christianity have been used to legitimize the accumulation of wealth and market capitalism as well as religiosocial movements such as those of Francis of Assisi and, in the twentieth century, Dorothy Day's Catholic Worker Movement, and liberation theology in Latin and Central America. The process continues today regarding issues of gender relations, birth control, abortion, homosexuality, and social justice, yielding multiple and diverse positions. While using the same text and referring to a common history, people come out with different interpretations. Islam too is an ideal that has taken many forms historically and has been capable of multiple interpretations, conditioned by reason and social contexts. For example, much of the debate over the relationship of Islam to women's rights must be seen in terms not only of religion but also, as in other religions, of patriarchy. The status and role of Muslim women in law and society was defined in a patriarchal past and by the male religious elites who were the interpreters of religion.

This is a time to remember the events of September 11 and to respond: a time to remember the victims, those who died and their families. It is also a time for the international community, governments, religious leaders, opinion makers, intellectuals, academics, and citizens to respond. The United States–led coalition has brought an end to Taliban rule, the first major step in the war against global terrorism. Whether Osama bin Laden is captured and however successful are attempts to contain al-Qaeda, religious terrorism in the Muslim world and beyond will continue to be a threat to nations and to the international community.

As President George W. Bush and other political leaders have recognized, we will not defeat global terrorism solely by military or economic means. Public diplomacy must be a critical component. There can be no excuse for terrorism in the name of Islam. Suicide attacks, bombings, assassinations in the name of any cause, whether justified in the name of God, justice, or state security, are still terrorism. Quick and easy responses, such as moves to quiet the Arab street through overwhelming force, may be emotionally satisfying but will in the long run prove ineffective and contribute to greater radicalization and anti-Americanism. While some forms of terrorism, like some forms of cancer, respond to radical surgery, this deadly disease can only be effectively countered first by understanding how it originates, grows stronger, and spreads and then by taking action. The cancer of global terrorism will continue to afflict the international body until we address its political and economic causes, causes that will otherwise continue to provide a breeding ground for hatred and radicalism, the rise of extremist movements, and recruits for the bin Ladens of the world.

Notes

Chapter 1

1. Indira A.R. Lakshmanan, *Boston Globe*, September 26, 2001.
2. About the bin Laden Family, PBS Online and WGBH/*Frontline*: http://www.pbs.org/wgbh/pages/frontline/shows/binladen/who/family.html
3. Ibid.
4. A Biography of Osama bin Laden, PBS Online and WGBH/*Frontline*: http://www.pbs.org/wgbh/pages/frontline/shows/binladen/who/bio.html
5. Ibid.
6. Ibid.
7. Yossef Bodansky, *Bin Laden: The Man Who Declared War on America* (New York: Prima, 2001), p. 5.
8. John K. Cooley, *Unholy War: Afghanistan, America and International Terrorism* (London: Pluto Press, 2000), p. 87.
9. As quoted in Peter L. Bergen, *Holy War Inc.: Inside the Secret World of Osama bin Laden* (New York: Free Press, 2002), p. 53.
10. Ibid.
11. Robert Fisk, "Anti-Soviet warrior puts his army on the road to peace," *The Independent*, December 6, 1993.
12. M. Nazif Shahrani, "Afghanistan," in *The Oxford Encyclopedia of the Modern Islamic World*, ed. John L. Esposito (New York: Oxford University Press, 1995), vol. 1, pp. 27–32.
13. Ahmed Rashid, *Taliban: Militant Islam, Oil and Fundamentalism in Central Asia*, (New Haven, Conn.: Yale University Press, 2000), p. 136.
14. Vernon Loeb Washington, "Terrorism Entrepreneur Unifies Groups Financially, Politically, *Washington Post*, August 23, 1998.
15. Ibid.
16. *Jane's Intelligence Review*, October 1, 1998.

17. Washington, *Washington Post*, August 23, 1998.
18. As quoted in Bergen, *Holy War Inc*, p. 88.
19. Richard Lacayo, "Public Enemy No. 2," Time.com, November 12, 2001, vol. 158.
20. Scott Baldauf, "The 'cave man' and Al Qaeda," *Christian Science Monitor*, October 31, 2001: http://www.csmonitor.com20001/1031/p6s1-wosc.html
21. *Reuters*, February 28, 1997.
22. "Bin Laden's Warning: Full Text," *BBC News*, Sunday, October 7, 2001: http://www.news.bbc.co.uk/hi/English/world/spout_asia/newsid_1585000/1585636.stm
23. Ibid.
24. Hamid Mir, "Osama claims he has nukes: If U.S. uses N-arms it will get same response," *Dawn: The Internet Edition*, November 10, 2001.
25. Interview with Osama bin Laden (May 1998), "Hunting the Enemy, " *Frontline*: http://www.pbs.org/wgbh/pages/frontline/shows/binladen/who/family.html
26. Ibid.
27. Ibid.
28. Ibid.
29. Ibid.
30. Ibid.
31. Ibid.

Chapter 2
1. Sayyid Qutb, *Milestones* (Stuttgart: Ernst Klett Printers, 1978), p. 21.
2. Ibid., pp. 88–89.
3. Bernard Lewis, *The Arabs in History* (New York: Harper & Row, 1966), p. 149; Daniel C. Peterson, "Ismailiyah," in *The Oxford Encyclopedia of the Modern Islamic World*, ed. John L. Esposito (New York: Oxford University Press, 1995), vol. 2, pp. 341–42.
4. Qutb, *Milestones,* pp. 32–33.
5. See John O. Voll, "Renewal and Reform in Islamic History: Tajdid and Islah," in *Voices of Resurgent Islam* (New York: Oxford University Press, 1983), ch. 2.
6. Emmanuel Sivan, *Radical Islam: Medieval Theology and Modern Politics* (New Haven, Conn.: Yale University Press, 1985), p. 96.
7. Ronald Nettler, "Ibn Taymiyya," in *The Oxford Encyclopedia of the Modern Islamic World*, ed. John L. Esposito (New York: Oxford University Press, 1995), vol. 2, p. 165.

8. Hasan al-Banna, "The New Renaissance," in *Islam in Transition*, ed. John L. Esposito and John J. Donohue (New York: Oxford University Press, 1992), p. 78.

9. As quoted in Christina Phelps Harris, *Nationalism and Revolution in Egypt* (The Hague: Mouton, 1964), p. 144.

10. David Cummins, "Hasan al-Banna (1906–49), in *Pioneers of Islamic Revival*, ed. Ali Rahnema (London: Zed Books, 1994), p. 136.

11. S. Abul A'la Mawdudi, *Jihad in Islam* (Pakistan: Islamic Publications, (Pvt.) Limited, 1998), p. 3.

12. Ibid., p. 15.

13. Ibid.

14. Ibid., pp. 4–5.

15. Ibid.

16. Ibid., p. 8.

17. Ibid., pp. 23–24.

18. Richard Mitchell, *The Society of Muslim Brothers* (New York: Oxford University Press, 1969), pp. 35–71.

19. Qutb, *Milestones,* p. 261.

20. Ashad S. Moussalli, *Radical Islamic Fundamentalism: The Ideology and Political Discourse of Sayyid Qutb* (Beirut: American University of Beirut, 1992), p. 42.

21. Qutb, *Milestones,* p. 12.

22. Ibid., p. 239.

23. Ibid., pp. 17–18.

24. Ibid., pp. 32–33.

25. Ibid., p. 34.

26. Ibid.

27. Ibid., p. 221.

28. Ruhollah Khomeini, *Islam and Revolution: Writings and Declarations of Imam Khomeini*, trans Hamid Algar (Berkeley: Mizan Press, 1983), pp. 75–76.

29. Johannes J. G. Jansen, *The Neglected Duty* (New York: Macmillan, 1986), p. 161.

30. Ibid.

31. Ibid., p. 193.

32. As quoted in Saad Eddin Ibraham, *Egypt, Islam and Democracy* (Cairo: The American University of Cairo, 1966), p. 63.

33. *Jihad and Shahadat: Struggle and Martyrdom in Islam*, ed. Mehdi Abedi and Gary Tegenhausen (Houston, Tex.: Institute for Research and Islamic Studies, 1986), p. vi.

34. Ibn Khaldun, *The Muqqadimah: An Introduction*, trans. Franz Rosenthal (Princeton, N.J.: Princeton University Press, 1967), p. 183.
35. Ibid., pp. 109–10.
36. See Khaled Abou El Fadl, "The Place of Tolerance in Islam," *Boston Review*, December 2001/January 2002, 36.

Chapter 3

1. Joseph A. Kechichian, "Islamic Revivalism and Change in Saudi Arabia," *Muslim World* 80 (January 1990): 8–12.
2. "The hate that will not die," *Guardian,* December 17, 2001.
3. Ruhollah Khomeini, "Message to the Pilgrims," in *Islam and Revolution: Writings and Declarations of Imam Khomeini*, trans. Hamid Algar (Berkeley: Mizan Press, 1983), p. 195.
4. Taha Husayn, "The Future of Culture in Egypt," in *Islam in Transition: Muslim Perspectives*, ed. John J. Donohue and John L. Esposito (New York: Oxford University Press, 1982), p. 74–75.
5. *Egyptian Gazette*, February 1, 1979.
6. Fedwa El-Guindi, "The Killing of Sadat and After: A Current Assessment of Egypt's Islamic Movement," *Middle East Insight* 2 (January-February 1982): 21.
7. Saad Eddin Ibrahim, *Egypt, Islam and Democracy* (Cairo: The American University in Cairo Press, 1996), p. 212.
8. Ibid., p. 23.
9. Walid Mahmoud Abdelnasser, *The Islamic Movement in Egypt: Perceptions of International Relations, 1967–81* (London: Kegan Paul, 1994), pp. 239–43.
10. Chris Hedges, "Egypt Begins Crackdown on Strongest Opposition Group," *New York Times*, June 12, 1994.
11. Jack Kelley, "Devotion, desire drive youths to 'martyrdom'," *USA Today*, July 5, 2001.
12. *The Covenant of the Islamic Resistance Movement* (Jerusalem 1988), Article 1.
13. Ibid.
14. Interview with Hamas leader Mahmoud Zahar, quoted in Beverley Milton-Edwards, *Islamic Politics in Palestine* (London: Tauris Academic Studies, 1996), p. 186.
15. Hisham H. Ahmad, *Hamas: From Religious Salvation to Political Transformation* (Jerusalem: Palestinian Academic Society for the Study of International Affairs, 1994), p. 114.
16. Kelley, "Devotion, desire drive youths."

17. Anthony Shadid, *Legacy of the Prophet: Despots, Democrats and the New Politics of Islam* (Boulder, Colo.: Westview Press, 2001), p. 124.

18. Sayyid Abu Musameh, as quoted in Shadid, *Legacy of the Prophet: Despots, Democrats and the New Politics of Islam*, p. 124.

19. Kelley, "Devotion, desire drive youths."

20. For background and analysis see Dirk Vandewalle, "Islam in Algeria: Religion, Culture and Opposition in a Rentier State," in *Political Islam: Revolution, Radicalism, or Reform?*, ed. John L. Esposito (Boulder, Colo.: Lynne Rienner Publishers, 1997); I. Williams, "Algeria: A Deaf Ear to Amnesty," *Middle East International* 21 (November 1997): 15.

21. J. P. Entelis, "Bouteflika's Algeria: Prospects for a Democratic Peace," *Middle East Insight* 14 (November-December 1999): 7.

22. R. Tiemcani, "From Bullets to Ballots," *Middle East Insight* 14 (November-December 1999): 12.

23. H. Amirouche, "Algeria's Islamist Revolution: The People Versus Democracy?," *Middle East Policy* 5 (January 1998): 100.

24. Ahmed Rashid, "The Taliban: Exporting Extremism," *Foreign Affairs* 78 (November-December 1999): 22–35.

25. Ibid.

26. Ibid., p. 6.

Chapter 4

1. Francis E. Peters, "The Early Muslim Empires: Ummayads, Abbasids, Fatimids," in *Islam: The Religious and Political Life of a World Community* (New York: Praeger, 1984), p. 79.

2. See, for example, Daniel Lerner, *The Passing of Traditional Society: Modernizing the Middle East* (New York: Free Press, 1958); Manfield Halpren, *The Politics of Social Change in the Middle East and North Africa* (Princeton, N.J.: Princeton University Press, 1963). For an analysis and critique of the factors that influenced the development of modernization theory, see Fred R. von der Mehden, *Religion and Modernization in Southeast Asia* (Syracuse, N.Y.: Syracuse University Press, 1988).

3. See, for example, Harvey Cox, *The Secular City: Urbanization and Secularization in Theological Perspective* (New York: Macmillan, 1965), and *Religion in the Secular City: Toward a Post Modern Theology* (New York: Simon & Schuster, 1984); Dietrich Bonhoeffer, *Letters and Papers from Prison*, rev. ed. (New York: Macmillan, 1967); William Hamilton and Thomas Altizer, *Radical Theology and the Death of God* (Indianapolis: Bobbs Merrill, 1966).

4. Peter L. Berger, "The Desecularization of the World: A Global Over-view," in *The Desecularization of the World: Resurgent Religion and World Politics*, ed. Peter L. Berger (Washington, D.C.: Ethics and Public Policy Center, 1999), p. 2.

5. Samuel P. Huntington, "The Clash of Civilizations?," *Foreign Affairs* (Summer 1993): 22, 39.

6. Ibid., p. 31.

7. Ibid., p. 40.

8. Samuel P. Huntington, *The Clash of Civilizations and the Remaking of World Order* (New York: Simon & Schuster, 1997), p. 258.

9. Ibid., p. 217.

10. For a discussion of this point, see James Piscatori, *Islam in a World of Nation States* (Cambridge: Cambridge University Press, 1986), p. 149.

11. Maxime Rodinson, *Islam and Capitalism* (Austin: University of Texas Press, 1978), p. 76.

12. See Nikki Keddie's comments in "Introduction: Deciphering Middle Eastern Women's History," *Women in Middle Eastern History*, ed. Nikki R. Keddie and Beth Baron (New Haven: Yale University Press, 1991), pp. 1–2.

13. As quoted in Haleh Esfandiari, *Reconstructed Lives: Women and Iran's Islamic Revolution* (Baltimore: Johns Hopkins University Press, 1997), p. 85.

14. Valerie J. Hoffman-Ladd, "Women's Religious Observances," *The Oxford Encyclopedia of the Modern Islamic World*, ed. John L. Esposito (New York: Oxford University Press, 1995), vol. 4, p. 327.

15. Ibid., pp. 327–28.

16. This section is based on John L. Esposito and John Voll, "Islam and the West: Muslim Voices of Dialogue," *Millennium* (January 2001). See also our longer study *Makers of Contemporary Islam* (New York: Oxford University Press, 2001).

17. See, for example, Judith Nagata, "Religious Ideology and Social Change: The Islamic Revival in Malaysia," *Pacific Affairs* 53, no. 3 (1980): 425, and Fred R. von der Mehden, "Malaysia in 1980: Signals to Watch," *Asian Survey* 21, no. 2 (1981): 246.

18. Ian Johnson, "How Malaysia's Rulers Devoured Each Other and Much They Built," *Wall Street Journal*, October 30, 1998.

19. See, for example, the editorial "Malaysia on Trial," *New York Times*, November 4, 1998.

20. Ibid.
21. Anwar Ibrahim, "Development, Values, and Changing Political Ideas," *Sojourn: Social Issues in Southeast Asia* 1 (February 1986): 2.
22. Anwar Ibrahim, "The Ardent Moderates," *Time*, September 23, 1996, 24.
23. Address by Anwar Ibrahim at the Ismail Faruqi Award Presentation Ceremony, International Islamic University Malaysia, February 28, 1996.
24. Surah 49:13. The translation is as it was presented in the text of Ibrahim's "Islam and Confucianism."
25. Anwar Ibrahim, "The Need for Civilizational Dialogue," Occasion Papers Series, Center for Muslim-Christian Understanding, Georgetown University, 1995, p. 5.
26. Anwar Ibrahim, *The Asian Renaissance* (Singapore: Times Books International, 1996), p. 45.
27. Mohammad Khatami, *Islam, Liberty, and Development* (Binghamton, N.Y.: Institute of Global Cultural Studies, Binghamton University, 1987), p. 150.
28. The interview received extensive coverage in the news media. See Elaine Sciolino, "Seeking to Open a Door to U.S., Iranian Proposes Cultural Ties," *New York Times*, January 8, 1998; Barton Gellman, "Iranian Leader Urges Exchanges with U.S.," *Washington Post*, January 8, 1998; and "A whisper in the Wolf's Ear," *The Economist*, January 10, 1998.
29. An interesting contemporary analysis of the significance of the new approach is Saul Bakhash, "From Iran, an Understated Overture," *Washington Post*, December 18, 1997.
30. Elaine Sciolino, "At Khomeini's Tomb, Iran's President Switches Tune on U.S.," *New York Times*, January 20, 1998.
31. Khatami, *Islam, Liberty, and Development*, p. 24.
32. Ibid., pp. 28, 30.
33. Eighty-seven per cent of Indonesia's population of 220 million are Muslim.
34. Mujiburrahman, "Island and Politics in Indonesia: The Political Thought of Abdurrahman Wahid," *Journal of Islam and Christian-Muslim Relations* 10, no. 3 (1992): 342.
35. "Where To: Interview with Abdurrahman Wahid," *Inside Indonesia*, October 8, 1986, p. 3.
36. "An Islamic Awakening," *Economist*, April 17, 1993.
37. "Yes, I have enemies. But it is important that I do the right things," *Business Times* (Singapore), March 24, 1999.

38. Abdurrahman Wahid, "Reflections on the Need for a Concept of Man in Islam," Memorandum to the rector of the U.N. University, May 1, 1983, n.p., n.d, p. 3.

39. Ibid.

40. Ibid., p. 4.

41. Abdurrahman Wahid, "Religion, Ideology, and Development," n.p., n.d., p. 4.

42. Abdurrahman Wahid, "Islam, Nonviolence, and National Transformation," n.p., n.d., p. 3.

43. For an analysis of this issue, see John L. Esposito and John O. Voll, *Islam and Democracy* (New York: Oxford University Press, 1997); John L. Esposito and James P. Piscatori, "Democratization and Islam," *Middle East Journal* 45 (Summer 1991): 427–40; John O. Voll and John L. Esposito, "Islam and Democracy in a Violent World," *Humanities* (Fall 2002, forthcoming); Mahmoud Monshipouri and Christopher G. Kukla, "Islam and Democracy and Human Rights," *Middle East Policy* 3 (1994): 22–39; Robin Wright, "Islam, Democracy and the West," *Foreign Affairs* (Summer 1992): 131–45.

44. John O. Voll and John L. Esposito, "Islam's Democratic Essence," *Middle East Quarterly* (September 1994): 3–11, with ripostes, 12–19: Voll and Esposito reply, *Middle East Quarterly* (December 1994): 71–72.

45. *Mideast Mirror*, March 30,1992, p. 12.

46. Abdelwahab El-Affendi, *Islam* 21 (October 2000).

47. John L. Esposito and John D. Voll, "Islam and Democracy," *Humanities* (November-December 2001): 24.

48. Ibid.

49. R. Bianchi, "Islam and Democracy in Egypt," *Current History*, February 1989: 104.

50. Shibley Telhami, "Defeating Terror: Confront Supply and Demand," *Middle East Insight* 16 (November-December 2001): 7.

51. "American Muslim Poll" (Washington, D.C.: Project MAPS, Georgetown University, 2001), p. 7.

52. Robert Crane, "Re-thinking America's Mission: The Role of Islam," *American Journal of Islamic Social Sciences* 19, no. 2 (Spring 2002), forthcoming.

53. Paul Kennedy, "As Others See Us," *Wall Street Journal*, October 5, 2001.

54. *Al-Hayat*, Islamic Research Council of al-Aẑhar University, November 5, 2001.

Glossary

ayatollah (ayatullah) "Sign of God," title of a high-ranking Shii religious leader.

bida innovation, deviation from Islamic tradition.

caliph for Sunni Muslims, successor of Muhammad as leader of the Islamic community.

chador traditional garment, worn in public, covering a woman from head to foot.

dar al-harb "abode of war," non-Islamic territory.

dar al-Islam "abode of peace," Islamic territory, i.e., where Islamic law is in force.

dawah "call to Islam," propagation of the faith; more broadly, social welfare and missionary activities.

dhimmi "protected" or covenanted people; non-Muslim citizen who is subject to poll tax (jizya).

faqih (fuqaha) legal expert; jurisprudent.

fatwa formal legal opinion or decision of a mufti on a matter of Islamic law.

hadith narrative report of the Prophet Muhammad's sayings and actions.

hajj annual pilgrimage to Mecca required of all Muslims at least once in their lifetime.

halal permitted, lawful activities.

haraka   "movement."

haram   prohibited, unlawful activities.

hijab   veil or head covering worn by Muslim women in public.

hijra   emigration of Muhammad from Mecca to Medina in A.D. 622, where he established rule of the Muslim community-state.

hizbollah   party of God.

ijma   consensus, or agreement of the community, a source of Islamic law.

ijtihad   independent analysis or interpretation of Islamic law.

ikhwan   brotherhood.

imam   "Leader," prayer leader. In Shii Islam, refers to successor of Prophet Muhammad, descendant of Ali, who governs as divinely inspired religiopolitical leader of Islamic community.

iman   "faith," religious belief or conviction in the fundamental doctrines of Islam.

intifada   Palestinian "uprising" against Israeli occupation.

islah   reform or revitalization of the Muslim community through return to the Quran and example of the Prophet.

islam   submission or surrender to the will of God.

Islamist   Islamic political or social activist; often commonly referred to as a fundamentalist.

jahiliyyah   period of ignorance, i.e., pre-Islamic Arabia; used by contemporary revivalists to refer to un-Islamic behavior in society.

jihad   "strive, effort, struggle" to follow Islam; can include defense of faith, armed struggle, holy war.

jizya   poll-tax on dhimmi (non-Muslims) that entitled them to protection and to practice their faith.

kaba   cube-shaped shrine located in the center of the Grand Mosque in Mecca, the focal point for daily prayer and the pilgrimage.

kafir (var., kufir)   "unbeliever" or infidel, one who is "ungrateful" and rejects the message of Islam.

kalam "speech," theology.

madrasa religious college or university, seminary.

Mahdi divinely guided leader who is to come in the future to establish God's rule on earth and a socially just society.

majlis al-shura consultative council.

maslaha "public interest" or "human welfare."

mihrab "niche" in the wall of a mosque, indicating the direction of Mecca, which Muslims face when performing their daily prayers (salat).

mufti specialist on Islamic law competent to deliver a fatwa or legal interpretation or brief

mujaddid "renewer," one who brings about the renewal (tajdid) of Islam; a widely held Muslim belief based on Prophetic tradition teaches that God sends a mujaddid at the beginning of each century to restore or strengthen Islam.

mujahid (pl., mujahidin) soldier of God.

mujtahid one who practices ijtihad or interprets Islamic law.

mullah a local religious leader.

Muslim one who submits (islam) to God's will.

qadi judge who administers shariah law.

salafi "ancestors," the first generations of the Muslim community; because of their proximity to the Prophet Muhammad, their beliefs and practice are considered authoritative.

salat official prayer or worship observed five times daily.

shahadah the confession or profession of faith: "there is no god but Allah and Muhammad is His Prophet."

shahid martyr, witness to faith.

shariah "path," Islamic law.

shaykh head of a tribe or Sufi order; term applied to a ruler, religious teacher, or tribal leader.

Shii "party or faction" of Ali; those Muslims who believe that

Muhammad designated Ali and his rightful descendants to be the true leaders of the Muslim community.

shura   consultation.

Sufi   follower of Sufism, Islamic mysticism.

sultan   ruler, military commander in medieval Islamic states.

Sunnah   normative practice or exemplary behavior of Muhammad.

Sunni   Muslims, the majority community, who believe that they represent the authority of the Sunnah or example of the Prophet Muhammad and the early Muslin community.

tajdid   revival or renewal of Islam through return to its sources, the Quran, and the example of the prophet.

takfir   excommunication, the proclaiming of a fellow believer as an infidel.

taqlid   unquestioned imitation or following of tradition, past legal or doctrinal precedents; the opposite of ijtihad.

tawhid   unity of God (absolute monotheism); Allah's absolute sovereignty over the universe.

ulama   religious scholars or clergy.

ummah   Islamic community; refers to the worldwide Muslim community.

waqf   endowment of property for religious purposes such as building mosques, schools, hospitals.

zakat   annual alms tax or tithe of 2 + percent levied on wealth and distributed to the poor.

Index